DANIEL DEFOE

Daniel Defoe

AMBITION & INNOVATION

Paula R. Backscheider

THE UNIVERSITY PRESS OF KENTUCKY

Portions of chapter 4 appeared earlier as "Cross-Purposes: Defoe's *History of the Union*" in *CLIO* 11 (1982), and are reprinted by permission of the publisher. Portions of chapter 7 first appeared as "The Genesis of *Roxana*" in *The Eighteenth Century: Theory and Interpretation* 27 (1986) and are reprinted by permission of the publisher. An earlier version of part of chapter 8 appeared as "Defoe and the Geography of the Mind" in J.M. Armistead, ed., *The First English Novelists*, copyright © 1985 by The University of Tennessee Press, and is reprinted by permission of the publisher.

Scholarly publisher for the Commonwealth,
serving Bellarmine College, Berea College, Centre
College of Kentucky, Eastern Kentucky University,
The Filson Club, Georgetown College, Kentucky
Historical Society, Kentucky State University,
Morehead State University, Murray State University,
Northern Kentucky University, Transylvania University,
University of Kentucky, University of Louisville,
and Western Kentucky University.

Editorial and Sales Offices: Lexington, Kentucky 40506-0024

Library of Congress Cataloging-in-Publication Data

Backscheider, Paula.
    Daniel Defoe: ambition and innovation.

    Bibliography: p.
    Includes index.
    1. Defoe, Daniel, 1661?–1731—Criticism and
interpretation. I. Title.
PR3407.B33 1987   823'.5   86-12076
ISBN 0-8131-1596-5

TO MY SISTER
Gayle

CONTENTS

ACKNOWLEDGMENTS

I SHALL ALWAYS think of this book with pleasure because of the generous support of my colleagues. They shared their knowledge of the literature of other periods, listened to my enthusiasms and speculations, and read pages or chapters with alert, critical eyes. With affection, I offer thanks to Lewis White Beck, George Ford, Tom Gavin, Thomas Hahn, Tanya Page, and Joseph Summers. My debts to my husband, Nick Backscheider, to Marjorie Curry Woods, to J. Paul Hunter, and to my graduate assistant, Mary Ellen Potts, are particularly great. I am also grateful to friends from other universities who have answered questions, read chapters, and made helpful suggestions: Margaret Doody, J.A. Downie, Frank Ellis, and Louis A. Landa. Finally, I owe deep thanks to Maximillian E. Novak; at a time when I was ready to turn away from Defoe, he shared a world of enthusiasm.

The writing of this book was supported by the University of Rochester, the American Philosophical Society, and the National Endowment for the Humanities; their grants and the extraordinary work of University of Rochester librarians Phyllis Andrews and Shirley Ricker helped make my work pleasant and efficient.

I thank Sir John Clerk, the Massachusetts Historical Society, Harvard's Houghton Library, the Dr. Williams Library, the University of Edinburgh, the Scottish Record Office (S.R.O.), and the National Library of Scotland for permission to publish manuscript material. I also thank *CLIO*, *The Eighteenth Century: Theory and Interpretation*, and the University of Tennessee Press for permission to reprint previously published and earlier versions of parts of this book.

DANIEL DEFOE

ONE

THE BENT AND GENIUS
OF THE AGE

DEFOE WAS THE most English of the major writers of his time,
and therein lies the problem with his literary reputation. Although
he knew Latin, had studied the classics, and drew upon the
ancients frequently and with facility, Horace and Virgil did not
dominate his conception of literature. He brought to his work the
Renaissance awareness of the increase in human knowledge, of the
richness of experience, and of the complexity of human nature.
Widely read in historical collections, universal histories, travel
books, conduct books, sermons, political tracts, works of natural
science, and theoretical treatises on government and aware of
developing forms of prose fiction, such as the picaresque, French
memoirs, and novella, he accepted the noncanonical genres and
the mixing of forms. Intensely engaged with current issues, he
wanted to extend literature to engage rather than to arrest
experience.

Unlike his great contemporaries, he did not rely primarily on
classical dramatic and poetic forms nor did he attempt to create an
object of beauty, one worthy of contemplation because of its
structure, language, models, subject, unity, and completion. The
measure of art in the eighteenth century, however, has been
supplied by Milton and Dryden, Evelyn and Clarendon, Pope and
Fielding, and they are misleading and largely irrelevant guides to
an evaluation of Defoe. The terms of polarization are clear:
Chaucer was a court poet, Shakespeare was a member of the
King's Men, Ben Jonson was poet laureate, and they thought of

themselves in those terms. The identification of political power, social rank, and aesthetic superiority was handed down to such socially unlikely heirs as Milton, Addison, and Pope, and they located themselves in the classical tradition. Samuel Johnson spoke for them when he complained, "The province of writing was formerly left to those, who by study, or appearance of study, were supposed to have gained knowledge unattainable by the busy part of mankind. . . . "[1] Johnson went on to argue that only such men had the right to instruct others, and Matthew Arnold, T.S. Eliot, and others assumed the position that Pope and Fielding held as instructors and chastisers of "scribblers." The easy eloquence of their graceful, allusion-rich verse, the continuity of shared imagery and values, their subjects and themes, and the structure and control in all they wrote reinforced the concept of these poets as elite guardians of order, virtue, and power. They allied themselves, even when being critical, with the privileged and the governing. Some critics have found "Augustanism" as far back in English literature as "the circle of King Alfred" (c. 890-99), and others have called it "the 'orthodox' ethical and rhetorical tradition" resembling "a sort of central nervous system running through the whole eighteenth century."[2] Wherever one located its origins, its power as a cultural norm in Defoe's time meant that he contrasted with the writers who set the literary expectations of tradition, grace, and ease, and the modern reader therefore finds his work hard to place and to evaluate.

Some words for this conflict are court/country, Whig/Tory, trade/land, energy/order, empire/republic, and passion/virtue, and more come to mind. One side treated unpleasant social reality in mock pastorals, such as Swift's "Description of a City Shower," or in offhand references, as in canto 3, lines 19-23, of Pope's mock epic, *The Rape of the Lock.* To devote entire works to petty crime, trade, earning a living, faith in God, or other such embarrassingly mundane topics and to eschew classical models for loose prose was to sacrifice an Olympian position. Decorum, restraint, and reason legislated against these "low" subjects, against the psychological intensity of Robinson Crusoe on the island and H.F. in the midst of the plague, against the undisguised "middle-class morality" of *Colonel Jack,* and especially against such emotional fervor as found in *Farther Adventures* when Crusoe seizes the hand of a companion and exclaims, "Blessed be God, we are once again come among Christians."[3] Taught to value classical genres and to admire Dryden, Swift, and Pope, Defoe's contemporaries and our own accepted "Neoclassicism" and failed to find a place for Defoe in literary history.[4] Even his best modern biographer, James Sutherland, described him thus: "For one who was so widely read by his contemporaries he was a strangely isolated figure, both as a man and as a writer," and so discerning an admirer as James Joyce called him "the first English author . . . to create without literary models."[5]

What Defoe did was to join Dryden and other writers in extending the idea of literature beyond the narrow confines of the classical conception—to include periodical essays, history, biography, memoirs, and travel books, all forms that every era since the Renaissance has found troublesome.[6] If we grant only that literature is put forth as an act of imagination and interpretation rather than as mere representation and is deliberately written so that pleasure is to be found in its language and construction as well as its ideas, we must acknowledge that many of these noncanonical forms share the nature of literature. The complete acceptance of the requirement that literature should give pleasure and instruction meant that writers attended to purely imaginative forms and to *English* prose style as they never had before. The proliferation of essays on good English style and of prefaces in which the author promised that the writing would be one of the pleasures of reading testifies to the new self-consciousness of English writers.

Literature also came to accept the tasks of collecting knowledge and of interpreting events. Not only did writers draw historical parallels and point to the lessons of the past, but they also repeatedly expressed the fear that useful information and skills would be lost and reminded their contemporaries that other times and other cultures should be analyzed in order to record their contributions. In *The Order of Things*, Foucault has demonstrated the crucial centrality of the act of interpretation for the seventeenth and eighteenth centuries, when writers came to see themselves as bearing the principle responsibility for organizing and explaining data.

Out of this conception of literature came a wealth of unclassifiable and original Renaissance literature; the authors of *The Book Named the Governor, The Arcadia, The Unfortunate Traveller, The History of the World, Emblemes, The Anatomy of Melancholy,* and poetry such as *Poly-Olbion, The Faerie Queene,* and *Paradise Lost* found new uses for narrative, ignored generic purity, and experimented with a vigorous, distinctively English style. To this wealth of books was added a huge number of fine, new translations, including North's *Plutarch,* Chapman's *Homer,* and the King James Bible. Here is Defoe's literary world.

Defoe may have been more widely read than any of his literary contemporaries. A comparison of the evidence we have of Defoe's reading to that of, for example, Pope and Swift, suggests, first, that he read for ideas rather than to gain literary experience and models, and, second, that he read "the wrong books" consistently. For instance, he quotes Raleigh's *History of the World* rather than his poetry, Machiavelli's *Discourses on Livy* rather than *The Prince,* and Sallust rather than Tacitus. Careful analysis, however, reveals that the correct perception of his reading is that it is as astonishing as his own literary output. The allusions in his poetry alone are mind-boggling, and, in one essay, he discusses Taylor, Ussher, Tillotson, Burnet, Beveridge, Newton, Flamstead, Littleton, Coke, Milton, Chaucer, Spenser, Shakespeare, Dryden, Otway, Cowper, Butler, Addison, Pope, Garth, Rowe, Prior, Dennis, Congreve, Phillips, Jonson, Rochester, Sedley, Buckingham, Farquhar, Steele, Oldsworth, Horace, Virgil, Aristotle, Galen, and Cicero and judges each intelligently.[7] He knew Cowley well enough to use eight lines of *The Second Olympique Ode of Pindar* in the preface to *The True-Born Englishman,* and he could quote Waller's "The Muses Friend, Tea, do's the Fancy aid" in an essay on tea in *Mist's Journal;* he knew Sidney and Bacon well enough to refer to "speaking pictures" throughout *A Journal of the Plague Year.* He quotes Milton and Rochester, writes a life of Sedley, and draws examples from almost all of the Roman histories, but he was also steeped in Renaissance historical collections and books on travel, magic, crime, science, government, and ethics. References and quotations abound from such men as Joseph Glanvill, Thomas Heywood,

Richard Brathwait, Thomas Elyot, Peter Heylin, and from translations of Mexia, Grotius, and Bossuet.

After he came to see himself as a professional writer (albeit one in the service of political interests), he seems to have read nearly everything printed, including, predictably, tracts on political and religious controversies, periodicals, poetry, and books on "the present state" of various countries as well as, less predictably, French memoirs, economic geographies, and the new forms of English prose fiction. All of this reading shaped his mind and his writing. He blended the traditional and timeless with fads and invented new forms and invigorated old. He was often a conscious innovator, occasionally pointing out the "improvements" he had made. He singled out some of his novels as being exceptionally good examples of a type or as especially well written. In these works, he was a writer aware of his roots and dedicated to the idea that writers have special gifts of insight and prophecy that allow them to describe social, psychic, and moral phenomena in ways that enlighten and even influence readers.[8]

In many ways, the canonical writers call their readers back to values and ways of seeing the world. Because they see themselves as bearers of an ideal, a norm, even a Platonic form, their art is constantly moving toward abstraction and affirms permanence. Emotions and even people are described and objectified so that we can see abstraction, understand the moral, and recognize that people are more alike than different. Pope can write, "My Life's amusements have been just the same, / Before, and after Standing Armies came" (Satire II, ii, 153-54), and Swift can give us Count Munodi in Book III of *Gulliver's Travels*. Defoe and writers like him demand that their readers see change, admit the complexities and confusions in the world, and, above all, recognize the possibility of progress in the world, in society, and even in human nature. The restraint, aloofness, and order so characteristic of the writing of men like Addison, Dryden, and Pope even in the times they were most embroiled in immediate events contrast with the sprawling, apparently disorderly, open-endedness of much of Defoe's best work. His aim is to focus the reader's attention on a continuous experience rather than upon a finished performance or what would be, in Corneille's terms, the crucial point in a work with unity of action. Most of Defoe's works give satisfaction by repeatedly arousing interest and by duplicating the experience of a life in progress rather than by fulfilling the expectation that the work will be "finished." Significantly, the greatest of the early novelists do the same things, most obviously perhaps in Sterne but also in Richardson, as evidenced by Samuel Johnson's comment that anyone who reads Richardson for the story "would be so much fretted" as to hang himself. Fielding manages to deliver the same satisfactions as well as to give the experience of a finished work of art because he deliberately shapes, or tries to give the appearance of shaping, his novels according to classical models.

Defoe's generation absorbed these literary changes and redefined literature's relation to reality. Classical and Christian writers had seen the strongest bond as that between man and the supernatural world, whether it was conceived as Platonic forms, fate, or providential order. Defoe brought the relationship of man to society to the foreground, kept this relationship within an eternal world, and gradually replaced "man" with "the individual" in the triangle. By doing so, he adapted fiction to reflect the Renaissance awareness of the diversity and complexity of human nature and experience and of the dynamic interactions that made so many of the greatest thinkers creators of utopias, or what we might call psychological anthropologists. The concentration on the individual, the particular, "man and society," and interiority, which became some of the novel's most distinguishing qualities and necessitated such characteristics as the smooth movement between the external world and the characters' thoughts, came from the reordering of relationships and redefining of personality.

Defoe shared with his contemporaries a view of literature common since before Sidney, who had written, "it is that feigning notable images of virtues, vices, or what else, with that delightful teaching, which must be the right describing note to know a poet by." They believed that art, especially painting, could express "in natural symbols moral and psychological truth."[9] The art of Dryden, of Pope, and of Swift, however, was *obviously* art and signalled itself to be so from its opening sentences. Defoe had inherited from earlier controversialists a rich literature that was familiar, idiomatic, often intended to sound like the account of an eyewitness or an individual with strong opinions, and sometimes written in forms perceived to be "true," such as history, biography, journal, and sermon. As prose fiction disguised itself as memoirs, criminal biography, and history and was combined with forms incorporating such kinds of "truth" as allegory, spiritual autobiography, and travel literature, new protests arose that prose fiction was "Lye" and dangerous deception.

Defoe absorbed these developments, considered the protests, and joined a number of other writers in suggesting a new relationship between the writer and reader, a relationship that reaffirmed even as it transformed the artistic expression of moral and psychological truth. Instead of reporting experiences or feelings, rather than imitating life or art, he invented the imitation of reporting and imitating. He used historical and social actuality to create illusion rather than to render accurately or artificially and, by doing so, redefined art and referential truth. The test of truth came to be within the reader rather than in Nature or the world. As Scholes and Kellogg have said, a shift from rhetorical to psychological presentation and from the creation of the actual to the typical came about,[10] and Defoe was central to its discovery and development. Even in his pamphlets, Defoe wanted to communicate a picture of the world that would reveal a truth deeper than the accurate rendering of its surface. Because his primary goal was to move beneath event to causes and implications and to give his readers a picture created from his experience—political, social, religious, *and* emotional—he often deliberately chose to create "fictions." By translating his *Weltanschauung* along with his perception of events into coherent, carefully designed linguistic structures, he moved beyond reportage to art.[11] He could accept and convey the seriality of experience, the complication of multiple perceptions and opinions, and the formlessness of life[12] without sacrificing the useful instruction and poetic justice he promised in his prefaces, introductions, and dedications to his poetry, fiction, histories, and even travel books.

Novelists since have articulated Defoe's conception. E.M. Forster complained that "Beauty has arrived, but in too tyrannous a guise" and argued that the demands for polished structure and unity cannot be "combined with the immense richness of material which life provides."[13] Norman Mailer, a writer who won the Pulitzer Prize and National Book Award while in his twenties but whose relationship to the literary establishment has come to resemble Defoe's, admitted that his desire "to have one's immediate say on contemporary matters kept diverting the novelistic impulse" but argued that "at precisely that point where experience is sufficiently emotional, spiritual, psychical, moral, existential, or supernatural" fiction must take over from history and journalism.[14] What Mailer knew is that certain kinds of involvement with the present and certain kinds of innovation are judged inartistic by many in the establishment.

In this study, I trace Defoe's development as a teller of tales, argue the intensity and integrity of his artistic ambitions, and demonstrate that everything that Defoe wrote rests solidly upon his extensive reading of books published in England, his understanding of the reading tastes of his contemporaries, and his engagement with the issues and events of his time. For example, a stagnant English economy and a new recession raised new interest in colonization in the early 1720s even as countless new fictitious and factual travel books joined new editions of Renaissance classics by Hakluyt, Raleigh, and Knox, and *Robinson Crusoe, Farther Adventures,* and *Captain Singleton* appeared and bore evidence to a lifetime of reading history, economic geography, and travel books. Similarly, a number of collections of cases of spirit appearances, such as John Aubrey's *Miscellanies,* were reprinted at a time when new fears of the growth of atheism and heresy were widespread, and Defoe drew upon his reading of similar books by authors as diverse as Thomas Vaughan and Richard Baxter to produce his *History of Apparitions* and important thematic incidents in *Moll Flanders.*

To see Defoe in relation to the writing of his time is to understand his artistic theories. He tells us, for example, that the beauty of the style will be part of the pleasure in *Memoirs of a Cavalier.* One of his narrators, Robinson Crusoe, comments on his writing and self-consciously compares it to works similar to *Farther Adventures.* In the preface to the second volume of *A Tour Thro' the Whole Island of Great Britain,* Defoe explains that his method "is giving an account by way of essay, or, as the moderns call it, by memoirs of the present state of things, in a familiar manner." He will be content, he says, "to have it compar'd with any that have gone before it."[15] Time after time, he indicates that he is aware that he is writing within established literary traditions and conventions. To see Defoe in the context of English literary history is to understand his conceptions and to find revisionist readings of some of the major novels, even as we come to see him as the indisputable father of the English novel.

· TWO ·

POETRY

ALTHOUGH NO ONE today thinks of Defoe as a poet, he wrote more verse than Milton or Dryden, and the signature he used most frequently on his published works identified him as the author of a poem. Some of Defoe's poems were indisputably popular. *The True-Born Englishman* (1700) went through ten authorized editions and at least twelve pirated editions in the first year. *The Mock-Mourners* (1702) was in its seventh edition less than a year after its publication, *A Hymn to Victory* had at least four editions in 1704, subscribers clamored for *Jure Divino* (1706), which was soon published as a chapbook, and *Caledonia* (1706) appeared as a lavish volume supported by the Edinburgh Town Council and most of the important Scots of Defoe's time. As Frank Ellis has pointed out, Defoe dominates Volume 6 of the Yale *Poems on Affairs of State* as Andrew Marvell does Volume 1.[1]

The interest of Defoe's poetry for us is in the ways it reveals why men wrote poetry in the late seventeenth and early eighteenth centuries and in the sophisticated uses Defoe makes of some fashionable and traditional poetic techniques and forms. Through his poetry, he begins to learn to combine the imaginative and the factual, the entertaining and the political. A close look at his poetry reveals that it deserves consideration alongside the poetry of William Walsh, George Granville, Samuel Garth, William Congreve, Joseph Addison, and Matthew Prior.[2] The poetic careers of these men begin with occasional, often idealistic verse, turn to verse in which ideals are inseparable from the celebration of men and political parties, and conclude with the subordination of the artistic and idealistic to propaganda or something very close to it. It is necessary in order to understand Defoe's poetry to begin with a survey of the peculiar literary landscape in which Defoe began publishing it.

Rachel Trickett has argued that the "peculiar circumstances of the Restoration and eighteenth century" gave rise to three clearly distinguishable kinds of poets: the dedicated men of letters, the gentlemen amateurs, and the hacks.[3] In the eighteenth century the "gentleman amateur" was usually a public servant. This classification system is no modern abstraction. Time after time, Defoe and his contemporaries referred to it as if it were familiar and accepted. The most obvious early expression of the idea is in Charles Montagu's *Epistle to My Lord Chamberlain* (1690), which called on Dorset to eulogize King William on the occasion of the victory at Boyne. From this point on, the call for a worthy poet willing to dedicate his life to the service of his country and to art, coupled with the writer's statement of his own unworthiness and lack of poetic ambition, became almost conventional. Dryden's retirement and death, and the deaths of John Oldham and Rochester, had broken the line of great English poets able to immortalize England's heroes, but the poets at the turn of the century wrote about desire as much as about talent. Aaron Hill, for example, in *Advice to the Poets,* wrote that rather than be a great poet, he would "Look round the busy world, and hug my rest." Matthew Prior cast critical eyes on "Drudge Dryden," and Addison wrote no serious poetry after his appointment as Secretary to Sir Charles Hedges.[4] Defoe himself described the arduous work of the serious poet in *A Vindication of the Press* (1718). "Haste," he wrote, "is attended with a fatal Consequence," and he went on to contrast the relative ease of prose writing to the composition and revision of poetry.[5]

None of these men disputed the value of poetry; in fact, they all glorified it. William Congreve cautioned Montagu, now Lord Halifax, not to undervalue the praise he earned as a poet: "If not the Greatest, the most Lasting Name."[6] Aaron Hill, by arguing that poets have made Augustus's name greater than the name of Julius Caesar or Vespasian and created saints, heroes, and philosophers, attempted to demonstrate the poets' superiority to these great men.[7] Because they can give immortality, George Granville, in "To the Immortal Memory of Mr. Edmund Waller," described poets as "partaking of celestial fire" and as creators of gods.

These poets not only affirmed the traditional functions of public poetry, but they also saw the usefulness of poetry as a mode of discourse or even argument. Taught from youth to write poetry and to imitate classical and English themes and forms, they naturally saw poetry as one of many means of effective expression.[8] Defoe and his contemporaries took their ability to "versify" for granted; the collections of poems published in memory of deceased classmates, the volumes of verse produced by young men, and the frequent requests for occasional poems made by friends to men not known as poets testify to the unremarkable nature of poetry writing. A representative example is one of Defoe's Newington Green classmates, Samuel Wesley, who published a miscellany of verse called *Maggots* (or "whimsies") when he was in his early twenties and who continued to refer to himself as a poet well into his life as a clergyman. Another childhood friend, John Dunton, published much of Wesley's poetry and solicited at least two poems from Defoe. Their teacher Charles Morton had followed the common practice of assigning them to write poetry, and Morton himself habitually used couplets to sum up sections of his lectures on logic, ethics, and even physics. He explained in a postscript that books should be read three times and that he arranged his lessons so that the student read them in prose, "in verse memorial," and "in schemes."[9] From him, too, Defoe and Wesley learned to see poetry as a salvo to be launched at the enemies of truth and righteousness.[10]

All of the great poets of the earlier generation—Cleveland, Waller, Denham, Cowley, Davenant, Milton, Marvell, Butler, Oldham, Rochester, and Dryden—had written political poetry, and these men fought the battles and championed the causes that pamphleteers and journalists would a generation later. Some critics have gone so far as to say that panegyric was transformed from a type of oratory into a kind of journalism.[11] Many of these early political satires reviewed the situation in a biased manner, characterized the major participants, and insisted that only fools or knaves could hold the opinion opposed by the author. Clandestinely printed or circulated in manuscript, they were often passed out in London Common Council or even in Parliament. The poems were often idiomatic, loosely constructed, and inartistic; at best, they had a single devastating epithet or a memorable couplet. Because newspapers were not so numerous, the poems had to review events and identify the major personalities. The event was usually treated as an aberration and set in contrast to eternal standards of order and virtue. The poetry, then, was designed to educate readers and to reinforce conceptions of reprehensible and laudable behavior. Most ended with panegyric passages reminiscent of Cowley's *On His Majesty's Return Out of Scotland*. Councils of Miltonic devils and contemptible biblical characters populated many English political disputes, and references to historical parallels gave political events extraordinary tonal resonance. As Joseph Summers has pointed out, the language in these passages came to approach the language of apotheosis.[12] The poet at this time attempted to place such minor events as the election of the lord mayor in a framework of history and of providential design in a way that would influence opinion.

As poetry assumed increasing importance as a means of informing and influencing Englishmen, as satire on public affairs became the dominant poetic genre, and as evidence of such poetry's popularity grew, the writing of poetry came to be seen as a means of achieving recognition and appointment to a party position. A number of men, including Samuel Wesley, William Congreve, Matthew Prior, and Joseph Addison, did receive government appointments after writing successful poems. Once appointed, the man often felt he was expected to continue to publish an occasional gentlemanly poem. Addison wrote that England's "prudent Bards" began to build up "stores of Flights and Magazines of Rhimes, / Prepar'd already in Exalted Verse / The yet unpurchas'd trophies to reherse."[13] Prior sent Dorset's companion Fleetwood Shepherd an epistle whose "business, Sir, you'll quickly guess, / Is to desire some little Place" (1690). As late as 1706, Prior implied that he had to produce a laudatory poem about the year's victories. "I thought myself indispensably obliged, upon the present Occasion," he wrote in the preface to "An Ode, Humbly Inscrib'd to the Queen."

Thus, these poets openly acknowledged that they did not aspire to be professional poets of the highest order, yet they justifiably distinguished themselves from the anonymous or near-anonymous mercenaries like John Oldmixon, George Ridpath, and John Tutchin.[14] They saw verse as a form of public poetry, an extension of their work, and an endeavor requiring a graceful art. Both of the other groups of poets saw their poetry as their work and as a primary means of earning a living, but these gentlemen poets—more accurately called "gentlemen civil servants"—knew poetry was ancillary. Their poetry had to be better than the hacks' and less transparently self-serving. It had to partake of the traditions and trends evident in the greatest poetry of the time even as it articulated party interpretations of history and event. Defoe might have been speaking for all of them when he praised John Somers as statesman and poet: "So sweet his Voice, and all his Thoughts so strong, / So smooth his Numbers, and so soft his Song, / Eternal Musick dwells upon his Tongue. . . ."[15] They balanced an understanding of what good poetry was with a pragmatic dedication to party poetry. After all, as great as Dryden's *Annus Mirabilis* was, it had been written to counter three seditious pamphlets on the Great Fire,[16] and, although few could aspire to Dryden's heights, many could do as well as the worst of Granville, Walsh, Addison, and even Dryden and Marvell.

Defoe's first published poem is very much in the manner of the professional civil servant. *A New Discovery of an Old Intreague* (1691) is an utterly typical contribution to the hurriedly written satires about city politics.[17] Defoe uses the loose narrative framework grown popular after *Paradise Lost,* and his metaphors and allusions are the clichés of his time: the unthinking extremists are "Jehu-driven" and Englishmen are compared unfavorably to the grumbling, discontented Hebrews of Saul's time. Defoe conventionally traces recent English history and ridicules the years of James's rule as "A Protestant Body with a Popish Head." Rough-and-ready satiric portraits of men like the Earl of Feversham and Sir Peter Rich seldom rise above the level of turn-of-the-century abuse: "As much a Souldier, and as much an Ass. . . . "

As mediocre as this poem is, *A New Discovery* exemplifies what Defoe and his generation had learned from Waller, Cowley, Cleveland, and the best of the seventeenth-century topical poets.

Most notably, they gave political events cosmic reverberations. Like them, Defoe used history as setting and precedent, satiric portraits, and allusions selected to establish typology. The final verses especially show the strong influence of the tradition. John Dryden's *Absalom and Achitophel* (1681) had become a model for that kind of poem, and Defoe deliberately echoes Dryden's great poem in his own "Conclusion" to *A New Discovery*. Dryden begins, "Thus from his royal throne, by Heav'n inspir'd, / The godlike David spoke." Defoe writes, "Great Nassau from his envied Throne look't down." Defoe describes King William's contempt and impatience with his subjects' behavior and explains how "His Conquering Mercy did his Justice stay." Dryden has Charles speak: "Thus long have I, by native mercy sway'd" and "Must I at length the sword of justice draw?" Both Dryden and Defoe anchor the conclusions with images of thunder and lightning. Although Defoe's poem lacks the strong fable and smooth verse of Dryden's work, it is considerably better than most of the city-politics poems.

Defoe's second published poem, "To the Athenian Society" (1692), appeared in Charles Gildon's *The History of the Athenian Society,* his attempt to capitalize on the popularity of John Dunton's question periodical, *The Athenian Mercury.* Again, Defoe demonstrated his awareness of poetic practice, for he used the classics, a conceit, and historical allusions. Even here Defoe could not let pass a chance to show a parallel to recent history. King Ignorance (whose reign began with the Tower of Babel) like James had influence behind the throne and his child, Sloth, is heir to the throne because none of the Old Monarch's "numerous Progeny" can inherit the throne. The parallel, however, is undeveloped, and the poem turns immediately to the Old Monarch's twins, Wisdom and Learning, who inspire respectively Rome and Athens. These twins become the forces that drive Ignorance from the world, and the Athenian Society members are among the viceroys of Wisdom and Learning. Except for the opening stanza, the poem is ingenious and well-constructed. The statement that Athens, for which the Society is named, excels Rome, which excels the world, and the story leading to the final tribute to the Society as the "faithful Agents" are concise and graceful.[18] Other poems in *The History of the Athenian Society* were contributed by

Nahum Tate, then poet laureate, and Peter Motteux, the successful dramatist; Defoe's poem compares well to theirs.

In the next few years, Defoe published several more public poems. Among these were his elegy for his childhood pastor, Dr. Samuel Annesley, *The Pacificator* (1700), which was part of the Garth/Blackmore paper war,[19] and *An Encomium upon a Parliament,* which was an ironic address to the M.P.'s who opposed William's requests for funding for the war.

In 1700 Defoe published *The True-Born Englishman,* a second poem supporting William. This poem made him famous and appeared in fifty editions by midcentury. At last ready to speak in a more distinctive poetic voice, he used inversions of conventional techniques, idiomatic language and metaphors, startling fictions, and incorporations of fairly sophisticated philosophical arguments to create a highly original apologia for William's kingship. In addition to a fable, Defoe championed William by including a panegyric for him sung by Brittania, two satiric portraits designed to illustrate the despicable nature of the typical grumbler against William, and poetic paraphrases of sections of John Locke's *Two Treatises on Government* on the obligations and rights of kings and subjects.

The introduction addresses Satyr as the most appropriate one to explain English behavior. Here, Defoe, like so many writers of his time, insults his age by insisting that they deserve satire, and he opens the poem by outlining its intentions and naming the object of its attack. Satyr, we presume, accepts the charge to explain and thus establishes a daring setting and provides a principal character that corresponds to the numbered parts of the poem. The world is the Devil's kingdom and England is a fallen woman; Part I explains English history and Part II, English character. Satan's vice-gerents, Pride, Lust, and others, have divided the world and rule without challenge because the temper of each nation now matches its ruler (e.g., Avarice: the Dutch, England's trading rival). The verse introducing England is quite suggestive:

> *England,* unknown as yet, unpeopled lay;
> Happy, had she remain'd so to this day,
> And not to ev'ry Nation been a Prey.
> Her Open Harbours, and her Fertile Plains,

> The Merchants Glory these, and those the Swains,
> To ev'ry Barbarous Nation have betray'd her,
> Who conquer her as oft as they Invade her.
> *So Beauty guarded but by Innocence,*
> *That ruins her which should be her Defence.*

Should the sexual nuances of "Open Harbours," "Fertile Plains," "betray'd her," and "Invade her" be overlooked, the final couplet insists upon this interpretation. The devil given her is Ingratitude, and he ruins her. He "possessed" her first and subjects her to "Crowds of Wandring Thieves" so that she is "oft subdu'd" and her children "oft undone." Like the incestuous triumvirate of Death, Sin, and Satan in *Paradise Lost,* England, Satan, and the first children mingle. She is "undone," not by nature evil. Wave after wave of immigrants—some conquerors, some opportunists, some refugees—come in a variant on the seventeenth-century satiric poem's review of actual historical events, until Defoe concludes "[England's] Rank Daughters, to the Parents just, / Receiv'd all Nations with Promiscuous Lust" and "still the Ladies lov'd the Conquerors." Defoe includes details designed to remind the reader of the facts of reproduction; for example, the red hair of the descendants of invading Norsemen and Charles's "Bastard Dukes" are named and described explicitly. Words like "medley," "common," "mixture," and "jumbled" are repeated and multiplied until the idea that "A *True-Born Englishman's* a Contradiction, / In Speech an Irony, in Fact a Fiction" becomes an indisputable conclusion.

Just as Englishmen bear the physical signs of their mixed heritage, so they suffer from inherited, incompatible temperaments, and this is the subject of Part II. They have the characters of soldiers, thieves, drunkards, opportunists, vagabonds, and religious refugees. The spirit that made their ancestors adventurers rather than settled family men lives on and mixes with the conquered's tendencies toward such things as "Submit to Love with a reluctant Mind" and "never love, where they accept Relief." They value wealth and power inordinately yet feel alienated from it and grumble against it. Both parts of the poem ridicule and condemn Englishmen even as they provide an excuse for the national temper.

The remarkable achievement of *The True-Born Englishman* is that it boldly calls Englishmen the children of the devil's vicegerent and a whore, lashes their faults in character and behavior, and yet becomes a moving, nationalistic statement. The most powerful appeal in it is to the common man who has been "bubbled" and is not contending for place, but the poem also makes common cause with those able to laugh at the contradiction of tracing titles back to Norman conquerors at the polyglot of "noble names," and to admit that the ancestry of "a Turkish horse" is better known. In this fiction, William becomes the archetypal Englishman. He is a brave, warlike immigrant but, unlike earlier kings, has come to free Englishmen. The final sections of the poem offer the reader two models: Sir Charles Duncomb who has behaved like the worst Englishmen by advancing himself through ingratitude, betrayal, and dishonesty and the "new Englishman" who sees the humor in boasting about his ancestors and acts upon the precept given in the concluding lines of the poem, "'Tis Personal Virtue only makes us great." Brittania's song begins: "The Fame of Virtue 'tis for which I sound, / And Heroes with Immortal Triumphs crown'd." The final two sections, then, imply that William makes no claims about his ancestry but is entitled to every claim because of his virtue. Defoe prods his countrymen to laugh and to go forward even as he praises William and makes a covert argument for Parliamentary monarchy.[20] He succeeds in defining the Englishman as essentially invincible, able to recognize and reward virtue, and irrationally proud of his stubbornness, irascibility, and rowdyism. In this poem Defoe's various strategies work together, producing a highly unified poem with the theme that virtue alone makes men and nations great.

Defoe always attributed his acquaintance with King William to *The True-Born Englishman*, and much of the poetry that followed can be explained in this light. He had come to see poetry as a means to recognition and position, had begun to write specifically to support government policies and positions, and he set out to celebrate the ruling party's success. In a number of his poems he attempted to regain from Queen Anne and her ministers the attention and approval that he had enjoyed during William's reign. *The Mock Mourners* testifies to the reality of Defoe's aspirations. It is an elegy for William and typical of the many turned out after the king's death in that it is unified by the presentation of good government and ideal kingship which finds William "An Emblem of the Government above." In fact, Defoe wrote many more moving elegies for William,[21] and this poem is more concerned with giving Anne lessons for her reign and paying tribute to her. He and dozens of other contemporary poets made her a typological descendant of Queen Elizabeth I: "And let it once more to the World be seen, / *Nothing can make us Greater than a Queen.*"[22]

Another less than successful attempt followed a few months later. *The Spanish Descent,* written to celebrate the victory at Vigo, again compared Anne to Elizabeth. The cosmic theme that poets used to set the immediate in historical and providential schemes made *The Spanish Descent* more ludicrous than grand. Defoe tried to use the battles of Cadiz (a defeat) and of Vigo (the victory) to illustrate God's actions in the affairs of men and man's limited vision. The poem did use psychology in an interesting way; it presented man's "fancies" regarding news of the war in Spain and described his ambitions, his guilt over defeat, and his elation at victory. The concentration on states of mind rather than on troops and men made the war and its meaning more immediate and unified Englishmen, whether at home or in Spain.

Although poems to commemorate victories and other significant national events were more typical of the poems ambitious poets wrote, others were written to support the monarch's favorite causes. Different from the shorter, cruder propagandistic poems, these were often written in the forms of "higher" poetry and were designed to appear disinterested. Defoe wrote four poems of this type in support of national moral reform, a movement he approved wholeheartedly, which had begun with Queen Mary, and then had been embraced by William when he returned from the wars, and had been supported by Queen Anne in her turn: *The Pacificator* (1700); *Reformation of Manners* (1702); *Good Advice to the Ladies* (1702); and *More Reformation* (1703). These four poems in heroic couplets are more interesting as representative of the sub-genre than as poems.

These poems are full of insinuations about covert motives and

political maneuvers. They use references to contemporary philosophical and literary issues to make highly political statements. In
them, Defoe continues to show his maturing comfort with traditional classical poetic themes, values, and forms and his growing
ability to rely on biblical narrative and allusion. In *The Pacificator*,
for example, Defoe uses the structure of opposing armies, which
Swift's *Battle of the Books* and Addison's *Spectator* essays on wit
would later exploit with more range and humor. In a poem
ostensibly about other things, Defoe draws a telling parallel
between factional turmoil and paper war, between the committed
and the mercenary, and between the unethical practices of journalists and the temper (and illness) of the nation. "The Pen's the
certain Herald of a War," he writes, and then he identifies the
writers who he believes worsen political situations by exacerbating
suspicions and emphasizing conflicts. These "Bawling Curs"
contrast to Cowley, Milton, Rochester, Waller, Roscommon, and
even Aphra Behn, who were dedicated both to truth and art. Defoe
continues to chronicle the effect of the increasing amount of party
poetry. "But now the fashion of the Times, / Makes Poets Damn
the Men without the Crimes," he writes in 1704 in *An Elegy on the
Author of the True-Born Englishman*. In *More Reformation*, he
attacks political satire at the end of the section on conscience. The
"Modern Tool" is the person who ignores conscience to write for
party, "As Prospects govern, and Success directs" (p. 50). At this
point, Defoe draws a parallel between the Dissenter who assents to
Occasional Conformity and the modern party poet; in the first,
Defoe finds the perversion and wilful misunderstanding of religion; in the second, the perversion and betrayal of English
patriotism.

Reformation of Manners (1702) is a typical verse satire in
heroic couplets. It compares London unfavorably to Sodom and,
like Defoe's early poems, laments the bad influence prominent
people have, in this instance, London sheriffs, magistrates, and
other city officials who "Punish the poor Men's Faults, but hide
their own"; merchants who form fraudulent stock companies,
burn their own ships, and engage in the slave trade; corrupt judges
and lawyers; and men in responsible positions who drink excessively. The poem shows Defoe's continued interest in city affairs
and his ability to bring symptoms together to describe a national

disease, but it could have been written by any of two dozen of his contemporaries. The theme that virtue is the key to happiness and the "wit writing" contrasting the virtuous with the evil done in workmanlike but uninspired heroic couplets appear repeatedly in similar poems: "*Vertue*'s the Friend of Life, the Soul of Health, / The Poor Man's Comfort, and the rich Man's Wealth: / *Vice* is a Thief, a Traytor in the Mind. . . . "

Between *Reformation* and *More Reformation* (1703) came *The Shortest Way with the Dissenters,* the pamphlet for which Defoe was convicted of seditious libel and pilloried, and the cathexis of this experience on earlier themes is poignant. Published only a week after Defoe's sentencing, *More Reformation* is the first of several poems in which Defoe combined personal experience and intense feeling with the familiar themes of his public poetry and in which he showed a new experimentation with verse forms.

The preface and text of *More Reformation* make the same three points: Defoe has been misunderstood in an incredible, perhaps dishonest way; he is being attacked while he is defenseless; and he knows what laudatory satire is and has practiced it. The tone of the preface is offended and belligerent, that of the poem somewhat abstract and somber. The long central section on conscience is complexly conceived and moves in three frames of reference. The immediate subject is Occasional Conformity, which Defoe continues to oppose vigorously; the more important subject is conscience as concept ("The secret Trepedation" that can "rack" souls and is stronger than courage, resolution, or law), and both subjects work toward the defense of his own publication of *The Shortest Way.* Defoe's use of typology here is among the most effective in all of his poetry. For example, he refutes the argument that the Dissenters who accept Occasional Conformity are like St. Paul ("ToDay would Christian Proselytes Baptise, / To Morrow Hebrew Converts Circumcise"). In four devastating lines, Defoe dismisses those who adopt these spurious arguments: "To talk where Pride and Profits are to come, / Is Preaching Gospel to a Kettle-Drum. / Interest, like one of Jeroboam's Calves, / In all Religions will at least go halves. . . . "

More Reformation is more pessimistic than *Reformation of Manners* but touches the same themes and makes many of the same points that the poems published after the pillory do. In

Reformation, Defoe finds that "Wit has lately got the start of Sence" and sees a decline from the time he wrote *The Pacificator.* He has found satire ineffectual, but in *More Reformation,* he says men will make the satirist a devil and persecute him rather than merely ignoring him and allowing him to starve. To Defoe, modern poets are worse than Rochester because they use his immoral themes without either his perceptiveness or his repentance: "Pleas'd with the Lines, he wish'd he had not Writ, / They Court his Folly, and pass by his Wit."

Defoe puts himself in *More Reformation,* and the tone of the poem becomes scathing, ironic, and bitter. He tells his story indirectly and sees himself from a number of points of view as he reflects on the reception and consequences of *The Shortest Way.* In portraying himself, Defoe obliquely suggests some reasons for his persecution and broods over his mistakes. He had believed himself to be the public-spirited, outspoken voice of his "True-Born Englishman." He had thought people understood his motives and respected his character. The confidence in the voice and the signature, "By the Author of the True-Born Englishman," in *The Mock Mourners* and *The Spanish Descent* became an ironic initiation for the reader, for Defoe establishes an immediate link to Rochester's *Satyr against Reason and Mankind* by choosing "A Satyr upon Himself" as the subtitle for *More Reformation.* Now Defoe sees that the prevalence and nature of political journalism subjected him to the charge of being a "party" writer and exposed him to the extremism of the current situation. From the description of what he believes others see when they look at him, he moves to describing himself as a fool: "A *Fool* indeed to Advocate for such"; "A *Fool* as by the Consequence appears"; "A *Fool* to tell the Nation of their Crimes." Finally, he sees himself as he will be: "learn thy sinking Fortunes to despise, / And all thy *Coward Friends* turn'd Enemies." He believes that his popular, public poetry has made his honesty suspect rather than communicating his principles. The alternation of verses describing the actions of men with verses giving advice to personified Satyr gives a doubly cynical view of the world. Men will be knaves, and satire must be cautious and politic. Charity, good will, and fair play cannot be expected. The tone, however, is restrained and reasonable rather than bitter because so much of the language is general and because the poem carefully approximates the dozens of contemporary poems on poetry writing. Even when Defoe refers to the three ministers who refused to pray with him, he might be describing a type rather than Howe, Spademan, and Fleming.

A Hymn to the Pillory is the release of the undercurrents in *More Reformation*. Written with the reality of the pillory, the fine, and the seven years of good conduct before him, the poem is close to Walter Ong's conception of literature as cry. The theme is "who can judge of Crimes by Punishment, / Where Parties Rule, and Law's Subservient." In this poem, specific examples and familiar names replace abstraction, and unequivocal declarations abound. Defoe turns the scaffold into a stage and parades across it those who have committed real crimes against the nation. He sharpens reference after reference from *More Reformation*, giving each bite: "Thou like a True-born *English* Tool, / Hast from their Composition stole, / And now art like to smart for being a Fool." This line compresses the way he described himself as perceived as "Tool" and naively being a "Fool" in the earlier poem even as the opening reminds the reader that, contradictorily, he is the much-praised author of *The True-Born Englishman*. He assumes the stance of the feared and, therefore, persecuted poet who dares speak truth. Defoe uses Sappho, Urania, Diadora, and others from *More Reformation* to show how people claim to see actual individuals in such satiric portraits; in *Hymn* he parades them as gaudy whores who harm their country. The poem builds to the portrait of the solitary, patriotic Defoe, "an Example made, / To make Men of their Honesty afraid. . . . "[23]

Defoe's *Hymn* is his first mature use of the Cowleyan ode, a dignified, respected form allowing thematic discursiveness and personal revelation. Defoe had experimented with Pindarics in his *Meditations*,[24] and he knew the form well. Abraham Cowley himself had summed up the attraction of this popular late seventeenth-century form in *Upon Liberty:*

> If Life should a well-order'd Poem be
>   (In which he only hits the white
> Who joyns true Profit with the best Delight)
> The more Heroique strain let others take,
>   Mine the Pindarique way I'le make.

The Matter Shall be Grave, the Numbers loose and free.
It shall not keep one setled pace of Time,
In the same Tune it shall not always Chime,
Nor shall each day just to his Neighbor Rhime;
A thousand Liberties it shall dispense,
And yet shall mannage all without offence;
Or to the sweetness of the Sound, or greatness of the Sence;
Nor shall it never from one Subject start,
    Nor seek Transitions to depart,
Nor its set way o're Stiles and Bridges make,
    Nor thorough Lanes a Compass take
As if it fear'd some trespass to commit,
    When the wide Air's a Road for it.

Cowley maintained the serious, stately character of the Pindaric ode but freed it from the elaborate, rigid structure.[25] He varied stanza, line length, and meter, but, more significantly, he defined the distinguishing feature of the ode as consisting "more in *Digressions,* than in the main *subject.*" Moreover, he recognized that Pindar often wrote about his own art and admonished the reader "not to be chocqued to hear him speak so often of his own Muse; for that is a *Liberty* which this kind of *Poetry* can hardly live without."[26] Cowley, then, combined thematic discursiveness with formal freedom and allowed for a significant amount of highly personal comment.

Recognizing the vitality the personal references contributed in the words "can hardly live without," Cowley set the stage for a new kind of more personal "public poetry." The ode traditionally encouraged serious and often personal reflections on important occasions, and the late seventeenth-century poet found the looser Pindaric ode ideal for the expression of deep feeling about national directions. Those poets in search of ways to explain, then to evaluate, specific events even as they set that action in historical and ethical contexts found that the new Pindaric ode easily allowed explication of process and shifts from the particular to the abstract. In the hands of poets such as Dryden, the ode had become increasingly narrative and emblematic. *Threnodia Augustalis,* for example, begins with the "story" of Charles's death and concludes with an idealized vision of James's coming reign. Dryden, too, had successfully integrated deeply personal statements into public poetry, as he does in *The Hind and the Panther* in lines such as these:

> If joyes hereafter must be purchas'd here
> With loss of all that mortals hold so dear,
> Then welcome infamy and publick shame,
> And, last, a long farwell to worldly fame.
> 'Tis said with ease, but oh, how hardly try'd
> By haughty souls to humane honour ty'd!
>
> [Part III, ll. 281-86]

It is in his Pindaric odes, however, that his poetry on this theme takes on lyrical power and beauty:

> Happy the Man, and happy he alone,
> He, who can call to day his own:
> He, who secure within, can say
> To morrow do thy worst, for I have liv'd to day.
> Be fair, or foul, or rain, or shine,
> The joys I have possesst, in spight of fate are mine.
> Not Heav'n it self upon the past has pow'r;
> But what has been, has been, and I have had my hour.
>
> [ll. 65-72]

Dryden, and Defoe in his turn, imposed restraint on what they saw as Cowley's extravagance,[27] but the opportunity to unite the private with the public held powerful appeal for poets "in opposition." As Defoe continued to use the form, he combined the most common metrical patterns of his time with experimental variations. Most of the longer lines of his odes are composed of heroic couplets with iambic hexameter indented lines, but he uses Alexandrines, dactylic feet, and alliteration to emphasize meter often enough to give the odes force and unusual beauty. Although he continues to analyze the moral state of his country and concentrates on one manifestation of English sickness (the arbitrariness of English law) he feels more free to use himself as example and to include more affective imagery. These odes, for example, develop an image that can be easily overlooked in *More Reformation*: that of Death. In *Reformation*, he compares the satirist to Icarus who risks death, but the odes and especially *An*

Elegy on the Author of the True-Born Englishman (1704) are
filled with images of death, shadows, shades, ghosts, graves, and
ashes. He turns himself into personified Satyr and extends what
has happened to him into an object lesson for other poets, a
"Memento Mori."

In the odes, Defoe is close to the traditional satiric themes and
stances that Alexander Pope would exploit in his late poetry.
Pope's interlocutors return repeatedly to the public perception of
the poet as tool or fool or both, and the poet himself insists that he
is a misunderstood, courageous patriot who suffers because he
scorned interest and flattery. The conception of the poet as an
independent, moral legislator fearlessly using satire as judicial
power draws force from its lonely, heroic, but immortal character.
Dryden had called satire "Our last Redress" and our "*Court* of
Chancery" in "To my Ingenious Friend, Mr. Henry Higdon," and
Pope would rise to his famous apostrophe, "O sacred Weapon! left
for Truth's defence / Sole Dread of Folly, Vice, and Insolence!" in
Dialogue II of the *Epilogue to the Satires*. In *More Reformation*,
Defoe writes,

> New Satyrs will their Crimes reveal;
> More Poets from my Monument shall rise;
> Who shall like me their Power despise
> Who shall condemn a vitious Court,
> And make the Nation's Knaves the Nation's sport.
> Naked as Nature's first Original
> Vice shall before the Bar of Truth appear,
> Keen Satyrs shall to Judgment call,
> And Power shall not protect them there. . . .
>
> Satyr shall keep those Knaves in awe,
> Who are too cunning for the Law.
>
> [pp. 9-10]

Defoe, like the other poets, associates Satyr with Heaven's truth
and justice. He promises an unbroken line of poets "like me" who
are willing to risk ruin and even death for truth. He and Pope point
out that Satyr shames men who ignore law and religion. Defoe

shows such men brought naked, and, therefore, embarrassed and vulnerable like Adam and Eve after they ate the fruit, before the "Bar of Truth." For Pope as well, "Truth" was an ultimate, certain standard by which actions and even intention were finally judged in light of the nation's highest interest. "Truth guards the Poet, sanctifies the line," Pope says, and Defoe insists, "But lasting Verse shall make the matter clear, / And what the Nation feels, the World shall hear." Both speak of the irresponsibility, even impossibility, of keeping silent, and both express public and private defiance. Defoe says, "Oppression makes a Poet."

The self-dramatization so effective in the late poetry of Pope is in *An Elegy* by Defoe as well. Defoe, like Pope, is both the real person in actual circumstances and synecdoche for a conventional poetic stance. The poet, armed with more than ordinary perception and his poetic ability, confronts sophisticated, widespread corruption. As Maynard Mack has pointed out, the poet is both public citizen and naif. He tells what he sees and then reacts in real (or feigned) surprise at the abuse heaped on him. He finds himself the object of attempts to silence him. Defoe tells his own story in *An Elegy* much as Pope does in *An Epistle to Arbuthnot,* defends his actions, condemns those who persecute him with their own actions, and asserts the independence of satire, which will inevitably be championed by time and the recognition of honest, ordinary men. Such self-presentation not only exposes vice but establishes unsentimental sympathy for the poet. The weariness and isolation of the beleaguered poet so well articulated in Dryden's "To my Dear Friend Mr. Congreve" appears in Defoe's prison poems. Dryden's elegant lines find echoes in Defoe's:

> Already I am worn with Cares and Age . . .
> Be kind to my Remains; and oh defend,
> Against Your Judgment Your departed Friend!
> [Dryden, ll. 66, 72-74]

> Let not the Insulting Foe my Fame pursue. . . .
> he must be void of Sense,
> Who dare stand up in my Defence
> [Defoe, *Elegy,* p. 5]

> He's bad indeed, who when he dyes
> Has none to mourn his Obsequies. . . .
>   [Defoe, *Elegy*, p. 15]

The poet is isolated, then, not only by the vicious but also by the pragmatic. A person must go "against his judgment" to defend the satirist, and Pope's comic dialogues ("Hold! for God-sake—you'll offend") are but dramatizations of this kind of conventional mingling of the individual poet and the traditional stance as defender of Truth.

An Elegy is the closest Defoe came to writing the traditional satiric *apologia*. One of the ways he demonstrates the kind of satire he wrote, the satiric objects he chose, and the allegedly, high-minded verse he wrote is to use lines from his earlier poems. He uses "True-Born English" repeatedly to refer to his just tributes to William and incorporates lines from *The Character of . . . Samuel Annesley*, *The Pacificator*, and *A Hymn to the Pillory* among others. Sometimes the lines bear important thematic weight as "[the Poor] suffer for the Crimes the Rich commit, / For want of Money, not for want of Wit"[28] or "*Was ever God All-mighty banter'd so?*"[29] Sometimes the lines merely call to mind Defoe's public poetry, as his repetition of the opening lines of *The Address to the Pillory* does: "Ye Men of Might and *muckle Power*. . . . "[30] At other times, he reworks lines already pressed into service twice; in *An Elegy*, he writes,

> And Damn'd the Author, tho' he lov'd the Book. (p. 23)
> They like the Doctrine, but they hate the Man (p. 24)

These lines are based on the lovely, reminiscing tribute to another man persecuted by repressive laws, Samuel Annesley:

> *His native Candor, and familiar Stile,*
> Which did so oft his Hearers Hours beguile,
> *Charm'd us with Godliness,* and while he spoke,
> We lov'd the *Doctrine* for the Teacher's sake.[31]

In *More Reformation*, Defoe changes "lov'd" to "hate" to show human nature's ungrateful spirit:

We'll hate the Doctrine for the Teacher's sake
As School Boys, when Corrected for a Fault
Like what they learn, but hate the Man that taught. [l. 2]

The mingling of the personal and the public with a statement of the poet's artistic intentions makes these lines representative Cowleyan odes. They use Defoe's experience to illustrate the debasement of law into a servile instrument of the government and maintain a running commentary on the duty of the poet and the function of satire. Poetry and law, satire and the pillory should be the servants of truth and the voice of virtue. The Cowleyan tendency toward extravagant affective imagery further frees Defoe. *A Hymn to the Pillory* is unified by the opening "Hail! *Hi'roglyphick* State *Machin*." The pillory becomes a symbol of national law, a "character" that can be read. Defoe exploits the image by referring irreverently to its "Lofty Loops," "opening Vacancys," "great Counterscarp," "spreading Stage," and "Wooden Wings" and by calling upon it to replace satire as the voice of truth. Both *A Hymn* and *The True-Born Englishman* appeal to common sense and common men; the people knew that men profiting from England's wars and corrupt magistrates were more destructive than writers but that they were safe from the pillory and that most of the writers punished had simply angered men in power. "They that in vast Employment rob the State . . . , / Who carry untold Summs away, / From little Places, with but little Pay: / Who Costly Palaces Erect . . . ." has the timeless appeal to common men. The human distrust, antipathy, and envy toward authority can be fanned by clever allusions and subtle images. Those in power are largely portrayed as an amorphous group, those in the pillory as lonely but dignified individuals. The current scandals carried out by nameless villains—the plundering of Cartagena, the military excesses at Port St. Mary's, the Irish Transport Debts—are set against " . . . *Bastwick*, *Pryn*, *Hunt*, *Hollingsby*, and *Pye*, / Men of unspotted Honesty; / Men that had Learning, Wit and Sence . . . . " *An Elegy* uses the poet's corpse as a unifying image and describes law as a machine with "Thousands of little Wheels, and unseen Parts" that "rings the Tune 'tis set to, *like the Chimes*." Both poems explain Defoe's satiric theory, give us a rare glimpse of the deep feelings of the man, and are forceful satires of contemporary events.

Defoe emerged from Newgate Prison an employee of the ministry, and his poetry immediately reflected the change in his situation. No one until Alexander Pope produced satires as full of autobiographical references and personal emotion as Defoe's 1703-4 poems, but many wrote poems very much like those he published after the Battle of Blenheim. His poetry became more pragmatic, more specifically in harmony with party position, and less personal. He already knew the rewards poetry could bring, and he and his contemporaries seemed to understand that in accepting an office appointed through patronage, they accepted an obligation to argue cases and to celebrate important events. That they and Defoe were very serious about their poetic art, however, cannot be disputed; the number and ambitiousness of Defoe's poetic projects as well as his continued experimentation with the forms of verse that had become the conventional modes of public poetry suggest a considerable degree of dedication. Perhaps Defoe believed he could mend his fortune and his reputation. Certainly he entered what he saw as a competition with other poet-civil servants and, just as certainly, realized that he could not compete.

Defoe's post-prison poetry was an ambitious attempt that assumes importance for literary history by revealing the hidden motives and forgotten vogues in the poetry of the first decade of the eighteenth century. On 29 August 1704, sixteen days after the news of the Duke of Marlborough's victory at Blenheim, Defoe published his first work as one of the voices of the Harley/ Godolphin ministry—*A Hymn to Victory*. This ode was quite successful; it required a second edition almost immediately. Then Defoe began preparing *The Double Welcome* to celebrate Marlborough's return to England, but, between the publication of his two Blenheim poems, he was reminded of the realities of the connections between politics and poetry, for Joseph Addison was commissioned to write *The Campaign* and rewarded by Godolphin with the position of Commissioner of Appeal in Excise.

Defoe saw Addison's poem puffed and its publication orchestrated to coincide with Marlborough's arrival in London on 14 December. *The Campaign* went through three editions in rapid succession, and it resulted in widespread acclaim of Addison's "genius"; whatever he published found an eager audience.[32] So familiar was the poem that it was even quoted in the dedications of novels such as Mary Hearne's *Female Deserters* (1719). A very short time later, Addison became Under-Secretary of State for the Southern Region. How galling this appointment was to Defoe can be seen from his observation that he is the "one Author in the Nation that writes for 'em for nothing," while Addison would not write *The Campaign* "till he had 200 l. per Annum secur'd to him";[33] £200 was the exact income from the office of Commissioner.

In *The Double Welcome*, Defoe undercut his compliment to Addison as "our Modern Virgil" with the snide observation that "he had never sung" had they not "fix'd his Pension first." More poignant is his implied comparison to himself: "Envy and Party-Spleen h' has never known, / No humbling Jayls has pull'd his Fancy down: / The Towring Youth with high Success aspires, / And sings as one whose Song the World Admires."[34] In contrast, in his *Hymn to Victory*, he had described himself as "the meanest of the Inspir'd Train, / *Supprest* by Fate, and *humbl'd* with Disdain" and "Under the Blast of *Personal Pique* to die."[35] Addison, twelve years younger than Defoe, seemed to have accomplished what Defoe himself longed for. Already he suffered from Harley's irregular payments and vague instructions; how much more he would have chafed had he known that Harley had engaged John Philips to write *Blenheim* and that Philips had done it in Bolingbroke's house.[36] Even Defoe's schoolmate Samuel Wesley benefitted from Blenheim; he received a chaplainship in the army for "Marlborough, or the Fate of Europe."[37] The position given Addison was roughly comparable to the one Defoe had held as auditor and was well within his old ambitions.

Defoe's *Hymn to Victory*, while lacking the ease and elegance of *The Campaign*, is not much its inferior. The topical matter and formulaic tribute are anchored in abstraction of an "eternal" truth—that the English have finally united cause and man, and, therefore, victory is assured. The poem strains a bit but is a genuine meditation on God's action in the affairs of men and contains some good expressions of patriotic fervor. *The Double Welcome* has a somewhat broader political vision; Marlborough's triumph is a "double victory" because he heals divisions at home even as he wins battles abroad ("you *our Hearts* as well *as Troops* Command").

Another object of Defoe's envy was Matthew Prior, whom Defoe had characterized in *The Pacificator* as born to "Flatter Kings in Panegyrick." Defoe thought Prior's rise unmerited and attacked him again in *Reformation of Manners*. Prior, he said, "Was for his Wit and Wickedness advanc'd" and

> While out of Pocket, and his Spirits low,
> He'd beg, write Panegyricks, cringe and bow;
> But when good Pensions had his Labours crown'd,
> His Panegyricks into Satyrs turn'd,
> And with a true Mechanick Spirit curst,
> Abus'd his Royal Benefactor first.[38]

Prior, too, had written a Blenheim ode. His, very nearly the equal of *The Campaign* and a good description of the role of the public poet, is a witty monologue asking Boileau ("hir'd for Life") how he will explain Blenheim and lamenting the difficulty of writing public poetry. Prior concluded by saying that his own poetic genius had been lost "In Prose and Business," but that he knew England had poets equal to the challenge. The classical grace of Addison and the range of Prior's wit show Defoe outmatched by men who had studied poetry more systematically and more deeply, yet Defoe continued to write serious poetry through 1706, the year in which he published *A Hymn to Peace, A Hymn to Thanksgiving, On the Fight at Ramellies, Jure Divino, Caledonia,* and *A Scots Poem*, more than four thousand lines of verse. After 1706 his poems tended to be short occasional poems and lampoons.[39] The drudgery, especially of *Jure Divino*, was out of proportion to the reward.

Jure Divino is the project of a man certain of public interest in his writing, even literary writing. Begun while Defoe was in Newgate but not published until 1706, it carries some of the *animus* of 1703 as exhibited in the vigorous attacks on "Despotick Power," religious persecution, and legal injustice and in the hymns about liberty and the fortune of nations with good government, but much of it shows lack of inspiration and signs of sporadic rather than sustained composition.[40] Defoe himself admitted that he sacrificed poetry for argument and history,[41] but the poem is unquestionably an ambitious *literary* undertaking with its twelve books of heroic couplets and its roots in the popular verse treatises of the Renaissance.

To the modern reader, the printing history and sale of the book is astonishing. Benjamin Bragg, one of Defoe's former printers, went to the trouble to have page proofs stolen, and his cheaper, pirated edition went on sale within days of the authorized edition. A chapbook, also pirated, soon followed as certain testimony to Defoe's commercial value. Defoe's poem argues that "jure divino" derives from the will of the people who choose their monarch and submit to his or her rule. "*Justest Title, viz.* the Revolution, and Parliamentary Settlement, from which, whoever reigns in *England*, has without a doubt, a *Divine Right* to the Crown, and possesses it by the *best Tenure* in the World," he concluded. Hereditary versus Parliamentary succession was still a deeply felt, much debated topic. The best evidence for this assertion may be the number and widespread nature of the Jacobite uprisings at the time of King George's accession, but the contemporary publications on the subject and conclusions of modern historians underscore it. Defoe's title page advertised that it is "By the Author of the True-Born Englishman," and he signed the preface "DEFOE." He was well known for *The True-Born Englishman* and *Legion's Memorial*, and the pillory and poems such as *A Hymn to the Pillory* had made him notorious to some and a champion of liberty to others. His opinion would be expected to be forthright, clear, pro-Protestant Settlement, and a bit provocative—all recommendations for the poem. In fact, *Jure Divino* is a pastiche of philosophical clichés, and long sections paraphrase familiar ideas, especially from Hobbes and from Locke's *Two Treatises of Government*.[42] Defoe argued from biblical and secular history that men, not God, choose and set up kings, that they do so to defend property, and that it is man's responsibility and a "natural" behavior for him to end tyrannic rule. He was at pains to demonstrate these points, to define "tyrant," and to praise the English constitution and the Queen from a philosophical perspective. *Jure Divino* did have a greater readership than Locke's *Two Treatises* and, for many, must have stood in relationship to the great works on political theory, as Addison's *Spectator* papers did to Locke's *Essay concerning*

Human Understanding[43] and Pope's *An Essay on Man* did to contemporary ethical treatises.

Although Defoe has structured *Jure Divino* very carefully,[44] he never achieves the concentration, compression, control, and power of poems like Rochester's *A Satyr against Reason and Mankind* or the "extensive overview" of poems like Johnson's *Vanity of Human Wishes*. Books VII and VIII, which give a historical survey designed to show that all nations in all ages have resisted tyranny, offer Defoe the opportunity to do a number of things for which similar poems by Rochester, Pope, and Johnson are admired. Defoe, however, does not identify the historical examples that would provide the best cases nor does he have the ability to write the tight, devastating satiric portraits that the form demands and for which Pope is so justly praised. Defoe's discussion of Sardanapoulus, which rambles for ten pages, and his obscure comparison of Arbaces to William III are but two examples of the problems with Defoe's technique. Defoe uses Richelieu, Nottingham, Filmer, Buckingham, Algernon Sidney, thirteen English kings, Ninus, Darius, Nebuchadnezzar, Cambyses, Tarquin, Justinian II, and others to make a variety of points without achieving thematic unity. Time after time, the notes are more affective than the poetry. After one long section in Book VIII, Defoe writes, "Not *Charles* the First parted with his beloved *Strafford*; not *Charles* the Second with the *Habeas Corpus* Act and *Star-Chamber*, not King *James* with his Crown, or King *William* with his Blue Guards, with a fortieth Part of the Reluctance [of Darius with Daniel]."[45]

Even his best verses are full of clichés and lack sustained musicality. As he encourages his readers to accept his arguments in favor of contract government, for example, he writes,

> Fear not the untrod Path of endless Thought,
> This straight to those *vast Seas of Light* lead out.
> The bright pacifick *Sea of Knowledge* stands,
> Behind these tow'ring Clifts, those threatning Sands,
> And if with steady Sail thou canst but pass,
> *Time* will present thee there with Nature's Glass. . . . [46]

Cliffs, seas, sand, sail, and the play on "glass" are all predictable and the stock images of poetry on the same topic. That Defoe goes on to say that only Milton has sailed so far is unexplained and unrelated to the theme of *Jure Divino*, unless one is given to reading an extremely radical opinion here.

The limitation of the poem springs, I believe, from a fact of Defoe's entire artistic life; he was engaged with the topical rather than with the abstract. He never learned to use current events with restraint and artistic objectivity. Instead, the immediate overwhelmed the larger subject. After all, he himself had been persecuted for some of the issues raised in *Jure Divino*, he wanted to support the Protestant Succession, and he was acutely aware of the immediate context: he wanted to compliment Anne, Godolphin, and the ministry and was at pains to show himself a loyal Englishman not liable to arrest and prosecution. He does not have the lofty perspective of the poets like Rochester and Pope, who were writing about the nature of man. Although Defoe makes numerous statements about the nature of man and his motives and actions, his poem uses them to explain events and to argue "rights" rather than to do the reverse: to describe the nature of man. Defoe is not interested in defining and satirizing man but in justifying an action that he makes identical to England's Act of Settlement. The sheer number and miscellaneous nature of his examples suggest the engagement Defoe felt with his own time; that he concludes with comments on Scotland and the need for union is but one example of the intrusion of an immediate political situation only tangentially related (and then only by Defoe's special pleading). In sacrificing musicality, Defoe was in agreement with the poets of his time. Dryden, for example, had explained in the address to the reader that the second part of *The Hind and the Panther* was "as plain and perspicuous" as possible "yet not wholly neglecting the Numbers" and that the third part was "more free and familiar."

When Defoe went to Scotland in 1706 to work for the Union of England and Scotland, his poetry came to illustrate the modes he saw as most helpful in furthering his political work. Some of them, like *The Vision*, were merely lengthy lampoons, but *Caledonia, A Scots Poem*, and *The True-Born Britain* were major efforts. All of them praise Scotland, especially for her military prowess and her economic potential, and rehearse the reasons for the Union in specific enough detail that such fine points as the salt tax are mentioned. In spite of the fact that Defoe could write cynically to Robert Harley that he had designed *Caledonia* to fool the Scots into thinking that he intended to settle there,[47] the poem is carefully done, shows deep appreciation for the country and its people, and carries the trappings of an ambitious, major poetic effort.

Caledonia is a topographical poem in the traditions of Michael Drayton's *Poly-Olbion* (1622) and Sir John Denham's *Cooper's Hill* (1642).[48] By Defoe's time, the combination of descriptions of prospects with moral, historical, and political reflections dominated the form, and didactic purposes were taken for granted. In addition to the overriding purpose of acquainting readers with the beauties and advantages of a region, these three topographical poems share a number of features. For example, they praise agriculture and commerce, give catalogues of notable men, include legends and fragments of history, and characterize the region and its people. All include several types of verse, such as satire, panegyric, and narrative.

Here again we see that Defoe was well aware of the structure, conventions, and purposes of a popular early eighteenth-century verse form and that he was able to adapt it for his own purposes, in this case to present many of the propagandistic points being made in his prose writings about Scotland and the advantages of the Union. Like the best of the topographical poets, Defoe infuses his descriptions with emotional and intellectual significance and finds a dynamic relationship among man, nature, and God. God's creation and purposes are made manifest in the correspondence between the country and its people. Rather than making description an end in itself, the eighteenth-century topographical poems used descriptions of nature to illuminate personal, social, and theological correspondences, as the lines in *Caledonia* that compare "Hearts of Stone" to the Scottish crags.

Defoe establishes very early the correspondence between the land and the people. The title of the poem reminds the reader of the first settlers, who successfully resisted the Roman attempt to conquer the entire island of Great Britain. Defoe's opening imitates Drayton's in that it concentrates on climate, winds, and light/dark imagery, but the two countries are depicted as quite different. Drayton writes, "where heate kills not the cold, nor cold expells the heat, / The calmes too mildly small, nor winds too roughly great. . . . "[49] Defoe, in contrast, gives the overall impression of forbidding cold and brutal elements. "Where Winds incessant blow, and Waves incessant roll" and "Inclement Air, Inhospitable Clime" are part of a Nature that "seldom smiles" but wears a "constant Frown." Numerous passages throughout the poem compliment the Scots for their fortitude in settling and developing their land, for example:

> Suited to no mens Temper like thy own:
> Wealth that well suits a hardy Race like thine,
> That dares through Storms and Death pursue the Mine.
> Wealth hid from Cowards, and the fainting Hand,
> Scar'd with the Sea's content to starve by Land.[50]

Caledonia is divided into three parts and moves from a survey of the land and climate to answer the question of why Scotland is still so poor. The first part gives some of the derogatory "myths" about Scotland, corrects them, and identifies fish as Scotland's gold. The second part describes the common people and reviews their military successes, especially with Sweden's Gustavus Adolphus and England's King William. Part III compliments individual families, praises Scotland's cultural achievements, answers the question regarding her poverty, and calls upon the Scots to be industrious and support the Union. The poem is united by the image of England as the right hand and Scotland the left and by the argument that poverty is enslaving. Throughout, the poem balances an awareness of a forgotten, even betrayed, valuable past with a vision of Scotland's potential. The people have bravery, virtue, honesty, and friendship but need to rouse themselves from their "long *Lethargic* Dream" (p. 59). Defoe argues that Union is "natural" and will bring Scotland to a glorious future. Most of the topographical poems include such political arguments, and Defoe's is no more intrusive than most. *Poly-Olbion* also included satire and prophecies, and *Cooper's Hill* ends on a political note. The type enjoyed considerable popularity; William Diaper's *Dryades* (1713) combined history, topography, politics, and patriotic sentiments in the form of prophecy and has been praised in our century by Pat Rogers. These poems, like the Cowleyan ode,

accommodated the age's affinity for variety and allowed considerable digression within a poem, purporting to place the immediate
in the context of history and of God's plan.

Defoe undertook no major poetic projects after the Scottish
Union, although he continued to write verse for his periodical and
nonfiction works. His earlier poems had expressed deeply felt
opinions or even emotions, but *Jure Divino* and perhaps
Caledonia had taught him how laborious and unrewarded writing
poetry could be. By this time, too, Defoe must have known that his
place in life was circumscribed; he was not going to be rewarded
as Prior, Addison, and Swift had been. On the horizon, too, was
Alexander Pope, a professional poet fully dedicated to the highest
ideals of his art and familiar with the traditions and classical
themes, allusions, and techniques as Defoe could never be. Yet
Defoe was unwilling to sink to the level of the second-rate
scribblers, who increased in number each year and who merely
lashed out at people by repeating political positions without
insight or commitment. His sanest comments about poetry were
made in later works such as *A Vindication of the Press*, in which
he discussed the rigors of poetry writing; his saddest were in the
Review, when he explained why he had not produced a tribute to
Marlborough upon the 1708 victory at Oudenarde: "I am not
qualify'd."[51]

Defoe stands, then, as a fine example of the group of nonpro-
fessional, public poets. He had modest talent, above average
learning, and mastery of the poetic forms and fashions of his time
at a superficial level, and he used his poetry for the same purposes.
He could never gain the public rewards given to so many of his
contemporaries, however, because he could not minimize the ways
he was different from the English ruling class. Oldham's father
was a Nonconformist minister, Addison's was a country parson,
Robert Harley was a Dissenter, and Prior had worked in a tavern,
but that was seldom mentioned, while Defoe's origin and past
were continually brought to mind by his behavior, his arrests, the
point of view he took, and the habit he had of speaking out
provocatively on Dissenting issues.

His poetry is interesting partly because it represents the modes
and purposes of turn-of-the-century poetry. When William was
king and personality dominated government and conceptions of

history, Defoe and his contemporaries wrote panegyric and satire; as English government became an oligarchy of ministers and the country became dominated by mercantile considerations, the poets turned to verse essays and topographical poems. Defoe tried to follow the path to success; he began by writing as a rather disinterested observer on social and political issues that concerned him, turned to the celebration of the ruling party, and finally, by ironic means, joined the poets who used their art to explain and to support the causes of their employers. Defoe's poetry has additional interest because of the period during which he tried to win favor with Anne and overcome the stigma of being pilloried. The 1703-4 poems include highly personal, powerful passages and interesting formal experiments.

That pragmatic rather than artistic concerns dominated Defoe's poetic ambitions does not mean that he was uninterested in art. Among the poets he praised are Milton, Marvell, Cowley, Rochester, and Dryden; he quoted and imitated a dozen poets of the seventeenth century and knew poetry well enough to do such things as use the first eight lines of the last stanza of Cowley's *Second Olympique Ode of Pindar* on ingratitude in the preface to *The True-Born Englishman*, the poem about ingratitude to William. When he praised poets, he was aesthetically correct, as he was when he said of Sedley that he had "an exuberant Fancy in Composing, and a Happiness beyond most Men in expressing himself."[52] Over and over Defoe praised others for grace and ease of expression, commented upon the revisions necessary to achieve it, and lamented rightly that these were his greatest failings as a poet. In another place he said that good literature "has always been my Ambition and Delight."[53] His poetry shows seriousness, wide reading, and considerable understanding of contemporary poetic forms and intentions. He experimented with many, many popular forms, including satire, hymns, epistles, addresses, ballads, and numerous mock forms. In the time between Dryden and Pope when Addison's best known poem was described by Richard Steele as "a Chronicle" and by Joseph Warton as a "Gazette in rhyme," Defoe was far above average in reputation, sales, and ability.

· THREE ·

PAMPHLETS
AND POLITICS

DANIEL DEFOE was a writer for almost thirty years before he published *Robinson Crusoe,* and, in his own lifetime, his fame rested primarily upon his pamphlet and periodical publications. As a journalist and controversialist he dwarfed even the greatest of his contemporaries. Richard Steele, Joseph Addison, Jonathan Swift, and dozens of the best minds of his generation engaged him in party warfare, but he was finally declared the "Goliath of his Party." More than any other single writer, Defoe demonstrated the potential of this important means of opinion shaping.

Just as some of the most ingenious writing today is in American advertising, so it was in propaganda in the eighteenth century. Writers often developed distinctive techniques, and the caliber of the writing was extraordinary. The *Tatler,* for example, used dreams and letters to expose predictable consequences and hidden motives; always interested in science, Steele often created pseudoscientific instruments, such as the political barometer, ecclesiastical thermometer, and "Gyge's ring" (a means of becoming invisible). Both the *Rehearsal* and the *Observator* used dialogues. Joseph Addison's *Whig Examiner* included poems, riddles, classical analogies, fables, and literary allusions to explain the Whig position on such things as foreign policy and Parliamentary Succession. Jonathan Swift used far more classical satiric devices, such as mock definitions, parody, fables, burlesque, and *reductio ad absurdem.*

Defoe and these writers took part in one of the most significant developments in English literary history. The late sixteenth century saw the rise of the prose pamphlet written in English. By the turn of the century, "pamphlet" had come to mean a treatise on some social, economic, political, religious, or philosophical issue of current interest.[1] These pamphlets met an immediate desire for information and were conceived as part of a controversy or concern and, even in the mind of the writer, as ephemera. They were often written hastily and aimed at a literate rather than a literary reading public. These readers were accustomed to hearing sermons and speeches and reading conduct books, proverbs, and jest books, and the Renaissance pamphlets often followed these models. Such readers were accustomed to obtrusive moralizing and a familiar tone. Writers often addressed readers directly, remarked on shared opinions or reactions to scandalous behavior, and made observations on their own writing. Such casual statements as "Now back to the main point" and "but I have gone on too long about" were common. Because of the readership and the interest in the immediate, the style tended to be far plainer, more denotative and economical than Renaissance prose. Access rather than beauty was the ideal, and English prose became marvelously flexible and varied. George Saintsbury recognized the result in Dryden's prose, which he described as "now easy, now forcible, now combative, now playful, admirably suited for narrative, and as admirably for exposition and argument, but essentially conversational, and, in virtue of that very quality, expressly eschewing and almost ostentatiously abjuring the complicated fugue-solos of the generation of his youth."[2] That description might fit any number of pamphlet writers of the seventeenth and eighteenth centuries.

The most original aspect of this native English prose style was its familiarity. The reader was assumed to enter into a relationship with the writer at once and to follow his reasoning. The reader was to recognize accepted moral judgments in familiar allusion and fable; more amazingly, he was to sense changes in speakers, tones, and even levels of "truth." Pamphlet writers felt free to include such "fictional" material as dialogue, vision, parody, personae, and mock speeches. Changes of tense and syntax became clues to interpretation, and subtle shifts in the level of diction signalled changes in relationship to reader or in point of view. Writers pretended to have overheard conversations, to have found other people's writings, and to have discovered strange almanacks.[3] Pamphlet readers from the beginning accepted these devices as means of presenting positions and opinions and relied upon their instincts to recognize the "cock and bull" story.

Although many pamphlets were carefully structured as sermons, rhetorical orations, or dialogues, others were deliberately formless and digressive. As late as 1685, Dryden explained:

> To conclude, I am sensible that I have written this too hastily and too loosly . . . it comes out from the first draught, and uncorrected. This I grant is no excuse; for it may be reasonably urg'd, why did he not write with more leisure. . . . The objection is unanswerable, but in part of recompense, let me assure the Reader, that in hasty productions, he is sure to meet with an Authors present sence, which cooler thoughts wou'd possibly have disguised. There is undoubtedly more of spirit, though not of judgment in these uncorrect Essays, and consequently though my hazard be the greater, yet the Readers pleasure is not the less.[4]

Here he promised both truth and immediacy of a new kind without lessening the reader's pleasure. The apparent artlessness and informality was meant to decrease the distance between writer and reader and to allow blatant appeals to shared moral values, emotion, and even "reason." If the reader followed the writer's thoughts, would he not agree at the conclusion?

The early pamphlets included rogue biographies, accounts of topical scandals, opinions on issues such as the Puritan controversies, and news of all sorts. Because of their length, they could be more moralistic, speculative, and dramatic than modern news stories. Although the writer usually assumed the stance of observer and reporter of experience, his need to attract readers necessitated liveliness, vigor, and sensational details. Pamphlet production reached its peak during the political unrest of 1642, but when patronage shifted from the court to the political party during William's reign, readership increased and the rewards for the writer rose.[5] A hack named William Arnall reputedly earned £10,000 in four years in the early eighteenth century.[6] By 1711 the total sale of periodicals had reached 44,000 per week,[7] and a controversy such as the Sacheverell trial or the change in the Queen's ministry might provoke ten or twelve pamphlets a week.

In order to attract readers, these writers had to be endlessly inventive. Defoe was the best of them all. Before he died, he had written over sixty-five individual works on issues affecting the Dissenters, another fifty-five or so on the recurrent threat of the Jacobites, some thirty-five on the Scottish Union, more than thirty on the debates that led to the Peace of Utrecht, and dozens of others on such controversies as the benefits of William's Partition Treaty, the standing army, the Act of Settlement, reactions to the 1710 change of ministry, and the accession of George I. In other works, he discussed European wars and rumors of wars, the Africa and South Sea trades, Parliamentary elections, and the Bangorian controversy. He wrote about duels, bankrupts, stockjobbers, the press, and servants and about the social and legal conditions that affected them. He offered numerous plans for insurance, academies, institutions for the elderly and mentally ill, and colonization, and he published evaluations of, criticisms of, and plans for English trade throughout his career. He never ceased haranguing his countrymen to be moderate, enterprising, grateful, and loyal. More than anyone else, Defoe exploited and extended the strategies of pamphlet writers. His output, his effectiveness, and his virtuousity were unmatched. He used his periodicals and pamphlets to explain events, to unfold foreign and domestic situations, to persuade, to ridicule, and to solidify opinion.

His impulse to write came from the burgeoning market for information about current events, from the number of issues important to him personally, and from the same sense of duty that inclined Dissenters to the classroom and the pulpit. Defoe's earliest known pamphlets were addressed to his own group, the Dissenters, and attempted to explain clandestine motives and undesirable consequences of actions being contemplated by Parliament or by the Dissenters themselves. His first, *A Letter to a Dissenter from his friend at the Hague* (1688), was part of the literature warning Dissenters that James II's Declaration of Indulgence was hypocritically manipulative and coercive. He insisted that the true beneficiaries of the Declaration would be Catholics and used insinuation to raise suspicion: "There are many things which would make a wise man suspect that there is some farther Design than Liberty of Conscience in all this zeal for repealing the Penals Laws and Test."[8] From this modest beginning with such limited issues as the

Dissenters' welfare and a London city election, Defoe went on to write hundreds of words championing various causes directed at thousands of his countrymen.

Without a doubt, a good part of Defoe's contempory personal and literary reputation rested primarily on these essays. Ironically, but understandably and justifiably, they have almost no current readership. Propaganda by its very nature is ephemeral. The modern reader must painstakingly reconstruct the context, delineate the issues, and recognize the stances assumed and held (and those are not always the same) by men living in a different time and place. The specialist finds important information and is delighted by the care with which Defoe analyzes the Baltic trade or estimates the average income of major social groups in England, but the general reader has no reason to search out these tracts and read them.

They are, however, important apprentice pieces for Defoe's novels, and familiarity with them allows us to see the developing artist and the full range of his technical cratsmanship. In his nonfiction, he experiments with point of view, dialogue, narrative voices, and literary forms such as memoirs, allegory, comedy, and satire. He develops his skill with irony and argument, learns to use affective repetition of images, metaphors, and phrases, and comes to write concise, clear prose. Furthermore, Defoe analyzes human psychology. He studies the way people reason and make decisions. He analyzes villainy and virtue. He describes the way history influences people, the ways government, laws, and social mores shape individual action, and the ways individuals face common problems and temptations. As short as the 1716 *A Conference with a Jacobite* is, we can see the dialogue as prelude to Quaker William's comic exchange with Captain Singleton, the presentation of complex issues and personal prejudices as rehearsal for some of the situations in *Robinson Crusoe,* and the characters' reflections upon alternative courses of action behind Moll Flanders's and Roxana's reasoning.

In this chapter, I shall discuss the development of Defoe's prose style in relation to three groups of polemical essays: those on Dissenting causes, those on politics, and those on trade. The emphasis in the first group is on exposition and point of view, in the second on characterization, the use of factual detail, and irony, and the third on fictional techniques. Over the years Defoe became genuinely and impressively original in the ways he clothed his arguments and theories with satire, allegory, symbol, and drama and in the ways he incorporates these arguments and theories into his fiction.

The group of pamphlets that shows Defoe's development as an expository writer most clearly consists of those on Dissenting issues. These pamphlets cluster around the times when significant legislature regarding the Dissenters came before Parliament: 1702 (the time of the Occasional Conformity Bill), 1710 (the time before its passage), 1714 (the passage of the Schism Bill), and 1717 (when Parliament considered restoring full rights to the Dissenters). In them, he needs to address Whigs and Tories, Dissenters and Conformists, and he learns to do so in a variety of ways, including multiple points of view, a range of tones, and an adept blending of surveys of history, descriptions of the contemporary situation, and appeals to justice. He develops the confident, moderate cadences of the *Review* and the elaborate fictions of *Moll Flanders*. As he matures and gains experience, he solves many of his problems with style and structure and learns how to move his readers relentlessly through his arguments, often numbering the points made and using strong adverbial transition elements.

Defoe's most famous pamphlet is undoubtedly *The Shortest Way with the Dissenters,* the one that got him pilloried.[9] This tract is probably responsible for teaching Defoe that pamphlet writing is an art and must be a considered, responsible action; it undoubtedly turned him into a professional writer. *The Shortest Way* was one of three pamphlets that Defoe published shortly after Queen Anne came to the throne in 1702 and began her reign by asserting her desire to strengthen the Church of England. The House of Commons responded with the Occasional Conformity Bill, a proposal that would have required all those qualified for public office to take communion in the Anglican church at least once a year. The provocative nature of Defoe's pamphlets is astonishing considering that Defoe was forty-two years old, had already published over forty essays and poems on political subjects, and had proved himself to be an effective proponent of King William's

policies in difficult times. In his defense, it might be argued that the
reign of William had not called upon him to write on Dissenting
issues. Although William's Comprehension Bill had failed, the Act
of Toleration had passed, and William's benign attitude toward
the Dissenters prevented persecution. In the winter of 1702-3,
Defoe blundered in every possible way. In *An Enquiry into
Occasional Conformity* and *The Opinion of a Known Dissenter
on the Bill for Preventing Occasional Conformity,* Defoe argues
that the Bill is a matter of indifference to Dissenters because no
true Dissenter is an Occasional Conformist. He bluntly calls
Occasional Conformity a sin, accuses those who practice it of
"prostituting" their religion, and asks, "And how can you take it
as a Civil Action in one place and a Relgious Act in another? This
is playing *Bo peep* with God Almighty. . . . "[10]

In fact, many sincere Nonconformists attended the Anglican
church now and then and took communion, and men like Richard
Baxter and Edmund Calamy defended the practice. Furthermore,
the passage of the Bill would have had serious consequences for
the Dissenters as a group. It would have substantially reduced the
number of magistrates and officials who were friendly to the
Dissenters, weakened the Whig party in Parliament and the
London City Corporation, and prevented Dissenting initiative in
politics.[11] Defoe's inflammatory language and uncompromising
position angered moderate Dissenters and branded anyone who
defended Occasional Conformity a hypocrite.[12]

Defoe published the third pamphlet, *The Shortest Way with the
Dissenters,* to coincide with the House of Lords' debate on the
Occasional Conformity Bill in December. It was, according to two
of his biographers, "the biggest mistake Defoe ever made" and
"the worst error of judgment in his career."[13] Defoe intended for
The Shortest Way to be recognized as a burlesque of the immoderate language of High Church sermons and pamphlets. He
included and drew attention to all the parts of a typical sermon:
"Scripture," explication of Scripture, explication of doctrine,
application to the congregations' lives, confutation, and "prayer."
In this mock sermon, he argued that England should eliminate the
Dissenters for the good of posterity and that the time was right;
metaphors that described the Dissenters as butchers, rats, snakes,
poison, weeds, and wounds reinforced the case. Unfortunately for

Defoe, the pamphlet was taken at face value by many people and acclaimed and quoted by the High Church. In the face of Defoe's emotional language and the charged political atmosphere, the mocking sacrilege of substituting a L'Estrange fable for Scripture, the inversion of the story of the thieves at Calvary, and Defoe's demonstration that Dissenting loyalty and charity are greater than patriotism and charity among the Anglicans, his true purpose could easily be overlooked. Furthermore, Defoe failed to develop his narrator's personality, dwelled more upon the "happy consequences" than the inhuman means recommended, and undercut the force of advocating extinction by insisting that threats would be enough to get most Dissenters to conform. Soon the Tories who had approved so enthusiastically of *The Shortest Way* learned that they had been lured into revealing their fanaticism.[14]

The government could hardly allow the leaders of the national church to be called genocides, and a warrant for his arrest was issued. As soon as Defoe realized the effect of his satire, he tried to pacify the angry parties. *A Brief Explanation of a late Pamphlet* appeared in the first week of January, and he wrote eight more essays and poems on the subject in the next year. " . . . It seems Impossible to imagine it should pass for any thing but a Banter upon the High-flying Church Men," he wrote and went on to remind his readers that he had consistently been an opponent of both Occasional Conformity and High Church extremism. He could hardly expect to influence the Tories who had been fooled into approving *The Shortest Way,* and no one of any political or religious persuasion could benefit from championing Defoe. His writings had been rash, inflammatory, and self-righteous, and, in July 1703, he stood in the pillory for the pamphlet.

The Bill for Preventing Occasional Conformity came back up for debate in Parliament in December 1703 and November 1704, and each time Defoe contributed to the paper wars. Although his tracts continued to defend his own character and to explain *The Shortest Way,* they were quite different from his pre-pillory ones. Now Defoe described the loyalty of the Dissenters in detail and argued the advantages of "peace and union" between the Protestant sects.[15] For example, in *A Serious Inquiry into This Grand Question; Whether a Law to prevent the Occasional Conformity of Dissenters, Would not be Inconsistent with the Act of Tolerance*

(1704) he contradicted his earlier statements by admitting that Dissenters had "publickly declar'd" that "Occasional Communion [is] Lawful in it self" and that there were several kinds of Dissenters, some of whom could take communion in Anglican churches without violating their consciences.[16] He finally insisted that the Bill was unjust and unreasonable, that it would deprive the Dissenters of their civil rights, and that it would have seriously deleterious effects on his people.[17]

These pamphlets show his increasing control of argument and diction. He continues to write from the points of view of Dissenters and moderate Anglicans and develops a subtle range of tones. Many pieces appear as by the "author of The True-Born Englishman," the poem he saw as proving his patriotism and writing talent, and this voice becomes the voice of the *Review*. At this time, too, he begins to struggle with more elaborate fictions. In *The Consolidator,* he develops some of the ideas he no longer expresses openly by creating the conflict between the Crolians and the Solunarians. For example, the Crolians (the Dissenters) form a federation with considerable political and economic power, a vision of the influence united Dissenters might have.

The final group of Defoe's writings about the Dissenters came in 1717, when George I gave them hope that the Occasional Conformity, Schism, Corporation, and Test Acts might be repealed. Coming after the 1710 passage of the Occasional Conformity Act and the 1714 Schism Act (which forbade Nonconformists from teaching), the 1717 pamphlets are those of a seasoned fighter and are among his best. They are carefully structured and closely argued; he effectively blends the history of the previous thirty years and evidence of Dissenters' loyalty and England's needs with appeals to justice. In them, his prose often rings with biblical dignity: of freeing the Dissenters to serve in the military he writes, "that their Hands may not be any longer tied from fighting. . . ."[18] In light of the outcome, the power and near-ebullience of *The Question Fairly Stated* is rather poignant. He wrote, "there seems Room to hope, and Reason to expect our Deliverance from these Burthens . . . of persecuting Laws, and of unrighteous Distinctions, and [we] shall be restored to that Freedom which as Englishmen [we] have a native right to, and which as Christians [we] have a Divine Right to. . . ."[19] When Parliament failed to repeal the Acts in 1718, Defoe used *A Letter from some Protestant Dissenting Laymen* to lament that they, as "Fellow-Protestant Subjects and Free-born Englishmen," were yet deprived of their rights.

As considerable and recurring as the anxiety and fear Defoe felt, his most intense and frequent feelings regarding the Dissenters were probably personal frustration and resentment. Not only did he see the government as inconsistent, short-sighted, and unjust, but also his relationship with his own people was stormy.[20] In no other cause were Defoe's efforts so unappreciated and futile, yet he remained the defender of the Dissenters' loyalty to the Crown and the tireless, self-appointed guardian of their rights and interests. This situation forced him to struggle with rhetorical problems and to analyze the results of his work. The resentment he aroused came largely from the discrepancy readers felt between his position and the tone of his pamphlets. In spite of the fact that he was a pilloried bankrupt and frequently in the government's employ, he was blunt in criticizing political exigencies behind actions, lucid in his summaries of history, and ready to name names. Defoe could be pedantic, and many of his pamphlets about issues affecting the Dissenters openly purport to explain events and to recommend actions. He sets his opinions above those with more apparent right to instruct and, furthermore, often usurps the role of spokesman. He insists upon his position's moral superiority in the face of common practice and historical prejudice. When, for example, he points out that the Dissenters could be a powerful political and economic force, he raises the specter of the Commonwealth even as he states an undeniable fact. Few men could see Defoe's vision of this force as one for English and Protestant good without also remembering the repression, fines, confiscations, and Parliamentary chaos of the Cromwell years. In order to avoid being misunderstood, Dissenters saw many benefits in denying Defoe's position.

As he matured and gained experience, Defoe solved many of his problems with tone, and these pamphlets illustrate well the development of his middle style and argumentative structure. Some of Defoe's most vivid imagery appears in these tracts and testifies to his emotional involvement. He calls the Dissenters the "out-works" of the fortress that is England in the battle against Catholicism, and in *A Speech of a Stone Chimney-Piece* finds the

hearts of the Whigs who voted for the Bill to Prevent Occasional
Conformity harder than the stones in the famous chimney in the
House of Lords.[21] In his letters, he grumbles that the Dissenters
are stubborn and Issachar-like, but he produces some of his best
propaganda in their behalf.

Propaganda must be clear, persuasive, and carefully pitched. Its
purpose is to solidify the support of those who are inclined toward
their opinion and to furnish believers with additional arguments
and tracts to disseminate, for there is no hope of reaching resolute
opponents. It is not enough for propagandists to discuss the large
questions; rather, it is their work to recount battles over fine
points. It was not enough, for example, to point out the serious
threat to England that closer ties between France and Scotland in
1706 would pose. After all, England had been at war with France
almost continually since 1689, and everyone knew that Queen
Anne would surely die without a Protestant heir to the throne,
which would leave England vulnerable to the claims of James III,
the "Old Pretender," now living in France and recognized by Louis
XIV as England's legitimate monarch. Propagandists must be
prepared to explain the fine details and implications that are the
sticking points of ordinary readers; for example, they had to
comprehend the connotations of Darien, the salt and malt taxes,
and the means of distributing both the seats in the English House
of Lords and the cash payment to Scotland known as the
Equivalent.

The supreme test of propagandists, however, is the ability to
repeat an argument day after day without losing their readers'
interest. In spite of having only a limited number of things to say,
they must continue to amuse, touch, and even surprise their
readers. In *Spectator* no. 452, Addison points out how remarkable
it is that "half a dozen ingenious men" can live "very plentifully
upon [the] curiosity of their fellow subjects" since they all receive
"the same advices from abroad, and very often in the same
words. . . . " The appeal, he explains, is in the ways "of cooking."
Defoe became the master of "cooking" and, therefore, the acknowledged premier journalist of the eighteenth century. His
pamphlets tend to cluster around an issue, illuminating it from

several perspectives, each with appropriate emphases. The Quaker might see hypocrisy, the Whig trade, and the Tory taxation. Some pamphlets were long, closely argued, carefully structured orations, others were dialogues, some dramatic monologues, some numbered lists, and other brief explanations of a single point, action, or public figure. He included emblems, historical examples, anecdotes, and colloquial speeches. As Bonamy Dobrée has pointed out, Defoe's style was flexible and lively. He describes a representative quotation from *Everybody's Business is Nobody's Business* (1725) as "brilliant, 'higher vernacular,' an instrument evolved from infinite practice. . . ."[22] Defoe was attacked, feared, and imitated, however, because he could hold his readers' interest through hundreds of issues of the *Review, Mercutor,* and *Manufacturer,* and in dozens of pamphlets on much-discussed topics.

Defoe was deeply committed to explanation and always concentrated more upon issues than upon personality. His writing from his earliest publications was straightforward, factual, and admirably clear. Although he could use satire, epistle, and persuasive essays as the other propagandists did, he developed unusual strength and virtuosity in characterization, which exhibited itself in many ways, including increasing use of dialogue, detail, imagery, and irony. From the time of the pillory, Defoe supported himself and his family primarily by writing. Over the years, he was employed in a variety of ways by the governments of William, Anne, and George and wrote a significant number of pamphlets for booksellers or on his own hunches of what would sell. By the time he died, he had written on almost every major political issue that arose between 1693 and 1730.

During William's reign, Defoe developed the plain, easy, straightforward style that he would use throughout his life, and he began to experiment with point of view. The great challenges of William's reign were to contain the growing strength and ambition of France, to resolve the related problem of the succession to the Spanish throne, to secure the Protestant succession to the English throne, and to translate the Revolutionary Settlement of 1688 into a set of practical procedures for governing the country. Because of her leadership and out of necessity, England developed the modern military and fiscal structures that allowed her to become and to remain a major power for nearly two hundred fifty years. Defoe, like most of his contemporaries, equated France with Roman Catholicism and Catholicism with tyranny. Therefore, he believed in the necessity of the war against France. More important, he saw the interrelationships of the issues. If Louis XIV succeeded in placing his grandson Philip on the Spanish throne, the combined power of these Catholic countries might be sufficient to return the Stuarts to the English throne. In an England weakened by internal faction and Jacobitism, such an event became more of a possibility. After all, it had taken England two years and William's presence to turn back the 1689 Jacobite invasion of Ireland.

In Defoe's opinion, Englishmen had to face the French threat squarely and had to establish secure funding for a formidable British military force. His Williamite tracts largely concentrate on strengthening the Protestant interest. Before the 1697 Treaty of Ryswick, Defoe wrote *The Englishman's Choice, and True Interest: In a Vigorous Prosecution of the War against France.* After 1697, he entered the debate over William's request for a standing army and joined with those who believed that England should insist on Louis's conformity to the treaty's terms. He soon came to realize that the opposition to William was in Parliament[23] and began to address the M.P.'s and to insist that most Englishmen saw the wisdom of William's requests and would say so through the next election. In contrast to the reasoned and restrained early pamphlets, tracts such as *The Six Distinguishing Characters of a Parliament-Man* and *The Free-Holders Plea against Stock-Jobbing Elections* expressed outrage at Parliament. They exposed election abuses and advised men to avoid voting for atheists, socinians, heretics, fools, and supporters of King James. In addition to constructing such prejudicial groups, he conjured up the image of the sturdy yeoman whose common sense, patriotism, and morality have always strengthened England, and he explained the importance of the election and the duties of M.P.'s to them. He began to unify his pamphlets with the voice of the English freeholder.

Defoe was not alone in his opinion that Parliament's behavior was myopic and risky. Among the appeals sent to the new Parliament asking that the French military power be matched was one from the justices, grand jury, and others of Kent, the English county closest to France. "The Country People began to say to one another in their Language, *That they had sow'd their Corn, and the* French *were a coming to Reap it.*" Using the Act against tumultuous petitioning (1664), Commons declared the petition "Scandalous, Insolent, and Seditious," and the five men who had brought the petition from Kent were arrested and imprisoned. As Defoe wrote, the action "had neither Reason, Law, pretence, nor policy in it."[24]

Defoe's response was nothing like the moderate, respectful Kentish petition. *Legion's Memorial* was addressed to Speaker Harley and began, "you are commanded by Two Hundred Thousand *Englishmen* to deliver [the enclosed Memorial] to the H[ouse] of C[ommon]s." He insisted that the people of England had the "Right to Require, and Power to Compel" Parliament to do its duty and listed fifteen examples of Commons' misconduct. The four-page tract ends unequivocally:

These things we think proper to declare, as the unquestion'd Right of the People of *England,* whom you serve. . . . We do publickly protest against all your foresaid Illegal Actions, and in the names of our Selves, and of all the good People of *England,* do
Require and Demand.

There followed seven strongly worded demands calling for such things as the immediate release of "all Persons *illegally imprison'd*" and the recognition of the French threat and the need to supply the army. He concluded: "for *Englishmen* are no more to be Slaves to *Parliaments,* than to a King. *Our Name is Legion, and we are Many.*" Before Parliament adjourned that day, the Kentish men were released. In his *History of the Kentish Petition,* he remarked that imprisoning Englishmen for petitioning is "Illegal, and a Dishonor to English Parliaments."[25] Defoe could be justly proud of *Legion's Memorial*; few pieces of propaganda ever have such a recognizable impact on decisions.[26]

Defoe often wrote about the necessity of being "all things to all men,"[27] and his work during Anne's reign showed continued development of points of view and "voices." Anne inherited, along with her crown, William's war with the French and the problems of the Spanish and English successions. During her reign, England became an awesome military and economic power, the union between England and Scotland was finally accomplished, and a lasting peace was made with France. In spite of these great

accomplishments, Anne's reign was characterized by almost continuous party turmoil and intrigue. For this reason, Defoe's and
other journalists' propaganda in the time of Anne considered
people as well as issues as it never did during the reign of William.
For Defoe and his contemporaries, Marlborough, Sacheverell, and
others *were* issues.

Defoe was employed by one of the men who contributed
substantially to the achievements of Anne's reign and who was an
issue for his contemporaries. Robert Harley was Speaker of the
House of Commons when Defoe was appealing for justice and
relief from Newgate Prison, and it was Harley who arranged
Defoe's release on the understanding that Defoe would be his
secret employee. Shortly after his release, Defoe was given the
assignment that would engage nearly all of his energy for three and
a half years: he was to work in Scotland for the Union between
Scotland and England. Relations with England and Scotland had
deteriorated steadily since 1702, and Scotland moved ever closer
to forming a dangerous alliance with France. The Scottish Act of
Security and the English Aliens Act awakened everyone to the
damage each nation could inflict on the other, and early in 1706
serious negotiations designed to bring about an incorporate union
began. By July the commissioners from the two nations had agreed
upon a treaty, and in September Defoe was sent to Edinburgh to
work for the Union during the crucial time when the Scottish
Parliament voted ratification. Discontent and protest continued
after the vote, and Defoe remained in Scotland to keep Harley
informed of the situation, to explain the Scots and mollify
English resentment of them when possible, and to explain the
advantages of the Union to the Scots in an attempt to relieve their
anxieties. In these interests, Defoe wrote approximately forty
poems and pamphlets, a very large number of *Review* essays, and
his voluminous *History of the Union* and *Memoirs of the Church
of Scotland*.[28]

Defoe's Scottish writings can be divided into three groups:
ostensibly informative, objective prose, satires of individuals or of
publications, and poetry praising the Scots. While he was still in
England, Defoe began writing the series of essays called "At
Removing National Prejudices." The first two were addressed to
Englishmen and argued that England would benefit from a union

more than Scotland and had nothing to fear from economic competition. In Scotland, Defoe explained away a variety of Scottish reservations about their trade, their Church, and their national prerogatives. His pamphlets, he said, would explain away the national aversions and prejudices that "are the Mountains, which must be levell'd, to make smooth this Valley of Peace."[29] Defoe never lost sight of the fact that England's motives were political—to confirm the Protestant Succession and to prevent destructive and expensive fighting with Scotland—but Scots had to be persuaded primarily on economic grounds. Defoe brought little or no specialized knowledge and no original arguments to his tracts. Some of them were disorganized, and others showed a tendency to rely on emotionally persuasive analogies instead of clear arguments. Many of these analogies emphasized the dangers of failure to ratify the Treaty of Union, accused opponents of the Union of lying and cowardice, and insisted that mischief, not scruples, lay behind many objections. He expanded upon biblical and mythic metaphors in order to give his readers a vision of the satisfaction of danger that would be avoided when the union was completed:

As a Man that is safely landed on a firm and high Rock out of the Reach of the insulting Waves, by which he was in Danger of Shipwreck, surveys the distant Dangers with Inexpressible Satisfaction, from both the Sence of his Security, and the more clear Discovery of the Reality of the Hazards he had run, which perhaps he did not perfectly see before.

So it will be an inexpressible Pleasure to us to *look back,* and see the Dangers we shall be delivered from in *both Nations,* when this happy Union shall be obtained.

Many metaphors were mundane and attempted to evoke common sense and familiar experience, "you will not have the Trade for fear of the Customs; you will not Catch Fish for fear you weet [*sic*] your Feet. . . . "[30]

It is easy to understand the modern historian P.W.J. Riley's barely concealed anger at Defoe. Riley says, Defoe "was an English agent saying what he was paid to say,"[31] and the Scotch works do not show Defoe at his best. He relies heavily on ridicule and even appears to think the Scots not worth his usual careful organization and reasoning. He equivocates and presents partial

cases. In his sixth Essay—*Two Great Questions Considered*—
Defoe uses the Kentish petition issue to illustrate how governments
can legitimately resent the manner of a petition without attacking
the people's right to petition. In light of his outraged writing about
the Kentish petition at the time it was presented and his pride in
Legion's Memorial, this crass use of the incident is nothing short
of shocking. In his defense, it may be said that Defoe undoubtedly
believed in the Union and probably could not take objections to it
terribly seriously. As an Englishman who considered Scotland
united with England under one monarch since the time of James I,
who felt as ambivalent about oaths as most men of his time who
had been subjected to far too many contradictory or trivial ones,
who saw the Protestant interest to be far more important than the
admonition in the Solemn League and Covenant that Scots work
for "the reformation of religion in the Church of England," and
who could hardly grieve for the end of the Scotch Parliament and
nation as the natives could, he may be partially excused. The
Treaty of Union was, after all, ratified by the Scots Parliament
with little real difficulty.

Defoe left Scotland in early 1710 to participate in the greatest
political upheaval of Queen Anne's reign. At first, he joined the
pamphlet war associated with the Sacheverell trial and, in this
cause, we gain a rare look at his ability to mount an ad hominem
attack. The well-known Anglican clergyman from Oxford, Henry
Sacheverell, selected Guy Fawkes Day, the anniversary of the
discovery of the plot to blow up Westminster Palace, to attack the
Act of Succession by preaching the subject's duty to support the
doctrine of nonresistance to hereditary monarchy. The sermon at
St. Paul's before the Lord Mayor and other city dignitaries was
memorable. Witnesses described the "goggling wildness of
Sacheverell's eyes" and marveled, "I could not have imagined if I
had not actually heard it myself, that so much heat, passion,
violence and scurrilous language could have come from a Protestant pulpit. . . . "[32] In the sermon, Sacheverell attacked the
bishops, Queen Anne's council, the Dissenters, and, by implication, the Toleration, the Revolution of 1688 and the legality of the
Act of Settlement. Although almost everyone hoped the sermon
would soon be forgotten, its occasion, manner of delivery, printing, and defiant "Epistle Dedicatory" assured that it would not be.

Sixty thousand copies of the sermon were sold by the end of the year, and wherever Sacheverell preached huge crowds gathered.

That the content and intent of the November sermon were seditious could not be denied. On 14 December, Commons voted to impeach Sacheverell. It was Sacheverell's sermon style that Defoe had parodied in *The Shortest Way with the Dissenters*,[33] and his hatred for the man and his position emerge in the care and subtlety of his arguments and in ad hominem attacks. Defoe seems to have recognized the volatility of the situation, and the *Review* advises letting Sacheverell exhaust himself as a runaway horse or a barking dog does. After all, "would all the *High-Flying* Clergymen preach at that extravagant Rate . . . they would every Day lessen the Number of their *High-Flying* Hearers; Moderation always got Ground by the hare-brain'd Measures and wild Excesses of its Enemies. . . . " Defoe says he is one of those who "think they should let this Beast break Wind, for it is no other; let him belch, his Breath stinks so vilely, it will make their whole Cause smell of it. . . . " Once Parliament had voted impeachment, Defoe continued to ridicule Sacheverell and explained his own change of mind about prosecution by saying, "The Disease grew contagious."[34] In *A Speech without Doors*, Defoe explains that Sacheverell was convicted for denying the validity of the Act of Settlement. In it and in several other works, such as *Instructions from Rome*, Defoe intensified the personal nature of his attack. *Instructions from Rome*, allegedly a letter from the Pope "to his Sons" "who are as Infallible as my self," allies Sacheverell with superstition and the mob and stoops to some of the most insulting tactics Defoe ever used; in it he claims that the Pope encourages his priests to use sex to convert and influence Protestants: "We indulge 'tis true, the Use of the Carnal Weapon, even to Impunity, as it is an Instrument to convey Good to the Fair sex. . . . "[35]

Sacheverell was convicted by a narrow vote. That and the light sentence imposed did much to bring down the Whig ministry, to end the power of Godolphin and Marlborough, and to provoke the backlash that resulted in the large Tory majority of the 1710 election and the return of Robert Harley to power. Queen Anne's desire to change her ministry, Harley's scheming, and England's war weariness fed the fires kindled by the trial, and by August

Godolphin had been replaced by Harley as chief adviser to the Queen.

Now Defoe could put aside his complicated disguises and write with genuine understanding and intensity about serious political issues that were also related to some of his most deeply felt beliefs. In these pamphlets, Defoe's ability to appeal to a number of different audiences and to give broad interpretation to immediate events is at its height.

Defoe began at once to address the most pressing problem of the new ministry, financing the war. In this interest, Defoe wrote a vigorous series of pamphlets and *Review* articles designed to explain credit, to demonstrate its necessity for the war effort, to persuade his readers to uphold credit, and to reassure them that the Tory ministers were moderate men. The *Review* appealed to a primarily Whig readership whom it would be useful to persuade that the change in leadership was more in men than in temper or policies. Defoe skillfully appealed to their interests and patriotism and exaggerated the distance between courses of action. He reminded them of their investments, used familiar analogies to trade to discuss England's reputation and influence abroad, and equated England's strength with her ability to wage war.

In order to reach a broader audience and to exploit arguments and techniques inappropriate for a Whig paper, he wrote pamphlets such as *An Essay upon Publick Credit* (1710). This tract, one of the best he ever wrote, quickly went through three editions. It is a tightly unified, eloquently written argument demonstrating that credit is the expression of English history, principles, and ingenuity; in other words, credit is by definition and by manifestation "national," rather than the product of time, party, or particular event. Credit is not "pinn'd to the Girdle" of one man, not even Godolphin. Such personifications found their finest expression in the emblematic Lady Credit. Created in the 1 August *Review*, Credit, the daughter of Prudence and Probity, continued to embody principles and provide an allegorical vehicle for Defoe's presentation of events for the next few years.[36]

Almost simultaneously Defoe began to work for the Tory peace. *The British Visions,* written from the point of view of Isaac Bickerstaff, sets the tone of war weariness: "The Confederates Struggle hard, but Things do not answer the Expence" and "they

[will] end the Campaign with mutual Loss, mutual Mischief, and having mutually done nothing worth Notice."[37] In *Reasons Why This Nation Ought to Put a Speedy End to this Expensive War, Armageddon: Or, The Necessity of Carrying on the War, The Ballance of Europe,* and many other essays, Defoe insisted that trade and the domestic economy were suffering dangerously but that England had to continue to prosecute the war. Defoe was always careful to explain that he did not mean for England to sue for peace and "take such Conditions as [France] shall impose upon us." "But by putting an End to the War, is here to be understood, listening to a Treaty with a sincere Desire and Resolution; if the Enemy may be brought to make just, reasonable, and fair Proposals. . . . "[38]

Here we see Defoe, the polemical writer, at his best. Without difficulty, he addresses Whigs, Tories, and factions within each party. He works for a good peace and, therefore, for both the continued financing of the war effort and the recognition of the need for dignified negotiations. His pamphlets are relentlessly argued; dependent upon rhetorical questions, upon the summary of recent events with clever assignment of cause/effect relationships, and upon the repetition of persuasive clauses such as "But the Case is alter'd Now," the tracts appear to consider all sides of a question, weigh alternatives, and meet objections. Many paragraphs begin, "If we take any step here," "As to separate Views," "It hath been answered," and "But this is not all." Now and then he will shift into the language of satire. Defoe's pamphlets sound at times like Jonathan Swift's more famous *Conduct of the Allies,* such as when he describes the war as "reducing" France at the "rate of one Town every Summer" or asks, "But how lie the Bones of 22000 of the best and bravest Soldiers in Christendom sacrifieced [*sic*] . . . to decide . . . who should possess the Hedges of *Taniers* or be Masters of the little Coppice of *Blareignes*. . . . "[39] Throughout 1712, Defoe continued to support the peace negotiations and treaty, and he was one of the most effective propagandists set to work to discredit the Allies in order to justify England's separate negotiations with France. Between the publication of *An Essay upon Publick Credit* (in 1710) and *A View of the Real Dangers of the Succession, From the Peace of France* (in 1713), Defoe had written over fifty pamphlets and numerous periodical essays.

Robert Harley was dismissed from office on 27 July 1714, the Queen died on 1 August, and King George landed at Greenwich in mid-September, to be greeted by riots in all parts of England. By this time, Defoe had no income except from his writing, and he was accustomed to writing for the government. To his credit, he wrote numerous pamphlets defending Harley and his ministry; in addition, he strongly supported George's Accession and, by the summer of 1715, was securely employed by Townshend, one of George I's Secretaries of State.

The most significant constitutional achievement of Defoe's lifetime was the establishment of parliamentary rather than hereditary succession to the English throne. As W.A. Speck said, the problem plagued "British politics in one form or another until the final defeat of the Jacobite rebels in 1746."[40] Most of Defoe's 1714-18 propaganda was directed toward preventing the growth of Jacobitism. He used traditional tactics of propaganda, such as name calling, setting up disciminatory categories, and assigning pejorative motives to his adversaries. Defoe enjoyed enumerating the guarantees and benefits of the Protestant settlement and plaguing the Jacobites with questions about James Edward's legitimacy and their own Abjuration Oaths. He found irony to be the appropriate tone to describe the contradictions in the Jacobites' position and began to expand his uses of it. Notably, he used the technique of Swift's Bickerstaff papers and *A Modest Proposal*—the object of attack being allowed to speak for himself, thereby exposing and condemning himself with his own words. *Reasons against the Succession of the House of Hanover, And What if the Pretender Should Come?* and *What if the Queen should Die?* all acclaimed mock advantages of the Pretender's reign; for example, tyranny would end controversies over religion, over a standing army, over taxation, and over alleged outrages of the press; because of Louis XIV's influence on James, England would no longer need to fear France; and England would be saved the expense of Parliament and elections.

Most of Defoe's irony occurred when he showed contradictions in arguments or revealed lack of self-awareness in others; his irony was often combined with an impressive number of statistics and factual details. For example, in *A View of the Scots Rebellion* (1715) he described the Highland rebels, estimated the number of fighting men they could muster, gave detailed information about the geography of Scotland, and outlined the means to defeat them. He implicitly discouraged those who might join them with specific, telling details that predicted their defeat; he found, for example, their fighting strategies old-fashioned and ineffectual and their supplies and money easy to cut off. Using the strategies he had honed in Scotland, Defoe worked to place the blame almost wholly on a few individuals and to reconcile England to the Scots, whom he portrayed as deluded and betrayed, but brave. For example, in *A True Account of the Proceedings at Perth* and in the introduction to *A Journal of the Earl of Marr's Proceedings*, he ridiculed the leaders of the Scotch rebellion and prepared the way for the relatively lenient treatment of the rank-and-file rebels.

In other pamphlets he compared the causes of earlier rebellions, such as Monmouth's, to the 1715 ones and pointed out the moderation of George's response in contrast to the persecution and injustice that Charles II and James I visited upon the rebels in their time.[41] One of these tracts, *An Account of the Proceedings against the Rebels,* went through three editions in a single year. *A History of the Clemency of Our English Monarchs* (1717), written to support King George's Act of Grace, used a combination of the strategies of earlier pamphlets. In a straightforward manner, he compared the clemency of English monarchs from Edward VI to George, answered the objections to George's actions, and concluded that George had shown mercy, good sense, and justice in the timing and provisions of his act.

The Jacobite tracts demonstrate Defoe's knowledge of English history and mature ability to reach a variety of readers. He writes easily in the voices of the Whigs, Tories, Quakers, or a country parson and uses addresses, proclamations, and rebels' speeches. The use of details gives the same sense of verisimilitude that is much praised in his fiction. In some of his pamphlets he presents the most obvious objections to the Pretender in simple language, while in others he explicates philosophical discussions of divine right. Defoe admirably performs the propagandist's task of presenting the same points in a variety of ways in order to hold an audience's attention and goes on to turn his experience with Jacobitism into one of his earliest sustained fictions, *The Memoirs of Major Alexander Ramkins.*[42]

Because Defoe's chief government work during King George's reign was to infiltrate Tory newspapers in order to weaken the effectiveness of their opposition to the Whigs, he published far less on political issues. He wrote about the 1715 elections, the Triennial Bill in 1716, the factions in the Walpole cabinet in 1717, and post-Peace of Utrecht foreign policy particularly in regard to France, Italy, Sweden, and Spain. He continued to use the techniques of apparently straightforward exposition, of irony, of answering the replies of his adversaries, and of dialogues, letters, and secret memoirs written from a variety of stances. None are especially memorable, but all are clear, respectable performances.

During this time, he added a new political sub-genre to his repertoire: annals. His *The Annals of King George* (1717, 1718), *The History of the Reign of King George* (1719), and *The Political State of Great Britain* (1730) were volumes in existing series registering notable events, publications, and Parliamentary actions. *Mercurius Politicus,* which Defoe edited from May 1716 until October 1720, and *Mercurius Britannicus* (1718-19) were popular monthly chronicles of the same type. During the last years of his life, Defoe was, however, primarily a free-lance writer, and he experimented with nearly every form of popular literature. His somewhat autobiographical *An Appeal to Honour and Justice,* his *The Secret History of the Secret History of the White Staff* (both 1715) and *A Vindication of the Press* (1718) give the reader important insights into how Defoe saw his writing, how the publishing world worked, and how he functioned in it.

The subject of Defoe's final *Review* essay was "modern Whoredom," by which he meant a personal passion courted, fawned upon, and caressed like a mistress. In this piece, a man asks Mr. Review, "And what Whore are you for?" and he answers, "Writing upon Trade was the Whore I really doated upon. . . ."[43] Defoe was, after all, descended from tradesmen on both sides of his family, was admitted a liveryman of the City of London in 1688, and believed his future was in trade until he was nearly forty-five years old. For a time, he had been quite successful as a merchant in the export/import business and as a brick and tile manufacturer. He had traveled widely, speculated, and dabbled with a number of investments, including a diving bell, a linen factory, and civet cats. He entered business during one of the few decades of expansion of trade in his lifetime (before the 1689 renewal of the war with France, when English trade with Spain and the American colonies flourished), and his later writings show the influence of this period. His opinions about English commerce were consistent: he championed the development of new markets, a favorable balance of payments, the expansion of English trading interests, the explorers' spirit that had made England rich, high wages, a vigorous inland trade highly dependent upon a transportation system ("circulation of trade"), and nurturing the production, manufacture, and sale of wool (his idea of the backbone of the English economy).[44]

Defoe's writings on trade illustrate his astonishing technical virtuosity and range of information more fully than his writings about religion. He entered controversies over monopolies for stock companies, lashed stock jobbers, defended keelboat men, suggested ways to make the poor productive, explained the trading ramifications of treaties, and published a few tracts about distillers, the Turkey Company, smuggling, Wood's private coinage, and Laws's scheme for retiring the French national debt. Furthermore, he produced two periodicals and five substantial books averaging 360 pages each; these include an economic history of the world (*A General History of Discoveries and Improvements*), a "conduct book" for aspiring and established merchants (*The Compleat English Tradesman*), and a strikingly beautiful economic geography (*Atlas Maritimus*). Peter Earle said, "A very wide knowledge of business is clear in all of Defoe's works,"[45] and that is evident in his detailed analyses of technical points and statistics, his familiarity with the ethical dilemmas businessmen face, his recognition of large issues, and his comprehension of the global landscape. Most of his writing about trade was not associated with controversies and was in forms other than pamphlets.

Ironically, Defoe's propaganda on trade is his most transparently mercenary. He is often engaged on the side he probably would not have chosen. He manages not to violate his most basic principles and beliefs, but he does a good deal of special pleading and intricate sidestepping. A case in point is his most extended engagement over an issue of trade: the 1713 Tory bill to put the eighth and ninth

articles of the Treaty of Commerce into effect.[46] These articles
would have lowered the duties on French goods and raised them on
selected imports from other nations. In spite of misgivings about the
threat to the English wool, linen, and silk industries and Hanoverian opposition to the treaty, Defoe wrote several pamphlets, numerous *Review* essays, and created the *Mercator* to support the bill.
He hammered away at the idea that, on balance, the treaty would
benefit England by improving the balance of payments, by stimulating several segments of the British economy, by increasing the
amount of trade and the circulation of goods, and by giving England an edge over her traditional commercial rivals, the Dutch. All
of this, he asserts, would compensate for the additional care that
the government would have to take to protect the cloth industries.
By this time, he knew well the advantages of a newspaper over a
pamphlet campaign. He could repeat his points, establish a philosophy, answer objections promptly, create ongoing discussions,
and introduce metaphoric characters and key phrases that could be
played upon, developed, and repeated with the persuasive force of
modern advertising campaigns.

All of these things he did to good effect, but a few of his
pamphlets, which can only be described as written "in opposition"
to the two articles, are equally good. For example, *Considerations
upon the Eighth and Ninth Articles of the Treaty of Commerce* is
tighter and more energetic than *An Essay on the Treaty of
Congress.* In the latter Defoe gives the history of trade agreements,
quotes them, and insists that the Treaty of Commerce is more to
Britain's advantage than to France's. Unfortunately in rehearsing
the reason for trade restrictions after the Treaty of Ryswick, he
reminds the reader of the reasons to distrust the 1713 treaty. In
Considerations he alludes to history but concentrates on the
present. In *An Essay,* Defoe is on the defensive; most of the
pamphlet answers objections to the treaty. *Considerations,* in
contrast, seems factual, full of information, and vigorous. It moves
expeditiously through each article and points out the dangers to
English trade. Most of all, it seems to hide nothing; even the
opening definition of "tariff" is given in a good-natured, confident
way. *An Essay* seems to be the work of a man driven to argue
technical points and to beg the most significant questions; *Considerations* appears to be by a man in full command of his subject

and at ease with his position. Nothing in *An Essay* compares to Defoe's statistics, his reminder that the Treaty contradicts the earlier Methuen Treaty, or his discussion of France as the rival to the English wool trade. No sentence catches the threat of unregulated trade as vividly as "The *French* are an Industrious People; they work cheap, and work well; their Fancy in contriving Fashions, Figures and Fancies in their Work, is very bright and quick, and these Things recommend their Goods to us."[47]

Once the Bill of Commerce was defeated, Defoe attempted to demonstrate his own independence and consistency and to vindicate himself by explaining the reasons for the defeat of the bill and by predicting the consequences. The most creative of these efforts was *Memoirs of Count Tariff*, a ninety-five page "secret history" of an emblematic character. Here, as in *The Consolidator*, Defoe uses a fictional form to interpret events and to open his countrymen's eyes to truths that they have been too complacent or prejudiced to see. The "characters" of *Memoirs* act out the parts Defoe sees behind the Parliamentary vote: Mynheer Coopsmanschap, the greedy Dutch tradesman; Alderman Traffick, an English merchant; Harry Woolpack, a manufacturer; Sir Politick Falshood, a self-interested Whig; and Count Tariff himself, a Frenchman. Defoe presents Tariff as misunderstood, explains how Traffick (merchants) and Woolpack (manufacturers) were set against each other, reveals the crass political motives springing from knowledge of Anne's ill health, and, thus, argues that the Bill was defeated for every reason but its own content. Defoe had made similar arguments earlier,[48] but *Memoirs* is particularly interesting because of the way Defoe's emblematic characters work in a well-developed fictional structure, illustrate the dynamic relationship between individuals, opinions, and events, and are examples of yet another of Defoe's techniques of translating premises into cause/effect narration. Defoe's characters are fairly well developed, and Coopsmanschap and Sir Politick bluster, lie, and make amusing Jonsonian fools of themselves.

Most of Defoe's tracts on trade have the weaknesses and strengths of the Bill of Commerce writings. Defoe often casts accounts, reviews history, quotes documents, and answers objections. His strategies tend to be unsophisticated but evidence of genuine understanding of complex concepts and large issues. In order to explain terms or questions, he will often use a comparison to an individual; he will use a situation facing a homeowner, small businessman, bankrupt, or country gentleman to explain broad issues and concepts, just as he had Traffick speak for an entire interest group caught in complicated negotiations involving domestic and international factions. He appeals disconcertingly often to his readers' self-interest in an unrefined manner, and he often reassures his readers—without much evidence—that time will prove him right. His views on the wool trade, the balance of payments, and the necessity of scattering industries throughout England in order to create jobs in distribution become monotonous.

In the last years of his life, Defoe finally faced the stagnant condition of England's economy; he accused his countrymen of being in a "lethargic Dream" and urged them in book after book to take to the seas and to expand into Africa and throughout the Americas. He reminded his countrymen of the spirit of Raleigh, that trade was "power and wealth," and that individuals could explore, trade, and invest without help from Parliament. Much of his later writing bordered on the fantastic, but it was the fantasy that sent explorers from Europe around the world and that provided much of the imaginative power of *Robinson Crusoe, Captain Singleton,* and *Captain Roberts.* Furthermore, this fantasy was joined to the practical experience and pragmatic understanding of a man who had lived and had analyzed imperial England for over half a century.

Defoe was more often the historian, projector, or interpreter than the controversialist when he wrote about trade. As G.D.H. Cole said in his classic introduction to *A Tour thro' the Whole Island of Great Britain,* Defoe "looked at England with the eye of a tradesman, appraising most things in the light of their contribution to the economics of the national life, and most people in accordance with their place in the economic rather than the social system."[49] Almost nothing Defoe wrote was free of references to trade or of themes and arguments based on his economic knowledge and theories.

Defoe moved beyond controversies, answering "answers" and "replies," and propaganda, to produce other commercially successful forms of literature, such as conduct and travel books, histories, and memoirs. The experience he gained as a propagandist provided him with ideas, rich material, depth of insight, and stylistic virtuosity. He had assumed voices and points of view different from his own, written dialogues, histories, scandalous and counterfeit memoirs, "visions," and ironic polemics. He was accustomed to interpreting history, explaining events and their implications, and prescribing to the nation. The experience of fifteen years as a propagandist invigorated his later novels, historical memoirs, travel books, conduct books, and projects. Just as Defoe was genuinely impressive and original in the ways he clothed economic, political, or religious arguments and theories with satire, allegory, symbol, and comedy in the tracts and periodical essays, so was he a master of using these same arguments and theories to give his histories and fiction profundity, depth, and lasting interest. The clarity, knowledge, virtuosity, and dramatic voices developed and polished in the pamphlets stand behind the great works of the last fifteen years of his life.

· FOUR ·

THE HISTORIES

WE DO NOT THINK of the early eighteenth century as an important time in the development of history writing for not one great history was written; yet more than one hundred works of history were published in England alone between 1700 and 1754, and the evolution that would move history away from Raleigh's *History of the World* toward the histories of Hume, Robertson, and Gibbon was well under way. Defoe and his nameless fellow historians were caught in the crucial moment of the struggle to resolve the contemporary demand for the empirical with the eternal compulsion to find pattern and order in the universe.

Defoe and his contemporaries inherited a tradition of history writing that emphasized "the changeless patterns and structures which underlie the world of change."[1] Such a Uniformitarian view encompassed both the Christian conception of a Providential world and the classical idea of Nature. Both lent themselves to the belief that history was educationally essential. A commonplace of the age defined history as "philosophy teaching by example," and the benefits of the study of history were listed unvaryingly and with the tone of complete certainty found in Hobbes's preface to his translation of *Thucydides*: "For the principal and proper work of history being to instruct and enable men, by the knowledge of actions past, to bear themselves prudently in the present and providently towards the future."[2]

Defoe's contemporaries could not deny change, however. They saw that the relationship between the Church and the Constitution was evolving; they knew that economic and legal institutions were being created; they saw the differences scientific discoveries had made in medicine, navigation, and industry. Their conscious minds, despite the discomfort of their consciences, admitted the ideas of progress and the symbiotic nature of society. In reponse to this troubling perception of the world and to the empirical, scientific impulses of scholars of their time, they often emphasized the gathering and objective presentation of evidence. This tendency, like the earlier conceptions of history, did not admit imaginative interpretation and exploration of impact. Just as the age's scientists set about the collection of data with faith rather than with knowledge of applications, so did the historians. These historians put together narratives that moved and were animated by papers, often reproduced in full, rather than by interpretation. Tacitly arguing that the papers spoke for themselves, they produced history that they presented as and believed to be objective and free from error. The talent and energy of Henry Savile, William Cave, Henry Wharton, John Selden, Henry Spelman, John Strype, White Kennett, and Thomas Hearne went into the preservation and accurate publication of the relics of English history. Their work included such diverse volumes as Savile's *Scriptores post Bedam*, which is a collection of Medieval chronicles, and Kennett's *The History of England from . . . the Reign of Charles I to the end of the Reign of William III*, which transcribed nearly every document mentioned in it.

Concomitant with this sustained, scholarly movement came the rise of political parties with the resulting propagandistic history writing. Even as the century recognized and turned away from the ideological aspects of histories such as Clarendon's and Evelyn's, they appreciated the power history had to sway opinion and began to write accounts of events, often events in progress, that unabashedly used fictional techniques. While some men meticulously collected and transcribed Medieval manuscripts, others created a mistress or an aide-de-camp to reveal the secrets of a great man. As the political party came to replace religion for the Englishman,[3] the power to turn history to political purposes assumed great importance. Anyone reading the pamphlets of controversies between 1690 and 1715 would be struck by the change from arguments based on Scripture to arguments based on history. In fact, biblical examples came to be used as precepts rather than typologies as classical ones were, and argument from biblical exegesis all but disappears.

From his youth, Defoe was more interested in history than any other subject. His 1682 *Historical Collections* shows him already widely read, for he paraphrases and reworks stories from Bede, Plutarch, Ælian, Thomas Fuller, George Fox, and others, and in 1700 he tells his readers that he had read "all the Histories of Europe, that are Extant in our Language, and some in other Languages."[4] His poetry, religious and political pamphlets, and the *Review* are rich in historical examples, surprising in their number, diversity, and appropriateness. *The Consolidator* and *The Storm* are apprentice histories of quite innovative sorts. He was deeply convinced of the importance of history writing, and his histories provide valuable insights into his fictional career. In this chapter, I shall discuss *The History of the Union*, the Great Northern War histories, and *A General History of Discoveries and Improvements* as representative examples of types of early eighteenth-century historiography.

Defoe's personal impulses and purposes in writing *The History of the Union between Scotland and England*[5] were as complicated and inharmonious as those of history writing itself. He had written to Robert Harley on 27 January 1707 to boast that he had conceived the design of writing the history as one more means of explaining his continued stay in Scotland and as a way of gaining access to people and papers ordinarily beyond his reach. But despite this apparent lack of literary ambition for his project, he planned a lavish folio edition with his portrait as frontispiece and advertised for subscribers for eight months in his *Review*.[6] Before publication, he received praise and probably financial assistance from some of the most important men in Scotland, but he was also embroiled in petty bickering with a Glasgow clergyman and saw the worst printer in Scotland bring his book out in jumbled, piecemeal fashion more than two years after its conception.

He shared the common opinion that the Union was one of the most important events in Scottish history and a "distinguishing glory" of Anne's reign. Defoe, like Chamberlayne, Anderson, Cromarty, and other historians, made this point and celebrated the

Union as the fulfillment of Providential design. In the dedication to Anne and in his preface, Defoe drew a comparison between the attempts at union and Old Testament stories in which God withholds the completion of a laudatory task until a worthy, chosen instrument appears. Defoe explained these failures by quoting Psalm 78:37, a Psalm reciting the history of Israel: "Because their Hearts were not right with Him, neither were they stedfast in his Covenant. . . . " Now, however, he believed "the Connection of Providences in the Affairs of this World, and the various Turns the Island of *Britain* has had in the Compass of a few past Years" "have had their direct Tendency to this great Event."[7] Similarly, Chamberlayne observed that the Union "has now made the Inhabitants of this Noble Island to become again One People, as they formerly were, as the Great Author of Nature seems originally to have design'd they should always be."[8]

Scots saw especially pressing reasons for histories about their nation. George MacKenzie, one of the most distinguished and respected historians of his time, pointed out that "all the Wise Nations in the World, have, with great Care and Diligence, transmitted to their Posterity, the Lives and Actions of their Illustrious Predecessors, that they, seeing the Rewards and Honours that were conferr'd upon them for their Vertues, might be thereby excited to Imitate them in their Actions: And tho' our Nation has produc'd as Great Men as any other Nation in the World, yet we have been so unjust to their memories and to our Posterity, that hitherto there has not been made a Collection of their Lives."[9] Furthermore, increasing communication between England and Scotland had revealed an appalling amount of prejudice and ignorance about Scots. Chamberlayne did not exaggerate when he wrote that "very few, even of our most Inquisitive Men, have a just Idea of the Condition of [Scotland]; and many Parts of *Africa* and the *Indies* (to our Shame be it spoken) are better known than a Region which is contiguous to our own, and which We have always had so great a Concern for."[10]

Defoe, then, came to the composition of the *History of the Union* believing that his task included familiarizing his readers with the history, characteristics, and situation of Scotland; arranging and explaining the events related to the Union; and reproducing the most significant documents associated with the Union, both to substantiate his report and to give readers material of great interest. To him and his contemporaries, he was writing one of the forms of civic history, the kind intended to "propound" or "represent" "an action." Such histories had natural time limits determined by the event itself and avoided the deficiencies of the other two kinds of histories: that of "times," which must pass over "the smaller . . . motions of men" and which may reveal important motives, and that of "lives," which may also have to pass over important matters if unrelated to the subject of the life. Believed to be the most complete, truthful, and "sincere," histories of actions were seen as following the models of Xenophon's *Anabasis*, Sallust's *Catilina*, and Thucydides' *History of the Peloponnesian War*. Francis Bacon and others noted the ease with which such histories lent themselves to an instructive argument, and, above all, Defoe's intentions were irenic. He wanted to depict the Scots' resistance to the Union in a way that would avert English resentment and heal divisions and to explain the benefits and ramifications of the individual Articles of Union. Not surprisingly, these pacific themes often worked against the first three.

Defoe's conception of history writing and his own purposes explain the nature of *The History of the Union*. The decisions Defoe made about structure, interpretation, and rhetoric based upon these ideas shape the book.

❦ *Structure*. Defoe chose to begin *The History of the Union* with the time of the Picts and Saxons and to catalog the wars between England and Scotland and their attempts at Union. Like his contemporaries, however, he moved quickly to recent history (by page thirty-six, he was discussing Glenco). Renaissance men might begin with the creation of the world, as Raleigh did, or open the history of Parliament with Elizabeth's reign, as Thomas May did, but the early eighteenth-century historian usually defined the beginning and conclusion of a historical event quite narrowly. Hesiod might propose the ages of gold, silver, bronze, and iron, but Defoe's contemporaries believed their task to be discovering sequence and pointing out relationships within this sequence. Hesiod and others moved beyond episode in history and speculated from a philosophical, political, or even religious base, which historians in the eighteenth century had come to distrust.

With the work of the historian so narrowed, the most influential decisions Defoe makes are structural. The way the historian arranges his material determines far more than clarity; it implies relationships—temporal, spatial, causal, and analogical; it reproduces multiple reactions to single events; it indicates simultaneity or unrelatedness as well as sequence; and, most crucially, it shapes the readers' understanding and reaction, both rational and emotional: that is, it determines impact.

Defoe divided *The History of the Union* into six parts. The sections (I. *A General History of Unions in Britain*; II. *Of Affairs in Both Kingdoms*; III. *Of the Last Treaty, Properly Called the Union*; IV. *Of the Carrying on of the Treaty in Scotland*; V. *An Abstract of the Proceedings on the Treaty of Union Within the Parliament of Scotland*; and VI, an appendix divided into *Containing an Account of Transactions in both Parts of the United Kingdom subsequent to the* UNION, and copies of documents) necessarily repeat each other.[11] Section III concentrates upon the events in Scottish/English history that worked against the Union and in it Defoe argued that Anne had moved to heal many of these breaches and that both nations now needed a union more than before. In the next part, Defoe elaborated on which aspects of union were essential to each side, thereby repeating material in Section III, and described the ratification of the Treaty in Edinburgh, covering material to be included in Section V.

Section V alternates a transcription of the minutes of the Scotch Parliament for this same period with Defoe's "Observations" on them. Rather than interpretation, the "Observations" are elaborations and provide information about such things as length of debate and identification of major speakers. The first three sections of the *History of the Union* (I through III) provide essential background information and prepare for the amount of resistance from the common people and for the significance of such issues as religion and sovereignty. The repetition of motives for union in Sections III and IV/V is perhaps unavoidable yet shades toward the kind of overarguing we associate with propaganda. Sections IV and V, however, duplicate more than repeat, for they cover the same time period, first "without doors" and then "within doors" as Defoe habitually described outside and inside Parliament. The *History of the Union*, then, divides into parts devoted to the sources of national differences and animosities, the events and attitudes that made union possible, and to the months during which the Scottish Parliament considered the Treaty. Because of the delay in publication, Defoe was able to add Section VI, the Appendix. Part I of this Appendix duplicates the arrangement of the *History* in miniature; first, it recounts the reactions to events resulting from the Union ("without doors") and then explains government action ("within doors"). Part II summarizes the modifications of such things as the legal and monetary systems necessitated by the Union. This section gives the book a kind of symmetry but contributes nothing to unity or impact.

The unity of the *History* comes primarily from its subject but also from the drama of the passage of the Articles of the Treaty. The battle is fought on two fronts: in the streets and in Parliament. Defoe describes the general desire for union apparently shared by most Scots before the Parliament begins to meet in October. Once the Articles are read in Parliament and printed, public resistance grows, only to decline as the voting on the Articles proceeds. Simultaneously, the quiet but firm support for the union gives way to increasingly determined resistance and delays by the anti-union M.P.'s. The threat to union, then, moves from the general public to the Parliament members who begin to add amendments.

Defoe's methods contribute to his aims: the presentation of how the resistance and the Union came to be, the depiction of the Scots so as to avert English resentment of Scots' "ingratitude" for the Union, the portrayal of opponents to the Union so as to heal divisions without celebrating Scottish nationalism, and the explanation of the benefits and ramifications of the individual Articles of Union. His description of the opponents to union illustrates his tactics: "like true Souldiers, tho in a Bad Cause, they fought their Ground by inches. From Article to Article, they Disputed every Word, every Clause, Casting Difficulties and Doubts in the way of every Argument, Twisting and Turning every Question, and continually Starting Objections to gain Time; and, if possible, to throw some Unsurmountable Obstacle in the way."[12] Here Defoe compliments the gallantry of the opposition even as he reminds the reader of the futility of their effort.

The overall structure contributes considerably to Defoe's aims. He needs to keep considerations of Parliament, the Church of Scotland, and the common people alive throughout the *History*, and his mode of organization allows him to demonstrate how each group affects the other, how much more difficult outside opinion made the ratification and enforcement of the Treaty, and how the Queen and M.P.'s were wiser, steadier, and more farsighted than the people. The Queen and Parliament grow in stature because of their resistance and handling of the combined forces of history and of contemporary prejudices expressed in mob action, addresses, and anti-union pamphlets. Defoe often sees the larger implications of events and debates, as he does when he writes: "The Parliament were all this while Debating the Generals of the Treaty, and therefore the Debates were also in general: The Work of this Day was not at all debating what number of Members should be the Proportion of the Parliament, or how, or in what manner they should be chosen, and the like; but whether *Britain*, as now to be United, should be Represented by one and the same Parliament, yea or no."[13] His stylistic powers are such that he can present material briefly and clearly; he can undercut the merit of the common people's objections to union by compressing them into a single paragraph; he can capture the base fear of high taxes even as it mingles with Scottish nationalism. He can present the mood of the people in paragraphs resting upon clusters of images. In one, he says that the "Nation seemed as in Agony" and refers to the "Dying Constitution," the "Dying Country," and the "last Degree of Concern." Certainly in Part IV (*Of the Carrying on of the Treaty*), he catches the atmosphere in the city; the reader has a sense of powerful men acting clandestinely and groups of citizens caught, whirled about, and incited to act in frightening ways. Few of these people, inciters or rabble, have names, and this adds to the sense of threat and unpredictability. In contrast, in Part V (*An Abstract of the Proceedings*), he follows the minutes relentlessly, includes entire speeches, and names some of the principal actors. In IV, Defoe usually blames the opponents of the union for the mobs' actions but does not specify the exact tactics; in III he presents the opponents' strategems with an explanation of timing and motive and then defines the countermove by the union's supporters. In IV, both action and reaction are labeled ("misleading" and "outrageous"), but in III, they are identified specifically.

The forces of Parliament, Church, and citizenry came into play most dramatically between 23 October and 4 November 1706 in the two events that Defoe's contemporaries and generations of historians of the Union have agreed are the most significant. Defoe's handling of the riot of 23 October and the passage of Article 1 illustrates the most important aspects of the style of the *History* and provides a basis for the evaluation of Defoe as historian. Each event marks a pinnacle of resistance that becomes a defeat for anti-union forces and a prophecy of union.

Two Events. The fullest accounts of the 23 October riot begin with what had become a nightly occurrence: a crowd would wait for the Duke of Hamilton to come out of Parliament and then follow his chair, cheering him for resisting the Union. Rather than going to his own house in the Abbey, on the evening of 23 October Hamilton went to the house of the other leading opponent to the Union, the Duke of Atholl, who lived near Patrick Johnson, a member of the Commission that had written the Treaty, and Lord Loudoun, a member of the Scottish Parliament and a supporter of the Union. The mob attacked Johnson's house, was routed by the town guard, and then began roaming through the city, breaking windows and assaulting pedestrians. Eventually foot and horse guards were called to secure the Netherbow Port, Parliament Close, the Cannon Gate, and the Weighhouse. The next day's debate in Parliament made clear that intimidation was an issue and that calling in the guard was unprecedented.

Defoe's first account of 23 October begins with a paragraph presenting Hamilton as too reputable and too wise to have incited the mob.[14] His account of events is concise and agrees with dozens of other eyewitness accounts. The only sections that he could be said to have extended beyond an outline are an account of the attack on Johnson's house (which includes the story of Mrs. Johnson's call for help and Captain Richardson's driving the mob down the stairs), and a description of the reluctance of Lord Provost McClellan to call the guard into the city. Defoe's second account begins: "This was the Fatal Day of the Tumult in the Streets, and the House was no less warm within, proportionably speaking, than the Gentlemen were without, all which had its Share in Agitating the publick Confusions: I am far from saying, that the Arguments used within Doors, occasioned the Rabble, but the Improvement a Party without Doors made of them, and the manner in which things now said in the Parliament were Represented without, concurr'd to encrease the Ferment of the Nation" (*An Abstract of the Proceedings*, V. 15-20). Again Defoe begins by implying responsibility for inciting the mob while denying that is his intention. He follows this paragraph with an account of the debate concerning the eighteenth article, which he characterizes as warm, full of reproaches, and marked by "Universal" "ill Behavior" and frequent "Indecencies." The discussion involved some of the most controversial parts of the proposed tax and excise reforms: salt, beer, and ale.[15] Defoe next gives the Minutes for 25 October, when Parliament debated thanking the Privy Council for their actions on the evening of 23 October. In the "Observation" he says that Queensberry as Lord Commissioner ordered the guard into the city, and Defoe then recounts the debate with extended comment. He quotes the Marquess of Annandale as saying that the guard threatened freedom of speech, "awed" the House, and was "Arbitrary Government." Defoe comments that without the guard "the Members of Parliament would be Aw'd, and the Treaters Massacred by the Mob," and he argues that the guard was necessary, in the Parliament's power, and merely intended to keep the peace. He defends the guard at length and includes a particular incident in which "a certain great Person" tried to provoke them.

The second crucial event was the passage of Article 1 of the Treaty. To pass this article was to effect an incorporating union between Scotland and England, for it read: "That the Two Kingdoms of *England* and *Scotland* shall upon the First Day of *May*, which shall be in the Year One Thousand Seven Hundred and Seven, and for ever after, be United into one Kingdom by the name of GREAT-BRITAIN. And that the Ensigns Armorial of the said United Kingdom be such as her Majesty shall appoint, and the Crosses of St. *George* and St. *Andrews* be conjoyned in such manner as Her Majesty shall think fit, and used in all Flaggs, Banners, Standards and Ensigns, both at Sea and Land." The Earl

of Marchmont moved that Parliament proceed to the consideration of the individual articles "in order to Approve them or not,
and to begin with and Read the first Article." With this motion on
1 November 1706, the battle began. The Opposition knew, largely
because of the test-of-strength vote regarding seating Sir
Alexander Bruce,[16] that they could not defeat a motion to pass
the article, and so they began delaying tactics. They asked for a
delay until England had ratified the Treaty, until the M.P.'s had
had a chance to consult their constituents, until the other articles
had been considered and passed, until the security of the Church
of Scotland was assured, until a possible conflict with the Claim of
Right had been resolved, and until conflicts of interest between the
two countries ended. In addition, Parliament accepted and read
more than ninety petitions against an incorporating union, read
the Charter of Scottish Liberties and the letter of the Estates to
King William, heard speeches such as the famous ones by Seton of
Pitmedden and by Lord Belhaven, rejected an alternate proposal
for union, and accepted a protest entered by sixty-five members. It
was 2 November before Parliament agreed to vote on Article 1.
The passage of the motion stating that acceptance of Article 1 was
conditional upon the approval of the other articles helped a bit,
and the article was passed on 4 November by a margin of about
thirty votes.[17]

Defoe interrupts his account of the reading of the Articles in *Of
the Carrying on of the Treaty* with an account of popular
disturbances and protests and with the actions of the Church of
Scotland, tracing these strands into the middle of November. At
this point, he uses a rudimentary transition, "I must desire the
Reader, to go back a little to the Parliament" (p. 43). He makes no
attempt to discuss the passage of Article 1 but points out that the
vote really determined the Union, refers the reader to the Minutes,
and includes a noteworthy observation on the date of the vote as
omen: "It was Voted on the most remarkable Day for Publick
Deliverance, that ever happened to this Island" [William's birthday and landing in England] (p. 43). "And yet it was impossible to
observe, without some Emotion of the mind, and without some
Presage of the good Issue of this Matter; That the first Article,
being the Great and Essential Part of the Union, was Voted and
Approved on that remarkable 4th Day of *November*. . . . Happy

Day! Happy to Britain! Happy to all Europe!" (p. 44). He concludes the section with a description of the effect that the debate had on various groups and a reminder that "every word, every Clause" in the rest of the Treaty would be disputed tenaciously.

Were this the only account of the passage of Article 1, William Ferguson's accusation that Defoe did not comprehend the full significance of the debate might have some merit. Certainly the four pages in *Of the Carrying on of the Treaty* are hardly history. In Section III, however, he devotes twenty-seven pages to the episode. Besides the minutes, Defoe quotes the motions, the letter of Estates to William, and the speeches of Seton of Pitmedden and Lord Belhaven; his observations reinforce the historic significance. He begins, "The great Question came now to be Determined—, Whether they should go upon the Treaty, or no." Later Defoe makes a point of Queensberry's desire to be listed with those who voted for Article 1, for it was "the main Tryal of Skill" (p. 51). His paragraphs catch the sense of struggle; proposal and objection alternate paragraph after paragraph, and conjunctions and verbs contribute to the tone: "not withstanding," "but then," "and after long reasoning," "renewed the Debate," "brought in Addresses," "it being objected," "then they objected," "so Playing one against another." His conclusion records the opposers' weariness and defeat: "Upon the whole, the other Party soon saw in the House, it would go against them, and therefore, before it was put to the Vote, the Duke of A—ole gave in his Protest . . . " (p. 49). Furthermore, Defoe begins his Observation for 6 November thus: "the Fatigue of the last day was so great that both sides seem'd as it were, to take Breath . . . " (p. 50). He notes that he has already explained the work of the Commission of the Church of Scotland and covers the passage of the Act of Security so briefly as to make it appear less controversial than it was. Again Defoe insists that because the Article was passed on William's birthday, it has special meaning for England: "On the same day, now a second time, the Fate of *Britain* had a new Turn."

Accounts by other witnesses corroborate Defoe's facts. Discrepancies are trivial; for example, Bennet of Grubbet says that the guard entered Edinburgh "about" midnight, and Defoe says "about" one o'clock.[18] The Earl of Mar tells David Nairn that

Hamilton left Atholl's after a short visit and that the mob followed Hamilton home and then returned to Johnson's.[19] Since Mar was at dinner near Johnson's, he might have been a better witness, and yet he may have been inattentive to events outside for periods of time. Defoe seems to have exaggerated only once: when he says the treaters might have been massacred; Mar describes walking through the streets unmolested, but his letters do second Defoe's reading of the situation as volatile, dangerous, and intimidating: "we in my Ld Loudoun's were expecting to be attacqued every minut so we resolved to go out & walk down the streets, we saw a great number of the rable w^t stones in their hands, but as soon as they saw us they dropt them & let us pass. . . . If one stone had been thrown at us, there had been five hundred," and "I'm not very timerous and yet I tell you that every day here wee are in hazard of our lives, wee cannot goe on the streets, but wee are insulted, as I and some others were just now."[20]

Within the accounts, Defoe makes selections and judgments. He concludes that the mob action came so early as to be ineffectual, and even George Lockhart, who despised Defoe, agreed with this analysis.[21] His commentary explains necessity, uses tone to convey judgment (admiration for Queensberry's courage and firmness, wonder at Annandale's speech), and suggests rather than re-creates what it was like to be present on individual days. We know from other accounts that Fletcher of Saltoun said the mob acted in the spirit of "Reformation and Revolution" and that others said equally immoderate things; but we can also guess because Defoe gives two specific examples and tells us that the debate went on a long time. In the account of the debate over Article 1, Defoe says that many speeches were given, but Seton's and Belhaven's represent the major arguments and tactics of the two groups. Defoe's prose is usually terse, full of specific detail, and noncontroversial. For example, he says that the address from Midlothian had but twelve signatures although two hundred could have signed, and he explains why the pro-union M.P.'s discouraged addresses supporting the union. Defoe is present as observer, but his actions, words, and feeling are omitted.

Just as Defoe and his contemporaries were conservative about appropriate evidence in these histories, so they were about interpretation. They excluded myths, legends, and even literature, and they would never have included the fictitious orations commonly employed by classical historians such as Livy and Tacitus.[22] They tried to limit interpretation to efforts to clarify, and Defoe's "Observations" and expository sections conform to this closely. Beneath the spare prose, however, we can glimpse Defoe's political purposes and his own opinion of first cause. Just as he excluded the motives of malice, self-aggrandizement, and viciousness, he implied that the kingdom was moving inevitably toward union.

❦ *Interpretation and Rhetoric. The History of the Union* is a fascinating example of a work produced at the moment in history when men distrusted and rejected histories that explained events as the result of divine action or as the result of the personality and actions of a single brilliant man, and when men were turning away from the attempt to produce unadorned compilations of facts and documents. Like the French, Italian, and Dutch historians of the late seventeenth century, they struggled to explain events and, in so doing, analyzed forms of government, "natural law," the nature and limits of kingship, property rights, and the relationship between Church and state. As Hugh Trevor-Roper says, they had decided that history should be an explanation of social change illuminated by criticism and philosophy and intended to show the progress of mankind.[23] These historians groped for causes in human nature, in national character, in chance, in religion, or in government. Because they wrote this way, they, like Defoe, included more information about trade, industry, social life, and cultural developments than earlier historians.

Defoe faithfully records the economic and political mandates that pushed Scotland and England into union.[24] But Defoe also explains the union as the working out of Providential design, as the two nations being pulled toward Union as well as being pushed. Defoe points out repeatedly that the treaty came at a "critical moment" and that others, most notably the Queen, also recognized that fact. He says that his book will show "how Providence has led the Nations, as it were, by the Hand" (I, *A General History,* p. 1) and often remarks that God rescued men from being imposed upon, from a French invasion, from disappointment, and from other unfortunate happenings. The Union brings England closer to assuming the role of guardian of liberty and the

Protestant religion and thereby expresses the plan Defoe believes God has for England. As Maximillian E. Novak has observed, Defoe was a typical Whig historian in that he read "the present into the past in terms of the progress of liberty as evidence of the workings of Providence in the world."[25] Defoe, however, was intensely interested in the day-to-day maneuvers and the details of what he called "the strange Circulation of Causes" (*Of the Last Treaty*, p. 3). This fact prevents his consideration of God's actions in history in anything but the most superficial statements and, moreover, works against the sense of certainty in understanding cause and sequence. In this case as in others, Defoe refuses to pause for sweeping summaries of what conclusions might be drawn; he refuses to relate earlier speeches or actions specifically to later events, and he will not, even in Part I of the appendix, find a single, all-important cause or even a strain of attitudes or a set of personalities acting throughout the years he discusses.

Defoe's irenic purposes, his desire to record events accurately, his impulse to trace England's movement into a new age, and his vision of the pattern of God's action in history restrict each other, preventing the full exploration and elaboration of any. What Defoe creates is a verbal image of an event, distracting in its distance from the photographic, mirror, or metonymical images we expect to find in literature and history. We know, of course, that every writer constructs a verbal image when he does such things as impose plot, choose metaphors, and control pace and tempo. We accept the compression and expansion of material and the subordination of events and ideas. Bacon explains memory as the faculty required of historians, as imagination is required of poets and understanding of philosophers, and we know that we can perceive and comprehend new material because writers exercise these faculties. In order to communicate their vision, they choose to use the tools of the fiction writer and poet.[26] In the *History of the Union*, in contrast, Defoe seems to have been uncomfortable with the role of interpreter and uses the methods of rhetoric and fiction only when he could not avoid doing so. The result is a work that, in spite of its careful structure, accurate rendering of events, and profound generalizations, fails to project a unified painting worthy of contemplation.

Defoe is particularly cautious in his treatment of personality in the *History of the Union*. The emphasis on social change and documentary evidence had subordinated the role people played in other histories, but Defoe goes farther than most of his contemporaries in stripping history of heroes. In truth, Defoe would have distorted history had he elevated individuals. A great many people acted relatively important parts but none had a sustained major role. Queensberry, a man Defoe seems to have known and admired, might have been cast as a hero, but by 1706 his power was limited and he was not the "spirit of Union" in any sense.[27] The necessary strategy of both the pro- and anti-union forces was to divide responsibility for initiating pamphlets, debates, and motions. Because Defoe seldom names individuals, his *History of the Union* surrenders an important source of unity and drama, a memorable means of expressing conflict and providing profound examples from which abstractions might have been drawn. When he does name individuals, their identity tends to be essential to the narrative either because the event was extraordinary or because the person has some quality that explains the action. Both the Edinburgh and Glasgow riots were anomalies, and Hamilton and Clarke as individuals contribute to the explanations of events. In each case, the person has unusual influence on the riot and yet is a metonymy for others.

When Defoe writes of people, he simply records their action; when he writes of Hodges or Hepburn, their writing seems more real than they do, and the speeches of Belhaven replace description. We never know how these men spoke, moved, or thought. In this regard, Defoe deviates considerably from his contemporaries. The character, a short, complete description written "to show later ages what kind of men had directed the affairs and shaped the fortunes of the nation,"[28] used throughout English history and brilliantly so by Bede, Clarendon, Buchanan, and Evelyn, simply does not appear in the *History of the Union*.

A comparison of Clarendon's *History of the Rebellion* (begun 1646; 1702-4) and Gilbert Burnet's *History of the Reformation* (3 volumes; 1679, 1681, 1715) with Burnet's *History of My Own Time* (1724) illustrates the contrast with Defoe's *History of the Union* and the direction history writing was taking. Both of the earlier histories rely heavily upon personal experience, documents, and reliable witnesses. Clarendon resists giving names when to do so would automatically trigger a moral judgment; for example, he never refers to Lady Castlemaine as anything but "a lady" or "the lady." By the time Burnet wrote *My Own Time*, he and many others held the opinion that he expresses in the preface: "My chief design in writing was to give a true view of men and of counsels, leaving public transactions to gazettes and the public historians of the times. I writ with a design to make both my self and my readers wiser and better. . . . I have given the characters of men very impartially and copiously; for nothing guides one's judgment more truly in a relation of matters of fact, than the knowing the tempers and principles of the chief actors."[29] George Lockhart insists that without "characters" we could not get "a clear and full idea of what passed."[30]

To read Clarendon's *Rebellion* is to confront his intense, emphatic opinions and his complex personality; his learning, his continual sense of irony, and his integrity animate the book and make it unforgettable. In a different way, we remember that we read Burnet's *own* history. Defoe rejects this strategy and refuses to substitute his own personality for heroes and villains. His social rank and role in events precluded such a stance to some extent, and yet he solves the problem repeatedly in his later memoirs[31] and especially in *A Journal of the Plague Year*, in which H.F. is an observer and peripheral participant. After the early eighteenth century, the trend in history writing was toward the unabashed, assertive narrator who claimed public authority and yet admitted to an individual and somewhat personal perspective. The movement in prose fiction was toward concentration upon a single individual consciousness. In the *History of the Union*, Defoe retreated from both and subordinated himself and all of the other participants in order to avoid placing blame and exacerbating divisions and to refrain from reminding people of who belonged to which faction.

Although he came to be a master of collapsing time, Defoe is equally conservative in his use of time. He is particularly alert to simultaneity, and his virtuosity in expressing it perhaps surpasses that of any other writer. *The Storm* has sections that show simultaneous events vertically and horizontally; in one moment we may know events in a single house, in adjacent houses, in several parts of town, and in neighboring towns. The book locates events so closely together that the sequence seems to be a single event, each discrete part so integral to the whole that it is indistinguishable from the whole except in memory.[32] In his nonfiction work after the Union, Defoe is able to juxtapose present and past events to show their similarity and to reveal the pattern in, for example, England's injustice to the Dissenters. He can impose events in the northern and southern European war theaters upon situations in England. In fiction, he can give clues relating an event or scene to several different time periods simultaneously in order to emphasize the common aspects of human nature or to draw significant comparisons for thematic purposes.[33]

Had Defoe done some of these things in the *History of the Union*, he would have avoided certain problems. He was aware from the beginning of the danger of following "truth too near at the heels." In addition to the possibilities of legal prosecution, the history of the present faced enraged criticism from those who interpreted events differently, who had a more limited, more prejudiced, or more comprehensive perspective, or who had some vested interest in the account of an incident. Defoe quoted Raleigh very early in his *History of the Union*: "But there was yet some Political Difficulty to pass, and here being to Tread Truth almost on the Heels, those Readers that are willing to have it told plainest, must excuse me for naming Peoples Names: I have avoided, on all Occasions, the Mixing Satyr and Reflection in this Relation, as much as possible" (*Of the Last Treaty*, p. 2). Later Defoe would come to be an expert at talking about an immediate event and at making blunt judgments about it by appearing to talk about another time and event. In this history, he seemed unable to escape time, and the debilitating quibble with Clarke of Glasgow was but one destructive effect. Clarke's objections called into question the most important quality of a historian, the ability to observe and report fact. The extended controversy and its seriousness and vituperativeness compromised the history before its publication.[34]

Because Defoe eschewed analogies from other times, he could not move beyond the Union to generalizations about the political behavior of men, about the ways factions are formed and overcome, or to any number of other lessons to be learned from the events of 1706. More important, he could not escape that time to transcend the personalities and events of the era to discover

ethical, political, and philosophical truths. What Samuel Johnson
did so effortlessly in his portrait of Charles XII in the lines, "He
left the name, at which the world grew pale, / To point a moral, or
adorn a tale," Defoe would do in his portraits, in his life of the
Baron de Goertz, and in his novels. As a historian and a novelist,
Defoe would learn to integrate the past and present into a vision
with implications and usefulness for the future. Again, *A Journal
of the Plague Year* is an obvious example of the triumph of this
technique. Defoe could draw from the plagues of England's past,
the documents and stories left from his childhood, and then rely
upon the threat of plague and the anxiety over Walpole's Quarantine Act coming on the heels of the Toulon massacre to create a
novel showing the sane, exemplary behavior of the mayor and
aldermen, the survival of the city, and the developing wisdom of a
single citizen. In histories written late in Defoe's life, he comes to
plead with his countrymen to take to the seas and to increase
England's wealth. He evokes the memory of Drake and of Raleigh,
conjures up the spirit of Elizabeth and even of Marlborough, and
then carries his reader on a survey of declining England, a country
filled with stupefied luxury-lovers and struggling, languishing
tradesmen and laborers.[35]

Those who read the *Review*, *Legion's Memorial*, and *The
Consolidator* probably came away from *The History of the Union*
feeling as we do today who see Defoe as the worthy father of
Walter Scott, Charles Dickens, and Joyce Cary. We wish Defoe
had done more of what he does brilliantly. We wish he had used
factual detail as one strategy instead of subordinating everything
to the presentation of fact, and we wish he had given us a narrative
voice or a set of characters worthy of him. We miss the art that
could create an unforgettable scene, that could design an emblem
to explain something as mundane as credit, and that was so
various and so inexhaustible that Defoe could write on almost
every subject and in almost every genre of his time.

We must not forget, however, what Defoe accomplished. Quite
simply, every historian of the Union to this day must read the
History of the Union, and Scottish nationalism and the economy
in the last decade have focused new attention on Defoe's history.
Those who complain that the book is misleading can do so only by
attacking parts of the verbal image he wished to project: his

reluctance to depict the petty, self-serving nature of some Scots or his refusal to make the end of Scottish independence a tragedy.[36] His facts cannot be denied. He was far ahead of his time in summarizing the differences between the Scots and the English, identifying the events that embittered the Scots, recognizing the compelling necessity of the union in 1706, and isolating Scotland's and England's maneuvers to persuade each other of this necessity and then to compromise in order to make the union possible. He makes England and Scotland appear to be wary cocks, feinting and lunging, until they can retreat with dignity to ratify the Treaty of Union. His analysis of events such as the collapse of the Darien Company, the series of Parliamentary acts in the two years before the Commission met in London, and the passage of the economic articles is as good as that in the best modern histories. If Defoe is conservative with his evidence, his interpretation, and his rhetoric he is in good company. Voltaire was to say, "Ardent imagination, passion, desire—frequently deceived—produce the figurative style. We do not admit it into history, for too many metaphors are hurtful, not only to perspicuity, but also to truth, by saying more or less than the thing itself" (*Philosophical Dictionary* s.v. "History").

Defoe could not escape generic considerations, preconceptions about the purpose of his work, and the sense of his position while he composed the *History of the Union*. Only when he was free to assume an identity or to concentrate on a single personality did he begin to explore the larger themes and profounder insights of great histories.[37] The necessity to present mundane detail, to outline the varieties of political behavior, to integrate past, present, and future, and to acknowledge God's transcendent plan, and to do this in a way that would heal divisions within and between the two nations, worked against the imaginative force of the *History of the Union*.

The Great Northern War became of intense interest to England in 1715. It had major historical significance and considerable literary potential. It could be described in dramatic terms, as Voltaire did when he wrote, "And so, at a time when ice and snow force nations in temperate regions to suspend hostilities, Czar

Peter was besieging Narva only thirty degrees from the Pole, and Charles XII was advancing to its relief."[38] A set of magnificent characters struggled in a cold, unfamiliar land. This war, in contrast to the recently concluded War of Spanish Succession, offered tales of nations, not barrier towns, won and lost and of villages massacred, not garrisoned. Unlike the administrator-monarchs and aristocratic gentlemen-generals of England and France, Sweden and Russia had unpredictable, flamboyant kings who commanded armies to which the British press had given dramatic character. Charles Whitworth, special ambassador to Russia, captured the moment best: "How striking a picture might an author of genius form. . . . Peter recalled that Image of the Founders of Empires, of whom we read with much satisfaction and much incredulity in ancient Story. Charles the Twelfth, of those frantic Heroes of Poesy, of whom we read with perhaps more satisfaction and no credulity at all. Romulus and Achilles filled half our gazettes."[39]

For many Englishmen of Defoe's time, biography was what Sir Francis Bacon had called it, a form of history,[40] and the Great Northern War was the story of Charles XII and Peter I. Biography offered all of the benefits of history, yet it was deemed more affecting and enjoyable and, therefore, more effective in presenting examples for the instruction of readers. The distinguished Dissenting clergyman Edmund Calamy wrote in the preface to *Memoirs of the Life of the late Reverend Increase Mather, D.D.* that lives of eminent men "strike the Fancy in a very lively Manner, improve the Judgment, impress the Memory, raise and captivate the Affections, make the reaching great Attainments appear . . . practicable, and provoke . . . Imitation." Furthermore, they often offer proof "That God has not yet quite left our World."[41] Some even saw biography as a dramatized treatise on political philosophy. Historical biography with philosophical overtones had been popular since the Renaissance. The Italians particularly excelled in it, and books such as Boccaccio's *Life of Dante* continued to be read avidly.

Although Defoe shared these opinions about biography, his "histories" of Charles XII and Peter I are as partisan as *The History of the Union* and, therefore, use the techniques of historiography for a variety of purposes in combination with polemical strategies familiar to the readers of his tracts. The period between 1714 and 1720 was the time when Defoe was most active as a journalist (in contrast to a pamphleteer) and was, therefore, concerned with reporting the day-to-day events of the war as well as indicating their implications for the British. Among Defoe's Great Northern War publications are daily reports in periodicals such as *The Daily Post*, digests and summaries in monthly chronicles such as *Mercurius Politicus*, pamphlets such as *A Short View of the Conduct of the King of Sweden*, a "life" of the Baron de Goertz, *The History of the Wars of . . . Charles XII . . . of Sweden* (2 editions), *The Impartial History of the Life . . . of Peter [of Russia]* (2 editions), and a somewhat related historical novel—*Memoirs of a Cavalier*. The fact that these works are on the same subject, written in close proximity during the time he wrote most of his novels, and in a wide variety of modes makes them especially useful in analyzing Defoe's artistic strategies and methods of composition. We see what he does with gazetteer releases, how he assembles as much as writes some of his books, and how he reworks the same material for a variety of purposes. Defoe himself saw a close relationship between history and journalism, which he once called history writing "by Inches,"[42] and in this insight lies his special originality.

Here is the professional writer, the literary Defoe, the man whom his contemporaries read with zest; yet with the possible exception of *Memoirs of a Cavalier*, none of these works is read today. Their appeal for Defoe's time, however, is not hard to explain for they are close to books that have captured considerable readerships very recently. We need only think of *At Dawn We Slept*, *The Making of a President* series, and *Dispatches* to understand the satisfactions *The History of the Wars* offered. Defoe explained in the beginning of the 1715 edition that it was not enough to give "the History of Facts"; instead he would give his readers "a true Idea of the thing, and make him Master of the Causes, and Beginnings. . . . " His method, he says, will be to "fetch the Stories [of each nation] severally from their beginnings, shew the Pretences they made, the Steps they took, and in what Manner they all united to fall upon the King of Sweden. . . . "[43] Addison had recognized the advantages of these books over newspapers as early as 1712 when he wrote in *Spectator* no. 452,

"Why should not a man who takes delight in reading every thing that is new, apply himself to history, travels, and other writings of the same kind, where he will find . . . much more pleasure and improvement than in these papers of the week? He may read the news of a whole campaign in less time than he now bestows upon the products of any single post." Defoe, like the other writers of these books, uses many of the strategies of the contemporary journalists in combination with fictional techniques to create something of fiction's feeling while remaining nearly entirely factual. Like the practitioners of American "literary nonfiction" of the 1960s and 1970s, he draws together the observer and ποιητης and, by selection, arrangement, and emphasis gives an interpretation to factual materials. From the actual events, his subject gains significance and a sense of destiny and, from his fictional methods, it takes shape and is refracted through an ethical consciousness.[44] These modern books, like Defoe's, often blend essay, memoir, reportage, and biography, as does Truman Capote's *In Cold Blood*, for example.

Defoe's book, then, is for people who want to know more about important events and who want to understand causes and implications. The language of the passage quoted above and especially of words such as "Stories" shows that Defoe saw his purpose as narrative and his work as author to be that of narrator, the eternal seer/sayer who selects events and takes discrete experiences and orders them so that their relationship and meaning are open to others. He explains, interprets, and, at his best, gives universal, even mythic, significance to his story. When Defoe promises to show "the Pretences they made," he personifies nations and suggests that motives will be personal as well as political.

Perhaps more significant is Defoe's desire to give "a true Idea of the thing." "Idea" to the early eighteenth-century man was both closer to the Platonic meaning and far more suggestive than the world is for us today. The word still implied Plato's "form," a model and a standard or definition of perfection. To give an "Idea" of a thing was to give a perfect image, the most exact picture that could be rendered (OED). Defoe is promising that most reliable of all delights offered by fiction: identification. What would it be like to be—? to do—? to feel—? what would I then know? Furthermore, he offers it both as individual experience and as analysis of history. The reader can "be there" and also obtain an omniscient understanding of the war. Is that not why we read *If I Die in a Combat Zone?* We hope to understand the causes and duration of the Vietnam War, to understand why men enlisted, what it felt like to be there, and, by doing so, to understand what kept men there and contributed to their postwar attitudes. We want to understand the dynamics between our nation and that distant war, both as the participants were nations and as the participants were men, some quite ordinary men. We want to see the differences in experience and in judgment that "being there" made. Here is the appeal of what was called "the new journalism," of *Dispatches*, and of *The History of the Wars*.

It is only fair at this point to note that Defoe's contemporaries held the same reservations about such books as we do. They recognized that assigning causes was arbitrary and that the methods of the fiction writer had to be employed to give continuity, flavor, even credibility to narrative. In saying "this is what it was like," the writer had to construct a unified experience that was more subjective than "legitimate" history allowed. Samuel Johnson complained that "all the colouring, all the philosophy of history is conjecture." Even though they, like we, knew that they were to believe "pure" history written by professional scholars to be superior, they turned to these books for the pleasures, illumination, and coherence they offered. Moreover, they knew that "facts" were not yet truth. In discussing Tom Wolfe's book *The Right Stuff*, astronauts Scott Carpenter and Gordon Cooper described it as "100 percent accurate" and said, "There may be things that didn't happen factually, but [it brings the reader] closer to what the experience was like."[45] Even as critics debate such generic classifications, readers and subjects recognize intention and even method.

Neither the readers nor the writers of these books confused the methods and intentions of *The Impartial History . . . of Peter* with Kennet's *The History of England from . . . the Reign of Charles I to the end of the Reign of William III*, and yet some of the most successful professional writers and most acute thinkers wrote such books, even as Norman Mailer, Arthur Schlesinger, and Henry Kissinger have in our time. In these books, what we think of as evidence, often documentary evidence, and narrative tended to have a reciprocal relationship. The narrative explained the circumstances that led to the treaty or memorial and stated that the reader would be interested and would understand why the results were as they are because of the account that came before. The document verified the account because it repeated some of the information given and because it could not exist in its form had results not been as the narrator described. The documents authenticated some of the motives and "personalities" of kings and countries when such characteristics as generosity or perfidy appeared in the writing or aftermath of a treaty or letter. Moreover, some of the same pleasures existed in both narrative and evidence; for example, one could follow the gradual loss of Sweden's empire in either. The reader felt he was reading something serious and artful that, at its best, combined the objectivity of journalism and history with the intimacy of memoirs. After a brief explanation of the Great Northern War, I shall discuss Defoe's artistry in the "histories" of Charles XII of Sweden and Peter I of Russia, first emphasizing the uses of documentation and then narrative point of view.

❦ *The Great Northern War.* Quite simply, we know now that the Great Northern War made Russia a western nation and altered the balance of power in Europe, and eventually the world, to the present day. Sweden lost her empire, Poland was confirmed as the helpless, eternal pawn of her neighbors, and Russia gained the Baltic seaports that established her as a major military and economic force.

The war began in 1700 when King Augustus of Poland attacked Swedish Livonia. According to agreement, Denmark immediately threatened ducal Sleswig-Holstein and Russia besieged Narva. Charles XII, then only seventeen years old, had inherited the empire that his grandfather had amassed, which included Finland, Estonia, Ingria, and part of Poland. His father's refusal to form an alliance with either England or France during the War of Spanish Succession, however, had left Sweden without powerful allies. In the early years of the war, Charles had superior military forces, extraordinary advisors, and what can only be called an instinct for timing. He was able to intimidate first Frederick of Denmark, then Augustus's Saxons, and to defeat the Russians decisively.

Denmark, Poland, and Russia all had straightforward territorial

ambitions, but almost unbelievably tangled political considerations determined the progress of the war after the first year's
campaign. For example, Augustus's Saxon army was able to
quarter in the Holy Roman Empire, where Charles could not
pursue them without angering the powerful alliance of the Maritime Powers. With this army intact, the Swedes could not afford to
march on Peter and the Russians. Several nations maneuvered to
dethrone Poland's Augustus and determine his replacement. Sweden finally achieved a peace with Poland in 1704 and, by the end
of 1706, had forced Augustus's abdication. Charles XII was finally
free to march on the Russians, who had gradually taken more and
more Baltic territory and had begun the building of St. Petersburg,
the symbol of Russia's western presence and aspirations. The
decisive battle was fought at Poltava in 1709; the Swedes were
defeated, most of their demoralized army surrendered, and
Charles fled to Turkey, where he rather unwillingly remained for
five years.

When Charles finally returned to Sweden in 1714, he returned
to a nation that had managed to resist invasions from Denmark
and Norway and that had survived serious divisions between civil
and military leaders administering the government in Charles's
absence. He also faced a new and very serious political complication: the new king of England was also the Elector of Hanover.
George I as Elector wanted Bremen and Verden, two Swedish
territories now in Denmark's possession. In the spring of 1714, he
joined an alliance with Prussia and Denmark in return for these
states and soon after joined Russia in declaring war on Sweden.
The result was what Denmark wanted: the British navy became
unofficially involved, and the allies' naval supremacy over Sweden
was clear. Sweden lost her last two German possessions in the
winter of 1716 and, thereby, another barrier between her country
and her enemies. Her plan to invade Norway was never executed,
and Charles was killed by a stray bullet in November of 1718 in
the midst of a struggle over succession to the Swedish throne. For
England, things were hardly more promising with Russia, however. One contemporary observer of the Baltic and Mecklenburg
rivalries observed, "le czar était pour l'électeur un danger permanent, l'électeur était pour le czar un obstacle invincible." The
Northern War ended with the Treaty of Nystad in 1721.[46]

Although Britain had been interested in the Great Northern War from the beginning because of the Baltic trade, because of its possible ramifications for the War of Spanish Succession, and because of Sweden's traditional role as one of the protectors of the Protestant interest, it was not until George came to the throne that the Northern War became a matter of intense interest for ordinary Englishmen. It is true that Marlborough had been to see Charles in 1706 and that various degrees of frustration had been expressed because the Great Northern War diverted men and arms away from England's war against Spain and France, but a survey of the periodicals before 1714 shows what can only be called desultory interest.

George I's actions as Elector were extremely controversial in England. As the Jacobite riots made plain, he was not a safely popular king, and such actions as drafting a treaty with France as early as 1716 brought simmering fears and resentment into the open. Many Englishmen considered the actions of the British fleet sent into the Baltic, ostensibly to protect the British merchant fleet, a violation of the Act of Settlement clause forbidding English forces from participating in a war not involving British possessions without parliamentary approval. The divisions within George's ministry were deep and bitter. Townshend and Walpole sternly opposed and tenaciously hindered George's efforts to change England's political alliances in Europe while Stanhope and Sunderland sided with George I. Defoe at this time was in Townshend's service with the specific assignment of appearing to be in disgrace with the Whig party in order to infiltrate as many Tory periodicals as possible in order to "disable" and "enervate" them. When Townshend was sent in disgrace to be Lord Lieutenant of Ireland in December 1716, Sunderland assumed Defoe's employment until 1718, when he began to report to Stanhope, usually through Charles De la Faye, Undersecretary to the Secretary of State for the Northern Department.[47] These political considerations can be seen in Defoe's 1715 *History of the Wars* and the 1719 *Life of the Baron de Goertz*.

English attitudes toward the participants in the Great Northern War were successively complicated by the exposure of the Gyllenborg intrigue (in which Sweden apparently offered aid to the Jacobites), by the discovery of Swedish privateers' attacks on

British merchant ships, by the disclosure of Russian troops quartered in Hanoverian Mecklenburg, and by rumors of Russian-Jacobite negotiations. In 1717 England prohibited trade with Sweden, and in 1720 diplomatic relations with Russia were severed after several stormy years.[48] *The Minutes of Mesnager* (1717), the 1720 editions of *The History of the Wars* and *Memoirs of a Cavalier,* and *The Impartial History of the Life of Peter* (1723) came out of this milieu.

Structure. Many of Defoe's contemporaries believed that the best histories were written by eyewitnesses and that one of history's chief functions was to acquaint people with the men who had influenced events. These opinions, as well as the growing popularity of prose fiction with its emphasis on the individual, encouraged the writing of books such as Defoe's *History of the Wars* and *Impartial History of the Life of Peter* and contributed toward the breakdown of the distinctions between biography and history. Just as John Strype was convinced that his *Ecclesiastical Memorials* included a quite satisfactory biography of Edward VI, so did Defoe believe that a life of a ruler could be amply rendered in an account of a portion of his reign. Just as memoir writers customarily began by explaining that they intended to hurry over the uninteresting and irrelevant early events, so Defoe, Strype, and many others trusted the synecdochical approach. Since the early seventeenth century, English soldiers had served as "war correspondents" who wrote or translated news from, for example, the Thirty Years War; these accounts were published at frequent intervals as "relations" or "corantos" and then bound into collections. Defoe's Northern War histories are good examples of the blending of genres and techniques common to that branch of civil history which Bacon called "lives."

Both of Defoe's histories, like *The History of the Union,* describe events so recent and so well known that his readers can test their factual and experiential accuracy. In addition, he promises to explain causes, to give details, to correct mistakes, and to decipher implications. By combining the different methods of journalism, history, and fiction, Defoe does these things more easily than he could with one set, and he masks his political purposes more successfully. Certainly these books are more unified than *The History of the Union* and more enjoyable reading.

It is hard for the modern reader to appreciate the eighteenth-century affection for public documents.[49] Royal proclamations, memorials, acts, and speeches were routinely printed by the printer holding the royal patent; these same publications were reprinted, usually in their entirety, in periodicals, in annals, and in books like Defoe's. The numbers of collections that were made by private citizens of official documents associated with any number of public events surviving in British libraries attest to their popularity as do the innumerable requests for copies of various official publications found in correspondence. Readers expected to find the documents; buying certain kinds of books supplied the very collections they might have regretted not keeping, and the copies of treaties, speeches, and memorials were seen as important evidence. By the time Defoe wrote his Great Northern War histories, it was common to judge a historian by his ability to select, arrange, and unite records.

The 1715 *History of the Wars* includes thirty-three documents, accounting for 16 percent of its 400 pages, and the 1723 *Life of Peter* has thirty-nine, accounting for 38 percent of its 420 pages, and these totals do not include unacknowledged material quoted nearly verbatim from other books such as John Perry's *The State of Russia Under the Present Czar* (1716). *The History of the Wars* includes official memorials, declarations, treaties, manifestos, terms of surrenders, and resolutions that mark the passing of time and the results of events. Defoe tends to use such items to reinforce his assertions of causes or results, as he does when he gives us Charles XII's letter to the Confederacy urging the deposition of King Augustus of Poland in favor of Prince Sobieski, the declaration deposing Augustus, and Charles's agreement on the conditions during the interregnum in Poland, all of which appear to support the part Defoe says Charles played in this event and his reasons for interfering with Poland's monarchy.[50] Defoe also gives us somewhat more personal letters, such as General Lewenhaupt's account of the Livonian battle at Lesnaja addressed to Charles and allegedly private letters and excerpts from journals. These papers often repeat the narrator's story and are presented as evidence of his impartiality and accuracy. A letter from an officer in Peter's army to a friend in King Augustus's allows the reader to compare accounts of the event, how it felt, how its significance is regarded, and how each side explains the outcome, as well as adding a human element. Victors are often quoted and their opinions printed, but we are usually left to wonder what the beaten would say; the letters, however, give a voyeuristic view of their depression, regrets, rationalizations, and second guesses—things usually accessible only in fiction.

In *The Life of Peter* Defoe includes more documents and quotes extensively from a number of sources. Here we see the established, elderly, professional writer assembling and unifying material from his wide reading and previous publications. In addition to the kinds of official papers printed in *History of the Wars*, Defoe gives us inventories of troop and fleet size, more letters published to justify the conduct of nations and generals, and more documents exchanged between allies that clarify agreements. In general, Defoe is more concerned, as he must be, with putting Peter's actions in a favorable light and developing his readers' understanding of the Russian country and character. Because *The Life of Peter* covers a longer time period than *History of the Wars* and more events than the narrator could have been expected to witness, he uses accounts introduced as from "an eyewitness" or "one of the writers of the time" to present pertinent material or to reinforce or supplement the narrator's description. Defoe's sources were well chosen. For example, from Jodocus Crull, author of two of the best, hastily written books on Russia published at the time of Peter's visit to England, he borrows the description of the first rebellion against Peter and the defeat and death of the conspirators.[51] From John Perry, a canal builder and hydraulic engineer hired by Peter, he takes the account of the 1698 Strelitzer rebellion.[52] His favorite source, however, is his own *History of the Wars*. Occasionally he rewrites or summarizes *History of the Wars* in order to give a different interpretation or tone, but he often quotes verbatim, as he does when he reproduces accounts of the battle of Poltava or explains King Augustus's motives in 1701.[53] Because of the ignorance and prejudice about Russia, Defoe needs to produce a variety of witnesses and kinds of evidence to corroborate his narrator.

Defoe followed one of the patterns of his time by limiting his history to what he saw as a unit, a "story" with beginning, middle, end, and theme. Charles XII's life was his military career, and Defoe began with the concerted attack on Sweden and concluded with Charles's return to Sweden, ostensibly a new chapter in European history. Because *The Life of Peter* was the story of the transformation of Russia, it began with Peter's genealogy and birth and, after the demonstration of the military change at the battle of Poltava, shifted to complementary subjects, such as Russia's altered diplomatic and economic significance. As well as presenting the causes, progress, and outcome of the Great Northern War, Defoe gave a picture of "the tempers and principles of the chief actors." He combined "public transactions" with life writing in order to give his readers the fullest, most enjoyable account he could.

Both histories, then, move by the major events, diplomatic and military, in the Great Northern War, depend on public records, and by arrangement and commentary, reduce years of news reports and party pamphlets to a unified, coherent narrative. Defoe avoids the personal attacks and the suspicions and charges of serving party purposes that clouded the reception of *The History of the Union*, as he supplies a vehicle for comment and coherence by creating an attractive narrator with a consistent point of view.

Narrative Voice. The Scottish gentleman who is the narrator of *The History of the Wars* has a stronger personality than the British officer of *The Life of Peter*, but both are his readers' countrymen and, therefore, sympathetic and easily seen as reliable narrators. Englishmen and Scots in fairly large numbers had fought for several countries in the Great Northern War, and no one would have been surprised to meet such veterans.[54] Defoe's narrators are mercenaries more than patriots and, therefore, bring a perspective and objectivity even as they risk their lives. Because they are often on the front lines and relate details about individuals and specific numbers of casualties, their engagement is assured, yet they are continually observing and judging. These narrators provide the interest of a character in an exciting situation without making the point of view either too detached or too partisan.

In fact, Defoe takes some pains to establish these narrators as observers in the early pages of each book. The Scots, largely because of the poverty and lack of opportunity in their country, often enlisted in foreign armies, and the narrator of *History of the Wars* focuses on his mode, subject, and hero rather than on himself. We do not learn anything, for example, about the Scot's family or his means of joining the Swedes, but his discrimination and literary experience are established when he remarks with easy command that his account has "as many Glorious Actions, Battles, Sieges, and Gallant Enterprizes as any real History can" and his hero is the type that will "make his History Incredible, and turn it into Romance."[55] The Scot compares the pleasures of reading his book to those found in reading about Alexander and the Caesars, calls our attention to the limitations of real history that he faces, and remarks on his good fortune and opportunity because he can make Charles his protagonist.

Now and then the account is enlivened by an idiomatic word or phrase such as "trail a Pike" to mean "serve under," by a touch of humor as when the men watch tapestries, books, paintings, and even orange trees packed to be sent to Russia and wonder if two men in all of Muscovy can read, or by a brief personal observation such as the Scot's in *History of the Wars* when he says, "we did little else then [*sic*] subsist all Winter." Infrequent detailed descriptions of men, places, clothing, or sights relieve the accounts of marches and battles and help the reader mark time, differentiate events, and find various pleasures in the narrative. The beautiful description of the waterfalls on the Narva River is but one example of writing that "surprizes the Fancy": "The River of *Narva* which rises out of the Lake of *Pepis*, and Discharges it self into the Gulph of *Finland* is very rapid, and there is a Precipice in it, about half a League above the City, where the Water falls with much Violence and Noise, and by accident Produces a wonderful Effect, for the Sun Shining all the Morning upon the falling Water, causes the Appearance of a Rain-bow, as lovely as that which is seen in the Clouds."[56] In another place the Scot describes Charles's clothing as "a Plain blue Coat; a Buff Wastcoat and Breeches, and a Campaign Wig"; nevertheless, "he always look'd like a King" (*History of the Wars*, p. 137).

Far more important are the lively records of battles and the observations, speculations, and gossip that these points of view allow. As "participants" in the battles, as officers, and as seasoned fighters, they notice and remark upon aspects that ordinary men would not. The Scot, for example, says that "The Saxon push'd on their Attacks with a great deal of Vigour, and the Garrison defended themselves like men that understood their Duty, and were resolv'd to perform it . . . " (*History of the Wars*, p. 43). In balanced sentences so characteristic of the eighteenth century, Defoe gives a "soldierly"[57] comment on the work and attitudes of soldiers.

Defoe's descriptions of battles are as good as have ever been written and, considering his limited first-hand experience, stand up amazingly well to the tests of accuracy combatant-critics have devised.[58] Whether he is recounting the broad expanse of attacks, counterattacks, and shifting fronts at "Leipsick," the confined, linear battle of Narva, or the desperate, small skirmishes at Gloucester, he is clear, visual, and economical, yet combat—the prospect of it, the event, and the aftermath—dominates. The men are always depicted as marching toward a battle, memories of past battles color the perception of an impending engagement, and the survey of the field after the battle is always more poignant than triumphant. To fight on the day of a previous victory seems a good omen to Charles XII's men, and the Englishman marvels at the number of Russian bodies even as he recalls "every Body knows foot Soldiers are pretty cheap in *Muscovy*" (*History of the Wars*, p. 113). Defoe captures the spirit of the defensive, siege warfare of the post-Vaubon era[59] and takes for granted the composition of armies of men who were adventurers, employees, conscriptees, cannon fodder, and noblemen who believed in honor and in the inspiration an able leader could be.[60] As Jean Cru tells us that war is almost always an unequal fight between large groups of men; so Defoe shows it.[61] Man-to-man combat is rare, brief, and intense.

❦ *Interpretation.* Defoe's narrators contribute to his purposes by providing a vehicle for speculation and judgment and, by doing so, impose theme and interpretation. He shapes his material with great dexterity in order to manipulate his readers' responses.[62] For example, a large number of "coffeehouse politicians and generals" had difficulty understanding why Charles XII had left his Livonian subjects "at the mercy of" the Russians while he pursued

Augustus's Saxon troops in Poland. The British press had reported atrocity after atrocity and been free in their criticism of Charles. Defoe takes this familiar episode and writes about it from opposite sides in *History of the Wars* and *The Life of Peter*.

The Scot in *History of the Wars* deviates from his almost entirely favorable picture of Charles to admit that "it must be confessed it was our Opinion in the Army, that the King would have marched instantly back" (p. 145) and he describes the "Muscovite" cruelties, the way the badly outnumbered Swedish troops were "devoured" and "overlaid," and the eventual complete destruction and loss of Livonia. In *History of the Wars* Defoe condemns the behavior of the Russian soldiers on several occasions and includes one fairly lengthy paragraph on the specific fears of the Swedish soldiers, who saw capture as "the Fate of the War" and who saw themselves in "the Hands of Men of some Honour" except when captured by the Russians, who are characterized as devouring wolves (pp. 145-48). Defoe has no desire to exaggerate Charles's apparent insensitivity and his narrator is a soldier, but he knew more than he included, as his *Review* makes clear when he mentions "the Murthers, the Burnings, the Ravishments"; compares the Russians to the Cossacks in Africa, the Spaniards in America, and the Devil; and specifically describes the way the Russians tied people to spits and roasted them, put them in ovens, hung them from ceilings and lashed them, and sold them into slavery.[63] Because Peter's treatment of soldiers, civilians, and captives violated the all but universally respected rules for the conduct of war,[64] the world reacted with outrage. John Perry confirms Defoe's account in *The State of Russia under the Present Czar* (1716) and concludes that such behavior is evidence of the lingering primitivism of the Russians.[65]

In *History of the Wars*, Defoe's conclusion is, interestingly enough, the same as that held by most modern historians: Charles needed to defeat Augustus before turning to Livonia and the Russians.[66] By 1720 Defoe could call Charles the "implacable Enemy of the Country and Government, the King, and the Administration,"[67] and the Livonian incident became part of a pattern of responding to personal motives, especially to revenge, more often than to justice or benevolence.[68] The English officer, narrator of *The Life of Peter*, (1723) relates unequivocally that

Charles "abandon'd his faithful Subjects in *Livonia*" and sought personal glory "at the Expense of the Loss of his Dominions" (pp. 136-37). The Czar took land "equal in Wealth and Commerce to his whole Kingdom of *Sweden*," he says. In *History of the Wars* Defoe portrays Charles as hard-pressed and beleaguered on all sides; *The Life of Peter* shows him changing fronts before achieving complete victory anywhere and making decisions for personal reasons. For example, the Englishman says that Charles was driven by a "wicked Principle of Revenge," leaving Poland "not yet half subdued" in order to attack the Czar. "This chymerical Piece of Personality in War drew [h]is *Swedish* Majesty, otherwise a most gallant and experienc'd Prince, into so many wild and desperate Undertakings, as have never been heard of before; and into such Mistakes . . . as never any General of an Army run into. . . . "[69]

In *The Life of Peter*, Defoe was faced with the difficult necessity of explaining the Russian atrocities in Livonia even as he developed his central themes. The structure of this eight-page episode relies upon the tactics of Defoe's best pamphlets; most notably he uses a variety of tones that appear to shift point of view but that, in fact, reinforce each other.[70] He begins with a straightforward statement of the position and numbers of Peter's forces but quickly mentions Narva, the defeat of the Russians that will serve as comparison and motive for the Livonian incident. The narrator simultaneously shows that the Swedes suffered the same disadvantages at both battles and that the Russians avoided every earlier mistake; through him, Defoe launches a satiric attack reminiscent of his finest 1712 pamphlets on Charles XII: "Now had the King of *Sweden*, thought his Province of *Livonia* worth securing, or had he not flattered himself, that the *Russians* would not dare to appear in the Field, but that they would be frighted with the Names of the *Swedes*; that the Scripture Prophesie was to be fulfilled in *Livonia*, in favour of his Men, *That one should Chase a Thousand, and Two put ten Thousand to flight* . . . " (p. 123). Every reason the narrator gives chides the Swedes and reinforces the idea that the Russians knew the Swedes held them in contempt. We are told that the Swedish general did not even bother to entrench, are given the account they "sent to all the Courts of *Europe*," and are shown the press release printed in England and Holland.

At this point, the narrator offers the battle as proof of his statement that this Russian army is quite different and admits the Swedes were correct to say they "laid wast[e] the whole Province." Protesting that Peter does not like or usually allow such carnage, the narrator turns Peter's action into a bid for respect and a military necessity. In a single paragraph he tells us that Charles treated Peter with "personal Indignity," represents Peter's troops as "contemptible," and repeatedly insults him. Peter was, therefore, "oblig'd to shew his Resentment" in order to insure that he and his men would be treated by "Rules of Honor." The narrator also mentions the fact that Livonian citizens continued to fight the Russians and that Livonia could have provisioned Swedish troops, thereby prolonging the war. Since the Russian strategy was to force Charles's advances by making large parts of the country unable to support his troops, the destruction of Livonia seems to have been part of a common policy and somewhat provoked.

Such passages and others giving judgments and opinions establish themes for campaigns and battles as well as for the books, as they add interest to the chronological narration of events and identify the king with the history. The heroic Charles with his tactical genius is defender of the faith in the 1715 *History of the Wars*. Defoe uses a number of traditional images to show Charles as the central figure in a kind of history painting. When Charles comes out of the snow and mist at the head of his army to defeat the startled Russians at Narva, when the Russians superstitiously publish a prayer to St. Nicholas, and when Charles reviews his troops and reminds them that "God the Protector of Right" would strengthen them, he is depicted as the archetypal Christian warrior.

In a similar manner, Peter is the subject of *An Impartial History of the Life . . . of Peter Alexowitz . . . Czar of Muscovy*. He is made to be the mechanick man of genius who gradually transforms Russia and her army into a great power. The narrator catches the misconceptions others have of him, the contradiction of an army that could behave almost simultaneously as barbarians and as admirable professionals, and the significance of Peter's Baltic ambitions. Although one book was published in 1723, both first editions of the histories essentially conclude with the events of 1714. For this reason, the story of Peter's determination and struggle to become a western power provides an illuminating commentary on the saga of Charles's loss of his empire and decline of fortune. Peter's commitment, ingenuity, and resources finally overwhelm a brilliant general who lost his sense of mission and priorities.

Defoe's *A General History of Discoveries and Improvements* belongs in the company of Diodorus of Sicily's *Bibliotheca,* Vincent of Beauvais's *Speculum historiale,* Robert Fabyan's *The Cronycle of Fabyan,* John Stow's *A Summarie of English Chronicles,* William Howell's *Medulla Historiae Anglicanae,* James Ussher's *Britannicarum Ecclesiarum antiquitates,* Sir Walter Raleigh's *The History of the World,* and a host of other books similar to these.[71] It is an old-fashioned but indisputably literary form called "Universal history." The underlying assumptions of universal histories, pagan and Christian, were that the world was a single nation and that all men were brothers. As Diodorus says, the universal histories tried to "marshall all men, who, although united one to another by their kinship, are yet separated by space and time, into one and the same orderly body."[72] These histories analyzed the rise and fall of nations, changes caused by wars and trade, and the development of arts, sciences, religions, and customs and included speculations about the reasons that some nations achieved more than others.[73] Christianity gave new impetus to this kind of history writing because it provided a single God for all the world, made the world into an expression of God's works, and provided a beginning (Creation) and an end (Judgment Day) to history. Most men would have agreed with *Discours sur L'Histoire Universelle,* in which Bossuet explained that God had created the world so that all the parts of the whole depended upon each other.

During the seventeenth and eighteenth centuries, war and commerce came to involve more and more continents. For example, the War of Spanish Succession resulted in trade agreements relating the Americas, Africa, and Asia to various European countries in new ways. In the hands of midcentury writers such as Vico, Voltaire, and Turgot, universal histories came to reflect this situation and became more secular. Defoe's *History of Discoveries* incorporates many of the qualities of the new universal histories, but it is solidly in the tradition of the old. Like Vincent of Beauvais, he wants to survey all of the useful knowledge available to his countrymen and to offer it for their improvement. Like Fabyan, Stow, and Speed, he begins his history with the Flood,[74] and his opening chapters depend heavily upon biblical admonitions. His broadest purposes might be stated in Dionisius Petavius's words, which called his *History of the World* (1659) "a whole Library of History" written that people "mayest be inriched with the knowledge of the rarest and most material Transactions that have happened under the Conduct of Divine Providence ever since the World began."[75]

Like Defoe's other histories, *History of Discoveries* addressed an immediate situation and shared some purposes with very different kinds of works written by him at about the same time. England was in a period of economic recession, and Defoe saw increased exploration and colonization as aids to trade, which he saw as the heart of English prosperity. New markets for English manufacture such as wool cloth would open up even as less expensive sources for imports such as coffee, chocolate, and dyes would emerge. Walpole had recently removed the import duties on dyes, flax, and silk and put tea, coffee, coconuts, and chocolate under the bonded warehouse system.[76] These and other tax reforms looked to Defoe like strong encouragements to home industries. Even as England coped with the recession, her relations with Spain deteriorated rapidly. In 1725, Spain entered into a treaty with the Empire that pledged Spanish support for the Ostend trading company and the Empire's good offices in regaining Gibraltar and Minorca for Spain.[77] Both clauses threatened England's trade with the New World, and England responded by forming a Franco-Prussian alliance and sending a squadron to the West Indies to blockade Spanish ports. War with Spain over Gibraltar seemed imminent.

Defoe had addressed a life of Sir Walter Raleigh to the South Sea Company in 1720, urging them to adopt Raleigh's dream and colonize Guiana. He called his treatise an "answer" to Lewis Theobald's *Memoirs of Sir Walter Raleigh*, (1719), but Theobald, too, was summoning Raleigh's memory in order to inspire Englishmen. Theobald called Raleigh the "Scourge and Terror" of

Spain and praised the spirit of the "stirring Age" that encouraged Raleigh,[78] but Defoe found Theobald's account shallow and gossipy. In order to write his competing life, Defoe reviewed Raleigh's *History of the World* and surely recognized the similarities of the nation's position in 1725 when he wrote *A History of Discoveries*. After the rapid increase of cloth exports in the early sixteenth century, stagnation set in and widespread unemployment resulted, and Spain, of course, was England's nemesis. At the time Raleigh wrote his *History of the World*, Raleigh needed to defuse the charge that he was an atheist, but his purposes were those of a circle of men, including the Richard Hakluyts, who were the main proponents of an aggressive imperialist foreign policy.[79] *The History of the World*, then, followed the pattern of the most orthodox Christian universal histories even as it shared Defoe's immediate concerns. Cromwell recommended Raleigh's *History of the World* to stir "an active vain spirit,"[80] and Defoe's title page expressed the hope that his own history might "prompt the Indolent" and "animate the diligent." At several points, Defoe quoted or cited Raleigh, even trusting some of Raleigh's accounts of biblical history in a few places. By overtly linking his book to Raleigh's, Defoe reminded his countrymen simultaneously of their great past (Raleigh's voyages) and of chances missed (Raleigh's imprisonment and execution) even as he argued his timely case on two quite different levels.

Inspiration. Well-written universal histories have a natural majesty, and Defoe's is no exception. Sweeping linearly from the beginning of biblical time and horizontally around the world, the grand scale cannot fail to impress, especially when presided over by an omnipotent, benevolent, farsighted deity. The imagination, learning, and vision of the writer lead the reader to believe he is having new vistas opened and previously obscure relationships explained; the reader cannot fail to be impressed by the mind of his guide. The fact that these histories approximate compilations easily blends with their promise to absorb and present all knowledge; here, truly, the test of the historiographer is in the selection, arrangement, and application of his material. Defoe's clarity regarding the high purposes of history animate *A History of Discoveries*: "Looking into Antiquity, is a Dry, Empty, and Barren

Contemplation, any farther than as is brought down to our present Understanding, and to bear a steady Analogy to its parts, with the Things that are before us"(pp. 4-5), and history is "to show us what may be, by what has been" (p. 100).

Defoe is strikingly clear and direct about God's place in his history and agrees with most early modern historians. Long before this time, most historians confined God to first causes and defended their concentration on second causes. Thomas Twyne, for example, tells us that "God worketh evermore by second causes unless He worketh miracles which are against the common course of nature."[81] Raleigh, too, says, "For well we know, that God worketh all things here amongst us mediately by a secondary means."[82] Defoe wastes no time on apologiae, and his history is almost entirely secular.

The world of A History of Discoveries, however, is clearly God's world. He created it, and his purposes for the Flood and the Tower of Babel as stated in the Bible are accepted. All men, therefore, have a common origin and belong to a single family. Defoe is absolutely consistent in this; he even, for example, has the Carthaginians blunder upon the New World from West Africa, thereby avoiding the problem other historians had encountered with a "second creation." Defoe also uses orthodox Christianity to provide two important motifs for his History of Discoveries.

First, God intended men "to be fruitful and multiply" and "spread a numerous Race upon" the Earth.[83] Not only does this kind of verse explain the few times God took direct action in the world, but it establishes a value system. Those nations, like the Carthaginians and Phoenicians, who boldly took to the seas, established colonies, and encouraged trade become praiseworthy, in contrast to the Arabians who remained at home or the Romans who "planted for Conquest" (pp. 94-99, 124, 169). Furthermore, it becomes the duty of men to populate the earth; Defoe adds the biblical admonition to the patriotic and profit motives associated with colonization.

In the second month's volume, Defoe begins to establish a parallel between the Phoenicians, a people "naturally Industrious, and addicted to Commerce," and the English (pp. 68, 78-79). The Phoenicians were not inventors but "Improvers of what others invented," but they, like the Carthaginians, went to the sea with enterprise and daring. This comparison is actually a subtle criticism and a sign of Defoe's growing pessimism about the English spirit. In the same volume, Defoe calls Raleigh "the English Hanno" and compares his spirit to the Carthaginians, whom he praises more extensively than the Phoenicians.[84] The Carthaginians have "the adventurous Temper, the genius for Discovery, the Application to improvement, and planting, and cultivating" (pp. 106, 125). They are, then, a complete people in that they will discover, improve, and "cultivate" whereas the English have not been discoverers or inventors, and they have abandoned or neglected some of their colonies. In choosing to compare the English to the Phoenicians rather than to the Carthaginians, Defoe reveals his fairly moderate ambitions for his countrymen.

The second motif that Defoe draws from religion is that God designed the world as a treasure trove for man: "the undoubted design of that Providence that made the World, it may first or last be fully Improv'd, its Treasures fully Discover'd, and all that intrinsick Wealth which Heaven furnish'd the Globe with, be found out and made use of, as he certainly intended it shou'd be," and "I cannot believe that God ever design'd the Riches of the World to be useless to the World" (p. 6). With that clear statement, Defoe frees man to discover and experiment, to push the limits of knowledge, and to partake fully in a progressive theory of history. Again and again, Defoe tells us that each generation finds its lot improved by "discoveries and improvements." People learn to use the resources of the earth and to supply themselves with conveniences. Defoe gives us a world teeming with fish, plants, metals, and treasures that become food, medicine, machines, coats, and beauty in man's dexterous hands. Francis Bacon described God as giving men two books: the Bible, which reveals the will of God, and nature, the book of his works. He reflects that man was not intended to "rest only in the contemplation of the exterior of" God's creation for to do so would be to "judge or construe of the store of some excellent Jeweller, by that onely which is set out toward the streete in his shoppe," and he commends Solomon for saying, "The glorie of God is to conceale a thing, But the glorie of the King is to find it out."[85] Although Defoe would agree that nature reveals God, his annotations in his copy of *The Advancement of Learning* show that he believed strongly that the goal of knowledge should be the benefit of the human race; for example, he approved of Bacon's modification of the anecdote about Solomon because he felt that Bacon disguised Solomon's personal motives, presented him as "God's playfellow," and thereby encouraged men in a "Healthful" way.[86]

Not only does Defoe depict the earth as God's treasure for man, but he illustrates how nature leads men not only to discover but also to invent. Advances in navigation provide his most extended example. He relates how men observed the breast bone of the swan and designed the bottom of a ship, how they watched the eagle's flight and added the helm, and how they found lodestone and invented the compass. As poetic as this image is, Defoe was Adam's child and glorified fallen man's achievement: "Thus Navigation was founded in Reason, and the Nature of Things, and discover'd by slow degrees, the Improvement being the effect of daily Experiment, and great Application, besides Hazards, and Difficulties, ay and Loss too . . . " (p. 31). Men died, but on their dreams navigation grew. Like so many Englishmen, he finds special beauty in Psalm 107: "They that go down to the sea in ships, That do business in great waters; These see the works of the Lord, And his wonders in the deep. . . . Their soul is melted because of trouble" (p. 51). Defoe uses George Sandys's interpretation of the Icarus story for just such an exemplum.[87] Icarus, he says, had sails, not wings, and the sight of a boat so propelled astonished men for it seemed that he "flew from them as it were in the Air, and that his Sails were to him as Wings," but the sails were too large and the boat overturned (pp. 55-56). The abundance of the earth and its possibilities become not just God's gift to man but his admonition to them to explore the world and to put their discoveries to use regardless of the effort and cost.

"[T]he particular Genius of a People is, in a manner, hereditary," according to one of the earliest treatises on historiography.[88] Whether national character creates a country's history or whether its history creates character, Defoe repeatedly alludes to qualities he finds distinctively English and uses them to reinforce his argument. As in *Jure Divino*, he mingles genetic, geographical, religious, and political factors to list inclinations and uses history as the means of finding patterns of response to events. He evokes memories of past achievements and of times when Englishmen have been tested and have triumphed. This almost subliminal message is intended to draw his countrymen into holding a common conception of themselves which will give them the spirit and will to undertake ambitious new projects. With comparisons to the Phoenicians, references to England's navigational and commercial past, and allusions to the work of great men such as Milton, Newton, Camden, Raleigh, and Boyle, Defoe shows "improvements" to be very English and prods his countrymen to behave characteristically.

Defoe's vision of one world is most impressive in his presentation of the history of trade. As men spread out over the globe, they develop different areas of knowledge and find different natural resources. Trade becomes a way of improving people's lives and also an expression of the human desire to communicate, to "have commerce with" one's fellow men. Both motives are treated as natural and benign. The earth yields more and more as time passes until it is a cornucopia of pleasures. Gold, silver, jewels, cochineal, ivory, logwood, mahogany, teak, cocoa beans, tea, and spices pour in with the dyes, cloth, and foods made from foreign plants and the china, lacquer boxes, and silk screens made in distant countries. Beauty, ingenuity, variety—Defoe finds them all in the earth's produce.

His vision of the community of the world's people is illustrated by his description of the wool trade during the time of Queen Elizabeth I. He claims that English wool was superior to most of the world's, but that until Flemish immigrants taught their weaving methods to the English, other nations produced better cloth. Once the manufacture of wool was established, more and larger ships had to be built to meet the world's demand, and nations competed to find goods to sell to the English in return. The passage is rich in the names of English towns famous for the quality of their wool (Colchester, Norwich, Exeter, and Taunton), of emigrant families (Rebow, Papilon, and De Vink), of the cloth produced (bays, serge, says, and broadcloth), and of the rest of the world's cloths (raw silk, wrought silk, calico, cotton, and flax) and their sources (Persia, Smyrna, Scanderoon, Aleppo, and Ispahan) (pp. 213-15). He tells us that the "World lay open before" men and "wherever they went they found the Country pleasant" (p. 13) and "the Sea friendly" (p. 18). In spite of his admission that advances have cost much labor and many lives, Defoe makes the world seem to be a teeming warehouse ready for English hands.

❦ *And Beyond.* In *A History of Discoveries*, Defoe recommends three specific actions for England to take:

1. Taking and rebuilding the North Africa of Carthage
2. Establishing a South American colony in what is now southern Argentina
3. Studying climate and planting appropriately in order to get such products as coffee more cheaply

Although he pauses to discuss the benefits and practicality of each, he fits them smoothly into the larger narrative. Because he has stated that one of his purposes is to reclaim and recall forgotten knowledge, he can recommend the reestablishment of abandoned and neglected territories. Because he has said that he will present reasonable and feasible plans for projects that might be profitably undertaken under the directive that history should "show us what may be," he can spell out how the military alliance for the North African venture might work without violating the unity and tone unduly.

A History of Discoveries is actually a history of trade, and its movement is the spread of people through the world, especially the West, the building of cities, and the development of navigation.[89] Defoe calls navigation "the Parent of Trade," and, as the book progresses, he spends more and more time on the subject that he called "the Whore I really doated upon" in 1713. Every invention he singles out either aids sailing or provides uses for ships— astronomy, foundaries, magnets, mathematics, even building channels and dikes fit into his sense of a unified story. The early books contain far more ornamentation than the later and move from fable, symbolism, and the imaginative to solid economics and precise geography. Few passages in all of Defoe's work are as emotive as his recreation of the wonder with which Noah's descendents first regarded the Mediterranean Sea: "How Frightful in the Opinion of some; How Glorious in the Opinion of others . . . that when they came to the Brink of it, they could see no more Land, nothing but a vast endless Ocean of Water; and that Water subject to various Disorders, Storms, Tempests, . . . their Souls fill'd with Wonder and Amazement . . . " (p. 18). He makes the reader see the architecture of the early cities, the lines of the early ships, tiny boats inching around the coasts of great continents, understand Prometheus consumed by a desire for knowledge, and comprehend the glory of Tyre, "Mother of Merchants." By the time the book gives way to accurate, geographical descriptions and short essays on mundane, modern commodities like wool, the teeming world of endless possibility and magical beauty has been established. Men could still be Diaz, Cabot, or Cadmus in Defoe's picture of the world.

A History of Discoveries is part of a series of publications by Defoe on England's economic recession based on history and geography. As early as the War of Spanish Succession, Defoe had argued tirelessly for increased colonization in the Americas and had praised the profits of the African trade, but in the last ten years of his life, these economic arguments become increasingly developed, sustained, and imaginative. At first, he approaches England's economic problem in pamphlets, such as *A Brief State of the Question, between the printed and painted callicoes and the woollen and silk manufacture* (1719), and in periodical publications, such as "The Petition of Dorothy Distaff" (*Mercurius Politicus*, Dec. 1719), and he approaches the hostilities with Spain separately in pamphlets like *Observations and Remarks upon the Declaration of War against Spain* (1719). The two topics come together in the life of Raleigh and in the tracts on the South Sea, Turkey, and African companies and grow to an ambitious book in *A History of Discoveries*.

One of Defoe's great strengths as a writer of history was his knowledge of geography. Raleigh and the Hakluyts were pioneers in combining history and geography, and part of the lasting significance of *The History of the World* comes from its serious attention to geography. As an Elizabethan historian wrote, "geography without history hath life and motion, but very unstable and at random, yet history without geography, like a dead carcass, hath neither life nor motion at all, or moves at best but slowly on the understanding. . . . History, therefore, and geography, if joined together crown our reading with delight and profit."[90] Petavius had called chronology and geography the "two eyes of history." Much of the persuasive power of Defoe's case for increased colonization comes from the range and details of his geographic descriptions. Because he can name rivers, describe topography, and evaluate ports and then compare these as well as climate, plant life, and resistance to be encountered from natives and from other European nations in other locations that might be considered, his point of view assumes impressive authority. In some of his books, geography dominates (*Atlas Maritimus*, 1728) as history does in *The Plan of the English Commerce* (1728). Other books, such as *Captain Singleton* (1720) and *The Four Years Voyages of Captain George Roberts* (1726), take fictional forms.

In *A History of Discoveries*, however, Defoe blends history, fable, and geography in one of the first of his books to urge ordinary, private citizens to take on the task that he spent ten years badgering first the government and then the trading companies to assume. In making this shift, his writings shift focus from patriotism and security to profit and then to recalling the great spirit of the True-Born Englishman. The straightforward tactics of the *Review*s and tracts addressed to political parties and government become the combination of near-allegory and proposal that *An Historical Account of the Voyages and Adventures of Sir Walter Raleigh*, with its concluding address to the South Sea Company, is. This universal history begins by telling us that the "most glorious Empires" began with the "little Adventures of single Men, or the small Undertakings of the few" (p. iii). Defoe has taken his case to the people, in a form designed to define and to awaken national character.

A History of Discoveries is the first of five universal histories written in his old age. *An Essay upon Literature* (1726), a history of writing, "the most useful art of all," might have been a part of *A History of Discoveries*. As in *A History of Discoveries*, in it Defoe claims that the first writing was God's, on the tablets that were the Ten Commandments, and he chronicles improvements in the materials on and with which people wrote, in scripts, and from printing. Many of the descriptive passages and anecdotes are identical in the two books. Defoe describes printing, for example, as taking the labor out of making multiple copies, and repeats the story of Faustus in Paris. At times he extends speculations begun in *A History of Discoveries*. For instance, in *An Essay upon Literature*, Defoe examines the competing claims of Chinese and Egyptian writing to be earlier than the Ten Commandments. In *A History of Discoveries*, he discusses gunpowder immediately after printing and comments on how it has increased the noise of battle; in *An Essay upon Literature*, he tells us that without printing "The Noise of a Victory would have scarce been heard farther than the Noise of a Cannon" (pp. 114-15). Such similarities in organization suggest that Defoe may have had the text of *A History of Discoveries* before him as he wrote *An Essay upon Literature*.

The Political History of the Devil (1726), *A System of Magick* (1727), and *An Essay on the History of Apparitions* (1727),[91] all in the tradition of books such as Bodin's *De magorum dæmonomania* and Vaughan's *Magia adamica*, followed. Again, relationships to *A History of Discoveries* abound. The second part of the latter book includes a saying about the experiments of early men: "*The Egyptians convers'd with the* Gods, the *Phoenicians*, with Men, and the *Arabians* with the Devil" (p. 86). In the last section of *Political History of the Devil* and in the beginning of *A System of Magick*, he discusses the Chaldeans and Arabians, extending his discussion of their interest in the occult and alchemy. In all three books he traces the advancement of knowledge and the decline of superstition. The same reworkings of the tales of Faustus and Prometheus appear.[92]

These histories range the world and unite men throughout the ages and nations by demonstrating their common interests in a supernatural world, their attempts to find secrets, and their fears and superstitions. How ideas and folklore are passed from nation to nation resembles the ways scientific knowledge is transmitted in *A History of Discoveries*. Although some nations are more superstitious and more interested in the black arts even as some are less interested in colonies and are robbers, the brotherhood of man serves to give the topic interest and even significance because useful inventions and lessons in the appropriate uses of reason have come from the study of magic and the occult. The work of history, to teach by presenting past events and then by regulating the past to the present, continues in these books despite the considerable differences between them and *A History of Discoveries*.

Of these late histories even admirers of Defoe speak as James Sutherland did: "Unfortunately there seems to be no good reason for denying to Defoe the authorship of [these] works on the supernatural. . . . "[93] It is true that we are not now admirers of the universal histories and hold those who believe in ghosts in contempt, but there is a touch of ignorance and defensiveness in an easy dismissal of these books. C.A. Patrides tells us that the "avalanche" of universal histories continued into the eighteenth century.[94] *The Political History of the Devil* can trace its lineage through Swift's brilliant *Examiner* paper on "the Art of Political Lying" (No. 14 for 9 November 1710) to Milton's *Paradise Lost.* The character of Satan is the same, and one of the themes is Swift's—man now outdoes Satan in craftiness, dishonesty, and self-interest. Defoe says that Machiavelli could have taught the Devil new tricks, and Swift says that Godolphin could. Others have linked Defoe's ideas to Henry More. Defoe smoothly incorporates stories from the classics, history, the Bible, and recent English literature. He borrows from Bunyan's *Holy War,* for instance to describe "the Faculties of Man are a kind of Garrison in a strong Castle, which . . . they defend . . . under the Command of the reasoning Power of Man's Soul."[95] *The Political History of the Devil* saw two editions in two years (1726 and 1727), was translated into French by 1729 and into German by 1730, and continued to be reprinted throughout the century. Similar books were written by such distinguished men as Francis Hutchinson, Cotton Mather, Richard Baxter, Meric Casaubon, and Fontenelle and bore such titles as Nathaniel Crouch's *The Kingdom of Darkness: Or The History of Daemons, Specters, Witches, Apparitions, Possessions, Disturbances, and other wonderful and supernatural Delusions* (1688). So numerous are Defoe's writings on the supernatural that Sir Walter Scott, one of the earliest serious collectors of Defoe's works, calls them Defoe's "third [of four] species of composition."[96] The number and variety of folktales and anecdotes give new insight into oral history and must have been a source of great delight for contemporary readers.

The imaginative power of stories, such as the one repeated in *Moll Flanders* of the time when she steals the child's necklace and has a fleeting but strong impulse to kill the girl, is but one which might test modern defensiveness.[97] Perhaps every reader can remember a moment in his own life when he had a powerful urge to do something he believed wrong: to steal an object, to push a playmate, to deface a valued object. Defoe summons up the force of that impulse and the bewilderment and, yes, fear of the unknown source of the thought that followed the impulse. So can we recall times when we changed our minds for no apparent reason and benefitted, or we remember coincidences that seem too great for what Fielding calls probability. We may even continue to puzzle over dreams that seem to have held prophetic symbols or to have revealed to us some truth about an actual situation. Sir Walter Scott, sensing such defensiveness, begins his essay "On the Supernatural in Fictitious Composition" with these statements: "All professors of the Christian Religion believe that there was a time when the Divine Power showed itself more visibly on earth than in these our latter days. . . . [I]t is enough that a firm belief in the great truths of our religion has induced wise and good men, even in Protestant countries, to subscribe to Dr. Johnson's doubts respecting supernatural appearances."[98]

Quite simply, Defoe—and all Christians—lived in a spirit world. God is a spirit; the Holy Spirit is the third part of the Trinity; Christians are told to worship God "in spirit and in truth," and eternal life depends upon the immortality of the person's spirit. Defoe's histories catalog incidents that seem to be evidence of spirits, describe men's attempts to explain and master unnatural happenings, and condemn the modern world's immorality, indifference, and temporality. The person dead to spirits was dead to conscience. The quest for understanding is the same as Robinson Crusoe's attempt to understand God aright.

Universal histories had always tried to integrate the spiritual and temporal, the actions of men and the order or plan built into the universe, and the empirical and the inexplicable that worked together to make the story the history told. Men before Defoe had worked from investigations of the supernatural to explanations of the ordinary world instead of from the actions of men to their part in God's plan or in the cyclical plan of the universe. Because Defoe seems to believe so much more than we do and to feel ambivalent about so many more kinds of experiences and because he writes in this archaic genre, his books strike us as strange. In all of them, however, we find astonishing learning, delightful reworkings of familiar tales, gripping anecdotes, and a work that catches our imagination and shows us strange sights and distant people—a good story. Defoe gives us the stuff of our experience, as he does in his description of the memories of a dead loved one's face or a murderer's "haunted" dreams: "The Soul of the Murther'd Person seeks no Revenge . . . but the Soul of the Murtherer is like the Ocean in a Tempest . . . and the Guilt of the Fact, like the Winds of the Sea, lies on his Mind as a constant Pressure. . . . "[99] He also recalls the stuff of our fantasies, as he does through the tales of men who bragged that they could perform great deeds and then tricked the credulous with fireworks or phosphorescent chemicals or of the man who wanted the Devil to reveal the name of his wife's lover. Again and again, he demonstrates that "reason does not exclude [spirits], nature yields to the possibility, and experience with a cloud [sic] of witnesses in all ages confirm" the reality of the supernatural. Whether we move back to Francesco Gauzzo's *Compendium maleficarum* and Ludwig Lavater's *De Spectris* or forward to Aniela Jaffé's *Apparitions and Precognitions* (1963), we find people searching for knowledge about the nature of the world and about the meaning of events.[100] Of such inquiries were Defoe's fictions made.

FIVE

THE HISTORICAL NOVELS

HISTORICAL FICTION explicates the meaning of the past. Writers of historical novels try to understand why the past was as it was, how and why events took place, and how people thought and felt. They do not merely reproduce the furniture in a room but also the furniture in a mind: the influences, ideas, opinions, knowledge, and uncertainties that lead to actions. At its best, the historical novel re-creates the mind and experience of the past so intensely that the reader understands that time as an important influence on the present.

Defoe wrote three historical novels, each different and each deeply engaged with the conceptual issues common to all later historical fiction. Defoe's central concerns in these novels were to bring the past to bear on the present, thereby using the "lessons of history" to show men how "to bear themselves prudently in the present and providently towards the future" and to explore the long-term effects of the inadequacy of personal and public resources in a time of national crisis. His novels, like the best histories and later historical novels, attempted to give an accurate rendering of the past, explain how the past came to be the way it was, and then draw out the implications for the present and future. In particular, Defoe was obsessed with the way individuals make decisions and how those decisions reflect conscience and affect self-respect. Time after time, he created characters forced to cope with change and the inescapable ambiguities of human existence. Defoe's novels are historical because the characters' personal and social resources are inherited, the products of the national past. Change tests these resources, and, in the outcome, Defoe found the mood of the present and posited reasons for permanent alterations in his contemporaries' relationship to God and society.

The earliest of these novels, *The Memoirs of a Cavalier*, has sometimes been mistaken for a genuine account of a true experience. It follows the adventures of a young man from his coming of age through the Great Rebellion. The second novel, *A Journal of the Plague Year*, describes a mature tradesman's experiences during the Great Plague of 1665. *Memoirs of a Cavalier* unfolds and forges links from one past to another past and finally to the present while *A Journal of the Plague Year* concentrates upon a single, highly unified, past event with immediate interest for Defoe's readers. The last of Defoe's historical novels, *The History of Colonel Jack*, creates a more typical novelistic hero and returns to the literary models for *Memoirs of a Cavalier*. In addition, *Colonel Jack* inverts the processes of the two earlier novels by presenting a protagonist without a past who demonstrates the effects of less dramatic but more complex historical forces.

Defoe's novels share many of the characteristics of the "classical form" of the historical novel as identified by Herbert Butterfield, Gyorgy Lukács, Avrom Fleishman, and others,[1] and, for that reason, his novels are seminal to the development of the form. Sir Walter Scott, the writer most often identified as the father of the historical novel and the writer whom Lukács eloquently uses to derive his definition and to illustrate how the result is achieved, recognized Defoe's originality. In Scott's essay on Defoe, he writes that had Defoe never written *Robinson Crusoe*, his "second species of composition" exemplified by *Memoirs of a Cavalier* and *A Journal of the Plague Year* would have given him immortality. Scott finds Defoe's "vigorous genius" particularly well suited to writing about "great national convulsions" and discusses some half dozen ways that Defoe achieves his effects. It is Scott who made Defoe's method synonomous with two characteristics historical novelists must have: the ability to "identity himself with the child of his imagination," and the use of circumstantial details to give fiction "an air of reality." Defoe, Scott says, garnished his "imaginary history with all the minute accompaniments which distinguish a true one," and by so doing re-creates the physical setting and the spiritual consciousness of the past.[2] He sees that Defoe's novels are not merely stories set in the past, but stories in which a particular past supplies a good part of the plot and functions as setting, character, and to some extent theme.

Lukács saw Scott's novels "as the direct continuation of the great realistic social novel of the eighteenth century" but signifying "something entirely new."[3] Lukács is partly correct and partly wrong, but the basic difference between Defoe and Scott that his discussion fails to recognize helps explain the limitations of each man's novels and the particular type of influence each writer has had. In their selection of times of great national convulsions and their identification of the "character" of its outcome, in their attention to historical detail, in their use of the Hegelian *erhaltenden Individuen* as protagonist, and in their belief in historical progression, Defoe and Scott are alike. Both exemplify what Lukács calls the heart of the historical novel: a felt relationship between the past and the present that "brings the past close to us and allows us to experience its real and true being" and that gives "poetic life to those historical, social and human forces which, in the course of a long evolution, have made our present-day life what it is and as we experience it."[4]

But Scott (and Lukács) is concerned with national movements, especially those involving ideological clashes, while Defoe cares about the moral imperatives for decision making. His characters are just as fully English *erhaltenden Individuen* as Scott's, just as fully exemplary of people who "experience the smallest oscillations as immediate disturbances of their individual lives,"[5] but they are consciences, not classes. Defoe's protagonist is not primarily a historical pawn but a soul in search of the meaning of his, and therefore, mankind's existence. He does not represent "social trends and historical forces" so much as he embodies the quest for fulfillment as it is shaped by history. Therefore, Scott can look to Defoe and claim Dickens, Thackeray, Stevenson, James Fenimore Cooper, and countless formula writers as his progeny, while Defoe looks to the French memoir and spiritual autobiography and can claim Conrad, Twain, Bellow, and a special kind of *Bildungsroman*.

And this is why the *welthistorische Individuum* is always a dramatic presence in Scott's work but is often nearly absent in

Defoe's, and why Scott makes the physical milieu of his protagonists vivid and gripping while Defoe often fails to do so. Butterfield discusses the depiction of "The quiver through a whole people of some breath of national feeling . . . the throb of a whole nation in some intense crisis . . . caught into story . . . most apparent at the point at which it meets resistance, no theme is better for this kind of novel than that which describes in a people the bitter sense of national liberty thwarted, and of national aspirations refused. . . . "[6] This is a description of Scott, not Defoe. Defoe's characters want something both more individual and more eternal than "national liberty." The adventure for a Scott hero is bound to the historical event; for the Defoe character, to his own decisions and final state of mind. Scott is exploring how society came to be as it is; Defoe is asking how men came to see themselves and the world as they do. Lukács is quite wrong to say that writers before Scott had no "clear understanding" of history as "the concrete precondition of the present."[7] Defoe's three historical novels demonstrate that he did, for each novel offers an explanation of the mood of his contemporaries in the early 1720s.

Defoe probably wrote *The Memoirs of a Cavalier* to remind his contemporaries of the destruction caused by civil war.[8] By 1720, when he published this book, England was in the midst of a Jacobite crisis that had begun in 1715 upon the accession of George I and still showed no signs of abating. In fact, in 1720 both Sweden and Russia were conspiring with the Pretender and British Jacobites, and Defoe was able to begin that year's edition of *The History of the Wars of Charles XII* with the statement that the Swedish king had to be considered the "implacable Enemy" of England (p. 250). Indeed, people were so certain that the threat of invasion was serious that years later John Dalrymple could write that John, Earl of Stair, had helped thwart "a Design that was formed by *Charles the Twelfth* and the *Czar of Muscovy*, to set the Crown upon the Pretender's Head, in Revenge of the late King's purchasing *Breman* and *Verden*."[9] The fear in England was that the Pretender would lead English exiles and foreign troops in an invasion that would then be joined by the Jacobites in the British isles. Other books such as Bernard Mandeville's *Free Thoughts on*

Religion, the Church, and National Happiness (1720) demonstrate that many others shared Defoe's opinions and fears. Mandeville wrote,

let us cast an Eye on the Remedy they prescribe, and which so many of us hanker after in fear and silence, I mean the *Pretender*.

Many Years might we fight for nothing but dry blows.

But what shall we venture all this for? And which the mighty Prize to be obtain'd? The *Pretender* whose Legitimacy is at best but dubious, a Popish Bigot. . . .

The Question is, whether we shall be contented with the present . . . Blessings, which it is in our Power to enjoy . . . in Peace and Tranquillity, or renounce both to go in Quest of an Eutopia to be look'd for in Revolution [with] the Certain and Substantial Calamities, that ever must attend National Discord and Civil Wars. . . .[10]

The lasting power and appeal of *Memoirs of a Cavalier* come from its utterly unexceptional hero, its pessimism, and its philosophically nihilistic conclusion rather than from its evocation of the seventeenth or eighteenth century. The book is divided into two parts, the first about the young man's childhood, travel in Europe, and time in the army of Gustavus Adolphus, King of Sweden (1594-1632), and the second about his adulthood and experiences in the army of Charles I at the time of the Great Rebellion. In many ways, *The Memoirs of a Cavalier* is like Defoe's histories of Charles XII and Peter I. The Cavalier's attention is focused on Gustavus and Charles I, and the plot largely follows the progress of their wars. The Cavalier moves from battle to battle, and most of the narrative alternates between the relatively leisurely account of troop movement, army strategy, and layout of battlefields and, in contrast, the intense, concise descriptions of battles. The conclusion of the book seems hasty and artless; a disgruntled, apparently elderly man describes himself as "a melancholly Observator" and presents us with lists of evil events and bad omens. This narrator, however, is the representative of Defoe's contemporaries and a fine example of the *erhaltenden Individuen*. He is an ordinary man and, therefore, can illustrate historical forces, national character, and change. He brings the experiences and values of the past to bear upon the 1720 crisis and suggests changes in men and society based upon the effect of the experience on the central character and, by extension, men like him.

In order to relate past to present in a popular form, Defoe draws upon the well-established fictional French memoir. These books, in French, translated, or imitated, usually began with a sketchy genealogy, an account of a somewhat miraculous birth, and a tale of an unpromising youth punctuated by unusual adventures and amorous intrigues that draw the young man ever closer to court or to the great, public person who will add significance to the book. Signor Rozelli, for example, tells us that his conception killed his father and his birth his mother, and the Count de Rochefort is born four and one-half months prematurely after his mother's coach overturns, killing her. Before he is sixteen, De La Fontaine gets a curate's niece pregnant, and the Count de Grammont laughs at the problems that two court ladies have when they disguise themselves as orange wenches.[11] Defoe is careful to begin *Memoirs of a Cavalier* in a way that will identify his book with this form. The Cavalier's mother has vivid dreams, including one the night of his birth, and the child seems to have little promise as he drifts through part of an Oxford education and back home.

In fact, the first quarter of *The Memoirs of a Cavalier* mimics the French memoirs closely. It includes a number of surprising, miraculous, and unusual stories that appear unrelated; they seem merely the kinds of things that might be seen when traveling: a particularly ingenious theft that the Cavalier (anti-French like his countrymen) quickly labels as the first but typical "French Trick" he saw (pp. 8-9) and a riot in which men carried bread on pikes to protest the price (p. 15). Memoirs were expected to have amorous intrigues, often scandalous ones, and the Cavalier meets a charming, gracious Italian with a tasteful home who sings to a lute but is discovered to be, in his words, "a Punk of the Trade" (pp. 31-33).[12]

Most English dictionaries of the period define *memoirs* as "remarkable observations" with the connotation of events worth remembering,[13] and the title pages and prefaces of memoirs promise such records. *The Memoirs of Signor Rozelli* has "the most diverting History, and surprizing Events, ever yet made Publick"; there is "something remarkable" in the *Memoirs of the*

Baron de Brosse;[14] "George Psalmanazar" promises a "faithful narrative . . . of the remarkable accidents of my wretched life,"[15] and even *The History of His Own Time* about Matthew Prior lists one of the "compiler" Adrian Drift's "chief Materials" to be "curious Anecdotes" not found in any other memoirs of Prior.[16] The best contemporary definition, however, was given by Richard Steele in *Tatler* (no. 84 for 22 October 1709); he describes their content, comments on their number, and concludes, "the word Memoir is French for novel." Contemporary definitions of *novel* emphasize the story rather than "observations" upon it. Both Boyer (1699) and Bailey (1721) define *novel* as "an ingenious story of a pleasant intrigue." By using the memoir form in England, Defoe was able to exploit the expectation of interpretive commentary upon actual events without asserting the truth of the plot.

As Steele says, a very large number of the French fictional memoirs were military. Not only was it credible that men like the typical protagonist of memoirs would join an army, but military memoirs allowed travel, adventure, and contact with great historical figures. The second quarter of *The Memoirs of a Cavalier* begins the story of the Cavalier's military adventures. After observing General Tilly's army, he joins the Swedish Gustavus Adolphus's troops and participates in a number of battles. He drifts home after Gustavus's death, is bored and restless, and leaps at the chance to enlist with the Royalists, his father's side more than a serious choice of his own.

At this point, the value and art of Part I begin to assert themselves. The Cavalier has been a connoisseur of armies. The September 1631 battle between Charles and Tilly begins like a patterned dance with the "glorious and terrible" armies massed on opposite sides of a plain, becomes a contest of maneuvers, courage, and ferocity, and concludes with the vision of a last regiment of Cuirassiers[17] ranging the battlefield, both too fierce and too impotent to tempt engagement. Defoe catches the solemnity and suspense at the beginning, the unpredictability of the battle itself, and the part played by individual leaders' planning and actions. As the action increases, Defoe's language becomes more metaphoric; Charles's men, when pressed, "go to Wrack" and Cullenback's men are "overlaid," the word used to describe the smothering of an infant in its mother's or nurse's bed. Entire wings of the army are "cut down in a Moment." Without diminishing the concentration on the battle, Defoe builds up its drama: "indeed I never saw any Fight since maintained with such Gallantry, such desperate Valour, . . . such Dexterity of Management . . . " (p. 67). When Charles camps on the battlefields in spite of the severe cold and the temptation to pursue Tilly in order to instigate a rout, respect for Tilly grows.

Accounts of battles and evaluative descriptions of the men under the Duke of Saxony (p. 49), the Dutch Prince Maurice (p. 132), and others allow us to see the English armies as though we were there. The King's combination of "rabble" of footmen, servants, and gentlemen whose "Garb, Equipage, and Mien, did not look like War" face Parliament's motley collection of Scots, London trained bands, and poorly mounted squires, while clergymen are both sides' camp followers, implicitly and devastatingly likened to the camp followers in the Thirty Years War.

Ineptitude and accidents decide battles that are fought with dedication and ferocity. That such courage and determination are largely irrelevant because of political considerations and the lack of training and arms is but one moving and pessimistic note. Men who fought for Gustavus with the Cavalier are fighting on both sides of the Great Rebellion and serve as symbols of the divisions civil wars cause. The Cavalier mentions that he yearns to speak to some of his former comrades when he is on a mission to their camp but that he dares not. These old soldiers haunt each battlefield, struggling in the midst of armies that are hideous parodies of the disciplined Swedes.

The Cavalier records chances missed, advice not taken, mistakes repeated, and times when he and his men are cut off from their command. His frustration simmers but never breaks out because he is in a situation beyond his control. Ironically, some of the times when he is out of touch with his army work to the King's advantage while others contribute to his defeat. At one point he behaves as a disciplined soldier would and remains in position even though he hears the sounds of an assault on the town, and the result is that the entire army must withdraw (p. 222). The stray bullets that could kill Tilly and Adolphus become an infinite number of possibilities beyond the English commander's control.

In a rare instance, Defoe alters fact when he depicts Prince Rupert as habitually pursuing the enemy wing too far while the main battle is lost; in fact, Lord Goring did so at Marston Moor and Rupert at Naseby. That the Cavalier must follow Rupert even as Tilly's caution at Leipsick taunts him ("let [the Saxons] go, but let us beat the *Swedes*, too, and then all's our own," [pp. 177-78]) reduces the Cavalier to the level of the powerless, frustrated soldiers of books like *A Farewell to Arms*, *Catch 22*, and *If I Die in a Combat Zone*.

As the civil war continues, it becomes more ludicrous. A woman leads her servants to defeat a drunken major and his troop of cavalry, and Parliamentary supporters defend their town by using unfamiliar muskets as mallets and clubs. Some of the anecdotes in Part II are variations on those in Part I and, thus, reinforce Defoe's themes. For example, the Cavalier goes on a scouting expedition dressed as a farmer, feels so uncomfortable that he dares not speak, and meets the brother of the man from whom his horse was stolen while, in contrast, a man in Gustavus's army disguises himself as a plowman and tricks Tilly's sentries into revealing the width and depth of a river channel and the nature of both banks.

Defoe shows battle as reducing men to parts of an unpredictable mass whose efforts are futile. At best, the Cavalier can be a good gauge of his men and is sure to be affected by them. When he describes the Royalists' readiness to run away at Berwick, the Cavalier recognizes the signs (the "Men began to look one upon another, as they do in like Cases, when they are going to break"), is humiliated and frustrated, and yet we know he will be forced to retreat if they run and that he will do so for the same reasons they will: survival. Examples of noble, individual actions are rare compared to reports of the effect of events on group morale. An old soldier may raise his arm and rally his troops; a king may ride to the front of a yielding company, but such men usually die or are wounded and in ways that emphasize their pitiful mortality and the price of such foolhardiness. Much more common are reports that the men are "dispirited" because they sense mismanagement or are temporarily "heartened" by a victory. Defoe realistically but pessimistically shows victory or defeat to be the results of superior equipment, training, weapons, and numbers, but when the sides are nearly equal, the balance is a matter of accident or dependent upon the mind of the fighting men, presented as symbiotic and collective and accurate about their leader.

Like so many modern writers, Defoe suggests that winners are seldom better off than losers. Charles XII and Charles I die; Sweden loses her empire, and the reader knows that Charles II will be restored. The Russians will never be trusted, and the Presbyterians will be labeled as rebels for another hundred years. The Cavalier sees the hypocrisy in both sides and comments, " . . . Religion rightly practiced on both sides would have made us all better Friends." The frustration, helplessness, and disappointment in the Cavalier's final words could not come so effectively from another man. He is a quite ordinary adventurer, fights close to the greatest leaders of his time who should have given him a heroic vision if anyone could, and concludes his days at his family home, "a mellancholly Observator of the Misfortunes of the Times" and of "a World of Confusion" (p. 307). For those who read *The Memoirs of a Cavalier*, he is the dramatization of the powerful anti-war sentiment that would sweep England and the continent and find expression in the works of the greatest thinkers of the age: Hume, Gibbon, Adam Smith, Voltaire, and Rousseau.

Defoe's ambitions went beyond warning his countrymen against civil war; by analogy, he offered advice to George I and his advisers. A striking example occurs very near the beginning of the book, when the Cavalier compares the Queen Mother of France in 1632, who understood "the Management of Politicks, and the Clamour of the People" (p. 17), to Charles I of England: "Had this Princess been at the helm in *England*, she would have prevented all the Calamities of the Civil War here, and yet not have parted with what that good prince yielded in order to Peace neither; she would have yielded gradually, and then gained upon them gradually; she would have managed them to the Point she had designed them, as she did all Parties in France. . . . "[18] This description of the Queen Mother's method is almost exactly like the comments Defoe made in *Mercurius Politicus*.[19] Throughout the *Memoirs of a Cavalier*, Defoe offered examples and reflections that applied directly to England in 1720. He had long felt free to comment and to offer advice, although he had to protect himself from legal prosecution for appearing to criticize or to direct his king. In such pamphlets as *Some National Grievances, An Argument Proving that the*

Design of Employing and Enobling Foreigners, Reasons for a Royal Visitation (all 1717), and *Considerations on the Present State of Affairs in Great Britain* (1718), he reminded his countrymen—and their leaders—of such things as England's obligation to support Protestantism on the continent.

In these works, but especially in *Memoirs of a Cavalier*, Defoe is drawing upon the tradition of discourses for the education of princes dating back to the late Middle Ages. Defoe's participation in this tradition can be seen specifically in *Of Royall Education*[20] and in passages in his pamphlets that are like it. Englishmen usually began in the same way that Thomas Elyot did when he declared that his love and loyalty to his country and sovereign made it his duty "to rendre for that one litle talent delivered to me / to employe . . . to the increase of vertue [by setting] fourth some part of my studie. . . . I haue now enterprised to describe in our vulgare tunge / the fourme of a juste publicke weale. . . . " Common to books as diverse as Boccaccio's *De Casibus Virorum Illustrium*, Machiavelli's *Discourses on Livy*, and Castiglione's *The Courtier*, were the ideas that offering good counsel was one of the highest duties a subject owed his king and that such counsel should come both from "the sayenges of moste noble autours" and from experience.[21] All of these books were more related to the specific time and place than, for example, the writings of Erasmus, but the English usually managed to incorporate an image of the ideal and to emphasize moral goodness as well. Most included plans for the education of a prince or aristocrat that covered the topics to be found in later courtesy books and essays on political principles.

These discourses for the education of princes had great influence in the development of historiography and biography. Most of them illustrated definitions and precepts with historical anecdotes, and some went so far as to defend explicitly the use of apocryphal examples.[22] Writers in Defoe's time used such anecdotes to establish character and to present standards by which to judge contemporary actions. Such stories as Elyot's of Darius, who so personified majesty that the hangman sent to execute him dropped his sword, were much like the ones Defoe selected for his *Historical Collections*.[23] Firmer in their recommendation of pure virtue and closer to their classical sources, they contrasted to the practical applications of examples such as Machiavelli's Timasitheus, who refused to let his Corsairs keep the spoils of war intended for Apollo because he wanted the respect inspired by the *appearance* of virtue rather than the virtue itself (*Discourses on Livy* 29) or Catiglione's multiplication of amusing but uninspiring rustic conversation (a man being whipped about a market tells a well-meaning person who has suggested his punishment will end sooner if he runs, "When thou art whipped, goe at thy pleasure, for now will I goe as I shall thinke good").

Those discourses also used dialogues, developed characters, and even had stories introduced ingenuously as "to pause and take brethe / & also to create the reders / which fatigate with longe preceptes / desire varietie of mater / or some newe pleasaunt fable or history."[24] In the shadow of Chaucer and Boccaccio, these writers developed a didactic form that saw fable and history as highly similar—as pleasurable for the reader and as an effective way to instruct with a light touch. Years later, Oliver Goldsmith reiterated this opinion by explaining in his preface to Plutarch's *Lives* how unpleasant receiving advice could be: "Counsels, therefore, as well as compliments, are best conveyed in an indirect and oblique manner; and this renders biography, as well as fable, a most convenient vehicle for instruction."[25] Thomas More's *Richard III* went beyond these discourses to create a unified narrative with a "monster-king" complete with personality and motives. His series of character studies and the implications an examination of tyranny had for his own time suggested how much he drew from the education treatises; the fact that he did not complete and publish it suggested that he saw how it could be interpreted as addressed to Henry VIII.

More's *Richard III* was also innovative and a step toward modern historical biography because he began to emphasize his use of evidence for his opinions, most especially eyewitnesses. In the English version, he often included such clauses as "It is for trouth reported"; in the Latin version, he said that he learned certain information from his father. Although More was one of the few Renaissance writers to include such statements, Plutarch again was a model. In Plutarch's life of Demosthenes, he explained that the historian needs to be in a city in order to read "works not easy to be got in all places, nor written always in his own language" and to meet men who preserve things in their memories (5:2). Elyot said that history's lesson is "the mirrour of mannes life / expressing . . . the beaultie [sic] of vertue / & the deformitie and lothelyness of vice."[26] The discourse combined "history," then almost exclusively illustrative anecdotes, with essays on how to create and to maintain a good society; after all, even Machiavelli's *Prince* was directed toward the unification and liberation of Italy.

More's *Richard III* pointed the way to the division Dryden and his age would take for granted: annals, history, and biographia. In his "Life of Plutarch" in the 1683 edition of the *Lives*, Dryden asserted that the last "comprehends" the first two. Although he found it inferior in dignity and variety because it was confined to "the fortunes and actions" of one man, he believes that it excelled in pleasure and instruction and that it did so because the style could vary between the "plainness and nakedness" of annals and the "loftiness and gravity of general History" and could consider "minute circumstances, and trivial passages of life."[27] The historian most often cited as model by the French memoirists and Defoe's contemporaries was Plutarch, whose *Lives* they praised for recommending and teaching virtue.[28] Plutarch wanted to exemplify private virtue in great men and distinguished his work from history:

It must be borne in mind that my design is not to write histories, but lives. And the most glorious exploits do not always furnish us with the clearest discoveries of virtue or vice in men; sometimes a matter of less moment, an expression or a jest, informs us better of their characters and inclinations, than the most famous sieges, the greatest armaments, or the bloodiest battles whatsoever. Therefore as portrait-painters are more exact in the lines and features of the face, in which the chacter is seen, than in the other parts of the body, so I must be allowed to give my more particular attention to the marks and indications of the souls of men, and while I endeavor by these to portray the lives, may be free to leave more weighty matters and great battles to be treated of by others.[29]

Plutarch's favorite pattern was to discuss the family, education, ἦθος of his heroes, significant events in their lives, and the μεταβολαί of fortune. His use of anecdotes and vivid details and his style of alternating the reflective and narrative passages were imitated in histories, biographies, and memoirs. He said that "the virtues of these great men [serve] me as a sort of lookingglass, in which I may see how to adjust and adorn my own life" (*Life of Timoleon*, 2:107), and *The Mirrour for Magistrates* and other cautionary collections repeated his defense of biography.[30]

Defoe knew Plutarch well. His *Historical Collections* contained a number of stories from the *Lives*, and some of these appear in his fiction in revised form. Plutarch's account of Alexander's refusal to drink water in front of his thirsty men was transformed into an example of Charles XII's toughness and wisdom in *History of the Wars*; the story of Marius replying to Publius Silo's challenge, "If you are a great general, make me leave my camp and fight" became part of Gustavus's "not strong enough to fight, yet strong enough not to be forced to."[31] Like the Cavalier, Plutarch's heroes were often born soon after their mothers had significant, prophetic dreams. Pericles' mother, for example, dreamed that she bore a lion cub (1:321). The "embellishments" of illustrative stories, dialogue, and characterising gestures were quite acceptable to Defoe's age as long as they were probable, realistic, and contributed to the didactic purposes of the work. As early as the 1580s, Montaigne recognized the particular appeal of such lives: "Or ceux qui escrivent les vies, d'autant qu'ils s'amusent plus aux conseils qu'aux evenemens, plus à ce qui part du dedans qu à ce qui arrive au dehors, ceux là me sont plus propres voylà pourquoy, en toutes sortes, c'est mon homme que Plutarque."[32] Abel Boyer in his *Memoirs of the Life and Negotiations of Sir W. Temple* could have been paraphrasing Plutarch, as he expressed the same opinion in the eighteenth century: "the Particular Accounts of such Men's Lives as have had a share in the Management of Publick Affairs, are far more *Instructive* and *Entertaining* than *General Histories*: The latter, for the most part, being made up of bare jejune Relations of *Publick Transactions*; whereas the other acquaint us with the Characters of the principal *Actors*, and the most *Secret Springs* of their Actions."[33] In order to bring historical figures to life in this way, writers had to include actions, factual or fictitious, and they and their readers found delight in them.

Implicit, then, is the fact that Defoe's readers would have been quite adept at judging how important an objective presentation of fact was for the writer[34] and would have read the *Memoirs of a Cavalier* as a personal account rather than an objective history.

Only a few years later Defoe would write that readers are "not so unreasonable to expect" anyone to believe these long stories were true (*Mist*, vol. 4, no. 22). Readers could judge its verisimilitude by encountering well-established guides to the writer's intentions. Virulent, extreme statements and numerous pages devoted to explicitly described love affairs between people of widely different social statuses were, for instance, two clues that a work was highly fictionalized. Masses of reprinted papers and quotations from journals, such as we find in Prior's *History of His Own Time*, suggested an attempt to give an honest if necessarily incomplete picture.[35] Works such as Defoe's, openly assigned to a nameless narrator and following the pattern of the French memoir, told the reader that this was experiential truth, an account of how history felt, and, therefore, subjective and embellished as honest people's stories often are—they may not have the whole picture before them at the time of action, may be blind to certain possibilities, and have a tendency to make good stories better or single actions symbolic.

This expectation was related to another characteristic, found in the educational discourses and memoirs, that was not universally demanded of history or biography: the prose was to be pleasing in itself. Instead of valuing selection, arrangement, and interpretation, these forms demanded "ornament," a style that would heighten reading pleasure. Book after book claimed, as *The Memoirs of de Rochefort* did, that "none will ever find them tedious," and Defoe imitated them by using the preface to recommend *The Memoirs of a Cavalier* because his story was "inimitably told," gave "beautiful Ideas," and, once begun, would be hard to set down "till [the reader] has gone thro' it." The Cavalier's consistent use of colorful language, idiom, relish for repartee, and dramatic description contrasted to the relative infrequency of these literary touches in Defoe's histories of Peter I and Charles XII. For instance, like a man who knows he can tell a good joke, the Cavalier built his first conversation with Gustavus around a punchline: Tilly had two armies with him—one of soldiers and one of "Whores and their Attendants." Charles replied that the second army did as much harm as the first because it took food from the civilians (p. 61). Such an anecdote helped give the characters of both Charles XII and the Cavalier and, in a slightly old-fashioned way, made a moral judgment in the midst of an apparently secular narrative.

In contrast to the concern with process, causes, and conclusions in *Memoirs of a Cavalier, A Journal of the Plague Year* arrests a moment of collective consciousness. H.F. is the embodiment of that moment. More than recorder of events, more than novelistic character, he dramatizes the emotional crisis that the plague revealed. Defoe's generation had been battered by events that seemed to prove over and over again that religious, legal, and political beliefs and practices were inadequate. The Great Fire, the plague, political upheaval, and social problems seemed beyond rational explanation and human solution. The plague is more than plague; it is the threat of the triumph of Miltonic chaos.[36] Alfred Kazin once remarked, "Death in round numbers is by definition the death of strangers, and that is one of the outrages to the human imagination."[37] Not only does *A Journal of the Plague Year* describe the "outrage" that created a collective consciousness but also it vivifies in its main character the age's religious uncertainties and economic ambitions. H.F. comes to embody setting and theme even as his story brings a past time alive and makes that time relevant.

The immediate inspiration for *A Journal of the Plague Year* was the 1720 plague in Marseilles and the passage of the Quarantine Act in England. Suffering in Marseilles had been intensified by the behavior of officials and common people; therefore, Defoe saw a need to encourage Englishmen to behave in sober, orderly ways should plague break out. His first task, then, was to re-create the physical experience of a plague, and he methodically structured his descriptions to point out deplorable behavior and to praise and explain helpful conduct. In order to accomplish these things, Defoe relied heavily on documents and veridical material and made H.F.'s mind a replica of the work of the historical consciousness.

A Journal of the Plague Year is a great historical fiction because it simultaneously brings a past time alive, makes that time relevant, and goes on to use that past to delineate national character and to record a permanent alteration in people and society *by embodying setting and theme in a memorable character.* No matter how many critics have pointed out that H.F. might have been Defoe's Uncle Henry Foe, probably no reader has ever thought H.F. "real" or the "real author." Significantly, *Memoirs of a Cavalier* has been thought to be an authentic journal, but *A Journal of the Plague Year* never. It is simply too artful.

Memoirs of a Cavalier and *A Journal of the Plague Year* both draw upon personal forms, both usually recorded as events happen. Traditionally memoirs (like that of the Cavalier) had a public function and revealed the "secret springs" of action, while journals were written for private contemplation and taking stock. When journals were published, they had been judged to be exemplary and edifying rather than informative and instructive like memoirs. Although he uses both terms in both titles, Defoe follows the patterns rather closely; the Cavalier, who emphasizes "memoirs," has his eye on others, H.F., who subordinates "memoirs," on himself and God. The Cavalier does not agonize over his decisions; H.F.'s decision is the subject of his book. His mind is complex, and his dilemma gripping. Defoe has moved historical fiction closer to the psychological bent of the mainstream English novel and to the desire to convey the fullness of individual experience in a time of shared, national emergency. Without losing accurate reproduction of the time or the representative nature of character, he has expanded the reality fiction can convey.

Modern critics have increasingly recognized that H.F.'s "spiritual crisis is central to the book" and that the details about the plague are setting, not subject, but at least with *A Journal of the Plague Year*, they have not taken George Starr's admonition quite seriously enough: "apart from simple naming, Defoe is . . . less concerned with rendering [external things] objectively than with assigning them human significance and . . . this significance is broader, in some respects, than most commentators on Defoe have acknowledged." The "gaze" of Defoe's narrators "is obsessively purposeful."[38] And so it is in *A Journal of the Plague Year*, but it is also directed toward describing Defoe's own time.

When the plague begins, H.F. weighs leaving the city. At this point, he and his brother each represent a widely held opinion.[39] In the early part of the Novel, H.F. encounters a number of people who hold various opinions, but, as the novel progresses, debates

become increasingly interior and directed toward the final shape of
H.F.'s mind.

If Robinson Crusoe begins by casting himself as the prodigal
son, then H.F. chooses Jonah by staying in London to witness and
to warn. He assigns himself a role and tries to interpret through it.
At several points, London is compared to Nineveh; in both, the
initial reaction of the populace and of individuals is to deny the
danger or act as though believing it will pass them by will make
it so. H.F. finds the hand of Providence preventing his several
attempts to leave. Once committed to staying, H.F. rebukes
particularly profane or sinful people and specifically records and
reflects upon events that offer patterns and admonishments. At
one point, he says, " . . . I was mercifully preserved by that great
God whose Name they had Blasphemed and taken in vain, by
cursing and swearing in a dreadful Manner; and that I believed I
was preserv'd in particular, among other Ends, of his Goodness,
that I might reprove them for their audacious Boldness, in
behaving in such a Manner, and in such an awful Time as this
was . . . " (p. 80). He pauses at various times, as he does after
seeing the burial pit, to tell us that he wishes he could describe the
scene and its effects graphically enough that it would "alarm the
very soul" of the reader, for it is a "speaking sight." Repeatedly,
he calls his story "a caution and warning" and "a pattern" with a
"moral."

At the end of the time he spends considering leaving, he
summarizes the advice given him with the words, "Master, save
thyself." These were the words the thief on the cross spoke to
Christ, who had chosen to obey God and to die. The implication
is that H.F. believed he was intended to stay, and the theme of duty
versus self-preservation arises numerous times in various guises.
One of the most complicated passages in the book considers those
whom the city needed: physicians, clergymen, magistrates, aldermen, and other government officials. By this time (pp. 285-90), the
order and comfort they bring is undeniable, and H.F. says a record
"to the honour of such men" should exist.[40] Not only does he
provide another justification for his narrative—and he does, for
example, commend city government on at least fifteen specific
occasions—but also he proves not insensitive to the danger of the
plague: "A Plague is a formidable Enemy, and is arm'd with

Terrors, that every Man is not sufficiently fortified to resist, or prepar'd to stand the Shock against . . . " (p. 287); and "not an ordinary Strength [could support the terrors of the time]: it was not like appearing in the Head of an Army, or charging a Body of Horse in the Field; but it was charging Death itself on his pale Horse . . . " (p. 288). H.F. and these men, he says, thank God not only for their deliverance but also for allowing them to be useful.

Publishing his journal, then, becomes an act of redemption and thanksgiving, erasing the presumption he suspected in himself earlier. Because historians and other writers so frequently mentioned the duty a nation had to its public servants to immortalize their actions as a sign of gratitude, an act of patriotism, and an example for citizens, Defoe's readers would have recognized H.F.'s imitation of the historian's work and found amusement in his inept attempt to identify all of the dead magistrates, clergymen, and others whose public duty kept them in London.

Defoe's achievement in *A Journal of the Plague Year* is not in the character of H.F., of course, but in the re-creation of historical consciousness. Watson Nicholson and others have demonstrated the accuracy of Defoe's descriptions, and subsequent critics have suggested ways that readers respond to history in this guise, but no one has delineated the reproduction of the mind of those who lived through the plague nor pointed out how existential his recommendations are.

H.F. confronts the plague armed with orthodox piety and practical concern for his business. His indecision about leaving London was surely shared by almost everyone else; whether such considerations were brief and intensive or recurring and nagging surely depended upon circumstances as much as personality. Almost everyone in 1664 would have examined the plague as sign, tried to "read" it, first as applicable to themselves and then to their community, city, and nation. Economic aspects could not be ignored either in the commercial atmosphere of London.

The associations in H.F.'s mind are the source of some of the most subtle aspects of the re-creation of the historical consciousness and help identify H.F. as a representative Englishman. For example, the plague and the Great Fire are inextricably linked in the minds of all who survived both, and so H.F. presents them.[41] The initial images of the plague are those of the behavior of fire;

the plague flickers, darts into flame, fades, flickers, and slowly spreads. The plague is described in fire images such as "raging." The portents noticed by the people are the same before both events, H.F. says; both "defy" all remedies, and people react in similar ways—some run, some pray, some plunder (pp. 5-6, 241-42, 24, and 43, respectively). Numerous references show how prominently the fire was in people's minds (pp. 200-201, 272, 294); in their distress, some people actually cry "Fire." John, one of the few characters treated extensively, says he "must go out of my house if it is on fire," just as he must leave London when it is infected by plague (p. 151). People are equally helpless in both and reduced to an amorphous, reactive group. To the ends of their lives, those who lived through both would think of them contiguously.

H.F. tells us he is writing a history, not preaching a sermon, and *A Journal of the Plague Year* moves to some extent through documents, such as proclamations and mortality bills. The Lord Mayor's Orders alone, for example, comprise over one-thirtieth of the book[42] and had been published in 1721 by the bookseller of *A Journal of the Plague Year*. Most of the contemporary historians, such as John Evelyn, had remained in London during the plague and fire, and H.F. suggests that their role as "teacher" ranks them with magistrates and clergymen, among whose duty it was to stay if they were courageous enough. As in *History of the Union*, "the people" are usually undistinguished except by group tendencies, and anecdotes are more illustrative than intrinsically, individually important. In fact, at one point H.F. says that he will not "vouch to the truth of the particulars" (p. 141). The effect is that all who lived through the plague are bound together by the experience in ways that overshadow individual differences.

Defoe builds into the experience of passing weeks a subtle transformation that is the second part of what we call the "historical imagination" and that reinforces H.F.'s function as representative consciousness. Defoe converts the re-creation of the simple past into what the past always is: constructed, remembered experience, and here feeling may modify or even conflict with fact. To read the diaries, letters, and papers written at the time of the plague is to be struck by the number and power of anecdotes much like Defoe's. These anecdotes are often horrible, pathetic, moving;

others are "remarkable" and relate God to the suffering city, while
others are grotesquely funny. Mingled with anecdotes are documents such as mortality bills and extremely precise statistics. A
typical example reads, "A dreadful Plague raged this Summer in
London, and swept away 97309 Persons. It was usual for People
to drop down in the Streets as they went about their business; and
a story is reported for a certain Truth, That a Bagpiper being
excessively overcome with liquor, fell down in the Street."[43] The
bagpiper, or course, is picked up by the dead carts, but he awakens
in time and begins to play on his pipes.

The statistics refer to an incomprehensible horror that was a
concrete reality, but the anecdotes conflate the day-to-day experience into the recollected event. Paradoxically, the discrete and
sequential become a single, unified memory. People may say or
write that 97,309 died, but they remember the stories, the screams,
the "speaking sights." Defoe captures the way historical events are
remembered as symbolic vignettes. When the catastrophe is mentioned, the person says, "I will never forget . . . ," and a story
follows, the re-creation of an experience—felt as well as witnessed.
By recounting what H.F. saw and heard, Defoe upholds the
illusion of a chronicle even as he transforms his book into an
experience like the plague. The accumulation of anecdotes and
understated descriptions of H.F.'s reactions finally gives the reader
the sense of living through the plague. Who can remember
sequence? Who can be sure details from several stories have not
been blended? What matters is the helplessness, the struggle for
humanity and courage, the ugliness of the disease, the suffering
and the sense of time destroyed because of the similarities of
incidents, griefs, and the feeling that the plague was continuing
beyond prediction. The experience, the book, draws us into a
timeless nightmare—who can tell which incidents happen by day
and which at night? which in late fall and which in early spring?—
and becomes more powerful because of its contrast to the decep-
tively slow beginning of the plague and the rebirth of London as
people return to the streets at the end.

The Memoirs of a Cavalier moves from battle to battle,
following a geographical, chronological, and historical path. So,
too, does *A Journal of the Plague Year*; it is possible to map the
plague parish by parish and month by month, but the very

similarity underscores the contrast. To follow the Cavalier's campaigns is to move toward a predictable conclusion; to see an army advance through foreign territories or be pushed out of its capital city is a way to measure the coming of an end. Geographical and chronological movement promises no conclusion for London. The plague might sweep back to parishes struck first, might spread more extensively beyond the city walls, might linger for many more months, might conceivably last until London is abandoned. The ways we measure duration break down. What can be endured for a set period of time may be intolerable when experienced as unpredictable and open-ended, we are told by survivors of torture and war.[44] As the plague continues, usual measures of time become more irrelevant; H.F. locks himself up for various lengths of time; he goes out at night; he sees people in the day. But by what logic? London misjudges the end of the plague, and hundreds more die. What they and H.F. feel becomes more real than any external, standard measures of duration.

The third act of the historical imagination in to analyze resulting changes and even to suggest implications. The end of the plague is surprising, perhaps as unpredictable to the Londoners as the plague itself. When the plague is over, London finds itself triumphant. Maximillian E. Novak does not go far enough when he says that the London poor are the "collective hero," and the city "functions as the victory of life over death,"[45] nor is it enough to see in the Londoners' generally laudatory behavior that natural catastrophes can be a time of trial and testing rather than judgment and that men cannot always distinguish God's purposes. The conclusion is astonishing. People return to the streets, and images of spring and rebirth abound in A Journal of the Plague Year: "And wonderful it was to see how populous the City was again all on a sudden; so that a Stranger could not miss the Numbers that were lost . . . " (p. 278); and "a secret Surprise and Smile of Joy sat on every Bodies Face; they shook one another by the Hands in the Streets . . . " (p. 298). Trade increases greatly, and plans for a better London come from a dozen hands.

Even more significant than the growth of London is what Lukács calls an altered psychology. England becomes far more secular in its public utterances. Issues that had been discussed in theological terms become pragmatic and are not religious or even ethical, although in most cases civil and religious virtues were synonymous.[46] H.F.'s account has far more directions for the conduct of life than the practice of piety; he gives more instructions to magistrates than to clergymen. Government is far more important to the city even than pious men. Defoe is very close to Hume's idea of government as a means of compelling men to identify their private welfare with public good and to sacrifice their immediate interests for often distant benefits. Joining with the fading of the Puritan influence, the experience of the plague decreased the tendency to interpret every experience, no matter how trivial, as a message from God. Those who complain that H.F. leaves the reader with an ambiguous directive miss the point. He has looked for signs, looked to science and medicine, and come away sceptical and with the admonition to Job. Significantly, H.F. concludes his *Journal* with a short poem ending, "Yet I alive!" He does not explain his survival nor does he do more than compare himself to the "tenth leper," the only one who came back to thank Jesus for healing him. His experience, begun in pious questioning, ends in gratitude for his life but not in answers. Just as the huge growth of domestic manufacture and trade transformed England, so did the memoirs of men who survived the fire.

As Hobbes said, "the principal and proper work of history [is] to instruct and enable men . . . to bear themselves . . . providently towards the future." That Defoe intended *A Journal of the Plague Year* to instruct cannot be disputed. This book joined several other works, each written in a different mode, in making the same points, first to government and second to the people. The past, as Paul Alkon has said, becomes a means of depicting alternate, possible futures.[47] In periodicals, especially *Applebee's* and *The Commentator*, Defoe cautioned the people against foolishness and insensitivity and the government against increasing misery and panic through repressive, premature measures such as the Quarantine Act of 1721. Defoe said in *Due Preparations for the Plague* that he had deliberately selected cases from the past that suited circumstances to come and that he recommended the civic and religious pattern. Again, his technique was familiar and common. Abel Boyer, for example, explained that his *Life . . . of Temple* attempted to reconcile contemporary "*unhappy Divisions*" by a *tacit Parallel* between *former* and *late Transactions. . . .* "[48] The specific linking of past and possible future never fades from the narrative for very long; for example, in the family described most extensively, the matriarch had survived the plague of 1664. Many of these comparisons are stated in typological language, which reinforces the universally short-sighted behavior of people and the certainty of recurrent natural disasters; "we were Marrying and giving in Marriage to the very Day that it came upon us," the mother says, and she leads her family to prepare for and to survive the plague.

Defoe's periodicals concentrated on public conduct, *Due Preparations* presented a private family in the dialogue form Defoe used so well in conduct books such as *The Family Instructor* and *Religious Courtship*, and *A Journal of the Plague Year* united the civic and soterial admonitions in a less overtly didactic form. By this means, Defoe reached a very wide audience and produced two books that are more readable than many others in the flood of 1720-22 English plague literature. *Due Preparations* undoubtedly attracted the pious readers of conduct books, and the last sentence, a scriptural quotation (Psalm 112:7) would have been a comforting and predictable conclusion.

In contrast, *A Journal of the Plague Year* and H.F. are almost of another time. H.F. questions and searches; his mind is open to many more possibilities, and he asks more diverse questions. The catechismal questions of *Due Preparations* are little like H.F.'s issues, and H.F. is a fictional character for us because we believe that the situation may influence him, that he may learn new things, and that he may even change. He does not, like the matriarch's children, merely come to accept a well-known point of view. H.F. soon realizes that the plague is an unpredictable force and that business in London has been suspended. He turns to medicine, government, and science for answers and begins to look at such issues as class behavior and scientific attempts to diagnose, treat, and halt the plague. He, like Richard Baxter and many others, noticed that the poor were the principal sufferers.[49] By the end, he is recommending a number of measures to be taken by the city government and individuals, but admitting that at best they only decrease the number of cases of plague. He specifically rejects such theories of the cause of plague as the miasmatic and telluric and endorses contagion.[50] His answer, finally, however, is that com-

mon to most of Defoe's writings: plague spreads by natural causes
at the will of God. What those causes are, he does not know.

The ambiguity so often criticized in H.F. is the ambiguity of the
situation: he does not know cause; some people have a duty to stay
in London; some cannot leave because of poverty or physical
disability. The recommendations, then, are equivocal and problematic at worst and pragmatic at best: isolate the sick immediately; leave if possible; stock the home and remain sequestered;
behave prudently and hope for the best. Although his recommendations to the Court of Aldermen are more specific and extensive,
their goals, too, are order and relief, not preventative or curative.
But, we must never forget that H.F. is the tenth leper, the one who
does not forget to thank God.

Like an Enlightenment man, H.F. begins to engage himself with
the situation and to project plans of action for himself and for the
city, and the effects on him may be diverse, not limited to salvation
or damnation. The man, his experience, and the way the story is
told become a part of the message, and the book becomes a
historical novel—a fiction whose experiential and verifiable truths
bring the past alive even as it explains Defoe's contemporaries'
secular, sceptical bent of mind. Just as the Cavalier represents the
pessimism and antiwar sentiment of 1720, so H.F. embodies the
breakdown of faith in a personal God and the fruitless search for
certainty in Defoe's time.

Colonel Jack strikes the reader as more sociological than
historical, and yet it shows a wider range of the historical forces
acting on Englishmen than either *Memoirs of a Cavalier* or *A
Journal of the Plague Year*. Like the other two novels, it performs
the work of a critical history, for it unapologetically examines the
fabric of past life with moral commitment and understanding of
the common man. In contrast, however, it re-creates forces as
great as plagues and wars but far less immediately obvious because
of their complexity and lack of drama. The child, we are led to
believe, of some of the many immoral gentility in Restoration
England, Jack is left on his own by the death of his nurse. In the
course of his long life, Jack is an errand boy and thief (thereby
learning about goldsmiths' bills and Jews' diamonds), a soldier in

northern England, a kidnapped bondservant, a plantation owner and colonial trader, a gentleman traveler, a soldier in France and Italy on the side of France and Spain, a Jacobite who witnesses the battle at Preston (and, thereby, becomes a rebel), a captive of privateers, and a smuggler. He gives us glimpses, then, of England's foreign wars, the Jacobite threat, and major issues in the North American colonies.

More than Defoe's other novels, *Colonel Jack* draws upon and addresses issues discussed in his nonfiction. William McBurney and others have pointed out similarities between *Colonel Jack* and such books as *The Complete English Gentleman, The Family Instructor,* and *Of Royall Education.* In fact, the novel is more concerned with economics and politics than with manners. The relationship of episodes in the second half of the book to Defoe's writings on pirates, trade, and England's foreign affairs is obvious, and, in other places, he repeats his opinions and arguments in tracts such as *An Account of the Proceedings against the Rebels* (1716) and treats such issues as slavery, populating North America, and the trade rivalry in the colonies, which would lead to the series of wars beginning with the War of Jenkins's Ear in 1739.

The Cavalier and H.F. involved themselves in major historical events; Jack is more representative of the common man who is not a direct participant but behaves more like a simple biological organism that shifts slightly when touched but must be prodded to change colors or move. He is affected by social and political events that he does not analyze. The Cavalier and H.F. are observers, and they describe people at the moments when their essential natures are visible by arresting them in moments of crisis. Time after time, the Cavalier shows Gustavus or Charles at a moment of decision or a crucial turning point; time after time, H.F. gives us anecdotes of people pushed to the last drop of their emotional resources and displays them raving, swimming the Thames frantically, calling on God, or bringing their entire wages to their families. By using this technique, Defoe raises these moments to symbolic proportions. We see Charles I in a shabby inn in Newberry weeping over the dying Earl of Carnarvon (p. 214), and a woman opens a window, screams, and then cries out, "O! death, death, death!" over the silent, deserted, plague-ridden street.

The technique in *Colonel Jack* is the opposite. Here we have a single character whose life, whether he knows it or not, is the record of the impact of historical forces on ordinary people.[51] Upon contemplation, it is almost frightening how violent and unsettled Jack's world is. His parents have abandoned him, his nurse must be buried by the parish because her husband was killed when the ship carrying the Duke of York to Scotland in 1682 sank, and he becomes a London street child—without adequate clothing, food, or care. The indifference of society and of every institution that might be expected to feed or educate the child is taken for granted. Jack witnesses robberies, fights, drunkenness, pumpings, and Bridewell justice. The number of whippings witnessed approaches that in Smollett's most brutal novels. Jack himself is kidnapped, abused, has his nose slit, is held hostage, and is frequently afraid.[52] He lives in a world in which thirteen-year-old boys are ignored, then arrested and beaten brutally, then released to survive as they can. Jack knows people who are hanged and quartered in England, and one of his foster brothers is broken on the wheel in France. At one point, he fears being sent to the Spanish mines in Peru. His ships are sunk, captured, and confiscated, often leaving him economically or physically endangered. One estimate is that no fewer than 180 English ships were pillaged by the Spaniards in the West Indies between 1713 and 1731, and Jack's experiences are in harmony with this account.[53] His country seems to be continuously at war abroad and divided at home.

The brutality and callousness Jack encounters are depressing. During his youth, the only institution that seems to work is the legal system.[54] Although Jack's neighbors feed him and give him errands to run, nowhere do we see the attention and organization of the legal system approximated. Captain Jack, for example, is arrested after he commits a crime against someone prominent enough to set the process in motion, and he is sentenced to be whipped three times at Bridewell; this punishment was administered in a windowless room behind the courtroom so that those in court could hear the sentence executed. The criminal was stripped to the waist, tied to a post, and lashed with holly twigs "which will bend almost like Thongs, and lap round the Body: and these having little Knots upon them, tear the Skin and Flesh, and give extream Pain."[55] Defoe describes a living person, Alderman Turner, calmly lecturing Captain Jack as he "stamp'd, and danc'd, and roar'd out like a mad Boy" (p. 12). The lecture, delivered in such circumstances and to a person without education and religion, is a mockery.

Again and again, the legal system metes out drastic punishments in spite of social conditions that push men into crime and that have inherent contradictions. Jack notes that men have no chance for employment except in the military, and we see no signs of an apprenticeship or educational system; governments commission privateers as legal robbers and murderers, and men become traitors by preferring a former king over a present king. The brutality in the streets, in Edinburgh, on ships, on the plantation, and in private homes occurs regardless of Jack's wealth, status, or the country in which he happens to be. Men cheat each other, refuse to pay agreed-upon ransoms, intimidate and threaten, and demand payoffs. Women drink and commit adultery in their own beds. Jack can fight for France and be robbed by French privateers; he can, like the Cavalier, see former comrades-in-arms divided into opposing armies, and he can find a very few people willing to help and to educate him among those only too willing to laugh at him.

Jack is truly the product of his time, cut off from past values and past solutions and forced to cope with a world from which he cannot retire. Land no longer represents a source of continuity and stability but has come to be valued as it produces; it is something to administer, like a factory with workers and machines. He encounters dozens of people like himself who are basically unattached, rootless, opportunistic, and yet vulnerable. The plague, the fire, and urbanization have ended the orderly parish administration, and economics dominates his life. His is a world of credit and trade, and nations fight by plundering citizens as much as they fight with guns.[56] Time after time, people have no recollection of Jack, as is true with one of his robbery victims and of the Preston rebels of whom he is so afraid. Jack is transcendentally part of the mobile, impersonal, modern world that controls its citizens by intimidation rather than by recognition and admonishments.

Colonel Jack is closer to our idea of the novel partly because Jack was far less typical than the Cavalier or H.F. For this novel, Defoe drew extensively upon those French memoirs that were most obviously colored by the Spanish picaresque. Unlike the well-born protagonist of the memoir, the picaro was usually lower class or completely ignorant of his ancestry; his survival was far more precarious and his world more hostile. He was likely to commit real crimes and unlikely to rise to an influential post at court. These narratives, like the memoirs, were often first-person, retrospective, realistic, and coated with irony. Most often, the hero was "a naive youth wrestling endlessly with the problems of survival in a severely materialistic world."[57] Because he was young, he had some high ideals—often about his own possibilities or about love—but he was certain to discover that the world which espoused his ideals behaved in the most crass, dehumanizing ways.[58] His survival and personal fulfillment, then, had to be worked out alone and in spite of almost everyone around him.

The French writers, especially Lesage, increased the protagonist's desire for personal virtue and modified the fictional world so that poetic justice would be done. The Spanish "trickster" survived in the later stories because he was clever and flexible; the French maintained these qualities in the hero (although he often was better educated), but made him increasingly intelligent, witty, honest, socially adept, and a less protean personality who deserved his final success because of his inherent goodness.[59] Significantly, the French hero lived in a world in which virtue was rewarded while the traditional picaro did not. This change tended to make the tone of the narrative more problematical as the description of a harsh, realistic world blended with an overriding faith in providential order.

The subtitle of *Lazarillo de Tormes* is "*de sus fortunas y adversidas,*" and this emphasis remained dominant in the plots of memoirs and contributed to the complexity of tone. As Jean Sgard says, in Courtilz de Sandras we find the formula for the genre as it was practiced in 1700: "le heros de Sandras tient du picaro . . . "; and "le ton personnel, le fourmillement d'aventures et d'anecdotes qui font le tissu du roman, un cadre historique et géographique . . . les aventures de cape et d'épée. . . . "[60] Many heroes, such as Rozelli, are offered to the reader as candidates for the large gallery of "Men made famous by Adversity."[61] Colonel Jack adheres to this model well, and chance and adversity seem to affect his life at least as much as his own choices. Many of these early memoirs purport to justify a life and to discern the connection between events leading to the deserved happy ending. "George Psalmanazar" describes his memoirs as "amends" for his wretched life, and the Countess Dunois styles her memoirs as a "Vindication of the Female Sex" as well as an apology for her life.[62] Jack, like Psalmanazar, has been prompted to write by a "fit of sickness," in his case gout, during his enforced leisure at Vera Cruz, and he pauses at intervals to call attention to the "Chain of Causes" in his life that have brought him to prosperity and repentance.

The opening sections of *Colonel Jack* seem designed to place the novel in this Spanish-French tradition for contemporary readers. For example, Jack's obscure, but implied, upper-class background and his early association with rogues until "This Life began to grow irksom . . . for as my understanding increast I began to be asham'd of my self"[63] were standard to the genre. Jack's marital adventures are similar to those of de Rochefort's father, and de Sandras's book was extremely popular in England.[64] For much of the time, Defoe is writing in the spirit of de Sandras's preface to his *Memoirs of de Rochefort*: "should these Memoirs not prove so very profitable, I am confident they will be found to be very curious, discovering a great many things which are no where else to be met with. I believe too . . . that none will ever think them tedious." De Sandras means, of course, "profitable" to the soul, and his words recall Defoe's own in the preface to his *Memoirs of a Cavalier*. Jack notes that such lives are now extremely popular in England and urges his readers "that when they find their Lives come up in any degree to any Similitude of Cases" to ask if it is not now time to repent (pp. 307-9). Not only is the commercial motive brought to our attention, but also Defoe emphasizes the fictional nature of the book—few readers even in 1720 were likely to find themselves in many of Jack's predicaments. Scholars of the picaresque have long emphasized the secular and ironic intentions of the genre,[65] and Defoe finds these aspects useful in establishing the hostility and hypocrisy of Jack's world.

The combination of Spanish and French elements allows Defoe to create a harsh, unattractive world even as he presents an optimistic, even Romantic hero. Jack can remain spontaneous, adventurous, emotional, and also be an individual with special personal needs. In this somber and violent universe, Jack is a Huck

Finn, an Augie March. He is Romantic in his yearnings and his individuality. He has no home, no trade, and feels misplaced in the position society has assigned him. Because he wants personal fulfillment more than economic security, his inner life is as vivid and forceful as the depiction of the external world. He longs to direct his own life and yet he finds constraint at every point. By giving us a protagonist who knows no history and has no inheritance, Defoe delineates the historical forces that cannot be avoided or ignored and that will eventually shape the consciousness and choices of those living in that time in one of a relatively small number of predictable ways. Jack seems to be an individual with a life and destiny of his own, and yet he bears the ethical ambitions of an age through a specific, re-created past that we can recognize as the modern world.

Although Colonel Jack's life cannot be neatly plotted on an exact historical chart,[66] he is affected by almost every "national convulsion" in his time, and he stands as result and warning for Defoe's readers. The novel makes us aware of a few important events, such as the sinking of the Duke of York's ship, the attack on Cremona, and the invasion of the Pretender in 1708, of some major English endeavors such as colonialism and trans-Atlantic trade, but, even more significantly, of social and economic fluctuations. The last occur over relatively long periods of time and affect people more subtly but more universally. Jack, for example, is born during a depression marked by bankruptcies and a stop of Exchequer as well as in the tumultuous, reportedly immoral time after the Restoration. Except for a year or two, the time during which he is a homeless youth is prosperous, and this fact undoubtedly aids his survival as beggar, errand-boy, and thief. His early manhood is a period of recession and failed harvests, and he finds employment difficult; it is a good time to leave England for the colonies.

Jack experiences the breakdown of the earlier religio-social order that would have provided a different kind of childhood, and he observes the severe changes in the country's prosperity. These changes could be so great only in an economy undergoing drastic pressures and revisions; in Jack's time, war came to be financed in a completely new way and wealth to be measured in money and credit, not land.[67] From 1689 to 1721, the period of Jack's young manhood, Europe was continually at war, and Jack, like the Cavalier, fights in several wars and on several sides without much personal commitment. War was often a trade or an adventure to his generation. The European wars made the dangers and the opportunities for Jack's mercantile ventures. *Colonel Jack* faithfully captures the social flux of the time. Even the lack of moral standards and the bizarre pasts of his wives portray a more complex and disrupted world. The ambitious, opportunistic, confident spirit of the citizens of a nation that transformed their own economic system, became a major military power, and began to establish the empire that was the wonder of the modern world is personified in the characters in the novel. The willingness to use force, the careless brutality, the streaks of generosity, and, above all, the spirit of adventure that led to exploration of possibilities at home and abroad live in characters as diverse as Will, the sea captain who takes Jack to Virginia, his first wife, and, of course, Jack.

The novel ends shortly after the Preston battle in 1715 with a portrait of the now retired, allegedly repentant Jack. He bears the scars of the Jacobite uprising crushed so effectively by George I and the Whigs by such harsh measures as the Riot Act, Septennial Act, and the trials of the rebellious Scottish peers. Jack's fear and rapid conversion to George's side probably had many real-life analogues. Jack is not an old man in 1717, but he acts as if he were, and here Defoe presents a vision of the past's influence on the present. Jack's eventful life has left him tired and battered by forces he could not control; he longs for the same tranquillity and prosperity that made Walpole and his motto of *quieta non movere* appealing to Defoe's contemporaries; England longed for unbroken years of domestic tranquillity and isolationism.[68] Jack has absorbed English history, and his "memoirs" complete a historical act: they explain what and why a nation was.

CRIME AND ADVENTURE

"I SAW," "I SAW," "then I saw." These words occur thousands of times in the prose fiction of Defoe's time. Greedy for knowledge, experience, novelty, and opportunity, early eighteenth-century readers wanted to look through others' eyes at what they could not see and undergo themselves. New World plantations, Caribbean shipping, the Sahara, Siberia's tundra, even elephant herds and Asian idols were exotic and amazing. Freak accidents, gory murders, congenital deformities, and gallows behavior fascinated them. This craving for sensation contributed to a phenomenal rise in the popularity of travel and criminal literature.

The travel and criminal books of the time had much in common and much that appealed strongly to the average eighteenth-century reader. Both forms offered strange tales and vicarious experiences, intriguing personalities, and rambling lives. By Defoe's time, the heroes of these tales were usually restless, often rebellious and uprooted young men hungry for adventure, freedom, and economic gain, and this fact drew the forms closer together. Such men were willing to take risks and even engage in illegal activities from relatively minor, spontaneous theft or smuggling to full-scale, murderous piracy.[1] The narrative patterns of these books were similar, too. They alternated tales of unusual adventures with moral reflections. Moreover, like popular literature of all times, they always concluded by reinforcing the moral values and conventional choices of their readers. These didactic aspects increased their sales by making them acceptable to a larger reading public.

Daniel Defoe began writing in these forms after they had become popular and even formulaic. He had read them since boyhood, owned large numbers of travel books, and had included "crime reports" in his periodical writings for years. He drew upon his familiarity with them, then added elements from other kinds of writing, and expanded their purposes. More than any other writer, Defoe is responsible for leading other writers to see new potential in these forms and for giving them lasting vitality.

The craze for criminal literature, a craze partly created and certainly fed by Defoe, was at its height in the 1720s.[2] The broadsides ballads, chapbooks, newspapers, pamphlets, "anatomies," and criminal characters of the sixteenth and seventeenth centuries were augmented by the *Old Bailey Sessions Papers*, *The Ordinary of Newgate, his Account*, and collections such as *A Compleat Collection of Remarkable Tryals* and *The History of the Lives of the Most Noted Highway-men*. From the beginning, pirates were included with domestic housebreakers, infanticides, and frustrated lovers, and travel was often a part of the larger crime stories. Some literature borrowed freely from travel books: *The English Rogue*, for example, drew upon J.H. Linschoten's *Voyage to the East Indies*, and Defoe's *Captain Singleton* from Robert Knox's *An Historical Relation of Ceylon*.

This English crime literature was rigidly formulaic. In almost every case, the reader found a brief statement of the motive for the crime, a detailed account of the crime, and a description of the criminal's death. The Ordinary of Newgate added the facts of the trial (date, composition of the jury, magistrate, proceedings), his sermon, and an additional section that was often an essay on the type of crime committed or a statement allegedly made by the condemned and was similar in many ways to the traveler's "observations."[3] When a pirate was the subject, his life was depicted as miserable and chaotic. Until the middle of the eighteenth century, the motive for an individual crime was easy to overlook because it was assigned, often in single sentences, to a universal sinful tendency in human nature. As the compiler of the first volume of *The Newgate Calendar* said, "The criminal recorder has too often to detail the atrocity of ambition, the malignity of revenge, and the desperation of jealousy. . . ."[4] Furthermore, these crimes and their punishments always took place in a Providential world. Case after case observed that a just God would end the sinner's career sooner or later, and his punishment conformed in degree to that of a condemned *sinner* more than it was appropriate to the specific transgression of a *criminal*.

By 1720 travel literature, too, had become highly formulaic. The traveler was not the Renaissance patriot-dreamer but an opportunistic wanderer. These travelers were usually blown off course, shipwrecked, captured by pirates, or offered unexpected opportunities that put them in strange countries with exotic people, customs, and wildlife. The longer the narrative, the more often such accidents occurred. Factual and pseudofactual travel books described a set list of details about each nation: topography, climate, language, customs, laws, commerce, employments, government, history, religion, and rarities. Because the emphasis was on the place rather than on the protagonist, the narrator was usually unobtrusive for long sections of the book. He gave accurate, detailed descriptions, often including such things as latitude/longitude readings and heights of mountains, arranged information, and relayed curious, novel, or horrible stories with comment or reaction. Until midcentury, fiction duplicated these conventions and adopted their most frequent conclusion: the traveler retired to England grateful to God and usually penitent either for his dissatisfied, restless nature or for specific crimes.

Because historical, psychological, and anthropological as well as fictional accounts of the material in travel and criminal literature are commonplace to us, we must exert our imaginations to comprehend their fascination and power for early modern England. Yet it is a tribute to their writers that we find these subjects so familiar and see the adventure story as ubiquitous. When we consider that their travel and crime literature largely grew from trivial and especially rigid forms, that the heroes and heroines were often criminals, and that writers married the story to an explicitly, blatantly moral commentary called "observations," the enduring popularity of such books is remarkable.

In this chapter, I shall discuss four elements common to travel and crime literature, elements which Defoe recognized as strongly appealing to his age. By exploiting these characteristics and combining the forms and purposes of other literature, Defoe produced four respectably successful novels: *The Farther Adven-*

tures of Robinson Crusoe (1719), *Captain Singleton* (1720), *Moll Flanders* (1722), and *The Four Years Voyages of Captain George Roberts* (1726). Just as he brought his political writing and historical knowledge together in *Memoirs of a Cavalier, A Journal of the Plague Year,* and *Colonel Jack,* so he drew upon his knowledge of economic geography, rogue biography, and travel books for the four novels discussed in this chapter.

Defoe understood that a great part of the appeal of criminal and travel stories was the confrontation between ordinary, unheroic individuals and the unknown as these ordinary people struggled to fulfill a rags-to-riches fantasy. Owning less than Crusoe on his island, Defoe's heroes pit themselves against nations and men who apparently have all the advantages on their side. Without much education, "breeding," or money, they live out stories of adventure and economic gain and, in doing so, see almost all of the known world. "Known," however, is far from explored. In fact, the characters face situations, animals, people, and even natural features that are unpredictable and, therefore, horrifying. They cannot tell how much danger they are in. As Sir Walter Scott said, the reader admires "the advantageous light in which it places the human character as capable of . . . opposing itself . . . to a power of which it cannot estimate the force, of which it hath every reason to doubt the purpose, and at the idea of confronting [that power] our nature recoils."[5]

Captain Singleton, Defoe's most complete blending of the criminal and travel forms, came in the wake of the stunning success of *Robinson Crusoe* and while Defoe was one of John Applebee's crime reporters. His narrator, Bob Singleton, offers an entirely different consciousness from Robinson Crusoe. Because of his background, he is a kind of *tabula rasa,* coming to experiences fresh and reacting on the basis of very limited experience. Used by a beggar and then a gypsy to garner greater charity, cast on the parish, and transferred from ship to ship in his youth, Singleton observes all types of petty dishonesty and finally joins an unsuccessful mutiny. Unlike Colonel Jack, Singleton never finds disinterestedly good-hearted people; everyone who gives him food and shelter wants to use him, and most cheat or abuse him. As a marooned mutineer, he is "thoughtless" and "unconcern'd" for he has lost nothing and has no conception of the plight he is in. Never loved, never secure, never even well fed, he cannot imagine himself significantly worse off and lacks the education and experience to fear wild animals, cannibals, or starvation. He is forced to cross an unmapped continent and lacks the education that partially prepares Crusoe for his trip across Asia.

With this kind of character, Defoe gains two advantages: Singleton becomes a clear window to his adventures and to his own nature. Robinson Crusoe is driven to desperation by the memory of his former life and the list of his deprivations; a constant comparison focuses his experience. Singleton is free to share his experiences without the distraction of descriptions of his feelings. Crusoe obsessively searches for his sin; Singleton concentrates on survival. That Defoe and other writers sometimes saw emotion as distraction and directed attention away from it is often explicitly stated through transition phrases such as the one describing the death of Crusoe's wife in *Farther Adventures*: "It is not my Business here to write . . . " (2:117).[6] Truthful because he sees no gain for himself and transparent because he has been taught no moral code, Singleton allows the reader to experience and react to his exciting adventures.

Incident after incident challenges the courage and ingenuity of Singleton and the men with him. Many of the episodes are carefully structured for dramatic effect, and the book is rich in strange sights and sounds. Defoe well knows that terror comes from the shock of an unexpected or unfamiliar sight and that sustained, unnatural sounds erode courage and energy. The natives scream, wail, and make strange, eerie sounds, and interpretation is seldom immediate. In a number of places, Singleton and his men watch natives gather, and the white men puzzle over the implications of the sounds they are making. The nights are especially alive: "towards Night we began to hear the Wolves howl, the Lions bellow, and a great many wild Asses braying, and other ugly Noises which we did not understand" (p. 99). Even the deserts and wildernesses "howl" because of the wind. Huge animals suddenly appear, and the men must learn how to kill, for example, the armored crocodile. Ironically, what experience they have usually misleads them and increases their sense of being in an unpredictable, threatening land. For instance, they mistake the dust from a huge herd of elephants for an army on the march.

For the reader who enjoys exciting confrontations between an ordinary, unheroic person and a variety of adversaries, these books offer more than those by any other contemporary English writer. Defoe pits his protagonists against men, animals, large numbers of men, people who fight in different ways, accidents, the elements, and even natural disasters. The "heroes" scramble, improvise, seem doomed, and yet win. Defoe unified these books by the artistic selection of adventures. For instance, Crusoe's adversaries in *Farther Adventures* are usually men; Singleton struggles with terrain more consistently. Not only does this distinction reflect the state of each continent, but it also contributes to themes in the novels. Crusoe is a supremely social animal, deeply involved in world affairs, and analytical about national character; Singleton has no involvement with any nation and, until he comes to trust Quaker William, hardly distinguishes among men, animals, and weather. He is a lonely speck on the globe, expecting nothing from anything. At one point, he says, "We . . . often met with wild and terrible Beasts, which we could not call by their Names, but as they were like us, seeking their Prey, but were themselves good for nothing, so we disturbed them as little as possible" (p. 28). Crusoe shares our prejudices—he expects friendship from those like him and hostility from "heatherns" and Portuguese; Singleton makes no predictions until well into his career as a pirate.

Each of Defoe's adventure stories concludes with a vastly wealthier protagonist, and each contains two of the most popular strains of western rags-to-riches sagas. First, the protagonist is something of a trickster and the book a compendium of tricks. Singleton and Crusoe practice largely on natives in order to survive, but their stories and *The Four Years Voyages of Captain George Roberts* (1726) include significant numbers of descriptions of trading crimes. In order to sell their cargoes, they often must indulge in everything from smuggling to contract swindles. Like the heroes of jestbooks and fabliaux, they rob the anonymous, the selfish, the greedy, and the rich. Need or challenge supplies what motivation is given. Like an intriguing magician, the hero has his audience asking "what will he do next, and how does he do it?"

Sheer cleverness soundly resting upon psychology and ingenuity, even when employed in shameful enterprises, does glorify "the human character." Moll tricking another potential robber at a fire and getting away with her booty; Crusoe's capture of an entire hut of natives whom he forces to watch the destruction of their idol, and Quaker William's seige on the hollow tree full of natives carry the same suspenseful delight. Each has a measure of danger, each is spun out more dramatically than we expect, and each ends with the reader and trickster sharing a triumph that must be kept secret from a more cautious, rigidly moral, and even adult world. Crusoe most explicitly points out this reader/character secret in passages such as that describing the way he and his co-conspirators "appear'd among our Fellow Travellers exceeding busy" the day after they destroyed the idol (3:188-89).

The second element common to western success stories is the idea that hard work is guaranteed to bring material reward. No Defoe adventurer is afraid of hard work. One of the dominating images of *Captain Roberts* is that of him bent over his ship's pump. Often exhausted, ill, alone, and with no reason to believe his effort will do more than determine that he dies from starvation rather than drowning, he pumps on with what Defoe habitually calls "unwearied Industry." Defoe brings alive the position, the rhythm, and the monotony of Roberts's solitary pumping. In the preface of *Moll Flanders*, Defoe tells us that "unwearied Industry . . . will in time raise the meanest Creature." Singleton and his men must stop at intervals to build shelters or canoes, and the work is often described as tedious, heavy, and difficult. Often the work is futile, as it is with Crusoe's canoe and twice with Singleton's canoe building, but the faith in the success of work gives the character resilience and enduring interest. In a time when the streets of London could be compared to modern India with maimed and diseased beggars, orphans, scavengers, and pickpockets, Defoe's stories of Singleton and Moll, both "mean Creatures" who rose to appear in a "new Cast" in the world, must have had powerful appeal not only to the laboring poor but to the prosperous who wanted to believe in the work ethic.[7]

Just as the readers of Defoe's *History of the Wars* wanted to know more, to see beyond the bare report, so did those who went from periodical to pamphlet, from a report on a hanging to *The General History of the Pyrates*. The appeals of the periodical survive; modern readers expect to find elaboration of news stories in the paragraphs following the standard who-what-when-where opening, to find editorials, feature stories, and even serialized book chapters and articles on news and newsmakers, to be able to read more in news magazines, and even more in books. Paul Lorrain, one of the Newgate Ordinaries, explained that his *Accounts* brought "Things to Light which were before hidden in Darkness."[8] Even the progression from reports of Jonathan Wild's capture and trial to Defoe's and others' pamphlets to Fielding's *Jonathan Wild the Great* and Gay's *Beggar's Opera* have modern parallels, as anyone who knows the background of John Pielmeier's play *Agnes of God* understands.[9]

The English had always understood *news* to mean reports of the strange, bizarre, and puzzling as well as reports of serious political and economic events. Readers of these papers wanted to *see* more, to know more about aspects and parts of the world beyond their familiar world. Above all, they wanted to know things worth remarking upon. To read the periodicals of the time is to see these novels of Defoe's in miniature:

We hear from Jamaica, that within these 15 Months past they have hanged upwards of 250 Pirates. [*London Journal*, 10 Nov. 1722]

We are told, that no less than 16 large Cruisers are preparing to go to the Spanish West-Indies besides those that carry the Imperial Colours. . . .

Yesterday in the Fore-noon, a Lad about twelve Years of Age, presuming upon the Strength of the Ice, was unfortunately drown'd in *Wood's Close Pond*, a Place remarkable for the Loss of adventurous Youths both in Summer and Winter. He cried out for Help very much, bearing himself up with his Arms, but before the Assistance which was coming could be applied, he sank beneath the Ice, and rose no more. [*Whitehall Evening Post*, 23 Dec. 1718]

Last Tuesday Night a Boy about Eleven Years of Age, and a Girl about Fourteen, were both found dead in a Glass House-Yard in the Minories;

and it is supposed they died for Want. [*Universal Spectator*, 6 Feb. 1749]

[Two hundred eighty Englishmen and women who had been captives] marched in their Moorish habits in good Order through a great Part of this City to the Cathedral of St Paul's to return thanks to Almighty God. [*Whitehall Evening Post*, 9 Dec. 1721]

. . . The Prosecutor deposed, that [Prudence Price] came into the Shop, pretending to buy a Knot, and took her opportunity to take the Goods; and the Prosecutor was positive, that there was no Body else there but the Prisoner when the Goods were gone. Though she denyed the Fact, saying, She knew nothing of it; yet was [*sic*] known to be an old Offender. The Jury found her Guilty to the value of 4s. and 6d. [*The Proceedings on the Queen's Commission of the Peace*, 1703][10]

Londoners could turn to the back pages of their papers and read about a man who threw something at a maid but hit and killed his child instead, about a chimney that fell but missed a lady knitting in front of the fire, and about a potential suicide who came to thank his rescuers.

Unlike novel reading, newspaper reading is not almost entirely a solitary activity. Readers look up and remark on various items to companions or refer later to things they've read; they look for paragraphs on people's problems and actions even though they do not expect to see familiar names. Crime and suffering and "human interest" have always sold papers, and some of the best stories have a social nature: the engagement, battle, and outcome in a war; the arrest, trial, and hanging of a criminal; the sighting, arrival, and cargo of a ship. Even grisly notices such as the following appeal to readers' desire for "story": "The Person mention'd in a former Paper to have cut his Throat, and stab'd himself in several Places in the Body, near Kentish Town, proves to be a Mason, and a Person in good Circumstances: He is perfectly recovered . . . seem[s] sorry for that rash Action" (*London Journal*, 10 Nov. 1722).

Today's news stories rely on quotations, interviews, columns, and editorials for multiple points of view, while eighteenth-century papers often had a political voice or a "club" of writers. After the popularity of the John Dunton's Athenian Society, Defoe's Scandal Club, and the *Tatler* and *Spectator* clubs, examples are legion. *The*

Grumbler (1715) had the Grizzle family, and *The Tea-Table* (1724) included men and women, including the widow of a ship's commander. These periodicals frequently noted the taste for "strange, wild and absurd Notions" and "wandering" among a variety of topics as "Connection, Method, Proportion, Dependency of Parts upon the Whole . . . are . . . overlook'd by the Generality of Readers. . . . "[11] Gossip and hearsay also appear from the beginning of newspaper history; French *Nouvellistes*, for example, often met travelers on the roads to Paris, interviewed them about things they had seen and done, and then printed their comments about battles, prominent people, or village scandals as authenticated fact.[12] Periodicals had from the beginning included essays and stories with a broad tolerance for speculation, ornament, and even fiction.

As Clara Reeve said in *The Progress of Romance* (1785), "The word Novel in all languages signifies something new"; "The Novel gives a familiar relation of such things as pass every day before our eyes, such as may happen to our friend, or to ourselves."[13] That, of course, is also part of the newspapers' appeal. English journalism from the beginning fed on narrative. The eight to twenty-four page newsbooks, issued whenever enough material warranted publication, continued accounts and included "remarkable" stories often of atrocities or strange accidents. The recognition of the narrative nature of "news" can be seen in satires of typical items such as Addison's "We are informed from Pankridge, that a dozen weddings were lately celebrated . . . but are referred to the next letters for the names of the parties concerned" (*Spectator* No. 452). Intensely topical, newsbooks such as *Weekely Nevves from Italy, Germanie, Hungaria, Bohemia, the Palatinate, France, and the Low Countries* often included accounts of recent murders and competed directly with pamphlets with titles such as *Three Bloodie Murders* (1613) and *News from Fleetstreet* (1675).[14] An examination of a host of works such as *Sack-Full of Newes* (1557), *Tarleton's Newes Ovt of Pvrgatory* (1589), *Newes from the New Exchange* (1650), and *Strange News from Bartholomew Fair* (1661) indicates that readers associated "news" with the recent, the "remarkable," and the prying. Private family affairs—drownings, suicides, elopements—became public news, and the best journalists spun their material out into fiction or essay, as Ned

Ward did in his *London Spy* (1700) or Steele did in *The Tatler*. Just as the early novels promised a variety of "strange and suprizing" adventures, so the early newspapers were expected to produce incidents that would excite amazement in the reader who would respond by remarking, "Just listen to this!"

Like fiction, the papers felt free to report motive. The drowned "lad" had "presumed" upon the strength of the ice, a murderer "could neither bear the thought of forfeiting the esteem of a woman that he courted, nor of marrying her [whom he had seduced]."[15] John Dunton's *Pegasus* (to 1696) included a section called *Observation on Publick Occurrences*, which allowed him space to speculate about motive and moralize. Defoe's books, called the "crude products of the dawn of journalism" by Richard Altick,[16] added the power of a central personality facing unusual obstacles to unify the variety of incidents and the seriality of the journalistic rhythm.

Defoe converted the "characters" of the back pages of periodicals into heroes and heroines. Not one of his protagonists would seem to be worth the notice of more than a single day (usually in a report of the sentence to hanging), yet Defoe makes their lives remarkable. For example, George Roberts is an unprepossessing man sent to Virginia to pick up a sloop and a cargo. Captured by Captain Law, one of the most brutal Caribbean pirates,[17] Roberts is held in a state of constant terror before he is left to die on his stripped ship with two boys. Roberts is a winning combination of wit, courage, and piety. The same dry, religious wit that Bunyan used and that distinguishes Quaker William animates Roberts's character. For instance, Roberts tells us that he answers the swearing, threatening pirates politely on the advice of *Proverbs*: "When your Hand is in the Lion's Mouth, get it out as easie as you can" (p. 30).

Unable to recruit him, the pirates abide by their articles guaranteeing the freedom of married men with children, and they put Roberts on the leaky ship that his implacable enemy, Russell, has stripped of provisions, ammunition, and even sails. Roberts has been firm, sensible, and admirable, but, at this point, he becomes heroic. He and the boys find some food left on board, learn to prepare it and collect fresh water, and even fight and kill a giant shark. The almost constant need to pump out the ship dominates their days and nights. It limits their sleep, saps their strength, and calls for particular endurance and ingenuity from Roberts because his companions are children with limited strength.

Roberts's life becomes a series of frustrations. Because of the children's weakness, he will take so long to lower a boat that darkness comes, and he must pull it up again. He contracts a lingering fever. The younger boy falls asleep on watch, and the older boy and the rowboat are left behind. Now Roberts must pump alone. As he sails from port to port, friendly natives board sometimes to bring food and water but more often to tantalize him with dreams of rescue as they drink his scarce rum or simply swim away. When they spend the night on board but refuse to pump, the tired, debilitated, ill Roberts returns to the hold to pump while three healthy men rest above. Once the natives get him to Salt Point, he can neither climb the peak to get to the fruitful side of the island nor return to the ship. Although he has moments of intense frustration and near-despair, he always rallies and continues to struggle. When trapped on Salt Point, Roberts says, "if I can proceed no farther, and yet at high Water have not here so much Room to stand, or walk upon, as half a Ship's Quarter-Deck[,] I shall be worse than a Person pent up in a solitary close Prison all his Days" (p. 199). *The Four Years Voyages* uses many similar passages to repeat and emphasize Roberts's situation and also to give the reader access to feelings. The metaphor "a solitary close Prison" intensified by the adjectives "solitary" and "close" and the phrase "all his Days" suggest desperation and even horror.

Defoe is a master of these economical summaries. When Singleton and his men are too far from their last supply point to return, Singleton says, "our present Business was, what to do to get out of this dreadful Place we were in; behind us was a Wast[e]. . . . Before us was nothing but Horrour . . . so we resolv'd . . . to go on as far as we could . . . "(p. 138). Beneath the steady words is the vision of suffering and death called up by a statement of the situation and a few adjectives. The spare prose, suggesting rather than milking emotion, is related to journalism; we do not need to be told how a father felt when he accidentally killed his baby nor do we need verbal writhing to imagine Roberts's or Singleton's states of mind. The mastery is in the power to make us

see. To allow us to see the water rising toward a barren ledge on
Salt Point or to contemplate the vast land Singleton sees before
him is a kind of rhetorical discipline that reflects the control, the
refusal to despair, that is the character's greatest strength.

Although many modern readers find Defoe's novels episodic, the
eighteenth-century reader expected rhythm or narrative intensity
and reflective calm. This pattern easily accommodated the taste for
collections of the varied and the sensational. Periodicals ended
with lists of "Remarkable Providences," "Indifferent Things," and
"Remarkable Events," and books of hideous crimes, of lurid love
stories, of Oriental tales, of descriptions of exotic animals, of
events associated with earthquakes or storms, and of the deaths of
virtuous mothers were commercial successes. Writers after Defoe
explicitly noted the similarities of the appeal to the taste for the
varied and sensational in these collections, precursors of the
English novel, and the novel.

Sarah Fielding, for example, wrote in 1757, "From the same
Taste of being acquainted with the various surprising Incidents of
Mankind, arises our insatiable Curiosity for Novels or Romances;
Infatuated with a Sort of Knight errantry, we draw these fictitious
Characters into a real Existence; and thus, pleasingly deluded, we
find ourselves as warmly interested, and deeply affected by the
imaginary Scenes of *Arcadia*, the wonderful Atchievements of *Don
Quixote*, the merry Conceits of *Sancho*, rural Innoncence [*sic*] of
a *Joseph Andrews*. . . . "[18] Respectable citizens flocked to Tower
Bridge to see two-tailed sheep, hairless dogs, and deformed
children exhibited for a few coins, and they gobbled up tales of
coney catchers, saints, and kings' mistresses. Prose fiction embraced digressions, interpolated stories, and even other genres to
satisfy its readers in the ways that prose fiction since Sidney's
Arcadia had.

The reader of books such as *The English Rogue*, Chetwood's
Captain Falconer, or de Serviez's *The Lives and Amours of the
Empresses* (tr. 1723) will be immediately struck, however, by the
comparative unity of Defoe's narratives and the strength of the
personalities of his protagonists. Although *A Journal of the Plague
Year* is probably the best example of the use of a collection of

anecdotes for thematic and tonal force, in no Defoe novel are the episodes not literary in the strictest sense of the term. That he manages to give his readers the "sights" they wanted even as he subordinates them to his fictional intentions separates his books from those contemporary works most similar to his.

One of the most characteristic marks of eighteenth-century fiction is its use of interpolated, often sensational stories, and Defoe's novels have their share. For example, Crusoe discovers a starving boy gnawing on a half-eaten glove in *Farther Adventures*, and this boy and a servant girl tell their story; the exiled prince tells Crusoe part of his life story; Singleton finds a naked, sun-blotched white man in Africa, and they hear his "history." More often than not, a comparison of these anecdotes with the protagonist's past sets the protagonist in a more favorable light. Sometimes Defoe seems to have his narrators choose among life-histories. Moll, for example, suppresses Jemmy's and Mother Midnight's (noting that they are worth relating) but tells her mother's. This life is the same kind of repetition of Moll's own life and of the themes of the book that the tutor's history is in *Colonel Jack*.

Defoe's interpolated tales and incidents duplicate the plots, rhythm, pace, and types of characters and incidents of formulaic anecdotes, but he invests them with dramatic, even raw emotion. Many of these incidents still manage to carry the kind of moral implications that the anecdotes of the period do; they implicitly (or even explicitly) warn the reader against jealousy, rage, infatuation, or despair. Defoe, however, dramatizes them and draws out their full human vibrations.

Consider the end of Moll Flanders's first love affair. From its beginning, every reader winces at the implications of the class differences, the money given Moll, and the brother's easy "consider yourself married." That he is the *older* brother, that he occasionally is unkind to his family, that Moll is vain, increase the perception that the end is absolutely predictable. The lesson to be learned from the episode is equally unmistakable and utterly familiar. It is a trite story, even in 1722. Yet Defoe can still move us with it. When the lover tells her that his best advice is to marry his brother, Moll "gave him a look full of Horror" and turned "Pale as Death." Although she is sitting down, she nearly falls.

Her shock establishes her naiveté and promises deep grief and lengthy suffering. The vivid argument that follows is full of the clichés of betrayed love: "is this your Faith and Honour, your Love," she asks. His answers are the transparent excuses and placating promises of legions of lovers: he tells her "we might love as Friends all our Days, and perhaps with more Satisfaction" than if he married and were disinherited. Moll, of course, has no chance of winning him back. "Can you transfer my Affection?" she asks. And then she raises that question to a higher level of intensity: "Can you bid me cease loving you, and bid me love him?" And yet again the question assumes greater emotional force: "is it in my Power think you to make such a Change at Demand?" The answer, of course, is "no." Moll herself cannot *will* a transfer of affection, and here she apprehends the loneliness and impossibility of what she needs to do. Love is not so simple, temporary, or whimsical. To the end of her marriage to Robin, the older brother's face will appear to her, will haunt her very lovemaking.

Defoe has taken one of the most trite episodes of early English fiction and conduct books and reinvested it with emotional force. Moll's youth, vulnerability, trust, and optimism have been assaulted. The grim life of the working poor that has been her destiny since her infancy is now an emotional reality; she, and we, know this is no Cinderella story and that she will partake fully of the hardships and slurs of her social position. Moll is never again so trusting and vulnerable; only in the grief over separation from Jemmy do we see the same capacity for love. She accepts her lot, but her vulnerability had been established. That she is vulnerable is crucial to the rest of the novel. Without that quality, her actions would be despicable and her regrets hypocritical. It is not incongruous that she thinks of the woman's coming distress when she will discover that items saved from the fire are stolen or that Moll finds the thought of hurting the child she robbed horrifying. The girl who could ask, "is it in my Power . . . to make such a Change at Demand?" lives on in the woman. No need to look for psycho-social explanations, although they may be found; the quality of the heart, the genuineness of the human reaction, allows us at our hardest to view Moll with cynicism; we cannot dislike her or wish her hanged.

An equally emotional moment is when Quaker William's widowed sister sends her brother £5 and offers to let him move in with her and her four children. The incident occurs at a time when the narrative, and Singleton's and William's lives, have been arrested for some time. William, who was Singleton's adviser and strategist during their pirate career, has now become the means to his salvation. In addition to *Roxana*'s Amy's cleverness and loyalty, William has genuine goodness as well. He has led Singleton to retire with one of his understated, witty observations: "most People leave off Trading when they are satisfied with getting . . . " (p. 309). Gradually he brings Singleton to repent, encourages him through a suicidal period, and leads him to new hope. Even as serious, lengthy conversations "continually" give them pleasure and, thereby, signal to the reader that they are sincere converts, they struggle with the questions of converting their wealth into a manageable form and of what use they can most appropriately make of it.

It is after months of discussions that William writes his sister, "a poor relation," whom his money might benefit. At this point, he has given up his own hope to return to England. The irony of the contrast between her meager living from her small shop and the men's vast wealth emphasizes her generosity and moves both men to tears. Their wealth has been troublesome and described as "a Mass," "like Dirt under my Feet," and "no great Concern" when part of it had to be abandoned. For a man who had told William he has no home except where he is and that wherever he has been he has been "cheated and imposed upon, and used so ill" (p. 310), the long-neglected sister's simple, generous gesture seems as wondrous as William's loyalty. Singleton, characteristically extreme in danger or in friendship, first offers his friend's sister £5000 and then urges William to go to England without him. William, however, refuses in the words of the biblical Ruth, "I am resolved I'll never part with thee as long as I live, go where thou wilt, or stay where thou wilt" (p. 331). Over the next two years, William's loyalty and the sister's warm letters work on Singleton until he is willing to go to England disguised, although he still fears that someone will betray him out of avarice. The widow's touching letter, however, serves as the wedge that opens Singleton to an expression of trust and brotherhood and ends the most complete psychological and physical isolation of any eighteenth-century character.

Interested in the classification of experiences and the variations within a category, eighteenth-century readers came to narrative types assured of appropriate anecdotes. The ingenuity and skill of the writer determined how varied, how probable, how exciting, and how integrated these "cases" were. Furthermore, the reader expected certain types of stories with formulaic detail and predictable, exemplary endings. Just as Defoe could give emotional power to, for example, the formula story of the servant girl seduced by her master, he could sift the ingredients of the travel narrative and create a more unified, powerful form.

Readers of travel fiction expected the kind of geographical description found in primarily nonfiction books such as Bartolomé de Las Casas's *An Account of the First Voyages and Discoveries Made by the Spaniards in America* (1699). These passages tended to be specific, detailed, and in the manner of reports to the Royal Society. Las Casas, for example, included letters from other travelers along with his own reports. Representative passages read: "They unshale their Rice from its outward husk by beating it in a Mortar, or on the Ground more often; but some of these sorts of Rice must first be boyled in the husk, otherwise in beating it will break to powder"; or " . . . Capt. *Avery* . . . set all Hands at work in sounding the Bay of the *East* Side of the Island, in 15 Degrees 30 Minutes *South* Latitude, which was large and capacious, unexpos'd to the Fury of the most tempestuous Weather."[19] William Chetwood's *Captain Falconer* is quite typical in the way that he describes fish, insects, birds, and other elements common to nonfiction.[20]

Although Defoe is deeply concerned with geographical accuracy, he subordinates descriptions of the unfamiliar customs and clothing, for example, to the function these places and people serve in motivating adventures and affecting the opinions of his hero. Crusoe, his most self-conscious narrator, contrasts his story specifically to similar contemporary ones: "I shall not pester my Account, or the Reader, with Descriptions of Places, Journals of our Voyages, Variations of Compass, Latitudes, Meridian-Distances, Trade-Winds, Situation of Ports, and the like; such as almost all the Histories of long Navigation are full of, and makes the reading tiresome enough, and are perfectly unprofitable to all that read it, except only to those, who are to go to those Places themselves" (3:83; compare 3:154). Crusoe refers to the "Journals and Travels of *English* Men, of which, many I find are publish'd, and more promis'd every Day . . . " and recommends that readers consult those books for locations and details (3: 109). He will give anecdotes and adventures, then data. Crusoe's comments show that Defoe knew these books well enough to have analyzed their contents specifically and to imply that he was aware of the habitual, accepted borrowing of descriptions from one book to another.[21] He has gone beyond the recording of data to a somewhat deeper level of experience.

Defoe finds new fictional usefulness in the natural historians' data. First, he includes descriptions of what the age would call "sublime," then goes on to have his characters make observations that raise the readers' estimation of them. Defoe himself had written an instructive fable about two travel writers for the introduction to the third volume of his *Tour Thro' the Whole Island of Great Britain*. The foolish traveler kept "an exact journal" in which he notes such minutiae as the signs of the inns at which he ate, while the wise traveler takes "minutes . . . for his own satisfaction," and these he finds to be "critical" and "significant" and is able to write a "useful account" from them. Rather than a string of trifles, he produces a delightful book with an "abundance of useful observations."

Singleton sees huge waterfalls, deserts, lakes, and rivers, and he comes upon such beautiful sights as the three leopards on the river bank. Crusoe admires the house built of china and the Great Wall and notes the Tonguese who live in underground vaults and cover themselves and their vaults in fur. Descriptions such as these are so brief as to be mere notes; although they give additional credibility and interest to the narrative, they also serve as a vehicle for the characters' perceptive observations, the display of "judgment" so admired in the century. Crusoe finds the Great Wall impractical but he "wonders at it" because it is impressive in size and workmanship and represents monumental human endeavor; in fact, part of its marvelousness comes from its uselessness. Singleton can have the leopard killed and keep its pelt, but he continues to carry the visual image of the tableau of leopards and lush river bank.

These observations were supposed to spring easily from events and sights by the association of ideas and included moral, political, economic, and historical reflections and were sometimes extended into full-scale essays. There are, for example, some similarities between the incident in *Farther Adventures* when Crusoe destroys the idol and Joseph Addison's reflections on the errors of Catholicism after he describes religion in Italy in *Remarks on Several Parts of Italy* (1705). It was not even unusual to separate the recording of facts from the subjective (fictional or personal) commentary, as Defoe does in *Captain Roberts*.[22] Like the contemplation of any sublime object, the reflection upon these descriptions helped the reader understand his world and God's care of his creatures. The alternation of description and "observation" was a rigid convention in travel literature of the seventeenth century and often handled obtrusively, for more value was assigned to the observations than to descriptions. Since one underlying theme in Defoe's works is what should be valued, such "observations" contribute in fictional and artistic ways.

The second use Defoe makes of material common to geographical histories is to motivate adventure. In some ways, the killing of the crocodile in *Captain Singleton* resembles the zoologist's examination of a specimen, and yet it is a good story. The gunner finally runs up to the crocodile, thrusts the barrel of his gun into its mouth, and fires. He is so terrified, however, that he immediately runs away. Before the crocodile dies, it chews the iron barrel until it is marked like a stick worried by a dog. Such experiences try the ingenuity and courage of the travelers and make up the fabric of the plot. Defoe uses his knowledge of African and Asian rivers, of Caribbean sea ports, of climate, and of weather to complicate his plots, as he does when he has Crusoe cross Russia or Roberts lie ill at Salt Point. These episodes build the impression we have that the hero is courageous, persevering, and clever. Because these foes are usually unfamiliar, wild, or unnaturally large, they assume a threat enhanced by near-superstitious awe, the reaction Scott described as "our nature recoils."

By emphasizing characters' perceptions of objects and events or developing their emotional reactions, Defoe made his books unified, coherent linguistic structures. Without losing the appeal of the varied and sensational, he transformed the travel and criminal forms into stories that gave new delight in character and assured their continued vitality.

Finally, Defoe incorporates the satisfaction common to popular fiction, which has always explored fantasies and limits, but concluded by reinforcing the moral order a society believes exists. As press coverage expanded and increasing numbers of authentic and fictional memoirs appeared, readers' fantasies extended to wondering how the choice to join the pirates or to die would be met, what it would be like to be left to starve on a ship or on an island, to be on a ship with a crew of two boys, to be a pirate facing a man-of-war, or to be thrown in Newgate. Defoe knew that fantasies came from the experiences (direct or read) of their readers. From the sight of a boy being pumped comes speculation about his home life. From the shipping news come dreams of shipwrecks, pirates, and cargoes lost. From participation in a rag-tag mob following a constable with a pickpocket comes speculation about the motive for the theft.

Defoe's novels provide situation after situation designed to allow readers to compare their own solutions and fantasies to the action the character finally takes. Fantasies often involve escape from ordinary, social limits, and, more than Defoe's other novels, the four under discussion here free the protagonist from society's bonds. Singleton recognizes no government except the ones he himself designs, Moll insists her situation and her cleverness exempt her from ordinary rules, and Crusoe carries the mentality of the sole ruler of his island through his final trip. Each is a radical individual isolated from the everyday world. No rules exist to help Roberts deal with the pirates, the natives, or his exile on the ship. In fact, most of the dialogue in *The Four Years Voyages of Captain George Roberts* is argument; he reasons, explains, and pleads, and his hearers disagree. Not just cut off from but at odds with majority opinion, these characters are free to behave in ways that we can only imagine. Moll turns thief, Singleton pirate, and Crusoe judge and jury. None finds help from society, and all must make their own ways.

The emphasis in these novels by Defoe is on the adventure, the excitement, the dangers, and the escapes of the hero, and the world in which they operate is removed just enough from the readers' to permit action that would be offensive, improbable, or even impossible in a middle-class English family. For example, once Moll leaves Colchester she is part of a society few know. She is a completely unattached female; she does not even write to anyone in the town that was her home for twenty years. She is in a world in which she can meet and marry highwaymen, prowl the streets, and change her social class. Because Defoe's protagonists' situations are unfamiliar and quite threatening, they can be seen primarily as resourceful characters who exhibit humankind's strengths rather than as dubious examples. Unlike the readers of conduct books and novels such as Defoe's *Roxana* and Penelope Aubin's *Count de Vinevil*, the reader of these novels is encouraged to move from adventure to adventure without pause for moral judgment. The interest is in how Crusoe destroys the idol, not in his motives or in questions of his prudence, inconsistency, or even morality. What serious crimes Singleton commits as a pirate are swallowed up in the sighting and taking of ships; that he may have had to kill men to prevent his capture is acknowledged, but, when the need is debated, another solution occurs; comparable situations that ended, we may suppose, the other way, pass rapidly by the reader.

Injustice, crime, and immorality could appear in these novels and give pleasure to a reading public that demanded morally useful literature because they occur in a Providential world. Just as popular fiction produces popular fantasies so does it embody and support conventional ethical opinion. The reader of such fiction knew that the conclusion would affirm the moral processes and order in the universe. As John Cawelti explains, such novels indulged two human needs—for change and novelty and for order and security.[23] A deeply orthodox writer like Defoe could use this moral world and readers' expectations to increase suspense even as he relied upon it for what Ian Watt has called coherent moral structure.[24] Just as surely as the modern reader wonders if Moll or Singleton will get away with this theft or this piracy, the early eighteenth-century reader would have found reminders of the nature of the world in which these criminals acted.

Defoe establishes the moral framework of these four novels through manifestations of the eternal world that he believes encompasses the temporal one. Perhaps no other aspect of his novels is as foreign and even unattractive to the modern reader. Yet when Defoe depicts his character responding to premonitions, dreams, promptings, and the most conservative religious fundamentalism, he is carrying out one of the enduring imaginative endeavours of the novel. He is, in Richard Gilman's words, bringing us " 'news' of the invisible, of what exists beyond the recognitions of the naked eye, as possibility, alternative, redemption through a disbelief in what the world says about itself."[25] No matter how little Singleton knows of religion, he lives in God's world, and the reader (and the retrospective narrator) can locate moments when Providence seems to assert itself. Characters who have some religious education are unable to ignore it; they are never free from feeling the tension between what they do and what they ought to do. Their lives and events in their lives always come to serve as evidence of God's existence.

Lest anyone think religious faith came easily to Defoe's contemporaries, the list of serious, lengthy books proving the existence of God stands as grim evidence to the contrary. The philosophies of Hobbes, Descartes, Leibnitz, and the steady mathematization of the universe by the new science challenged the pious as never before. In addition, throughout the age, uncomplimentary terms hounded those who took religion too seriously or acknowledged their faith too publicly. Successful businessmen, ambitious politicians, and great literary figures endorsed the Christian rationalism of Addison's *Spectator* no. 465 but went no farther. Defoe's conduct books and his rigid opposition to Occasional Conformity seemed almost as old-fashioned to many of his contemporaries as they do to us. Defoe uses this climate of skepticism to provide themes and psychological tension in *Robinson Crusoe, A Journal of the Plague Year*, and *Roxana*. In the four novels discussed in this chapter, Defoe is writing adventure stories, and his emphasis in on the action, the plot, and the setting. One aspect of setting is the eternal world, and Defoe used it for artistic and didactic purposes.

Captain Singleton is one of the Defoe novels often criticized for its concluding, unconvincing conversion. In fact, Defoe has constructed the novel so that Singleton lives an amoral life within a highly moral universe. From the beginning of the narrative, the reader finds clues that indicate that God's grace operates in Singleton's life. As retrospective narrator, "Captain Bob" speaks of "a good Providence" that thwarted his numerous plans to murder the Portuguese captains when he was only a youth (pp. 11, 13). At other points, terrifying natural events, such as a violent storm with "Blasts" of lightning, remind him of the "Horrour" of his former life and of his need to repent. Time after time, accident or persuasion prevents Singleton from carrying out cold-blooded murders. Sometimes he and his men are attacked and must defend themselves, sometimes the natives or the ships slip away, sometimes someone suggests a more practical plan. Once Quaker William is taken on board, Singleton has a pragmatic "guardian angel" who stays constantly by him and unfailingly counsels mercy.

In contrast to these weak signs of Providence's plan, as the most devout of Defoe's readers would say, is the powerful tone created by Singleton's life. In brief, dramatic moments and through repetitive incidents, Defoe builds suspense regarding Singleton's ultimate capacity for violence and about his fate. Soon after he and the others are marooned, he suggests they take a boat by force, cruise the coast until they take a larger one, and continue the progression until they have an ocean-going vessel. At this point, he is a teenager, but he has summarized the way most of the pirates built their careers in *The General History of the . . . Pyrates* and is cheered by the men.[26] Here Defoe pauses in the narrative to include a striking incident. One of the most sympathetic and intelligent characters, the gunner, stops Singleton, catches his hand, studies his palm, then looks intently into his face and says "very gravely, My Lad, . . . thou art born to do a World of Mischief . . . " (p. 31). From that point until William Walters persuades Singleton to retire, he lives the most predatory life of any Defoe character. Only a few days after the vote to adopt Singleton's plan, the men's actions give the impression that they are criminals on the prowl. The natives *give* them food and yet they examine the earthenware containers covetously and draw out all the information they can about their neighbors' boats. As the men sail along the coast and cross Africa, they take what they are not given or cannot buy. Animals and men are left unmolested only when they are useless.

As a pirate, Singleton becomes a more ambitious predator. He prowls the seas not for the supplies he needs but for the wealth he wants. The men he captures are as anonymous as the natives and as quickly forgotten. If they are useful, he takes them; if not, his only interest in them is that they not endanger him. Into this world of men constantly on the lookout for an opportunity to rob comes William Walters. He begins to talk of home, retirement, and religion and finally leads Singleton through the process of salvation. He arouses his repentant feelings and then helps him move from suicidal despair to see that "to despair of God's Mercy was no Part of Repentance" (p. 326) and to build a new, reformed life.

Defoe draws upon contemporary opinions about the spiritual to explain Singleton's salvation. Not only is Walters a kind of good angel speaking directly to the pirate, but Singleton's dreams are of calls to repentance, not to evil. For example, he dreams that the devil asks his trade and has come to get him. This dream is no temptation, as those of beautiful, immoral women described in *The Political History of the Devil* are. Walters defines Singleton's suicidal thoughts as "the Devil's Notions" and, in harmony with his consistently wry pragmatism reminds Singleton that "on this side Death [*sic*] you can't be sure you will be damned at all, yet the Moment you step on the other side of Time, you are sure of it" (pp. 324-25).[27] Walters, his sister, and a dozen or more "accidents" exist as "instruments of God's grace." The fact that they have natural explanations and are treated economically would have seemed appropriate to Defoe's readers, who did not come to adventure fiction for the kind of intense interior drama that spiritual autobiography provided.

The setting of the Providential world is even more crucial in *Moll Flanders*. As I have argued elsewhere, much of the energy of the book comes from the reader's sense that she is being stalked by Newgate Prison, emblem of God's certain justice. Any reader of broadsides, pamphlets, and the Ordinary's *Accounts* would have encountered hundreds of sentences noting the "wonderful" way God "discovers" murderers, thieves, and other criminals and assurances that such actions are always found out. Moll specifically calls Newgate an "emblem" of hell, and Defoe's readers probably would have encountered the metaphor with elaboration before. *The English Rogue*, for example, describes the Compter in the same terms Defoe uses for Newgate: "Hell is a very proper denomination for it, since it is a place to be composed of nothing but disorder and confusion; a land of darkness, inhabited by calamity, horror, misery, and confusion. . . . A prison is the banishment of courtesy . . . the treasure of despair. . . . Here you may see one weeping, another singing; one sleeping, another swearing . . . a living tomb . . . a little wood of woe, a map of misery, a place that will learn a young man more villany . . . in six months, than at twenty gaming ordinaries, bowling-alleys, or bawdy-houses. . . . "[28] Prison often acted as symbol of the end of a criminal career, as re-creation of the atmosphere of Hell, and as emblem of the gateway to Hell in the literature of the time, and Moll's constant references to "the Place that had so long expected me" give Newgate more than ordinary meaning.

Having scruples rather than religion, Moll becomes a "creature" of the Devil. Her marriages are the product both of bad luck and the economic realities of her time, but she becomes increasingly predatory with men. She is willing to go beyond exaggerating her means to robbing "tricks." What has been called "hardening" carries the signs of spiritual warfare. A pattern representing the powers of good and evil emerges. Moll commits a crime and then reflects on the sinfulness of the act. At crucial moments, these reflections are intense and extended; for example, she agonizes over marrying Robin and describes "such terrors of mind" after her first robbery. The book becomes the alternation of a predicament quickly solved by an almost incredible opportunity for crime with Moll's guilty reflections on this action. The Devil provides the bait, and her conscience (as good angel) pinches her. The process may be seen in her first robbery. She hears a voice urging, "take the Bundle; be quick; do it this Moment" (2:4). The number of examples of such "promptings" from the Devil that could be drawn from spirit literature is nearly limitless. Richard Baxter, for instance, explains that "The temptations of Satan are sometimes so unnatural, so violent, that the tempted person even feels something besides himself persuading and urging him. . . . "[29] Moll tells us that " 'twas like a Voice spoken to me over my Shoulder. . . . " She describes the bundle as the Devil's bait, and, again, this idea was common.[30] Sometimes the temptation was a rehearsal in a dream, sometimes a waking opportunity, but time after time the criminal would cite his need, the irresistible clear stage, and say in all seriousness, "The Devil made me do it."[31]

When Moll is rich, she begins to wonder why she continues to steal. A number of contemporary theologians would have interpreted her behavior as additional evidence for the existence of the Devil. Only Satan's presence, they argued, could explain the number of ways men could sin and the fact that they continued in the face of their friends' warnings and exhortations. Until Moll is thrown in Newgate, she is unreachable, but there she is redeemed by love, as Singleton is. In Newgate, she sees Jemmy and is struck by the belief that she ruined him. He had, after all, spent his entire fortune to trick her into marrying him, and she reasons that his resultant poverty led him to crime. The regret she feels leads her to think of others whom she has led into sin and to pray for mercy. After she is condemned to death, she listens attentively to a minister sent by the Governess and relates a conversion experience.[32] Many elements in the story of Moll and Jemmy suggest Providential action. That their love is so strong that Moll can call him back to her, that they are finally united, and that one sight of him in prison has such a beneficial effect on her distinguish theirs from all of Moll's other marriages. It reinforces her capacity for sympathy for others, for love, and for friendship and reminds us of the girl who would have forgiven and been faithful to the older brother who seduced her had she been able to persuade him to abandon his plan to marry her to Robin. The pause in the narrative of adventure that describes her repentance returns her to society and even to her family. The movement and tone of the novel is broken by the description of Moll's conversations with the minister and, while the pattern of episodic adventures and complicated relationships resumes, the pattern of alternating seized opportunities for sin with reflections on the wrongfulness of the act ceases entirely. For an age that at the very least felt uneasy at rejecting the idea that the world was the field of active battle between the powers of good and evil, Moll's habitual guilty regrets would have seemed the soul's resistance to the Devil's "promptings," "baits," and "hardening."

Farther Adventures opens with a re-creation of the beginning of *Robinson Crusoe*. Quite simply, Crusoe is again obsessed with the idea of going to sea. He describes this obsession as "a chronical

Distemper" and laments, "I dream'd of it all Night, and my
Imagination run upon it all Day. . . . I talk'd of it in my Sleep, . . .
it made my Conversation tiresome . . . " (2:112). He struggles with
this inclination for years, until his wife offers to go with him since
she thinks it might be "some secret powerful Impulse of Providence." Her dramatic offer encourages him to conquer his "violent
Distemper," and he buys a farm and settles down, only to be cast
back into his original state by the death of his wife and his
nephew's unexpected offer to take him back to see his island
colony. The similarity between the beginnings of the two volumes
of *Robinson Crusoe* is deliberate. Many of the same arguments
against going to sea are marshalled; Crusoe and his wife are now
the aging couple aware of the happiness of the "middle station" of
life and the rashness of the proposal, and Crusoe does control his
impulse for a number of years. The acceptable reasons for such a
trip—poverty and ambition—are not augmented by youth, and
none justify Crusoe's journey. At sixty, he "plays the young man"
again.[33]

Immediately after the nephew invites Crusoe to join him, Defoe
writes, "Nothing can be a greater Demonstration of a future State,
and of the Existence of an invisible World, than the Concurrence
of second Causes, with the Ideas of Things, which we form in our
Minds . . ." (2:119). But Crusoe answers, "*What Devil sent you of
this unlucky Errand?*" And so he leaves his children and his
comfortable, retired life. A variation of this episode in the book
occurs at the end of *Farther Adventures* when the exiled Russian
prince refuses to leave Siberia with Crusoe: "How do you know
Sir, says he warmly, that instead of a Summons from Heaven, it
may not be a Feint of another Instrument? . . . let me remain . . .
banish'd from the Crimes of Life . . . " (3:207-8). There is an
element of superstition in the opening of *Farther Adventures* that
is partially dispelled by the Siberian dialogue. The purpose, the
value, of Crusoe's final odyssey is certainly not clear, and he has
been involved in "the Crimes of Life" even if he has not committed
any of the murders, rapes, and swindlings around him. What good
he has done—bringing Christianity to his island and rescuing the
prince's son—has been opportunistic rather than planned or even
described later as such. He was, as the prince pointed out by

implicit comparison, far more likely to find trouble and temptation than goodness.

Furthermore, the philosophical and theological writings of the time overwhelmingly suggest that Defoe's contemporaries would have seen the Devil rather than a good angel prompting the sequence of events that led to Crusoe's final voyage. The progress of Crusoe's decision conforms to Defoe's and dozens of other writers' descriptions of the actions of the Devil in the world. In *The Political History of the Devil*, Defoe tells us that the Devil "is with us, and sometimes in us" but not always suspected. The person who is calm and at peace with himself is "his own man" while the "ruffled," passionate man has the Devil in him.[34] Crusoe's incessant thinking and talking about his desire to travel resembles "possession."

Crusoe obviously regards himself as a Christian in *Farther Adventures*. He reflects on his actions and his duty; he is open to the manifestations of God in the world (3:142, 146-47). Neither a superstitious throwback nor a modern sceptic, Crusoe holds most of the attitudes of men of his time. He listens to the Spanish governor describe the premonitions that prepared him for the invasion of the cannibals: "I am satisfied our Spirits embodied have a Converse with, and receive Intelligence from the Spirits unembodied and inhabiting the invisible World, and this friendly Notice is given for our Advantage . . . " (2:166). Crusoe listens to this without comment. The Spaniard is expressing an opinion more common to the Renaissance than the Restoration and, although his anxieties prove to be well-founded, no further mention of the supernatural warning is made. The effect is to introduce the possibility of benign spirits without endorsement.[35] Defoe recounts a similar incident in his *History of Apparitions*. In this book of cases, a ship captain cannot sleep and, in his uneasiness, questions the mate who reassures him; as he leaves, however, he hears a voice say, "Heave the lead!" When he insists the mate do so, they find themselves in dangerously shallow water. Defoe concludes that this warning was not the work of Satan or an angel but "the work of a waking providence, by some invisible agent employed for that occasion. . . . " and uses it to ask, "how will those modern wits . . . account for this, who allow no God or

Providence, no invisible world, . . . kind and waking spirits, who, by a secret correspondence with our embodied spirits, give merciful hints to us of approaching mischiefs . . . ?"[36] Defoe is expressing a common opinion, one that can be found in books as diverse as Machiavelli's *Discourses on Livy* and Thomas Vaughan's *Magia Adamica*.[37] In *History of Apparitions*, he presents cases in much the way John Aubrey does in one of Defoe's acknowledged sources, *Miscellanies*,[38] and asks if the implications are not clear. In *Farther Adventures*, he uses a similar episode to add drama and to remind the reader that God's care for his creatures may be recognized whether or not man can explain an event rationally. Time after time, in *Farther Adventures* Defoe notes that people cannot always distinguish first or second causes, although second causes almost invariably act.[39]

Even more explicitly, Captain Roberts lives in a Providential world. His dedicatory epistle tells us that his book is a faithful relation of the "Dispensations of Providence." Ready to die in situations in which other Defoe characters compromise, Roberts steadfastly insists that he depends upon "the Blessing of God on my honest Endeavours" (p. 70), and his faith never wavers.[40] Marooned in the leaky ship, he recognizes his nearly hopeless situation but says, "if I was permitted to perish, I . . . doubted not but he would . . . receive me to his Everlasting Rest; and, what they had intended for my Misfortune, would be the Beginning of my Happiness; and that in the mean Time, I had nothing to do but to resign myself to his blessed Will and Protection, and bear my Lot with Patience" (p. 96). This passage might have been written by a contemporary of Bunyan, but its otherworldliness is undercut by the ingenuity and tenacity of Roberts's efforts to survive. As biblical as Roberts's language is and as many times as he refers to God, his physical survival dominates the narrative.[41] Because Roberts is so religious, he carries the moral world within him; Defoe does not need to supply reminders of it and he lets such incidents as Roberts's delirium on Salt Point pass without extraterrestial nuances.

Far from placing his heroines and heroes in an amoral world, Defoe uses the firmly ordered Christian world as his setting and makes this setting as important to the understanding of his themes as the concrete, historically accurate London Streets and West

Indian trade routes. Contemporary readers would have found suspense, delight, and outrage in his books because of it. They would have found affirmation of their hopes and confirmation of their moral choices. Above all, they would have found the mores of their society and their expectations of order and pattern in the narrative and in the world upheld and translated into art. Defoe gave them infinite variety and "surprizing adventures" within a comfortably predictable frame.

· SEVEN ·

ROXANA

DEFOE INTENDED *The Fortunate Mistress* to be a "woman's novel." By 1724 when Defoe published this book, which we call *Roxana*, novels for women were well established. Two full years had passed since the publication of Defoe's last novel, and those two years were unusually significant in the development of the English novel. In these years, Penelope Aubin published three novels and Eliza Haywood four. These works, Mary Davys's *The Reform'd Coquet* (1724), and Jane Barker's *A Patch-Work Screen* (1723) mark changes in these authors' own writings. A turning point had been reached in the history of the novel, and more tightly plotted love stories with emphatic psychological emphases began to outnumber scandalous memoirs, imaginary voyages, political allegories, and romantic novellas.[1]

Women already possessed a prose fictional form with plot lines, themes, and a tradition of its own.[2] In fact, women novelists outnumbered men, and prefaces appealed openly to female readers. Mary Hearne, for example, called *The Female Deserters* (1719) "this Woman's-Toy," "W.P." was careful that the language of *The Jamaica Lady* (1720) would not offend the "fair sex," and Jane Barker said that she chose the form of her *Patch-Work Screen* because of its particular appeal to women, whose "Tea-Table Entertainment" it resembled. Women writers acknowledged their debts and dedicated their books to other women writers, as Mary Hearne did to Delariviére Manley and "Ma[demoiselle] A." did to Eliza Haywood. That tradition may be what Ian Watt described pejoratively as "the characteristic kind of weakness and unreality to which the [novel] is liable—its tendency to restrict the field on which its psychological and intellectual discriminations operate to a small and arbitrary selection of human situations, a restriction which, since Fielding, has affected all but a very few English novels with a certain narrowing of the framework of experience and permitted attitude."[3] Whatever the tradition destroyed in breadth, however, it tended to compensate for in depth. It was almost as though both breadth and depth had to be established separately before the scope of Fielding could be combined with the psychological complexity of Austen and Eliot in the novels of Melville, Joyce, and Faulkner.[4]

Defoe's novels share the major characteristics of the woman's novel. Jane Barker remarks on the new taste for "Histories at Large" in the preface of *A Patch-Work Screen for the Ladies* and lists as responsible *Robinson Crusoe, Moll Flanders, Colonel Jack*, and *Sally Salisbury* "with many other *Heroes* and *Heroines*."[5] In fact, her own novel develops the character of Galesia in considerable depth and motivates the poems and interpolated tales carefully. This novel, Penelope Aubin's *Life of Madame de Beaumont* (1721), *The Noble Slaves*, and *The Life of Charlotte DuPont*, Arthur Blackmore's *Luck at Last*, and Eliza Haywood's *British Recluse* (all 1722), *Idalia, The Injur'd Husband*, and *Lasselia* (all 1723) developed the longer, more unified story that concentrated on a character's interior life even as it introduced more characters and more complicated decisions. Tom Brown in 1702 had argued that domestic settings and intrigues should be as popular as "Histories of Foreign Amours and Scenes laid beyond the Seas,"[6] and these novels also reflect the new preference for an English setting. Although most of the heroines travel, and often to exotic lands, these travels exist not so much to provide divertissement and adventure but to reveal new aspects of characters or to symbolize such psychological states as alienation. Plot, setting, and style serve character, which carries the weight of the theme.

The "woman's novel" of the early 1720s was still a courtship novel, but the heroines in increasing numbers came to be less conventional, less interested in marriage, more aware of their conflicts with society, which might be represented by parents, friends, or fiancé, more talented and intelligent, more students of books, people, and the world, more altruistic, and more likely to find partial fulfillment in life than to end in death, infamy, or bliss. (In contemporary novels by men, notably Croxall's *Ethelinda*, W.P.'s *Jamaica Lady*, Gildon's *Loves of Don Alonso*, and the anonymous *Perfidious Brethren*, society still imposed the punishment.) The situations in which the heroines found themselves, the obstacles encountered, and the choices made tended to be repetitious, but the novels gave strong reinforcement for the value of female intelligence and responsibility, motherhood, the search for a worthy mate, female friendship, and religious faith.[7]

Like most of the novels for women, the opening pages of *Roxana* sketch in the heroine's family situation and her accomplishments and introduce the man she is to marry. Defoe uses a number of phrases that would alert the eighteenth-century reader to Roxana's nature. As a child she "lov'd a Crowd, and to see a great-many fine Folks" (p. 8). She dances and is proud of her quick wits and tongue. What characteristics she has that are not vain are masculine, common-sensical rather than polished. Almost at once, Defoe mingles the authorial with the character voice. Roxana twice addresses her audience as "Ladies" and occasionally offers advice such as "O let no Woman slight the Temptation that being generously deliver'd from Trouble is" (p. 35). The assumed bond between reader and narrative voice is standard. Margaret Drabble has suggested that women readers approach characters in a different way from men; they ask "What does this say about my life?" Women writers also seem to see their characters as personal, as imaginative constructs that test possibilities rather than follow and verify patterns.[8] The number of semi-autobiographical novels by early women writers is significant, but more telling are the assumptions made in women's prefaces and periodical reviews that women's fiction reveals highly personal and authentic information about the woman author. In Defoe's elaborate fiction, the "Relator" of Roxana's story is a man who has "dressed up" her story for the world, but the voice we hear throughout the book is Roxana's, and it is a double voice, the woman describing events as they happened and the narrator commenting and judging. The "Relator" is forgotten, and Roxana is narrator and subject just as each woman who tells her story in novels like *The Life . . . of the Lady Lucy* or *The British Recluse* is, and all pause to admonish or explain to the reader, who comes to be identified with the characters listening to the protagonist's story.

Roxana also shares the situation of her novelistic sisters. She is left parentless and penniless early in the novel, faces poverty and the threat of disgrace, and meets a number of men who represent a wide range of socioeconomic classes and personalities. Many novels and numerous conduct books purported to help young girls learn to resist an unsuitable match (choice was not in their hands). Defoe's own *Religious Courtship* was such a book, and the young woman who read Haywood's *British Recluse* or Blackamore's *Luck at Last* carefully would learn similar lessons. In *The British Recluse*, Belinda rejects the virtuous if somewhat dull Worthly for the libertine Courtal. Although Haywood never suggests that Belinda should marry a man she does not love, Belinda is "ruined" by Courtal and sees her sister happily married to Worthly. Years later Fanny Burney explained the benefits of the novel as giving "a picture of supposed but natural and probably existence" that gives "knowledge of the world, without ruin or repentence; and the lessons of experience, without its tears."[9]

Defoe comes out strongly in favor of merchants as husbands— one English and one Dutch—and gives a picture of a slothful fool, an adulterous prince, and several perverted or luxury loving court-hangers on. The goodness of the merchants and their generosity and principles contrast sharply with the other men and with Roxana's own frivolous and avaricious approach to life. Colonel Jack tells us that he risks marriage a third time because "a settled family Life was the thing I Lov'd" (2:61), and even Moll Flanders tries time after time for a settled life. Only Roxana among Defoe's protagonists resists it. Modern critics have made much of Roxana's speeches about the disadvantages of marriage, but Defoe's readers would have heard her voice overcome by the calm reminders of the Dutch merchant that "the Labour of the Man was appointed to make the Woman live quiet and unconcern'd in the World" and "where there was a mutual Love, there cou'd be no Bondage; but . . . one Interest; one Aim; one Design. . . . "[10] Roxana's inability to settle down and be happy with the Dutchman has numerous parallels in earlier prose fiction; for example, Mademoiselle La Motte scorns her virtuous, hardworking husband in Haywood's *Injur'd Husband*.

In fact, Roxana's relationships with the Dutchman incorporate three strains already established in women's fiction. First, the reader is given numerous, conventional signals that she is one of the newly fascinating evil women. The opening references to her vanity and love for crowds and gaity are multiplied and then reinforced by other coded signals. She marries the brewer because he is handsome and a good dancer, their early arguments are over the use of the horses that she wants for her "chariot," and her chief dissatisfaction with him is that he embarrasses her in company. Not fifty pages into the book, Defoe has her yield to the landlord, and she pushes her maid Amy into bed with him. The words Defoe chooses to describe Roxana's actions are those usually given to male rapists or their victims: "do what I wou'd," "stript," "threw open the Bed," and "thrust her in" even though Amy resists to some extent. When Delariviére Manley's Caton helps Fauxgarde into bed with Mariana, the motive is unequivocally stated as resentment and revenge. In *A Patch-Work Screen*, the husband is to blame for a similar situation. Roxana says that "it was something design'd in my Thoughts, that my Maid should be a Whore too, and should not reproach me with it" (p. 47); in contrast, Caton admits that she resents Mariana's virtue and her reproofs when Caton is "amorous."[11] "Roxana refers to her part as being the "Devil's agent."

Second, Roxana is vain. Her seduction is directly related to her vanity and love of "fine Folks." It never occurs to her to become a servant girl, as does Sylvia in *Luck at Last* or Isabella in *The Female Deserters*. Time after time, Roxana tells us she was young and handsome or is "still young and handsome" and admits her vanity. She loves the benefits: "to be courted, caress'd, embrac'd," and admired. Vanity in women's novels is the "Foible of the Sex." Davys's Formator asks why women have "such a greedy thirst after that Praise, which every Man that has his eyes and ears, must give you . . . ," and warns Amoranda that when men see that flattery finds "so powerful an advocate" in the woman's heart, they "never despair of success"—vanity invariably subdues virtue and common sense, he says.[12] When the Prince begins to visit her, Roxana says "I was now become the vainest Creature upon Earth, and particularly, of my Beauty";[13] every day, she says, she became more in love with herself. These characteristics lead her to hold balls at her house in Pall Mall, to want to become the mistress of the King, and, when her ordinary beauty and clothes cannot attract enough attention, to dance in the Turkish costume. She parades her beauty, her dresses, her plate, and arranges her china to "make a fine show." She never learns what love is but moves from infatuation to gratitude to the desire for admiration. The excitement of receiving gifts and surprising the giver with her beauty, thrift, and feigned submissiveness dominates her consciousness. She makes it policy to ask for nothing, always expresses wonder at the generosity of her lover, and protests that she can never do enough for the one who cares for her so well. Revealingly, when she mets a man who does treat her as the free, equal woman she says she wants to be and who wants to take care of her in a permanent, secure way, she rejects him easily. The vain, energetic woman who loves society, excitement, and flirtation was already a character associated with women's anti-social tendencies, with frivolity and folly, and with feminine ruin.[14]

Before the 1700s such women were usually more foolish than evil and were punished by disgrace and death. In the 1720s such women became complex and "interesting."[15] A number of books, such as Alexander Smith's *The Secret History of the Lives of the most celebrated Beauties, Ladies of Quality, and Jilts from Fair Rosamond down to the Present Days* (1715) and the anonymous book "Extracted from Eminent Records," *The History of Fair Rosamond . . . and Jane Shore . . . Shewing How they came to be so; with their Lives, Remarkable Actions, and Unhappy Ends* (1716), had presented seduced maidens as complex psychological beings and as interesting, sympathetic characters. Eliza Haywood created five in a single year, and Ma. A.'s *Prude* (1724) was made in the same mold. These women characters tended to be conventionally reared, if a bit spoiled, unusually independent and enterprising, unwilling to behave conventionally, and strong in defeat. Idalia, for example, is described as having "Greatness of Spirit," as being "peremptory in following her own Will," and as being a coquette. Lasselia insists upon leaving the court in order to avoid becoming one of Louis XIV's mistresses. A.'s "prude" Elisinda and Haywood's Fantomina arrange one affair after another (in Fantomina's case, with the same man), enjoy themselves, and manage to be undiscovered for long time periods. They refuse to accept the roles their families and society have chosen for them, they work for their own material and sexual gratifications, and they remain unrepentant.

Roxana shares many aspects of these characters. Each of these women learns something unpleasant about men in her first experience with the opposite sex. All have successful and loving fathers, and, therefore, they are surprised by the characters of the men they meet. Florez, an overeducated page, takes advantage of Idalia's gullibility, turns her over to his master Ferdinand, who rapes her, and then Florez exposes her letters. De l'Amye is Lasselia's host and a married man when he seduces her. Fantomina sees the men in her social class preferring prostitutes.[16] Roxana's first husband is a "fool" who squanders their money and abandons her and their children; her brother loses her inheritance. These men are not mere seducers and fortune hunters: they are unprincipled and irresponsible. Gone are the stilted laments of lovers who say they cannot marry the ruined or the suddenly impoverished—laments that often conclude in marriages, as they do in Aphra Behn's *Adventures of the Black Lady*. These women learn quickly and adapt. Elisinda begins to acquire her own lovers. Fantomina enchants and holds Beauplaisir in the disguises of four different women; Idalia has the love of two men after Ferdinand, resists them, and demands marriage. Roxana, too, has learned to appear feminine and to suppress her desires and opinions in order to get what she wants.

Sir Robert Clayton comments "that he found few Women of [Roxana's] Mind, or that if they were, they wanted Resolution to go on with it" (p. 171). He smiles, and we sense a mixture of amusement, admiration, and surprise. Society is seldom so tolerant or kind. Haywood's women are clearly "ruined," and, even though we believe Idalia at least is a reformed and virtuous woman, normal marriage is not possible for her. Elisinda and Mme. La Motte are truly evil and cause destruction and even death. They and Roxana become social "monsters," characters so unusual in their behavior and "unnatural" in their motives and affections that they seem to be freaks of nature. Princess Halm-Eberstein in George Eliot's *Daniel Deronda* says, "Every woman is supposed to have the same set of motives, or else to be a monster." Society finds "few Women of [their] Mind" and "Resolution" and, therefore, is fascinated and repelled by them as if they were a sheep with three eyes displayed at Tower Bridge. That they are so beautiful is a necessary condition; like Webster's *White Devil*, the strength, ambition, resolution, and freedom from those emotions (constancy, love) that traditionally enslave women are less predictable and more difficult to guard against when clothed in beauty. Fantomina "had Discernment to foresee, and avoid all those Ills which might attend the Loss of her *Reputation*, but was wholly blind to those of the Ruin of her Virtue."[17] So, too, is Roxana. Many of the complex evil characters begin on a course of life that seems to indulge an important human characteristic without full realization of the moral and social implications. Fantomina's desire to know how the most elegant mistresses live and Roxana's initial liaison with her landlord are far from evil, and yet their effects and excesses warp apparently ordinary young women far beyond normal experience.

The third established but relatively new characteristic that Roxana shares is that she chooses to be a single woman throughout a long part of her life.[18] In fiction by men, this choice was often associated with the evil or "monster" women, but in fiction by women, such a life was often portrayed as viable, desirable, and even admirable. Haywood's *British Recluse*, which was published only a year before *Roxana*, has many similarities to Defoe's novel and to other novels such as *A Patch-Work Screen* and *The Female Deserters*. So independent, so capable, so strong, and so fascinating are these women that no one thinks of attaching the appellation "old maid" to them. Belinda and Cleomira in *The British Recluse* and Galesia in *A Patch-Work Screen* have earned their right to remain unmarried.[19] Cleomira has been seduced, buried her still-born child, and attempted suicide. She now lives closeted in a room, even eating her meals alone when Belinda, who has been seduced and is nearly responsible for a good man's death, rents a room in the same house. After exchanging stories, they agree to rent a house seventy miles from London "where they still live in a perfect Tranquillity, happy in the real Friendship of each other, despising the uncertain *Pleasures*, and free from all the *Hurries* and *Disquiets* which attend the Gaieties of the Town. . . ."[20] Galesia had yielded to her elderly mother's demands that she marry only to be spared by the suicide of her debauched fiancé. Her earlier experiences with men like Bosvil had given her "a secret Disgust against Matrimony," but she seems to believe her mother's argument that single women "frustrate the End of our Creation."[21] Solitude, peace of mind, and freedom from the hard work and physical rigors of marriage, pregnancy, and motherhood do not seem perverse or self-indulgent for all their pessimism about men. Experience and suffering seem to have earned them the right to retire with the dignity of widows.

Up to a point Roxana is like these women. She, too, has had several painful experiences with men and sees life with a man as comparatively upsetting, tumultuous, and uncertain. She cannot be abandoned, cheated, hurt, or robbed as easily; much more is in her control. She is slave neither to her affections nor to her social place. Roxana's defense of the single life is far more elaborate than that in any novel by a woman, but women novelists insist equally upon the integrity of their feelings. Belinda says, "if I never shou'd be [willing to marry], he ought not to expect I should do a Violence to my *own* Humour, to pleasure *his*" (p. 84). In every case, the woman is financially independent, certainly an admirable state for any person, male or female.

The portrayal of the self-sufficient, content single woman is the most optimistic expression of the theme of the heroine's alienation from her society. In novel after novel, women characters find their actions, values, and desires at odds with the world. If she is trusting, affectionate, and giving, she is often seduced and abandoned. If she expects generosity and altruism, she finds prodigality, guile, and greed. The fact that so many women's novels include both a scene of the woman alone in a garden and of her alone on a road are powerful evocations of the pattern in women's *Bildungsroman*. The garden has been a place of beauty, security, and pleasure in the character's girlhood; many have their first sexual experience in gardens, are "ruined" there, secluded there, and later are told or discover they have been abandoned there. Inchbald brilliantly sums up the significance of the garden when she has Hannah, in *Nature and Art*, consider committing suicide on the spot where she had lost her virginity. Roxana, child of the city, has a garden all gone to weeds for the landlord to restore, and the Prince hides her a country home with a beautiful garden. There he warns her dourly, "if once we come to talk of Repentance, we must talk of parting" (p. 82). The garden becomes fallen Paradise and another symbol of confinement.

Outsiders in literature have often been wanderers, and women are no exception. Forced out of their homes by an unacceptable engagement or fear of disgrace were their pregnancies to be discovered, eighteenth-century heroines dress as beggars, pilgrims, boys, servants, and visiting kin and look for ways to escape the role prepared for them. A few are gloriously successful (as Sylvia is in *Luck at Last*), but most find that they must appear even more submissive and uninteresting in order to escape recognition or new difficulties. The most successful become servants to virtuous women.

In spite of her desire for wealth, admiration, and adventure, Roxana's wandering is startlingly like that of her novelistic sisters. She has no real goal, and each time she moves, she is escaping and avoiding more than she is acquiring. Just as the pregnant, unmarried girl must leave to escape discovery and disgrace, so must Roxana when she leaves England, France, and Holland. Although her pregnancy is not mentioned as a reason for her leaving the Dutchman and Holland, had she stayed her condition would have determined that she marry or be disgraced. She moves from place to place, shedding an embarrassing and constricting identity, and escaping the penalties for her unconventional, socially unacceptable behavior. She, like they, hopes to find a place where she can maintain her independence and her lifestyle. She wants freedom, privacy, and respect; she hopes to find a place where, if she cannot fit in, she will at least be ignored. That Roxana comes closest to this state when disguised as a Quaker, part of the most radically nonconformist Protestant sect in England, and that the British recluses must retire seventy miles outside of London makes the same point about women's options in early eighteenth-century society.

How conscious Defoe was of the conventions of women's fiction and how analytical he was about them is unlikely ever to be known. The duplication of two tonal characteristics, however, does much to locate *Roxana* in the most significant path of fiction for women. Defoe's Roxana lives in a world that is both claustro-phobic and paranoid; furthermore, she is continually aware of herself "within and without." In other words, even as she is conscious of thinking and feeling, she is always watching herself act as if she were an auditor or looking in a mirror.

The protagonist of the early English novel for women usually becomes paranoid early. She soon comes to see her parents as determined to select and to force upon her an unsuitable male and to fear men as liars and seducers. People seem indifferent to her feelings. She cannot persuade, convince, or coerce anyone, and the affection she has been taught to rely upon in her youth seems to be converted into the right to make decisions about her life. Parents and suitors sweep away her opinions, feelings, and even principles. At any moment, her parents might insist that she marry a man she loathes and enforce that decision by verbally abusing her, locking her up, or even dragging her into the chapel. Men become unfamiliar creatures who are simultaneously connivers and slaves to the sex drive. They might court the woman for months, pledge eternal love and devotion, beg for favors, appear to spend every moment thinking about their love only to drop her within days after gaining "the last favor." Such men are also capable of such social breaches as walking into unlocked bedrooms and climbing in bed with the occupant or of committing violent rapes. One objection to women's fiction, of course, is the improbability of such plots and characterizations. The paranoia of the heroine, however, symbolizes the worst fears of the reader and the extent of change adulthood made in the life of a girl even as it provided a tone readers apparently enjoyed and the structure of a kind of psychological chase, two qualities the gothic novel would raise to high art.

Characters exhibit the classic symptoms of paranoia. They feel in opposition and come to expect hostility rather than understand-ing or sympathy. The number of characters who believe they must leave home, often in disguise, is quite striking. Neither Isabella in *The Female Deserters*, Adelasia in Manley's *Happy Fugitives*,[22] nor Sylvia in *Luck at Last* spend much time arguing. They feel conspicious and adopt the disguises of servants and beggars in order to avoid attention. In some cases, the heroine may become misanthropic or afraid of the entire male sex. In others, the paranoia comes to rest upon a single character, as it does with Roxana. Susan comes to symbolize the suspicions and judgments Roxana fears society would make if it knew her past. Roxana feels that everyone is curious about her, likely to recognize truths about her, and persecuting her by their very attention.

Closely linked to the characters' paranoia is the claustrophobic nature of many of the novels. Many characters are locked in rooms, sometimes with sealed windows. Even if they are not physically confined, their attractiveness restricts their movement. Unlike children who can come and go in safety, they risk undesirable men who will court them or criminals who might kidnap or rape them. They are not free to talk to certain kinds of people, to initiate conversations, or even to be in certain public places. Certain kinds of learning and intellectual interests are ruled inappropriate and forbidden. In fact, one form of rebellion attended with signs that the woman is now outside society and unlikely ever to marry is wide reading and serious study; for example, Cleomira and Galesia are free to read philosophy, history, and medical books only after they retire from society.[23] To indulge certain ambitions or to admit certain thoughts are also forbidden. Without question, the woman has to repress her sexual feelings, obscure the depth of her affections until marriage, and deny all desire for prominence, wealth, or professional achievement. Once married, she is often even more restricted.

Besides the obvious method of locking the woman up, heroines are confined by reminders of what they owe their parents, by economic necessity, and by society's expectations. *Fantomina* is a record of the sexual signals early eighteenth-century men knew. When the heroine dresses in a certain way and breaks the rules of modest behavior, Beauplaisir assumes she is available. Next she disguises herself as a servant girl, and as court records as well as fiction tell us, servant girls were always fair game.[24] As a widow she asks a favor and exchanges sex for protection. To violate the code of behavior for chaste women, no matter how impractical or irrational obeying it would be, is to telegraph sexual availability.[25] At one time or another, Roxana finds herself restricted in each of these ways. Her poverty keeps her trapped in the rented house after the brewer leaves her, then she must remain hidden in it to prevent the return of her children. Later she must stay in houses to avoid being recognized. The last section of the novel, however, makes confinement emotional as well as physical. In one of the most gripping chase stories in eighteenth-century fiction, *Roxana* creates a space growing smaller and smaller until the protagonist has nowhere to go.

Defoe has reworked the familiar confinement theme by denying that the amount of money a heroine has is directly proportional to the number of options she has and that being a "ruined" woman is to have no options at all.[26] In fact, the more money Roxana has, the more conspicuous she is. Although we see her life in France, at Pall Mall, and in retirement before she lives with the Quakeress as claustrophobic, she does not feel restricted. Because she needs to protect the Prince's or her reputation, she chooses houses with hidden entrances and disguises. Roxana tells us repeatedly that she does not feel confined, but once she is married to the Dutchman, she begins to feel her actual situation. Every day her daughter Susan comes closer to her, and soon the knowledge about the past, the lies she tells, and the truth she must reveal begin to give the Quakeress and then her husband damaging suspicions. Roxana is driven from place to place, and finally her conscience becomes her constant jailer. She can no longer assume a disguise, forget her past difficulties, and have fun. As Milton's Satan says, "myself am Hell."[27] She becomes the physical confinement, her own boundaries, and a state of mind keeping herself motionless. Psychological confinement has replaced physical.

As John Richetti has pointed out, Roxana is appropriately punished for her domestic sins by her daughter.[28] What modern readers have not seen, however, is the pathos of the character of Susan. When Amy as benefactor first accidentally meets Susan at the children's guardian's house, Susan cries like a heartbroken child. "Tho' she was a great Wench of Nineteen or Twenty Years old . . . she cou'd not be brought to speak a great-while" (p. 266) after Amy insists she is not their mother. Susan begs, "But O do not say you a'n't my Mother!" She asks, "what have I done that you won't own me" and insists upon her respectability, diligence, and good intentions. She promises not to disgrace Amy, to keep a secret even from her siblings, and cries that "it will break my Heart" to be denied.

Every time Susan sees Amy, she begs and cries "like a Child."

Amy and Roxana are more appalled than moved, and the hunt begins. Susan puts more and more fragments of stories together, bluntly states such things as that "her Mother had play'd the Whore" (p. 269), and finally guesses that, if Amy is not her mother, Roxana is. Rather than seeing that Susan wants to be united with her mother regardless of what Roxana did, Amy is infuriated that she cannot get Susan to accept the fiction she has created, and Roxana says discovery would ruin her "with my Husband, and everybody else too; I might as well have been the *German Princess*" (p. 271). Her reference to the notorious Mary Carleton, the "German Princess," locates *Roxana* in a fictional tradition and reduces Roxana's charade into the perspective Defoe wants. Mary Carleton was a simple girl from Canterbury, the wife of a shoemaker, who suddenly made an ostentatious appearance in London. She used forged letters, flashy fake jewelry, wit, and charm to give credibility to her story that she was a German noblewoman. John Carleton pretended to be a lord and tricked her into marriage. Almost immediately, Mary's deception was detected; she was arrested for bigamy but acquitted. She went on to act in a play about herself, *The German Princess* (1663), but was finally transported for theft and eventually hanged. A number of pamphlets, ballads, and fictionalized accounts of her exploits were published, the most contemporaneous to *Roxana* in 1714.[29] Although Carleton's life bears more similarity to Moll Flanders's adventures, the pretentious and daring central hoax that made Mary notorious is like Roxana's; the title page of *The Fortunate Mistress* had identified one of Roxana's aliases to be "the Countess de Wintselsheim in Germany."

Suddenly, Susan seems to appear everywhere: on the ship, at the Quakeress's, in the captain's remarks to the Dutchman, at Tunbridge, and, most persistently, in Roxana's thought and dreams. Susan continues to cry for her mother, and Roxana is once heartless enough to ask if she is dead (p. 283). Roxana feels rage and desperation and begins to swear as she never has before.[30] "The Clouds began to thicken about me, and I had Allarms on every side," Roxana says as more and more information comes to her husband and the Quakeress. Roxana not only sees that the Quakeress is "greatly mov'd indeed" but knows that neither she nor her husband will accept her past life. Finally, Susan follows the

Quakeress to Roxana's refuge in Tunbridge, persuades the Quakeress to try to persuade Roxana to see her, and insists she will follow Roxana even to Holland. Just as the circle seems to close in to the point that Roxana cannot maneuver at all, Susan and Amy disappear and reassuring reports begin to come from the Quakeress.

The tension in these fifty pages comes from Susan's steadily increasing knowledge and proximity to Roxana—time after time, she is in the room or in the next house—from the information Roxana's husband and the Quakeress receive, which seems too revealing and too damaging to the reader and to Roxana, and from the building rage in the women characters. First Amy begins to rave, finally Roxana begins to swear and shake with rage, Susan loses her temper and puts a curse on the Quakeress's children, and then the Quakeress loses her patience. The level of frustration and fury grows until an explosion seems inevitable. Instead we get the calm in the eye of the hurricane, and Roxana and the reader wait for the reappearance of Amy or Susan or both. "The Blast of Heaven" that comes seems both predictable and justifiable. As Defoe had remarked here as well as in criminal biographies and conduct books, "What a glorious Testimony it is to the Justice of Providence and to the Concern Providence has in guiding all the Affairs of Men (*even the least, as well as the greatest*) that the most secret Crimes are, by the most unforeseen Accidents, brought to light, and discover'd" (p. 297). Roxana's growing detestation of herself isolates her from others. She begins to feel evil when her husband embraces her, fears mixing her money with his, and feels that both Amy and Susan are persecuting her. She longs to embrace them, but orders them away. Throughout the episode Susan weeps, repeats her "dismal" story, and begs to throw herself at her parents' feet. Unable to love, to confess, to embrace, or to ask forgiveness, Roxana is locked into an existence dominated by loneliness, alienation, and nightmares.

Ironically, it is not her vision of herself that traps and destroys Roxana. It is Susan's image of her, and her again we see *The Fortunate Mistress*'s participation in a major theme in women's fiction. Women, real and fictional, seem to be conscious of themselves as actors; they watch themselves. John Berger has pointed out that "From earliest childhood [woman] has been taught and persuaded to survey herself continually."[31] Feminist critics have repeatedly pointed out that women have been encouraged to judge their value and even their virtue by this external physical appearance. Roxana often describes her appearance and especially her clothes in great detail. Although Defoe never gives the detail that women writers do, his use of clothing is deeply revealing. Manley, for example, gives us two paragraphs itemizing Adelasia's "rustic" dress in *The Happy Fugitives*, and Aubin uses paragraphs such as one including fine details ("cherry-colour Silk Petticoat" with silver flowers, braided hair, and straw hat) in *Madame de Beaumont*. These descriptions always increase the heroine's attractiveness, indicate her economic condition, and harmonize with her mental state.

Defoe goes beyond these descriptions to develop themes. A commonplace is that Roxana becomes her clothes; as Virginia Woolf said, clothes "mould our hearts, our brains, our tongues to their liking," and Roxana's do. Her Turkish costume becomes the sum of her character and an identity so firm that Susan can use it to stalk her. By Defoe's time, "Roxana" was a generic name conjuring up the image of harems and exotic, beautiful women. Contemporary play-goers would have thought of Alexander the Great's wife, of William Davenant's Roxalana (*Seige of Rhodes*, 1661), of Nathaniel Lee's ambitious "enchantress" (*Rival Queens*, 1677), and of Racine's vacillating and jealous Sultana Roxana (*Bajazet*, 1672) adapted into Charles Johson's love-sick, clinging Roxana (*The Sultaness*, 1717).[32] Novel readers, however, probably would have thought of *Memoirs of Count Grammont* and Montesquieu's *Lettres Persanes* translated in 1721 by John Ozell, and these associations are deeply suggestive. The *Memoirs of Count Grammont* includes a section in which a discussion of the disadvantages of marriage immediately precedes an account of the life of Betty Davenant, the actress who triumphed in *The Siege of Rhodes* as Roxalana. One lady instructs the other: "the Pleasures of Matrimony are so inconsiderable, in Comparison of its Inconveniences, that I can't imagine, how People can undergo that Yoke. Therefore be wise, and rather fly than court [it]. . . . How glittering soever the Bait may be, be sure not to be caught by it. Make not your Slave your Tyrant, and remember, that as long as you preserve your own Liberty, you'll be Mistress of that of others."[33] Then the lady relates the story of the actress who played the part of "Roxana." Betty Davenant, like Roxana of the novel, had "performed to perfection" and then disappeared from the public eye, becoming a powerful man's kept mistress. The common themes of liberty and of resistance to marriage in the *Memoirs of Count Grammont* and in Roxana's famous speech and the similarity in notorious performance/retirement suggest direct influence.

The influence of Montesquieu's *Lettres Persanes* is more subtle. A minor theme in *Lettres Persanes* is the subjugation of women, and Usbek, the chief letter writer, worries about his harem throughout the book. He receives letters from his eunuchs and slaves, and from his women Zachi, Zelie, and Roxane—Roxane least often. As his absence extends, disorder and rebellion in the harem grow, men are reportedly seen, and finally an incriminating letter is found. Roxane, believed by all to be the most modest and virtuous, is caught with a man.[34] After her lover is killed, she leaves a letter revealing her true nature and commits suicide:

Comment as-tu pensé que je fusse assez crédule pour m'imaginer que je ne fusse dans le monde que pour adorer tes caprices; que, pendant que tu te permets tout, tu eusses le droit d'affliger tous mes désirs! Non : j'ai pu vivre dans la servitude, mais j'ai toujours été libre. J'ai réformé tes lois sur celles de la nature; et mon esprit s'est toujours tenu dans l'indépendance.

Tu devrois me rendre grâces encore du sacrifice que je t'ai fait; de ce que je me suis abaissée jusqu'à te paroître fidèle; de ce que j'ai lâchement gardé dans mon coeur ce que j'aurois dû faire paroître à toute la terre; enfin, de ce que j'ai profané la vertu en souffrant qu'on appelât de ce nom ma soumission à tes fantaisies.

Tu étois étonné de ne point trouver en moi les transports de l'amour: si tu m'avois bien connue, tu y aurois trouvé toute la violence de la haine.[35]

Like Defoe's Roxana, she has shown herself to be a dissembler and actress. She was not submissive and did not even love Usbek. Her freedom of spirit, her rebellion, and her unwillingness to submit to woman's place lead her first to "monstrous" behavior and then despairing, self-destructive behavior. Both Roxanas, although appearing to be compliant women, have been the corrupting influences in virtuous men's attempts to establish orderly domestic lives. Both women are also symptoms of national corruption and of the evils of speculative corruption.[36]

Throughout her life, Roxana has gained and held admiration and power by the image of herself which she has deliberately projected. She dresses as well as she can for her landlord, but it is with the Prince that we see that image-making is a science for her. She tells him that she will put on the dress he likes best, and she does. Critics and psychologists have noted that women and women characters "read" people, that novels by women often teach such "reading," and that "reading" is an important source of influence.[37] That Roxana can choose the favorite dress demonstrates her understanding of the Prince and her power to please him. Time after time, she dresses and behaves so that others will confuse her external appearance with her internal self and will equate the beautiful lady who knows social forms and never appears greedy, discontent, or ambitious with the woman. That she is clever enough to choose a graceful French dance to overwhelm the revealing, pagan costume is another example of her ability to read people and shape their readings. Time after time, she notes what people think of her, and we never doubt her reports, as we sometimes do those of Moll Flanders.

Susan is her mother's own daughter; she bears her name and her ability to "read." She knows Roxana is her mother, and can accurately describe her magnetic appeal as she played the harlot at the Pall Mall house. Roxana cannot admit she is the woman Susan knows, and yet she cannot deny it. Not even the most severe and modest dress she can adopt, the Quaker's, can hide her from Susan's reading. Daughters are, after all, reflections of their mothers, and Susan becomes a glass for her mother. Roxana sees herself and loses her ability to change her shape in order to have others read her as she wants. She becomes trapped in her own form and, whenever she looks at herself, sees Susan's Roxana, which now matches the inner woman. Men in fiction are cautioned to beware the mask lest the face comes to fit; *Roxana* inverts that into the warning that women's novels often give: any attempt to counterfeit the female role as opposed to submitting to it will finally destroy what is both the source of woman's peace of mind and her only real claim to excellence—virtue. And the root of virtue is clearly the French "vertu" and the code that word

brings to mind—moral excellence practiced with modesty, courage, and benevolence.

For all its similarities to the early English novels by and for
women, no one can read more than a few pages of *The Fortunate
Mistress* without realizing that this is a novel by a man. Defoe may
have elucidated the subtext and conventions of the women's
novels by imitating them, but the style and the most significant
elements of the character's *Weltansicht* are utterly different.
Women writers from the mid-eighteenth century to the present
have remarked (often unhappily) on the contrast between man's
and woman's style.[38] Virginia Woolf once likened women's
writing to bird sounds. Matthew Arnold's comparison of the de
Guérins might be multiplied endlessly: "[Eugénie's style] is pretty
and graceful, but how different from the grave and pregnant
strokes of Maurice's pencil!"[39] In addition to whatever actual or
developed gender differences existed, the early novel struggled
against the artificiality of the language of translations, romances,
and novellas and tried to take into account the idea that literary
language necessarily differed from ordinary speech. No wonder
the style of the early novel was so often uneven, uncertain, and
distracting.

Reading Barker, Davys, Manley, and Haywood beside Defoe
defines the contrast inarguably in the word "command." Defoe is
clearly in command of his pen, his subject, his character, and her
society. He knows the reasons the French Huguenots came to
England,[40] he knows how a father/son brewery worked and how
a son so reared could ruin the business, he knows how to get from
France to Holland, how Robert Clayton might have managed
Roxana's money, and how men would react to a woman like her.
His prose is unself-conscious, expansive, explanatory, and filled
with the accurate, convincing details that Defoe made characteristic of every English novel after his. He is not afraid of the
subjective, of fantasies, of depicting long-term, successful immorality, of making judgments, of offending modesty, or of *asserting*
firmly. In other words, he is not afraid that he will be identified
with his heroine. He is confident as a writer, secure in his
knowlege of the world, and in command of the recently developed

tone that both asserted verisimilitude and yet signaled fiction, stories that "Come near us, and represent to us Intrigues . . . but not such as are wholly unusual. . . ."[41] Every sentence tells us that these might be people we have seen doing things that some people we know might be capable of doing, and yet the author sometimes "is writing to please my self" even as he keeps in mind pleasing the reader.[42] Defoe's twenty-five years as a journalist, historian, and allegorist as well as his earlier novels and memoirs give him the means of advancing plot, explaining, making transitions, and shifting from individual to context that some of his contemporary fiction writers were still working out.[43]

Roxana is an interesting character and resistant to archetypal interpretation because Defoe has omitted so many of the most dominant opinions and emotions traditionally assigned to women in novels and instead has included elements that, even as early as 1724, contradict the signals readers have learned to guide them to correct interpretation. Roxana, for example, does not fear what Isabella, Teresa, or Idalia does about herself or others. Furthermore, the quest that is her life and her relationship to God are not duplicated in other novels about women characters.

The most pervasive fear in women's fiction is not the protagonist's fear of a man or men but of herself.[44] She is never sure she is not naive, illogical, limited in intelligence, handicapped by inadequate education and experience, and subject to being "swept off her feet" by what would become the magnetic but evil Byronic hero. She is afraid she will get herself in trouble, and many novels such as *The Dumb Virgin* and *The Perjur'd Beauty* do seem to argue that seduced women get what they deserve. Even though Maria in *The Dumb Virgin* has struggled with Dangerfield an incredible two hours, Behn dooms her to suicide, perhaps because she "durst make no great Disturbance, 'thro fear of Alarming the Company below" or because she was finally "melted by his Embraces."[45] Victoria, *The Perjur'd Beauty*, is raped by her husband's father, who is also her own father.[46] Less sensational novels depict women fooled by simple strategies, unable to think of courses of action, and, very often, giving in to their love for fiancés. The woman is often physically overpowered, abandoned, and, should she find her seducer, driven away from him. These novels present a metaphoric hyperbole for what psychologists tell us are women's major sexual fears: of violence and pain.[47]

Roxana, however, exhibits the major male fear: about performance. This anxiety comes out in ways often seen as feminine when she wonders if she is clean enough, beautiful enough, and ingenious enough. In fact, however, at best all three are tied to male ideas, and her refusal to let sex bind her to anyone is more common to masculine behavior.[48] She pays men in sex sometimes because she had rather part with her body than her money. When the Dutchman becomes insistent that she marry him, she offers him money in a way that clearly equates sex or money as her signs of gratitude. That the sexual act has almost no meaning for her separates her from an unbroken string of heroines whose sexual initiation binds the fate of man and woman permanently.

The treatment of pregnancy and childbirth is an extension of the psychological meaning of the sex act. Just as women characters fear they have too little control over their lives and are likely to find their reason overwhelmed, so pregnancy is portrayed as the body out of control. The fact of the pregnancy is usually accompanied by horror and despair, then with attempts to conceal it, and finally with disgrace and death. The lassitude of pregnant heroines is striking. Belinda in *The British Recluse*, for example, mopes around the house where she has been seduced until sent to the country. The despair and anger and then the pains of childbirth are always described in terms of violence. The most common metaphor for birth is the rack. Whether the child lives or dies also seems to be completely beyond the mother's control. Although Roxana cannot prevent pregnancy, she resents it only once. Her concerns, again, are about performance. She wants fine, healthy children; she competes with Amy to have the landlord's children, grumbles that "the Charge, the Expence, the Travel" were all to do over because the first of her infants dies, and then gloats that the second was a "charming" boy. She invites the Prince in when she is in labor with his child and later worries that she is not *appearing* to be concerned enough over the Dutchman's son.

Quite rightly, seduced and abandoned women are enraged, and women, real and fictional, often feel angry because of social restrictions and pressures. The ways anger is expressed in women's novels are often subtle and are still being analyzed and debated by critics.[49] Some of the novels of the 1720s are crude enough that the rage is unmistakable. When a woman writer has a woman character slowly dismember her betrayer or has a lady forge dozens of letters causing a man great inconvenience, embarrassment, and expense, the message is clear. Aubin's story of the woman who rips out her eyes rather than see herself dishonored or semi-autobiographical fictions like Manley's *Rivella* are hardly more subtle. Characters who struggle not to show their distress in front of the men who have hurt them, who imagine stabbing or poisoning a man, and who threaten or actually turn violence against themselves are so common as to be tiresome. Unlike many of the women writers of the second half of the eighteenth century who, like Ann Radcliffe, were married or apparently contentedly single, like Maria Edgeworth and Jane Austen, a number of the early eighteenth-century novelists had had bad experiences with men or had been in situations that led to pessimistic analyses of society. Delariviére Manley had been tricked into a bigamous marriage at age fifteen; Haywood had left her husband after seven years; Behn and Davys were widowed early; and both Barker and Aubin were Catholic (Barker never married) and, therefore, discriminated against by English society. In their works, revenge episodes have considerable ingenuity and deep malice. They particularly like to bring men to spend all of their waking hours thinking about the beloved or to bring the proud seducer to grovel. Rather than a romantic picture of a lad and lassie mutually engrossed in each other, the woman is either genuinely indifferent or skillful enough at hiding her feelings that the man really suffers.[50] An inferior, unacceptable suitor is often treated in such a way, and his (and the woman's family's) presumption so punished. Coquettes, of course, are of this type and extort gifts, poems, letters, and promises. Modest young women, too, may behave this way as Davys's Amoranda does until she meets the model man (*Reform'd Coquette*, 1724). Such novels as *Love upon Tick* (1724) and the horrifying *The City Jilt* reduce the man to poverty and desperation. Glicera in *City Jilt*, for example, manages to hold Melladore's mortgage and greets news of his death as a soldier with "happy, Indifference." She is not, however, responsible for his poverty and even supplies him with the money for his military commission. That he has seduced Glicera rather than marrying her when her fortune is reduced is intended to justify Glicera's single-minded drive to humiliate him.

Roxana has more reason for anger than any of these characters. Her husband and brother have left her in poverty. The landlord insists on taking a trip she opposes, the Prince "reforms" and ends his relationship with her, and she has a series of superficial, even somewhat perverted affairs. She interprets things that happen to her more as accidents or as the nature of the world than as personal, and she goes to the next business of life with scarcely a glance back. Because she seems to see actions in broader perspective and life as open-ended, she is not arrested by any single experience. She does not brood, cry alone, or share her sorrows with another sequestered woman; instead, she contacts someone in the business world to sell her jewels, to change her bills, and to invest her money. Because she has many things to do and leaves her house, she meets new people and moves forward. Because she does not feel helpless and mistreated, she feels no need to assert herself or want revenge.

Most of the rage in early women's fiction comes from experiences that show that the woman is not valued or respected and has been exploited; in almost all cases, the woman suffers from unrequited love. Because men can take the initiative, their choices in women are greater then women's in men, and they do not feel the tension women do. Given the population imbalance in England at the turn of the century and the near-necessity that women marry, a man's courtship of a woman was a great relief. She was likely to seize upon the situation as the solution to the most important problem in her life rather than to see her conversations with him as a time for getting acquainted and as possibly one among many courtships. Conduct books, sermons, and novels admonish women to move slowly and to question men and warn women particularly against giving men virtues and attractions based upon imagination rather than experience and testing.[51] Time after time, however, novelists blame their heroines' errors on just this idealization of a man with whom they have not really had much contact, as Haywood does Cleomira in *The British Recluse* and Amanda in *Bath-Intrigues*. Once humiliated by having their love exposed, they lack the means of revenge given to fictional men: an immediate courtship of a more beautiful woman or rape.[52] Some feign gaiety and flirt, others weep and beg, many seclude themselves, and a few are given fantastic but satisfying recompense, as Glicera is.

Roxana's relationship to men is different because she is not dependent. In fact, most fictional women find verification of their worth[53] and purpose for their lives in a love relationship. Roxana does not allow herself to be exploited and, since she never loves, she cannot be rejected. The equation of women's love with dependence that is given such universal emotional and economic credence breaks down in *The Fortunate Mistress*. The closest thing to love for Roxana is her relationship with the Prince, but it soon becomes clear that status and show are the substance of the attraction. She does not expect the relationship to last and begins to prepare herself psychologically and financially from the beginning. When the Dutchman sketches the transitory nature of an adulterous affair, Roxana's experience provides dramatic example, but she feels no regret or need to protect herself from such another parting. She accepts the impermanence of human affection and relationships and looks for gratification in admiration, excitement, and change. Fromm has said that the need for excitement overwhelms the more common drive for security in some people, and Roxana is a fine example of the questing character who will initiate change when it does not come. Her love is, in Freudian terms, basically masculine in that it is narcissistic (seeking a love that will reinforce an image she has of herself) rather than feminine and, therefore, dependent (seeking a love with qualities and abilities she needs in order to be and function as what society calls an adult).

The heart of the contrast between *The Fortunate Mistress* and the other novels for women is the quest. Roxana is seeking neither a husband nor a settled life. Her story is more like that of Robinson Crusoe, Captain Singleton, Colonel Jack, and Moll Flanders, and more spiritual autobiography than picaresque. As illuminating as are the excellent books and articles published in the last twenty years on the themes and techniques Defoe shares with the writers of spiritual autobiography, they do not explain what is so radical about *The Fortunate Mistress*. Unlike the women characters before and after her, Roxana is more akin to Bunyan's Christian than she is to Richardson's Clarissa or Fielding's Amelia. These later characters find their destinies in marriage and their fate in a spouse; even Clarissa becomes the Protestant bride of Christ. Roxana, however, does not know exactly what she seeks and asks Christian's question, "What shall I do?" Her quest blends with a symbolic, moral landscape. Her story defines humankind's relationship to the world and especially to God.[54]

The novelist of the 1720s most like Defoe was probably Penelope Aubin, yet the differences are most illuminating. Her novels are long, characterized by extensive travel and adventure, and unapologetically pious. Although Haywood was more immediately popular, Aubin's books endured longer. Her characters, however, shared the goals of Behn's, Davys's, and Haywood's heroines—a settled life. Their piety was a source of strength and comfort and of a rigid and, to the modern reader at least, somewhat bizarre code of conduct. If Haywood's characters learned that society punished inappropriate behavior, Aubin's learned a rather horrifying Christian stoicism. Aubin's characters are admonished to die rather than to be dishonored or to fall below the ideal standard of behavior, and they act accordingly. In fact, Roxana summarizes their point of view: "without question, a Woman ought rather to die, than to prostitute her Virtue and Honour, let the Temptation be what it will" (p. 29). Roxana, however, almost immediately gives in to the landlord, and the course of her life is set. Aubin's heroines take the other path. If they can endure, they might have happiness thrust upon them. Madame de Beaumont has been forced into a convent, banished by her father-in-law, imprisoned and nearly starved, and reduced to living in a cave before her long lost husband is found. Maria in *The Noble Slaves* has been captured by the Turks, has torn her eyeballs out and thrown them at the emperor who wants to rape her, but finally is allowed to live on a desolate island with her husband. Teresa in the same novel is shipwrecked, nearly starves, is captured by pirates, has a stillborn child, is kidnapped by her husband's cousin, and is crippled for life. Of such experiences, Aubin writes, "Want, Sickness, Grief, nor the merciless Seas [could not] destroy them; because they trusted in God, and swerv'd not from their Duty."[55] Aubin called such characters "Christian heroes"; in *Popular Fiction before Richardson*, John Richetti calls Robinson Crusoe a religious hero because he insists upon the discovery of the religious meaning of his life in a time when to do so was controversial.[56] To cling to faith, and to find strength and joy in the midst of the kinds of suffering Aubin creates may be heroic, but it is also fairly passive. To search out the relationship between God and his creation, to learn to judge a life in terms of that relationship is active and, in Roxana's case, frightening. Women's fiction give us piety without quest; *Roxana* unites them.

Roxana's narrative never stops gauging her spiritual state. As George A. Starr pointed out in 1965, *The Fortunate Mistress* shares many characteristics of the spiritual autobiography and draws some of its thematic coherence from the form. What Roxana sees are the crucial moments in her life, which add up to missed opportunities for conversion.[57] Once she boards with the Quaker, she strains to repent, to move beyond the initial stages of the sinner's progress to eternity. The past, however, can neither be erased nor escaped. She sees that her refusal to marry the Dutchman in Holland was the moment of her most wanton act. Had she married him, the most excessive sins of her life would never have occurred. She was free of the poverty and helplessness that drove her to the landlord and the Prince. His was a virtuous proposal scorned for vain and presumptuous reasons, the scorning of Worthly for Courtal so to speak. When she agrees to marry the Dutchman, she finds him no more personally attractive; none of Moll's affection, concern, and generosity toward Jemmy appears. She hopes to go back, to turn time back. Her actions cannot be erased, and Susan, the child she could never claim, cannot be escaped. Roxana tells Amy that to wish Susan dead is the same as killing her, and her own reaction to Susan's death tells us that Roxana has wished Susan dead and is guilty by extension of Matthew 5:28. Roxana has never wanted her children, and Susan is the sign of a life in which every chance to repent and every chance to send for her children was deliberately rejected. Roxana was rich enough to take her children back when she returned to England; instead she sets up in the Pall Mall. The fact that Susan's life and hers converge and that Roxana's spectacular behavior gives Susan the means of identifying her mother further reinforces the crucial opportunity lost when Roxana leaves France.

Experience has taught Roxana, as it did Christian and Crusoe, that the question of life is "What shall I do to be saved?" Because of Defoe's reliance upon this theme of the spiritual autobiography, Roxana has unusual depth of character. Unlike Haywood's heroines, she possesses an inadequate code of honesty and chastity and, unlike Aubin's, she adheres to no fixed set of religious ideals.[58] Crusoe learns to trust God and to interpret,[59] Roxana to interpret but not to trust. Just as she could not depend on a man, she cannot surrender to God. Moll and Jack or Jemmy and his plantation wife can confess to each other and accept their own and their spouse's lives. Roxana conceals and conceals, builds layer upon layer of subterfuge. Her lies become increasingly elaborate, ingenious, and improbable.

Defoe makes Roxana such an arresting character partly by having her embody the most basic, archetypal fears men have of women. As her deceits and the conviction of her damnation grow, she becomes more fascinating and repugnant, less familiar, as mysterious as the "Blast of Heaven." The war within becomes more visible—she is overwhelmed by a surge of motherly love in the midst of her frustration with Susan,[60] she draws out Susan's description of her dance even as she tries to start a new life.

Psychologists, anthropologists, and psychosocial historians list four apparently universal, "dangerous" characteristics men assign to women:

(1) As "earth mothers" they give birth and nurture but they also may refuse to feed or demand sacrifice. This role is associated with ruthlessness.

(2) As temptresses they manipulate and weaken; they rob man of his reason and his will.[61] As Ecclesiastes 7:26 describes woman, her "heart is snares and nets."

(3) As manipulator she is unmatched. She will use any ploy, has few if any scruples and "she is a liar by nature, so in her speech she stings while she delights us."[62]

(4) As mystery she is incomprehensible, unreadable, and, therefore, can be assumed to be hostile, the adversarial other.[63]

Many studies of this topic list more fears or label them in slightly different ways, but analysis suggests that these four are reasonably comprehensive. Embedded in at least the first three is the Freudian notion that woman is castrator. She weakens and unmans. In some cultures, the vaginas of powerful women have teeth; D.H. Lawrence's Mellors tells Connie in *Lady Chatterley's Lover* that his wife like all "the old rompers have beaks between their legs,"[64] and, in most cultures, women are thought to be able to "feminize" and, therefore, weaken man, as Omphale did when she dressed Herakles as a woman. The argument seems to be that the man who does not feel like a man is not one, and the most extreme versions of the relationships between the sexes depict a war in which men fight for their manhood.

The dispute about marriage between Roxana and the Dutchman is an example of sexual warfare. She explains how the world is for men, how they have "Liberty, Estate, and Authority,"[65] then characterizes the options she has: the "She-Merchant" who is "a Masculine in her politick Capacity," "a Man in her separated Capacity," and free to "entertain a Man" (pp. 131, 148f.), or the wife. He argues from biblical and social precendent, and, finally, "he thinks of a Way, which, he flatter'd himself, wou'd not fail" to get Roxana to marry him and that is to "take me at an Advantage, and get to-Bed to me." In spite of Roxana's protests and "seeming Resistance," he succeeds, but she says his project "was a Bite upon himself, while he intended it for a Bite upon me" (pp. 142, 144). He has resorted to the most masculine argument, and one that allegedly puts him in a position to say that he will marry her "still" (p. 143). Not only is she to submit but also to be grateful.

Roxana, however, refuses and, by doing so, becomes a strange, unpredictable creature. The black actor Calvin Lockhart once spoke for many men when he said that he fears nothing but the unknown, that "God is the ultimate mystery, and women . . . come as close to that as anything else imaginable."[66] Roxana has become unreadable, unpersuadable, and, therefore, powerful and threatening. She does not do what "any other Woman in the World" (p. 142) would probably do. Scholars have often pointed out how many of men's fears of women see women as having anti-social influences. They may bring him to financial, legal, medical, social, or religious ruin, and Dalilah, Jezebel, Cleopatra, and Helen of Troy are powerful examples of women who diverted men from duty.[67] Most Restoration tragedies presented love (represented by the heroine) and duty (represented by father, friend, or country) to be in absolute, unreconcilable conflict. Roxana's example would destroy the family and the order of the working world, both reflections of the order eighteenth-century people saw in God's creation. The merchant resists, however, and leaves her, and the battle is a temporary stalemate.

Throughout the novel, Defoe has made Roxana mysterious. No matter how much she explains nor how well we think we know her, she keeps the power to mystify. At the heart of the fear of woman's mysterious quality is the fear of the unknown and what experience teaches: because the unknown is unpredictable, it may harm us, we cannot guard against it; and how do we interpret Roxana's putting Amy in bed with the landlord? her refusal of marriage? her behavior at the Pall Mall? the lost years before she comes back to London? or the sudden surges of maternal instinct in a lifetime of neglect for her children? How do we interpret her ability to charm the Prince, to hide so many of her thoughts and come up with ploy after ploy to hold his interest, and to mislead him so completely about her planning and avarice? Such questions horrify us. Disguise after disguise, life story after life story, Roxana seems to have depths we cannot imagine.[68] She is beautiful, deceitful, shameless, and apparently self-sufficient. How mysterious is the woman who does not need a man in our society and how many ways have been devised to prevent such a possibility. Psychologists believe that woman's independence and superiority are most threatening when they come from physical or economic skill, and Roxana is a dazzling financial success. Roxana is confident that she can get the advice and sex she wants on demand and does not bother to marry until she wants the appearance of respectability.

Most of the fears of women are linked to female biology. This description of academic woman sums the fear up well: "The male colleagues are likely to regard her as a Trojan horse, capable at any moment of disgorging, from within the pregnant cavities of her womanhood, an army of seductive wiles and irritating vapors upon their intellectual sanctuary."[69] She carries an enemy to them in her belly, she is "pregnant" with schemes, she does not act from or belong to their world and its rules and assumptions, "their intellectual sanctuary." "Wiles" and "vapors" rather than reason are her methods of influence, and Defoe makes Roxana's powers female. Roxana weeps, strikes pathetic poses, pleads helplessness, and flatters. She uses her adulterous pregnancies to advance her emotional and economic position with her lovers. She is beautiful and chooses clothes and settings to increase her effect on others. She sets herself up as a queen in the Pall Mall and dances in her Turkish costumes. When her children refuse to obey her, she withdraws all support, "starves" them as the Earth Mother was feared to do. By this means, she forces her son to marry the girl she has selected and brings about Susan's death.

Freud and others have made woman's womb the symbol of her mystery and have argued that a variant on her power to castrate is her power to consume. Roxana has that power. The Prince, a husband and also a habitual womanizer, is devoted to Roxana alone for years. His behavior toward her is not merely unprecedented but uncharacteristic. Roxana's darker aspects become more clear to us after her refusal to marry, and her power to consume and destroy is explicitly stated in the last episode. She fears mixing her money with the merchant's, and she is happy when he suggests separate accounts "that I should not bring my Husband under the Blast of a just Providence, for mingling my cursed ill-gotten Wealth with his honest Estate . . . " (p. 260). Later she calls herself "a Piece of meer Manage, and fram'd Conduct," "a She-Devil" in his arms (pp. 300-302), and suggests that she could corrupt him. Amy and Susan become sacrifices to her powerful personality as well.

Because Defoe encodes the archetypal fears of women in Roxana, he makes her a more magnetic and frightening character. He takes what has always been a popular novel plot and gives it gothic undertones. Roxana is, after all, the heroine in search of a destiny and that destiny is usually just what hers is—marriage to a suitable man. The men who choose her tell us how society sees her and should teach her how to value herself, and the men she chooses tell us how she sees herself and how that judgment conforms to society's. The men who choose Roxana are tradesmen and merchants like her father, but she can disguise herself and get noblemen to court her (but not marry her). This story tells us how presumptuous and daring Roxana is, how she belongs to that long list of heroines who will not "settle for" a solid, boring man and domestic drudgery. Daniel Deronda's mother said, "I wanted to

live out the life that was in me," and that life, like Roxana's, was
not what society saw as appropriate. These characters want to be
special, to be heroines as Rachel Brownstein puts it, and they pay
the price. Of course, a "Blast of Heaven" will put Roxana back in
her place as a child of Defoe's God and eighteenth-century
England, but it does take a blast of Heaven. Defoe has captured
the themes of longing and rebellion in the women's novels,
transformed them, and elaborated upon them until the implications are clear. Roxana's is a spiritual quest gone awry; she is the
reincarnation of Lillith, God's equal woman and man's deepest
fears about woman's nature.

Roxana might have provided useful correctives to some of the
characteristics developing in fiction for women. In context and
character, Defoe shifted toward the mainstream of the English
novel. The novels of the 1720s included large numbers of quite
improbable adventures set in places in which people like the
characters would be unlikely to be. Defoe's superior knowledge of
geography and trade routes protects him from the blunders and
vagueness of his contemporaries, and he motivates travel carefully.
Defoe tends to advance his plots through character action or
psychology in contrast to, for example, Aubin, whose characters
tend to be rather passive. Hers and Haywood's plots move by
means of forces outside of the character, such as by a father's
desire for an economic marriage or by coincidence. The unrealistic
nature of the moral universe contributes to both the passivity of
the characters and the improbability of character. Aubin describes
a world in which characters are not only expected to but do kill or
mutilate themselves to prevent "violation" by a pagan, while
Haywood posits a world in which virtue and honor are impossible.
When Aubin points out the amazing virtue of Lluelling and
Monsieur de Beaumont, she is participating in a dialogue with
Eliza Haywood, Jane Barker, and others who show the sexes in
ceaseless strife. Defoe, however, portrays good men and bad men,
people who sin in spite of themselves.

The direction of Haywood's fiction was to polarize the sexes.
Men were scheming, vicious, cold, mercenary libertines, and
women became increasingly stereotyped into the innocent, trust-

ing girl, swept away by her love. Because she had given in to her "inclinations," she was the emotional, irrational victim who could not be responsible for her actions. John Richetti is right to point out how narrow and degrading were the portraits of men in love stories: "Male sexuality is conceived as ruthlessly self-seeking, limited by economic and political realities (wives bring status, wealth, and stability, i.e., continuity of estates through children), and consistently degraded as simply another bodily appetite, regular and mechanical in its promptings rather than mysterious and spontaneous in the way of women's quasi-"spiritual" compulsions. Fiction such as this asks us to take sides . . . against unscrupulous masculine cunning."[70]

The heroine's maturation comes to mean her death or retirement from society; both conclusions symbolize her conflict with the world and lead to the "she-saint" that Clarissa will be. Roxana is a vast contrast. She is responsible for her actions, especially her sexual ones. She reflects, weighs, and chooses with such deliberation that she has been interpreted as passionless and cold. For example, she tells us "my Spirits were far from being high; my Blood had no Fire in it, to kindle the Flame of Desire" (p. 40) as she explains her reasons for becoming the landlord's mistress. Time after time, she minimizes or even denies sexual differences. She will be a "she-merchant" and choose her sexual partners; she will live her own life. Kathryn Rogers has pointed out that she has the ego-drives of men in that she wants wealth, public acclaim, and professional skill. Certainly her courage, resilience, and presence of mind contrast to feminine stereotypes of weakness and passivity.

Not only did *Roxana* not offer correctives, but it failed to attract imitators or even numerous readers. The reasons, I think, explain its rising popularity in our own time. The direction the English novel took in the second half of the eighteenth century was to minimize the differences between the sexes in novels for women and, incidentally, in all "sentimental" novels. The movement was unlike that in *Roxana*, however, for at first the male characters became more like fictional women. Both sexes became absorbed in courtship and commentary on small social groups until the harmony of opinion and "sensibility" became the unmistakable sign of a marriage made in Heaven. Defoe chose to make his

female characters more like fictional men. They were adventurers
and nonconformists, explorers and debaters, and they prefigured
the great characters of the nineteenth century and of the novels
about working women. The popular travel/adventure form did not
accommodate such women well, and for every female pirate there
were fifty pirate captives. We can imagine Defoe writing a novel
about a successful woman bookseller (after all, he published with
several, including the difficult Scot Agnes Campbell), but that life
would have been mundane in a time when settings were aristocratic ballrooms, desert islands, the Mint, and French forests
(where the wild boy had been found).

Second, the novel has always been a literary form that gives
readers conclusions. The demand for poetic justice was still very
strong in the eighteenth century.[71] Defoe denied his readers both
pleasures and, thereby, reduced Roxana's chance for popularity
and imitation. The very complexity of character and experience
that appeals to us today must have struck Defoe's readers as
unrealistic in a time when women's opportunities were so limited.
Roxana must have seemed exotic and improbable, and comparisons to "the German Princess" and Montesquieu's Roxane appropriate. In psychological conception, Roxana is not so far from
Eliot's Gwendolyn Harleth who dreams of a stage career or
Thackeray's Becky Sharp; authorial comment and plot, however,
shape them to the novel's traditional themes while Defoe puts
Roxana closer to the picaro's function as outcast exposing social
weakness.

Roxana is too strong and too unconventional. In an age when
novelists dedicated their books to Richard Steele in approval of his
Conscious Lovers and to Eliza Haywood in tribute for her portrait
of mother love in The Rash Resolve, The Fortunate Mistress
promised little profit, and yet Roxana is no isolated figure in the
history of the novel.

EIGHT

MELTED DOWN, FILLED WITH WONDERS

DEFOE's immortality will always rest on *Robinson Crusoe*, that immensely subtle, complex book with its simple plot. Defoe gives us a character of compelling reality who appears in one archetypal incident after another. Crusoe is, of course, living one of the most common fantasies of humankind: what if I were stranded in a foreign place? alone on an island? completely unable to escape? what if I had almost nothing with me on the island? Crusoe is both *isolated* and *imprisoned* and in an unfamiliar place. His questions are entirely predictable: Is survival possible? how can the most basic needs for food, water, warmth, safety, be met? Once these questions come to mind, the next are equally obvious: why did this happen? why to me? what does it mean? how will the experience affect me? As we follow Crusoe, we will watch physical, experiential, and mental resources brought to bear upon this common "what if" fantasy.

No one who conjures up this fantasy imagines himself succumbing to become a ragged savage howling and eating raw scavenger flesh. And Crusoe fully embodies this other element in the fantasy: he is successful. He will not starve; he will not rave, babble, and throw himself in the sea; he will not even fail to bake bread. He will survive; more than that, he will triumph—and to triumph, whether it be in our imaginations or in Crusoe's story, is to achieve an admirable standard of living and a heroic state of mind in the most elemental and moving way. He will master himself and his environment; he will create a civilized and satisfying life.

215

Quite simply, no other man could have written *Robinson Crusoe*. Everything Defoe wrote is full of stories and the love of good stories. He repeated his own and other people's. He lingered over even the most familiar: "the Sower, who went forth to sow, and sowed his Corn by the Highway Side."[1] His affection appeared in the way he took time to include the elements of the parable and made his prose caress the words, "The Sower . . . went forth to sow . . . and sowed."

His narrative bent is obvious to us from his earliest known writing, the poetic *Meditations*. His first impulse is to imagine a person and project feelings. The first meditation, "Fleeing for Refuge To the hope Sett before us," begins, "In Misadvertant Slaughters We are Told / Cittyes of refuge Were Prepar'd of Old;/ Thither He Fled who gave Unwilling Fate, / A guilt Misshap did (Not Designe) Creat." Immediately we have a dramatic situation and an individual "he." Defoe goes on to imagine himself fleeing to God and gives a vivid description of how the guilty feel when pursued and when the "refuge" appears before them. In "a Psalm of Thanksgiving," his soul is personified; and in "The Seige Raised," the "Will" is "Captain-General" of a garrison attacked by a "rabble of Desires"; two of the other meditations are dialogues. *The Historical Collections*, his second surviving manuscript, is a collection of anecdotes presented with lively dialogue and comments on motive and personality. The 1691 *Account of the Late Horrid Conspiracy* gives a narrative of the Preston plot and dramatizes such things as the rebels' meetings and their discovery on the boat to France. In his preface to the first volume of the *Review* he says, "The custom of the Antients in writing Fables, is my very Laudable Pattern for this . . . ," and his first numbers include *exempla* from history, the creation and business of the Scandalous Club, and illustrative stories that often begin, "This reminds me of a certain Story. . . . " The last things Defoe wrote, discourses on education and trade, are full of extended stories complete with setting and dialogue, and even his short 1728 piece for the *Universal Spectator* includes a mock conversation with "a timorous Friend" and ends thus: ". . . I ask Leave to conclude with a short Story. A certain Countryman travelling. . . ."[2]

Whenever Defoe wrote about his own writing, he wrote about "fable," as he did in his first *Review*, and he was almost never defensive about his fictionalizing. His most consistent explanation was that cliché of his age—he wanted to instruct and delight, or, in the words of his *Universal Spectator* piece, to "serve" and to "please." For Defoe, that meant a balance of "moral" and "fable," and he discussed the construction of the dynamics in such well-known places as the preface to *Moll Flanders* and "Robinson Crusoe's Preface" in *Serious Reflections . . . of Robinson Crusoe*. A character in *A New Family Instructor* (1727) argues that "for some Ages, it was the most usual, if not the only way of Teaching in the World; the brightest Part of Oratory, and was used in Cases of the last Moment, as the most Persuasive" (p. 53). Here summarized is Defoe's *apologia*; it is "the brightest," liveliest, most effective kind of writing, perhaps "the only Way of Teaching." The measure of good writers, according to Defoe, is their ability to tell a good story that makes a point.

The precedent for the writing of fables that Defoe cited most often was "our Saviour," although he brought classical and even Near-Eastern examples to bear as well. John Bunyan's "Apology for His Book" answered the objection "But it is feigned," similarly:

> Were not God's laws,
> His gospel laws, in olden times held forth
> By types, shadows, and metaphors?
>   Art thou for something rare and profitable?
> Wouldst thou see a truth within a fable?
> Art thou forgetful?
> . . . .
> Then read my fancies; they will stick like burs.
>   [*Pilgrim's Progress*]

Defoe, too, believed that well-told fables imprinted a lesson on the mind that was both durable and moving. He said, "By the Doctrine of Idea's it is allow'd, That to Describe a Thing, Ugly, Horrid, and Deform'd, is the best way to get Abhorrence in the Minds of the People—and this was the Method . . . in the Ages of Hieroglyphics, when Things were more accurately Describ'd by Emblems and Figures than Words; and even our Saviour himself took the Method . . . By Parables and Similitudes."[3] Defoe had been taught to regard fiction favorably since his youth. Charles Morton, his Newington Green teacher, explained, "Romances, parables, or fables that have no truth In the Matter, but Morall honesty In the Designe; As also Enlargement of stories, by variety of phrases, manner of expression (Provided they are no part of a testimony) are noe Lyes, but Ingenious Poesy (—In the propper Notion, distinct from the art of versifying, or poetry) or handsome Oratory, The better to Inculcate the virtue, or expose the vice they Designe to represent and are of singular Use in all Discourses."[4] Morton, like Defoe, found them beautiful, appropriate, and of "singular Use" in *all* kinds of writing. He was very close to Renaissance thinkers such as Sir Phillip Sidney, who wrote in his *Defense of Poesy*: "though he recount things not true, yet because he telleth them not for true, he lieth not. . . . with a tale forsooth he cometh to you, with a tale which holdeth children from play, and old men from the chimney corner." One of Defoe's most extended discussions of writing makes the same points. Fictions "told only the Design to deceive the Reader" are evil and rightly called lies, he said, but "even such we call *Romances*" that make solid "Impressions on the Mind" by recommending good and making wickedness abhorrent are "the most pungent Way of writing. . . ."[5] Like Morton, Defoe called them "handsome Oratory."

A lifetime of thinking like this and reading, writing, and collecting stories went into *Robinson Crusoe*, and the man who had learned to point out the economic, religious, and ethical facets to political issues concisely and clearly was ready to do a similar kind of synthesis in a book that combined the pilgrim, travel adventure, and memoir forms. He was ready to create a deeply spiritual character facing physical danger and economic opportunity with a nearly endless number of symbolic possibilities, both religious and secular. The shipwrecked man struggling for survival *and* meaning carried a powerful message about the possibilities for prose fiction.

What Defoe brought in knowledge, experience, piety, understanding of the book trade, and even theory made him absolutely singular. He was an activist, an analyst, and an artist. So intense as all three, so successful, and yet so irredeemably outside the literary establishment was he that he was free to create and transform. In pamphlet after pamphlet, he had experimented with dialogue, point of view, forms of fiction, and symbol. He had brought economic, political, and religious explanations and arguments to life with the techniques of imaginative literature. He had written histories of events and twelve biographical or pseudobiographical works. He had been a participant in two of the most prominent religious controversies of his time. He had read news releases daily and added to his considerable youthful knowledge of geography, history, and political theory by writing about wars, trade, treaties, and international relations. *The Consolidator* (1705), *The Memoirs of Count Tariff* (1713), and *The Memoirs of Major Ramkins* (1719) are full scale fictions, while *The Memoirs of John, Duke of Melfort* (1714), *The Family Instructor* (1715), and others are more fiction than exposition.

The publication of new editions of William Dampier's *New Voyage round the World* (1717), of Woodes Rogers's *Cruising Voyage round the World* (1718), and of a number of new travel books such as Daniel Beeckman's *Voyage to and from the Island of Borneo* (1718) came at a time when Defoe was not deeply engaged with any single issue but writing on a variety of subjects, including the politics and personalities within George I's court, Jacobitism, and the Bangorian controversy.[6] The variety of some of his 1718 titles suggests the nature of his writing: *Memoirs of the Life . . . of Daniel Williams*, *Miserere Cleri*, *A Vindication of the Press*, *The Family Instructor, Part II*, *A Continuation of Letters Written by a Turkish Spy*, and *A History of the Last Session of the Present Parliament*. Equally suggestive are his publishers. He did the Williams life for Curll, who produced a very large number of semi-respectable biographies in a few years,[7] and saw it sold by six booksellers, including Matthews who published *The Family Instructor* and would sponsor *Due Preparations for the Plague Year*. He published eight works with Boreham, including one he said was sponsored by the booksellers, and five with Warner who would join with others to publish *The Memoirs of a Cavalier*, *Captain Singleton*, and *Roxana*. He was, of course, working for Nathaniel Mist, and his *History of the Reign of King George* came out under Mist's imprint. Taylor, who would own the copyright for *Robinson Crusoe*, published the political allegory *Continuation of Letters Written by a Turkish Spy*. Defoe was obviously deeply involved in the publishing world, knew which booksellers specialized in particular types of books, and was accepting commissions.

The Stationers' Register shows that travel and geography books were selling better than anything other than religious works. Almost all contemporary travel accounts had strong religious content whether this was in repeated references to God's creations and care or in extended accounts of the narrator's religious experiences and beliefs. Robert Knox's *An Historical Relation of Ceylon* begins, for example, with the "Argument" that ends, "God set mee free from that Captivity . . . to whome be all Glory and prayse."[8] Defoe surely knew that many of the Renaissance travel books had been written to encourage exploration and colonization, and he was concerned with Britain's stagnant economy and factionalized colonial policy. A lifetime of reading gave him ample material and familiarity with the genre.[9] He had recently completed a conduct book, which had encouraged him to think about the uses and techniques of fiction, and had written a virtuoso list of at least a dozen pamphlets on the Bangorian controversy. Twenty years of combining moral and fable came together. The man who had been unable to hear a Bible passage without imagining how it would feel to be in that situation, how a person would act, and what the resolutions might be, and who turned to story whenever he wanted to emphasize his most important points or to fix an "idea" took the most striking common denominators of the best of the travel narratives and gave us the gripping human fantasy of the man alone on an island.[10]

Robinson Crusoe is far more than a good story, however. It still holds our attention because it absorbs and integrates so many of the most significant strains in western thought. Here are the ambivalences and ambitions that continue to occupy the mind. Cast into improbable and extraordinary circumstances time after time, Crusoe reacts in recognizably human and ordinary ways even as his thoughts reveal the diverse threads that lead to our opinions and decisions. Time after time, we are struck by the fullness of the mind Defoe has given Crusoe. Crusoe is truly what his critics have found him to be: adventurous, economic, political, religious, and yet ordinary. Almost any paragraph selected shows the rich blending of ideas: "I made abundance of things, even without Tools, and some with no more Tools than an Adze and a Hatchet, which perhaps were never made that way before, and that with infinite Labour. . . . But my Time or Labour was little worth, and so it was as well employ'd one way as another" (1:77). Here Crusoe notes his accomplishment with pride ("perhaps were never made that way before") and considers what we call "cost effectiveness" even as he tells us how he built his table and chairs and how it felt to build them that way. Society has taught him to compare the value of the time and effort with the worth of the product.

> . . . I came to an Opening . . . and the Country appear'd so fresh, so green, so flourishing . . . that it looked like a Planted Garden.
>   I descended a little on the Side of that delicious Vale, surveying it with a secret Kind of Pleasure, (tho' mixt with my other afflicting Thoughts) to think that this was all my own, that I was King and Lord of all this Country indefeasibly, and had a Right of Possession; and if I could convey it, I might have it in Inheritance. . . . [1:114]

Again we have the consciousness of the immediate, the physical experience joined inextricably to the feelings the experience awakened. Defoe was writing at the time when beautiful English formal gardens were highly valued, and he himself had helped his Scottish friends design gardens. The beauty and order of the scene remind Crusoe of England, and he feels again his exile but, more strongly, his ownership. His words, "King . . . indefeasibly," call to mind the political controversies of his age. For three generations Englishmen had quarreled over what constituted an "indefeasible," inalterable and uncancellable, right to rule, and here Crusoe finds it. Men of Defoe's time believed in the consent if not the design of Providence in the determination of kings, and Crusoe's "King and Lord" rings with biblical echoes. Finally, he remembers that this land could be an "inheritance," the day-to-day, legal embodiment of the right to rule, the most ordinary "right" a man had with his possessions.

"I might have rais'd Ship Loadings of Corn. . . . I had Timber enough to have built a Fleet of Ships. I had Grapes enough to have made Wine, or to have cur'd into Raisins, to have loaded that Fleet, when they had been built" (1:148); and "With these Reflections I work'd my Mind up, not only to the Will of God in the present Disposition of my Circumstances; but even to a sincere Thankfulness for my Condition . . . " (1:152).

Here Crusoe is master of his environment; he can produce far more than he can eat or use, and he muses about the products that England valued highly at that time. For example, writers separated as widely in time as Sir William Temple and Alexander Pope wrote about the patriotic duty English landowners had to raise trees for the Navy, and tracts such as *Mr. Williamson's Memoirs* (1717) explained how to make the Royal Navy's shipyards more productive and profitable. The detail of Defoe's economic thought is present in the idea of building a fleet and then loading the ships. Immediately after he surveys his island's wealth, Crusoe turns to religious "reflections" that are as mixed and predictable as his secular thoughts.

In the pages that follow he can be the seventeenth-century preacher who draws a moral: "all the good Things of this World, are no farther good to us, than they are for our Use." He can be superstitious enough to note the coincidence of significant dates in his life. He can be melodramatic enough to compare himself to Elijah fed by the ravens. He can be practical enough to see that he has every reason to expect more suffering on the island and spiritual enough to find the hand of "Providence" in the good fortune that brought the ship to the island. He can borrow from the language and aspirations of his religious upbringing to long for a "Mind entirely composed by resignation to the Will of God," and he is aware that he has led a "dreadful" life "perfectly destitute of the Knowledge and Fear of God."

In these passages, we see the elements of a wide variety of literary and subliterary forms, such as travel literature, spiritual autobiography, adventure story, pirate story, and memoirs, but we can also see that Defoe blended basically mono-referential forms into a fiction that satisfied readers' desires for adventure and for emotional exploration.[11] The "infinite Variety" and exciting incidents of travel books are more than setting and plot, however; they become the experiences upon which Robinson Crusoe broods. Crusoe is a rather ordinary, modern, secular man who asks if things happen in the world, and specifically to him, by accident or by design. He is a capitalist working out his relationship to God. Drawn to an active, enterprising, acquisitive life in spite of his desire to obey his parents and despite an understanding of the blessings of the "middle station," he builds a fortune on a Brazilian plantation and is on a slaving trip when he is shipwrecked. He is a castaway in the midst of the most active, most optimistic, and most opportunity-rich part of his life, and to endure that state of isolation for twenty-eight years while other men became rich and successful and lived out ordinary lives could drive the stongest men mad, and here we can see the enormous complexity of Defoe's novel, as he unites the economic ambitions, the psychological strains, and the most controversial religious tenets.

First of all, Crusoe is a realistic psychological being whose efforts to maintain his sanity are heroic, both in his large and small actions. To notice their number and variety is to see the degree of Defoe's artistry. In some ways, the small touches are the most impressive: the way Crusoe plans the day's work, the stick on which he records the passing days, the triumph he feels when he can predict the rainfall and the seasonal changes in order to produce better crops. He tells us, for example, "That I was very seldom idle; but having regularly divided my Time, according to several daily Employments." His struggle against despair recurs and changes in intensity, waxing and waning in spite of his efforts to moderate his emotions along with his life. Very late in his time on the island he again falls into the despair of the early week; he exclaims, "O that there had been but one or two; nay, or but one Soul sav'd out of this Ship, to have escap'd to me, that I might but have had one Companion, one Fellow-Creature to have spoken to me. . . . I believe I repeated the Words, *O that it had been but One*! a thousand Times . . . ," and this thought drives him to desperation (1:217-18).

Within this context and running parallel to Crusoe's efforts to find ways to occupy, to order, and to give meaning to the hours of his days, Crusoe's spiritual quest assumes thematic centrality, coherence, and credibility. Crusoe's initial question to God is the question of Job: why do I *suffer*? why do *I* suffer? He asks why a good God would "ruin" a "poor creature" and repeatedly describes himself as "singl'd out." Crusoe's religious questions are universal and yet gain intensity because of the seriousness with which his contemporaries discussed them. His pressing need to know if things happen to him by accident or by design summarizes questions about the existence and nature of God as well as about God's actions in the world. His distress at not being able to determine if events, dreams, and even thoughts are signs or messages from God raises the same issues. His questions and his answers are in many ways trite; philosophers and psychologists have long said that man would create God if there were none, and we can see this novel in the context of the age that constantly struggled against its own deep scepticism. When Addison admonishes his readers to remember the moment in which they felt faith and cling to that memory (*Spectator* no. 465), he speaks for a nation that wanted to believe in God as they thought their parents had and yet could not "prove" God's existence or rest on the assumptions of an earlier generation.

Were Crusoe not so ordinary and so worldly, these religious themes would have made *Robinson Crusoe* into a fable or a sermon. Instead they become part of a human being's desperate attempt to remain sane and to make sense of an experience harrowing almost beyond our imagination. *Robinson Crusoe* went through four editions in four months and opened new possibilities and directions for prose fiction.

Within a few months, Defoe himself published *Farther Adventures* and *The Life, Adventures and Pyracies of Captain Singleton*; soon William Chetwood published *The Voyages, Dangerous Adventures, and imminent Escapes of Captain Richard Falconer* (1720). All of these books are "adventures" and align themselves with that older form, but tighten the plot with a single, somewhat complex protagonist. The powerful bookseller Chetwood recognized some of the originality of *Robinson Crusoe* but was more aware of its blended nature. Taken with the opening pages, the preface of *Falconer* echoes *Robinson Crusoe* so closely as to approximate parody. *Crusoe* begins, "I was born in the Year 1632, in the City of York," and Chetwood's novel begins, "I was born at a Town call'd *Bruton*, in *Somersetshire*, of Parents tolerably well to pass in the World." Falconer's father says, "tell me what Calling you like best." The flippancy of this line and the compression of the opening suggest that Chetwood's preface carried a message for insiders. Chetwood has Falconer assert in the preface that he publishes "to get Money" because he has trouble balancing his budget and "to appear in print." Here he suggests the irony that men like

Chetwood must have felt in Defoe's authorship. He underscores the discrepancy between the pious assertions, such as *Crusoe's* prefatorial "to justify and honour the Wisdom of Providence," and the mundane motives Defoe had for writing.[12] Charles Gildon, whose fictional *The Post-boy Rob'd of his Mail* (1692), *The Golden Spy* (1709), and *Miscellanea Aurea* (1721) had been modest successes, reacted in the same way; Defoe simply did not deserve his success or any praise for his moral sentiments.[13] The anonymous author of *The Highland Rogue* (1723) insists that he is telling "Actions" as opposed to the "Adventures of a *Robinson Crusoe*, a *Colonel Jack*, or a *Moll Flanders*."[14] This author also attacks Alexander Smith's *The History of the Lives and Robberies of the most Noted Highway-Men* (1713) and cites Josephus as his model. His point is that speeches could be made up, but men and actions have to be "real." He is summarizing an opinion stated (if not rigorously followed) in such fictions as Sarah Butler's *Milesian Tales* (1719), in which Butler gives her historical sources and explains how she was willing to select names for some of her characters and make up dialogue but would not conclude with the conventional marriage because she could find no evidence that her lovers did not die single.

Defoe shook off such veridical demands and eliminated the conventional names, vocabulary, settings, and other signals of fiction. In fact, he specifically contrasted *Robinson Crusoe* to standard travel books in *Farther Adventures*, and *Roxana* to tales of "Knight Errantry," and explained what he would have written had he been writing in the older genres. Chetwood and others saw that he had unified travel fiction's observations and reflections, thereby elevating character.

Penelope Aubin, who seems to have seen the originality of *Robinson Crusoe* more clearly then her contemporaries, explicitly aligns *The Strange Adventures of the Count de Vinevil* (1721) with Defoe and reconsiders the standard authorial claim to a truthful narrative: "As for the Truth of what this Narrative contains, since *Robinson Crusoe* has been so well receiv'd, which is more improbable, I know no reason why this should be thought a Fiction."[15] *Count de Vinevil*, she says, is more probable than *Robinson Crusoe* and, therefore, should not be dismissed as a mere fiction. She takes note that Defoe has done something new, that he has redefined the relationship between life and the novel. He has rewritten the contract between the author and the reader. By choosing two of the most autobiographical forms and by then insisting upon the special kind of truth in *Robinson Crusoe*, he creates a new literary type. Instead of reporting experiences or feelings, rather than imitating life or art, he invents an imitation of reporting and imitating. He uses social and historical actuality to create illusion rather than to render accurately.

Aubin notes in her preface that "Religious Treatises grow mouldly on the Booksellers Shelves in the Back-Shops" and "that the few that honour Virtue, and wish well to our Nation, ought to study to reclaim our Giddy Youth; and since Reprehensions fail, try to win them to Vertue, by Methods where Delight and Instruction may go together." In her story, she says, "Divine Providence manifests itself in every Transaction. . . ."[16] The incorporation of the conduct book and even religious tract into the travel adventure succeeded for Aubin[17] and numerous other writers throughout the century. For example, the anonymous author of *The Jamaica Lady* (1720) distinguished this "novel" from translations and from those based on "some larger history" and argues that this novel is superior for it does not paint people in general but attempts to portray individuals. Poets had long glorified the attempt to go beyond the accurate rendering of the surface and used analogies to painting, as Dryden did in his "To the Pious Memory of Mrs. Killigrew"; contemporaries would have understood the *Jamaica* author's point.

Aubin also recognized the appeal of an English character. In the preface to *The Life of Madam de Beaumont* (1721) Aubin asserted that the story was for the "true-born English," which by being so labeled also revealed Defoe's influence on her. Ned Ward had said that native stories ought to appeal to his countrymen as much as foreign ones, but Robinson Crusoe was the most thoroughly English character yet produced. He had English prejudices, ambitions, skills, and ambivalences. He even set about reproducing his homeland on his island.[18] In 1721 Defoe was still well known as the author of *The True-Born Englishman*, and Aubin's phrase could not help but call the poem and its brave, virtue-loving Englishmen to mind. Madam de Beaumont concluded, "Such Histories as these ought to be published in this Age above all others, and if we would be like the worthy Persons whose Story we have here read, happy and bless'd with all Human Felicity; let us imitate their Virtues, since that is the only way to make us dear to God and Man, and the most certain and noble Method to perpetuate our Names, and render our Memories immortal, and our Souls eternally happy."[19] Here she explicitly paraphrased the theme of Defoe's popular poem: only virtue makes a man and a nation great and happy. She assumed the same aspirations and attitudes. After 1720, of course, more often than not English novels had English characters and the setting came to be England.

The single most original aspect of *Robinson Crusoe* did not escape Defoe's contemporaries. Jane Barker, for example, contrasted her *Patch-Work Screen* (1723) to "HISTORIES at Large" that "are so Fashionable in this Age; viz. *Robinson Crusoe*, and *Moll Flanders*; *Colonel Jack*, and *Sally Salisbury*; with many other *Heroes* and *Heroines*."[20] Chetwood, for all his chagrin at Defoe's success, borrowed from the opening of *Robinson Crusoe* in order to achieve the same advantages of sympathy and unity. Not only was his hero from a similar family, but also by the second page Falconer's family had been established as reputable and middle-class, and he must earn his own living and wanted to go to sea despite the family's opposition. Chetwood's borrowings were unmistakable, as this sample shows:

from *Robinson Crusoe*:
"He told me [the sea] was for men of desperate Fortunes on one Hand, or of aspiring, superior Fortunes on the other, who went abroad upon Adventures, to rise by Enterprize, and make themselves famous in Undertakings of a Nature out of the common Road" (2)

from *Captain Falconer*:
"he would often say, *Dick*, stay where you are, you know not the Hazard and Dangers attend a maritime Life" (2)

"He press'd me earnestly, and in the most affectionate manner, not to play the young Man" (4)

"Think no more of going to Sea, for I'll not have it so; I know it is only a Desire of Youth" (2)

"It was not till almost a Year after this that I broke loose, tho' in the mean time I continued obstinately deaf to all Proposals of settling to Business" (6)

"I liv'd two Years longer with him in Expectation of his Mind altering" (3)

The "history at large" offered some of the satisfactions of history, biography, and autobiography, all of which provided social contexts, concern with motive, and exemplary lives. Because of the opportunity for psychological depth and emotional exploration offered by *Robinson Crusoe*, the novella with its self-absorbed lovers with their elemental desires and conflicts might have found itself a genre apart or even died out had it not been for the second momentous publishing event of 1719: Eliza Haywood's *Love in Excess*.[21] Just as Defoe had drawn heavily from other forms of fiction, so did Haywood, and she moved the novel in the same directions as Defoe, but in a different way. If we can subordinate the impact of the extravagant tropical bedrooms and exaggerated passions, we see a carefully structured, although primitive *Bildungsroman*. D'Elmont is to be educated in Haywood's favorite subject, what love is; in order to be so, he suffers and grows as a human being and gives the narrative more focus and broader psychological and social concerns than the earlier love stories by Behn and Manley. In brief, D'Elmont "coldly" plots to seduce Amena, who is sent to a convent, marries Aloisa for her "Quality and vast Possessions," learns ideal virtuous love from Melliora, but must be punished for his adulterous schemes, wanders miserably over Europe, and resists such temptresses as Ciamara, who poisons herself before he is allowed to marry Melliora and have "a numerous and hopeful Issue."

Both of the 1719 novels are structurally "histories at large." They are long, unified by a central character with some psychological depth, posit complex and important relationships between the characters and society, substitute adventures and satisfactorily motivated, interpolated tales for the popular, loosely joined collections, and combine well-established forms. Characters change, develop, and reform; the work's central consciousness is more important than plot events and that consciousness assumes dimensions that reflect the complexity of human nature, moral questions, and society.

Defoe undoubtedly marked the success of *Love in Excess*, published, by the way, by Chetwood, Francklin, and Roberts. By 1722, when *Moll Flanders* and *Colonel Jack* appeared, he had seen the rise of Eliza Haywood and the accommodations made by Chetwood, Barker, Aubin, Davys, and others to combine the strategies of *Robinson Crusoe* with those of *Love in Excess*.[22] Some of Haywood's other novels competed in popularity with Defoe's—notably *The British Recluse, Idalia, The Injur'd Husband*, and *Lasselia. Idalia*, the "Unfortunate Mistress," had been expanded from 74 to 209 pages and was in a second edition in 1723. Defoe's novels increasingly emphasized the "history at large" aspects rather than travel adventures. For example, *Colonel Jack* was more like *Robinson Crusoe* than *Farther Adventures* or even *Captain Singleton* and was more ambitious than the novel with which it is more often paired, *Moll Flanders*.

Jack is attempting to marry well, to find a vocation, and to establish a satisfactory life in which he can take pride even as he is forced to grapple with a number of contemporary social and political situations. Unlike the Cavalier, his comprehension of situations and options is limited and, unlike H.F. in *Journal of the Plague Year*, he is not deep enough to explore sophisticated questions about God's relationship to the world. The pattern of Defoe's novels is the pattern of the development of the most characteristic English fiction. He places his protagonists into what Ian Watt calls "a stable and cohesive pattern of social relations."[23] He attempts to encompass more and more of the world, to draw in the social, political, philosophical, religious, and economic debates of his time. He is attempting to do what Thomas Hardy does with Jude, and he, too, chooses a character whose limitations will serve to underscore the complexity of the world and the difficulties of modern man.

In Defoe's novels, we find the characteristics of the mainstream English novel. Defoe found specificity in economic geographies, emotional depth in spiritual autobiographies, easy movement from the external world to the internal in travel adventures, concentration on the individual in crime literature, and shifting juxtapositions of fiction and contemporary event in political and fictional works such as the secret histories and French memoirs. Rosalie Colie, who dates the Renaissance from Petrarch through Swift, has pointed out that both the recognition of the complexity of human nature and the drive "to collect and transmit all knowledge" are distinctively characteristic of that time. She sees *King Lear* and *Paradise Lost* as the products of this drive, and it is equally accurate to see *Robinson Crusoe* this way. Her emphasis on forms and books well known to Defoe, such as *Don Quixote*, Burton's *Anatomy of Melancholy*—which she finds a *"florilegium"*—including versions of sermons and travels, Raleigh's and Agrippa d'Aubigné's histories, historical registers, and the *sylvae*, underscores the nonclassical but venerable concept of literature that Defoe held.[24] This view is open-ended because the traveler might travel again, the cartographer might map another continent—indeed, a new river or a new country might be discovered— the author of the spiritual autobiography could not describe his own death, and the collector of didactic kingship anecdotes could never record the last one. Economics, politics, religion, and personality were in dynamic relationships.

Robinson Crusoe, however, is different from Colie's two final examples, because in it Defoe blends the forms upon which he draws in such ways that a new genre, popular and promising enough to be canonized almost immediately, is born. As Ian Watt said, Defoe introduced a new subject, and other critics have reminded us that Defoe writes about the recurrent concerns of the English novel—the self in society, marriage and money, alienation and loneliness, personality under stress, guilt, and rags-to-riches.[25] Defoe's greatest contribution, however, may be his insight into the great problems of the early English novel: form and style. Indeed, when we define the novel, we often think in terms of the very characteristics most original and prominent in Defoe's fiction: its contemporaneity, its mixed and untidy form, its concentration upon the life of an individual, its formal realism, and its probing of the individual's psychological interaction with the empirical world, which makes that world representational even as it is referential.

Defoe habitually wrote from the first person point of view and was accustomed to assuming voices and to spinning a story out over several numbers of a periodical or throughout a political crisis. All of the titles of his novels include form-words that he used for polemical purposes. For example, he wrote *The Memoirs of a Cavalier*, *A Journal of the Plague Year*, the *life* of Singleton and of Crusoe, and the *history* of Jack and of Roxana. He, like so many of the earliest fiction writers, used the first-person point of view for all of his novels and insisted upon the truth that a personal, eyewitness account would bear. His novels, then, became pseudo-autobiographical and, in order to maintain the pretense, took on the characteristics of immediacy, familiarity, subjectivity, and structural untidiness. As a result, they gained the means to explore the character's inner life in great depth even as they presented adventures and experiences in the physical world. All of these characteristics continued to be important parts of our conception of the novel.

The shape of the English novel often reflects the shape of the life it describes. Because the nonfiction relatives of Defoe's forms provide this model, we often fail to recognize how easily he moves between his character's thoughts and experiences and how effectively he communicates the psychic being of even the least reflective characters. The realistic sounds made by the African animals become the symbols of Singleton's fear and awareness that he is in a strange, alien land, vast and unknown beyond imagination. The screams and cries in *A Journal of the Plague Year* seem both disembodied and massed and represent H.F.'s fear and the way London has become a foreign land to him. Singleton stands near the center of the wide part of the continent of Africa, looks ahead at a "horrour," remembers that he has just passed through a "horrour," and knows that he has but four days of supplies with him. This realization takes but a few lines, and yet it gives us a detailed description of the landscape and immediate understanding of his awe and weariness and, finally, fortitude.

Just as "novel" is characterized by its ability to move rapidly and smoothly between the external world and the character's thoughts, so it can recognize the power of the past. Defoe shapes his characters in part by giving them a personal as well as a national past. In *Robinson Crusoe*, *Memoirs of a Cavalier*, and *A Journal of the Plague Year* Defoe explicitly draws upon the Puritan past as it intersects the secularism and scepticism of the Restoration. That his characters find the faith of the Cromwellians and the most conservative of the plague victims ultimately unsatisfactory deepens his books because he shows his characters finding pathos, loss, disillusionment, and uncertainty more often than finding liberation or new certainty. The greatest of Defoe's characters vibrate deeply to their own personal histories as well as to their country's. Crusoe's and Roxana's tormenting guilt comes from the mingling of religious symbolism assimilated into the fiber of their minds with the consciousness of mistakes. The Puritan mind has given Crusoe the images of himself as Jonah, as the prodigal son, as the recalcitrant, petulant rebel. It has given Roxana the conception of the "Blast of Heaven." Singleton, Jack, Moll—each character looks back on a "dreadful life" and finds the sum nearly unbearable. The very list of sins that Moll enumerates to the minister seems to be nearly too long for the telling, numerous beyond the time available for the minister to hear her, and Singleton's despair is one of the most extended treatments of suicidal impulses in eighteenth-century literature. The personal past shaped in part by a cultural past is the most consistent source of psychological stress in Defoe's characters.

Defoe began to write prose fiction at a time when dramatists were seeking an artistic, appropriate, but more realistic language for a new time. The prose models available to him were as unsatisfactory as the bombast of heroic tragedy was to his generation. The deliberate artificiality of romances, novellas, *Euphues'* descendants, and even the rogue literature; the biblical and allegorical language of spiritual autobiography, pilgrim narrative, and homilies; and translations from Italian, French, Spanish, and Portuguese offered Defoe far less than the language of political treatises, periodicals, and conduct books. These nonfiction forms gave Defoe a style that was clear, straightforward, and yet capable of using metaphor, allegory, multiple points of view, and a number of other fictional strategies. The competition for readers of political argument was intense, and Defoe had learned the necessity for "liveliness," contemporaneity, and variety. Long accustomed to using dialogue, irony, imagery, analogy, and parable, to creating emblems and symbols, and to using history or contemporary places to sketch in a connotative setting, he developed the "middle style" of a novel that later writers have recognized and found of lasting value.

Defoe's style made him a great formal realist.[26] He does give us the streets, the objects, and the common events of his society, and he does seem to be reporting on human experience with a fullness and lack of manipulation that carries its own credibility. His work stands up well to the question consistently asked of fiction: how accurately does this novel reflect the time and describe the human condition.[27] His years as a journalist, his experience as a writer of lives that were designed to be published in periodicals or pamphlets, and his unequalled familiarity with the histories and travel literature of his time give him writing experience and knowledge unavailable to any writer before Melville. Whether he drew upon the pattern of crime literature, pirate biography, voyages to Ceylon, or accounts of the Great Northern War made little difference, for all depended upon an economical presentation of an exciting event in the present time, relied upon a variety of "strange and surprizing" incidents rather than upon the unity of plot and effect common to most poetry and drama, and reported not only events but also particular settings—readers knew that a crime was committed with a pistol on White Horse Lane, that a pirate took his first ship at a particular reading of latitude and longitude, that a ship coming from the New World was carrying rice, sugar, rum, and tobacco when it sank, and that the King of Sweden had 65,000 men at his command for the first battle of the year.

The particularity of historical detail exploited by Defoe contributed in unexpected ways to the very subjectivity and structural disorder of the novel. For example, the choice of detail depended upon the narrator even though travel literature had established a list of points to be covered, including topography, location of ports, major city, natural products, customs, and so on. Crusoe tells us several times in *Farther Adventures* that he is omitting things that are useful only to those who intend to travel, and Singleton is most interested in animals and natural things that can be used, for example, to build and to caulk a boat. Such selectivity reinforces the idea that Crusoe is an experienced, elderly traveler and that Singleton is fascinated by trees that yield a pitch substitute, alive to possibilities to save the labor of walking, and alert to the beauty and strangeness of the elephants, cats, birds, and other creatures.

A second way that particularity of historical detail contributed to the novelistic character of Defoe's work was that the reportorial nature of the forms he mimicked inclined him toward chronological presentation rather than toward the kind of artistic, thematic emphasis and studied composition that would have led to the aesthetic subordination of some topics in favor of others. Although each form met well-defined reader expectations and even had formulaic elements, all rejected the careful formal patterns and aesthetically pleasing structures that we find in some of the novels we admire so much by Eliot, Hardy, and James. Even retrospective narrators could not order their lives and recognize climax as well as Fielding's grand conductor or Austen's wry observer. Genuine autobiography is often admired for revealing more than the writer intends or even understands; in order to reproduce the pleasure of these biographical and autobiographical forms, Defoe needed some of the disorder of the forms. Later novelists have struggled with the critical demand for structurally beautiful novels, but even those who often achieved it often conclude by describing the novel in terms that remind us of *Robinson Crusoe*. Henry James, for example, in the preface to *Roderick Hudson* said,

[It] was my first attempt at a novel . . . . I recall again the quite uplifted sense with which my idea . . . permitted me at last to put quite out to sea. I had but hugged the shore . . . bumping about, to acquire skill, in the shallow waters and sandy coves of the "short story" . . . the breath of the spice-islands [seemed] to be already in the breeze. Yet it must even then have begun for me too, the ache of fear, that was to become so familiar, of being unduly tempted and led on by "developments"; which is but the desperate discipline of the question involved in them. They are of the very essence of the novelist's process . . . but they impose on him, through the principle of continuity that rides them, a proportionate anxiety. Up to what point is such and such a development indispensable to the interest? Where, for the complete expression of one's subject, does a particular relation stop . . . ?

Really, universally, relations stop nowhere. . . . [The novelist] is in the perpetual predicament that the continuity of things is the whole matter . . . . [28]

That is the discovery of Defoe's art and the distinctive lesson of his form.

That Defoe is a great formal realist and a master at reproducing the physical world of his characters does not necessarily mean that he had to sacrifice the kind of imaginative representations of the world that novelists use to reach deeper insights about experience and about the nature of the world. In fact, the very lack of introspection in the young Singleton helps us to see the callousness and immorality in the world, and the absence in Moll of the kind of emotional agonizing that Crusoe does reinforces our sense of her fortitude and the world's indifference. Time after time, Defoe isolates his characters and has them invent civilization all over, as he does most obviously with Crusoe and with Singleton, but also with Moll and with Jack. They invent ways to meet basic needs, they form governments, and they stratify society. Crusoe's island is not Lilliput, of course, but it does represent and comment upon English government and the nature of man. Moll Flanders is not Bigger Thomas, but she shows the destructive distance between the rich and the poor and her "life" criticizes her society; even her trial is as prejudiced, as predetermined, and even as political as his.

Defoe's novels reflect the fact that the novel was becoming an increasingly psychological form even as it clung to its referentiality and "density of specification."[29] He probes deeper and deeper into the ways that people think and respond to situations. Crusoe does, after all, embody the *form* of the spiritual autobiography, which was recognized as mimicking *the* path to salvation; in contrast, H.F. puzzles and reasons, Moll sometimes seems to be an unreliable reporter of external events, and Roxana moves farther and farther into her own private, inner world. The language of Crusoe is more traditionally biblical, more repetitious, and more expository than that of *Roxana*. Defoe increasingly creates private "emblems" and symbols as he does with Newgate Prison in *Moll Flanders* and the Turkish costume in *Roxana*. With growing daring, he begins to exploit secular themes (as he does in *Colonel Jack*) and to use fiction to collapse time in order to bring history to bear on human psychology and current events (as he does in *The Memoirs of a Cavalier*). He begins to play social, legal, and religious transgressions off against each other until he creates Roxana, a character who, if she breaks the law at all, is a "white collar" criminal, sins rather than commits crimes, and feels more pursued than either of the "notorious criminals" Moll and Singleton. Relationships become increasingly complex and psychological; William Walters and Singleton, Amy and Roxana, and the characters who have lived Moll's and Jack's own stories as her mother and his tutor have become vehicles for the development of character and theme.

The English novel has consistently developed great characters who feel limited, confined, and even alienated from their societies. Rather than finding their ideals reflected or their aspirations aided by social institutions, they find hypocrisy, corruption, and obstructionism. Perhaps no writer besides Dickens explores his idea in as many thematic and stylistic ways as does Defoe. Because of this conflict, the very act of defining the self becomes problematic in English society. If the character does not feel that society's place for him or her is correct, then who is he? After all, "place" is definition, determinant of education, occupation, recreations, and aspirations. What happens to the Bettys who cannot bear the thought of a lifetime of bedmaking and hearth scrubbing? to the Crusoes who feel a good trade would be as constricting as an out-of-the-way corner of a rural cottage? Educated beyond their stations, with ambitions beyond their expectations, they feel that they may be rebelling not simply against their stratified society but against the order of God's world denoted by their births. Without birth, money, education, religion, or the other tokens of society, many of Defoe's characters are nearly without identity, for "beggar" and "rabble" and "charity children" are amorphous terms reducing those they denote to indistinguishable parts of a dispensable group. In defining themselves, they must come not only to understand but also to redefine society's tokens of value until, in the words of Timothy J. Reiss, they are reconciled with society and society with them.[30] Later writers simplified the task by building in a fortunate discovery of a titled parent that elevated one character to the place of the beloved, as Fielding and Burney do, or by substituting a clear, superior moral value for a social value, as Richardson does in *Pamela*. Defoe takes a more difficult route. He attempts to make his readers accept ability, courage, leadership, and some combination of such qualities as equalizers and definers, and then he complicates his task by refusing to obscure the fact that money is often the middle term in the act of reconciliation. The result is a harsh vision of human nature, unpleasantly unlike the satisfactions of finding "virtue rewarded" in the good-hearted, the ebullient, and the pious.

Most readers would agree with Anthony Burgess that "it is character that counts" in the novel. We come to the novel to see "human beings in action" and to look for complex psychology and a story that grows from the clash of characters with ideas.[31] Defoe's clear apprehension of the complex relationship between the individual and society often gives us a modern sense of the great space between the longing, thinking interior of a character and the faceless social being. For example, Moll's disguises can make her all but invisible in the crowds with which she mingles in order to steal; signs of the life within, such as Jack's tears during the plantation master's speech, always surprise the other characters. The constant misperceptions that lead to such things as Jack's first marriage and Jemmy and Moll's, the desperate drama played out by Moll and her seducer in the midst of the Colchester family, and the horror of the interior lives led by Moll while married to her brother and by Roxana when married to the Dutchman are but a few of the ways Defoe works with perception and interiority.

The failures and inadequacies of religious codes and social institutions throw the characters back on their own resources and determine that the novels will be in the form of *individual* quests for the meaning of life. Just as Crusoe creates his own civilization, he works out his relationship to God and an understanding of how God operates in the world. Similarly, Jack and Moll wander through the world searching not merely for a means of earning a living but also for a "place" that brings together their moral, social, and economic aspirations. These characters are placing themselves within a complex society and Providential order in the face of definitions bearing the weight of parents, citizens, culture, and tradition.

Writers more than critics have recognized the pathos and power of Defoe's preoccupation with meaning and identity. Almost at once, women writers found the plot and setting of *Robinson Crusoe* useful for the trials of the virgin victim and the separated family, but it was the protagonist's alienation from the roles designated for him that appealed to them most strongly. Fanny

Burney, for example, specifically compares Juliet in *The Wanderer* to Robinson Crusoe in her concluding paragraphs:

> Here, and thus felicitously, ended . . . the DIFFICULTIES of the WAN-DERER;—a being who had been cast upon herself; a female Robinson Crusoe, as unaided and unprotected . . . as that imaginary hero in his uninhabited island, and reduced either to sink . . . or to be rescued from famine and death by such resources as she could find, independently, in herself.
>
> Yet, even DIFFICULTIES such as [hers] are not insurmountable, where mental courage, operating through patience, prudence, and principle, supply physical force, combat disappointment, and keep the untamed spirits superiour to failure, and even alive to hope.[32]

For Penelope Aubin, Fanny Burney, and others, Defoe's characters—especially Robinson Crusoe—represented the courageous persons whose own spirit and ingenuity allowed them to exert unexpected strength of mind and of body. They saw that women were as unprepared for the experiences of adults in the world as Crusoe had been for his island and that they could usually anticipate as little help, "though in the midst of company," as Crusoe received. The experience of desolation, loneliness, alienation, and the desire to make something of a life against all odds and expectations came to be the great organizing principle of the novel for men as well as women. We find it in *Pamela*, in *Tom Jones*, in *Roderick Random*, and we still find it in novels by writers as different as Mark Twain, William Faulkner, Ralph Ellison, Saul Bellow, Bernard Malamud, Joyce Carol Oates, Doris Lessing, and John Updike.

Although Defoe occasionally apologized in his nonfiction for neglecting to do revisions, he does not do so for his novels. In them, we can see the characteristics we have come to admire in eighteenth-century prose. *Moll Flanders* alone illustrates Defoe's ability to use balance, fine "judgment," and the kinds of sentences that come from the century's awareness of the signification of words. Moll, for example, "learn'd by Imitation and enquiry" what the Colchester daughters "learn'd by Instruction and Direction." She tells us that until her seduction, she had "the Character" as well as "the Reputation" of virtue; Mother Midnight explains "that whether [Moll] was a Whore or a Wife" she would "pass for a Whore" until she left the house "at the Sign of the *Cradle.*" References to "Moll Cut-Purse" and "Bills of Fare" from Mother Midnight, which call to mind the Drury Lane whores' advertisement bills, strengthen referentiality even as they illuminate character. Defoe's characters may spin out tales in the loose idiomatic way Moll does when she tricks the mercer who accuses her of theft, but the language is basically unadorned and admirably vigorous and efficient.

Joseph Conrad said in the preface to *The Nigger of the "Narcissus"* that the writer's task was "by the power of the written word to make you hear, to make you feel—it is, before all, to make you see. That—and no more, and it is everything. If I succeed, you shall find there . . . encouragement, consolation, fear, charm—all you demand—and, perhaps, also that glimpse of truth for which you have forgotten to ask."[33] Above all, this is what Defoe attempted. He let us know what it would be like to see, to do, to feel. He offered experience and understanding, novelty and adventure, identification, and new insight. The way Defoe transformed mundane reality can be seen from comparing his work to a commonplace quotation from a contemporary of his, Josiah Woodward: "If we ask any thief, strumpet or other malefactor what it was that brought them to their wicked way of life, they often reply that it was their want of an honest employment, and that they did it to get bread. And 'tis very probable that sometimes they speak the truth."[34] Not only does Defoe create great characters from these types, but he also shows us the complexity of "sometimes they speak the truth." Sometimes they do, and sometimes they feel they do, and sometimes they know they have ceased to. Through his work we forget that they are thief and strumpet, as he substitutes compassion and analysis for cynicism. His characters become human, and, for a short time, we identify with a character very unlike ourselves who is both complex and apparently invested with free will. We see how difficult it is to cope with life and to make moral judgments. We see what Moll does, feel her dilemmas, and come away with new ideas and judgments because of the vicarious experience. Time after time, a highly visual scene is the perfect mirror of a character's emotions and an exact reproduction of a feeling the reader recognizes as true. Moll zigzags through the winding, narrow streets of the Old City after her first theft; Jack frantically tries to get his first money out of the tree; Roxana sorts her rags and weeps.

Defoe not only presents the immediate, the things we like to know, to see, and to understand, but he also offers us characters who finally find meaning, pattern, and value in life. Out of poverty, hardship, and disaster come success and faith. Defoe pits his characters against problems that have immense but still unmeasured power and puts them in situations that are painful to imagine. Robinson Crusoe is enslaved, shipwrecked, threatened by cannibals; Singleton is marooned, crosses a known but unmapped continent; Moll is seduced, married to her own brother, convicted, and sentenced to hang; Jack is a homeless, uneducated boy, transported, married to a drunk, guilty of treason; Roberts is alone on a ship with two children, nearly dies of fever on a foreign island. Those characters, who appeared to have promising futures, become like Jack and Singleton, and yet all make something of themselves and their lives.

In Defoe's novels we find vicarious experience and the true landscape that was to be the novel's. "The moral consciousness of a child is as much a part of life as the islands of the Spanish main, and the one sort of geography seems to me to have . . . 'surprises' . . . quite as much as the other," Henry James said.[35] Defoe provides both in *Colonel Jack* alone. "When I remember Moll Flanders and all her teeming and rich fecundity like a market-place where all that had survived up to that time must bide and pass [I can wish I had written that book]," William Faulkner wrote.[36] Depth of personality and a picture of courage and endurance emerge in all of Defoe's novels, capture the imagination, and continue to open possibilities to all who write novels.

NOTES

For full bibliographic information on works cited here, see the Bibliography, beginning on page 267.

1. The Bent and Genius of the Age

"The Bent and Genius of the Age is best known in a free Country, by the Pamphlets and Papers that come daily out, as the Sense of Parties, and sometimes the Voice of the Nation." Preface to White Kennet, *A Register and Chronicle Ecclesiastical and Civil* (London, 1728).

1. Samuel Johnson, *Adventurer* no. 115 for 11 December 1753, in *The Idler and The Adventurer*, Vol. 2. Similar modern statements abound; see, for example, Bertrand Bronson, *Facets of the Enlightenment*, pp. 5-6.

2. Howard Erskine-Hill, *The Augustan Idea in English Literature*, p. xi; and Paul Fussell, *The Rhetorical World of Augustan Humanism*, p. vii.

3. Daniel Defoe, *Farther Adventures*, 3: 177. Unless otherwise noted, all references to Defoe's novels are to the Shakespeare Head Edition.

4. Ian Watt's *The Rise of the Novel* and Alan D. McKillop's *The Early Masters of English Fiction* were pioneering works, in which both authors argued that "Defoe's contribution to fiction has never been fully analyzed, interpreted, or even identified" (McKillop, *Early Masters*, p. 1).

5. James Sutherland, *Daniel Defoe: A Critical Study*, p. 233; James Joyce, "Daniel Defoe," p. 7. I could cite many other examples from the time of Swift's "I have forgot his name" to Ian Watt's "he is perhaps a unique example of a great writer who was very little interested in Literature" (*The Rise of the Novel*, p. 70) and Ioan Williams's "he showed no interest in the themes and preoccupations we think of as typical of the fiction of the period" (*The Idea of the Novel in Europe, 1600-1800*, p. 147). Moreover, it is still considered acceptable to begin studies of the novel with Samuel Richardson.

6. Phillip Sidney, for example, in *The Defense of Poesy*, says of writers of moral, historical, and natural philosophy, "whether they properly be poets or no let grammarians dispute." Tzvetan Todorov reminds us that the present usage of the word *literature* "barely dates back to the nineteenth century" and suggests that no "structural" definition can be formulated ("The Notion of Literature").

7. Daniel Defoe, *A Vindication of the Press*. His comments on Pope are

241

typical of his sound judgments. He remarks early in Pope's career that he "has few Superiors in this Age" and praises the translation of the *Iliad*.

8. Richard Gilman describes this conception of fiction and calls it "outdated" (*The Confusion of Realms*, pp. 143-50).

9. Jean Hagstrum, *The Sister Arts*, p. 177.

10. Robert Scholes and Robert Kellogg, *The Nature of Narrative*, pp. 86-88 et passim.

11. On this view of the distinguishing work of the literary artist, see Henri Bonnet, "Dichotomy of Artistic Genres," in *Theories of Literary Genre*, pp. 6-7.

12. Elizabeth D. Ermarth discusses the growth of realism in some of these terms in *Realism and Consensus in the English Novel*, esp. pp. x-xi, 3, 5, 25, 41, 50, 57.

13. E.M. Forster, "Pattern and Rhythm" in *Myth and Method*, p. 122.

14. Norman Mailer, *Existential Errands*, p. ix, and *The Armies of the Night*, p. 284.

15. Daniel Defoe, *A Tour Thro' the Whole Island of Great Britain*, 1: 251.

2. Poetry

1. Frank Ellis, *Poems on Affairs of State*, 6: xxxi. Ellis also notes that more than one half the total number of lines are Defoe's, (p. xxxii). The more customary state is represented by Pat Rogers's *Augustan Vision*, which surveys the poets of Defoe's time without mention of him (pp. 109-21).

2. Although some of these names will be recognized only by the specialist, in their time all were respected and imitated; see, for example, Pope's compliment to them in lines 135-44 of *Epistle to Arbuthnot*. Garth is a good example of the change in reputation (see Ellis, *Poems*, 6: xxxiv). So popular was he that he even appears as a sympathetic conspirator in Mary Hearne's novel *The Female Deserters*.

3. Rachel Trickett, *The Honest Muse*, p. 85. Vivian de S. Pinto gives an example in "Rochester and Dryden," *Renaissance and Modern Studies* 5 (1961): 29-48.

4. Matthew Prior, *Satyr on the Poets*, lines 149-50; Peter Smithers, *The Life of Joseph Addison*, p. 146.

5. Defoe discusses the qualifications of a poet in *Vindication*, pp. 28-30.

6. William Congreve, "Epistle to the Right Honourable Charles Lord Halifax" in *The Complete Works of William Congreve*, 4: 139.

7. Aaron Hill, *Advice to the Poets*, in *A Complete Edition of the Poets of Great Britain*, ed. Robert Anderson, 8: 682.

8. See, for example, Ruth Wallerstein, *Studies in Seventeenth-Century Poetic*, p. 11.

9. Postscript to Charles Morton's *System of Logick*. I am grateful to the Massachusetts Historical Society for permission to quote from this manuscript.

10. Charles Morton, "Pneumaticks or the Doctrine of Spirits," p. 32, and preface to *System of Logick;* Samuel Wesley, preface to "An Epistle to a Friend concerning Poetry," and Daniel Defoe, *Review*, vol. 1, for 1705, sig. A3v. All references to the *Review* are from A.W. Secord's facsimile edition.

11. See, C.A. Moore, "Whig Panegyric Verse, 1700-1760," pp. 362, 370;

Ruth Nevo, *The Dial of Virtue*, pp. 6, 19; James D. Garrison, *Dryden and the Tradition of Panegyric*, pp. 254-56.

12. This discussion is based upon Joseph Summers, "Some Apocalyptic Strains in Marvell's Poetry" in *Tricentenary Essays in Honor of Marvell*, p. 187; George de F. Lord, ed., *Poems on Affairs of State*, 1: vii; Moore, "Whig Panegyric Verse," pp. 370-400; Nevo, *Dial of Virtue*, pp. 37-42, 96 et passim; Warren L. Cherniak, "The Heroic Occasional Poem"; Trickett, *Honest Muse*, p. 71; Wallerstein, *Studies*, 136-37.

13. Joseph Addison, "To Halifax," p. 50. Samuel Johnson quotes Richard Savage as saying that he wrote a poem on the occasion of Princess Anne's departure after marriage "'because it was expected from him' and he was not willing to bar his own prospects by any appearance of neglect" (*Life of Savage*).

14. Poets of that time seemed quite certain of who belonged in this category (see Pope, *Epistle to Arbuthnot*, lines 145-46).

15. Daniel Defoe, *Jure Divino*, Book XII, 265-66.

16. Edward N. Hooker, "The Purpose of Dryden's *Annus Mirabilis*."

17. Other studies of this poem are Andrew Wilkinson's "Defoe's 'New Discovery' and 'Pacificator,'" and M.E. Campbell's *Defoe's First Poem*. James Sutherland has a useful chapter on his poetry in *Daniel Defoe: A Critical Study*.

18. Sutherland offers a different interpretation, *Daniel Defoe*, pp. 92-93.

19. The best discussion of *The Pacificator* is Albert Rosenberg, "Defoe's *Pacificator* Reconsidered"; see also Wilkinson, "Defoe's 'New Discovery' and 'Pacificator,'" pp. 497-98.

20. After the death of Queen Mary, succession to the throne became an issue.

21. See for example, Daniel Defoe, *The Storm, An Essay*, pp. 42-43, and Defoe's annual tributes to William in *The Review* (4 November).

22. A number of critics attempt to explain the uniform mediocrity of the elegies for William (see Moore, "Whig Panegyric Verse," p. 362; Arthur S. Williams, "Panegyric Decorum in the Reigns of William III and Anne," pp. 57-58). Ellis discussed *The Mock Mourners* in *Poems on Affairs of State*, 6: 372-75.

23. Daniel Defoe, *A Hymn to the Pillory*, lines 445-46; compare line 89.

24. Daniel Defoe, *Meditations*, available in G.H. Healey's edition.

25. Cowley's works went through twenty-five editions in Defoe's lifetime; Thomas Sprat's 1668 edition of the works saw twelve printings before 1721. The age was not unaware of Cowley's adaptation of the form; see Ben Jonson's "To . . . Sir Lucius Cary and Sir H. Morison" in *Under-Woods*, and William Congreve's "A Discourse on the Pindarique Ode" (1706), in *The Complete Works*, 4: 82-85.

26. Abraham Cowley, *Poems*, p. 157.

27. David Trotter discusses Cowley's changing reputation in *The Poetry of Abraham Cowley*, pp. 75, 113-19.

28. Compare this to Defoe, *Reformation of Manners*, pp. 8, 15.

29. Defoe, *Reformation of Manners*, pp. 19, 21.

30. Daniel Defoe, *Address to the Pillory*, p. 28.

31. Daniel Defoe, "The Character of Annesley," printed in *A True Collection of the Writings of The Author of the True-Born Englishman*, p. 113.

32. Peter Smithers, *The Life of Joseph Addison*, pp. 93-101.

33. Daniel Defoe, *The Consolidator*, p. 27.

34. Daniel Defoe, *The Double Welcome*, p. 12.

35. Daniel Defoe, dedication to *A Hymn to Victory*.

36. W.J. Courthope, *A History of English Poetry*, 5: 58.

37. Adam Clarke, *Memoirs of the Wesley Family*, p. 594.

38. Daniel Defoe, *The Pacificator* in Ellis, *Poems on Affairs of State*, 6: 179, and *Reformation of Manners*, pp. 30-31. "Mechanick" here is used as a pejorative and means low class, a manual laborer rather than a thinker. Prior's biographer, Charles K. Eves, explains Defoe's references to Prior's early employment in the popular Rhenish Tavern and the lampoon Defoe believed Prior wrote in *Matthew Prior. Poet and Diplomat* (pp. 12-14, 173-76).

39. This chapter omits discussion of Defoe's shorter satiric poems partly because of their ephemeral subject matter, because of their dubious "literary" stature, and because of the difficulty of assigning certain authorship.

40. Sutherland, *Daniel Defoe*, pp. 114-16; the best discussion of the ideas in *Jure Divino* is integrated in Maximillian E. Novak's *Defoe and the Nature of Man;* see also Novak's *Realism, Myth, and History in Defoe's Fiction*, p. 15, in which he calls the poem a history of mankind's struggle against tyranny. George Chalmers compares *Jure Divino* to *The Hind and the Panther* in *The Life of Defoe*, pp. 30-31. A full discussion of the composition and form of the poem is in my forthcoming biography, Chapter 8.

41. Defoe, preface to *Jure Divino*, p. xi.

42. See Novak, *Defoe and the Nature of Man;* he also identifies other influences such as Hobbes, Cumberland, Grotius, and Pufendorf; see esp. pp. 14, 18-20, 68.

43. See John V. Price's "The Reading of Philosophical Literature" in *Books and Their Readers in Eighteenth-Century England*, pp. 165-66, 176-78.

44. The twelve books examine the origins of kingship, its bases, and the ideal. They include a variety of forms such as the exempla and the hymn.

45. Defoe, *Jure Divino*, 8: 169.

46. Defoe, *Jure Divino*, 6: 146.

47. George Healey, ed. *The Letters of Daniel Defoe*, p. 141.

48. This discussion of topographical poetry has benefitted from Nevo, *Dial of Virtue*, p. 37; Bernard H. Newdigate, *Michael Drayton and His Circle;* and Robert A. Aubin, *Topographical Poetry in XVIII-Century England*, pp. 3, 20, 197.

49. Compare Defoe, *Caledonia*, pp. 1-2, with the opening of the first song in Drayton's *Poly-Olbion*, in *Works*, 4: 1.

50. Defoe, *Caledonia*, p. 12; compare p. 21.

51. Defoe, *Vindication*, pp. 28-30, and *Review* for 29 July 1708, 5: 212.

52. Defoe, "Some Account of the Life of Sir Charles Sedley," prefixed to *The Works of Sedley*, pp. 7-8.

53. Defoe, *Faction in Power*, p. 56.

3. Pamphlets and Politics

1. My discussion of pamphlet history is drawn from Sandra Clark, *The Elizabethan Pamphleteers;* her definition is on p. 23.

2. George Saintsbury, *A History of English Prose Rhythm*, p. 229; he discussed the balance in Defoe's prose on pp. 240-41.

3. These statements are all used by later fiction writers to give credibility to their works (see Clark, *Elizabethan Pamphleteers*, pp. 257-67).

4. Preface to *Sylvae, The Works of John Dryden*, 3: 18.

5. Philip Pinkus, *Grub Street Stripped Bare*, pp. 15-16; Lennard J. Davis, *Factual Fictions*, p. 78.

6. Harold Herd, *The March of Journalism*, p. 7.

7. Herd, *March of Journalism*, p. 44.

8. Defoe, *Letter to a Dissenter from his friend at the Hague*, p. 2. Defoe describes some of the persecution as "such Fines levied upon them, so many ruined, so many imprison'd, and so many murthered" (*Wise as Serpents*, pp. 9-10).

9. See James Sutherland, *Defoe*, pp. 83-109.

10. Defoe, *The Opinion of a Known Dissenter*, p. 2.

11. J.R. Jones, *Country and Court*, pp. 322-23.

12. Defoe had published the same opinion as early as 1698. In his 1715 *Appeal to Honour and Justice*, he says that he had made "many honest men angry."

13. Sutherland, *Defoe*, p. 86; Frank Bastian, *Defoe's Early Life*, p. 277.

14. Defoe, *A True Collection of the Writings of the Author of the True-Born Englishman*, A6v. Two excellent articles on *The Shortest Way* are Miriam Leranbaum, "'An Irony Not Unusual': Defoe's *Shortest Way with the Dissenters*," and Paul K. Alkon, "Defoe's Argument in *The Shortest Way with the Dissenters*."

15. See Defoe's 1703 *The Shortest Way to Peace and Union, A Challenge to Peace*, and *Peace without Union*, and the 1704 *The Dissenters Answer to the High-Church Challenge*.

16. Defoe, *A Serious Inquiry into This Grand Question*, pp. 5, 11-12.

17. Defoe, *A New Test of the Church of England's Honesty* and *Persecution Anatomiz'd*.

18. Defoe, *The Question Fairly Stated*, p. 5.

19. Defoe, *The Question Fairly Stated*, pp. 4-5.

20. Defoe was angered when three Dissenting ministers refused to come to Newgate to pray with him (see *More Reformation* in Ellis, *Poems on Affairs of State*, 6: 583-84; see also *An Appeal to Honour and Justice* in Defoe, *The Shortest Way with the Dissenters and other Pamphlets*, p. 233, and *The Letters of Daniel Defoe*, pp. 4, 68, 370, 379, 414 et passim).

21. Defoe, *A Letter to Mr. Steele*, pp. 39-40; [A Speech of a Stone Chimney-Piece].

22. Bonamy Dobrée, "Some Aspects of Defoe's Prose," in *Pope and his Contemporaries*, pp. 179-84.

23. William's relationships with Parliament were so difficult that he considered retiring to Holland; J.R. Jones, *Country and Court*, pp. 305-10; P. Yorke, ed. *Miscellaneous State Papers from 1501 to 1726*, 2: 362; Paul Grimblot, ed., *The Letters of William III and Louis XIV*, 2: 224 et passim.

24. Defoe, *The History of the Kentish Petition*, in *The Shortest Way With the Dissenters and Other Pamphlets*, pp. 79, 96.

25. Defoe, *Legion's Memorial*, pp. 111-12, and *Kentish Petition*, p. 98.

26. Jonathan Swift's *Conduct of the Allies* is another of the few examples (see Irvin Ehrenpreis, *Swift: The Man, His Works, and the Age*, 2: 500).

27. See Backscheider, "Personality and Biblical Allusion in Defoe's Letters."

28. Publication of *The History of the Union* was delayed until 1709; *Memoirs of the Church of Scotland* was not published until 1717, when it was released to support the case being made by the delegates from the General Assembly of the Church of Scotland that guarantees to the Church made at the time of the Union were being violated.

29. Defoe, *An Essay at Removing National Prejudices against a Union with Scotland*, part 1, p. 1.

30. Defoe, *Essay at Removing National Prejudices*, p. 25; and *A Letter Concerning Trade*, p. 10.

31. P.W.J. Riley, *The Union of England and Scotland*, p. 244.

32. Quoted in Geoffrey Holmes, *The Trial of Doctor Sacheverell*, pp. 63-64.

33. Defoe describes Sacheverell as holding the "Trumpet of Sedition in his Hand" in *A Hymn to the Pillory*, in *The Shortest Way with the Dissenters and Other Pamphlets*, p. 139; see also *Review*, VI, no. 114, p. 45, for 27 December 1709.

34. Defoe, *Review* VI, no. 107, p. 425, for 10 December 1709; VI, no. 112, p. 446, for 22 December 1709, and VI, no. 117, p. 466, for 5 January 1709/10.

35. Defoe, *Instructions from Rome*, p. 15. Satires of religious sects frequently resorted to accusations of sexual misconduct (see, for example, Albert M. Lyles, *Methodism Mocked*, pp. 69-70, 89-97).

36. See Backscheider, "Defoe's Lady Credit."

37. Defoe, *The British Visions*, pp. 6, 14.

38. Defoe, *Reasons Why This Nation Ought to Put a Speedy End to this Expensive War*, p. 10.

39. Defoe, *Reasons*, pp. 6, 9.

40. W.A. Speck, *Stability and Strife*, p. 152.

41. The most serious Jacobite uprisings were as follows: James Butler, Duke of Ormonde, tried to invade the Devonshire coast twice; John Erskine, Earl of Mar, led a rebellion in Scotland; and a third group of Jacobites harried northern England. Defoe wrote about all of these, but he concentrated on Scotland, where the most serious uprisings were and where he had lived for six years.

42. Major Ramkins, a Jacobite for twenty-eight years, loses his fortune and reflects in prison upon how James ruined himself and "Thousands of Families" and succeeded in nothing more than serving France's interests. Ramkins is offered as an instructive example of folly and short-sightedness. I discuss *The Memoirs of Major Alexander Ramkins* in *A Being More Intense*, pp. 165-67.

43. Defoe, *Review*, 9: 214, for 11 June 1713.

44. Some pamphlets that include nearly all of Defoe's fixed ideas are *Giving Alms No Charity*, *Reflections on the Prohibition Act*, and *A Brief State of the Inland or Home Trade*.

45. Peter Earle, *The World of Defoe*, p. 9.

46. Discussions of this campaign are in Maximillian E. Novak, *Economics and the Fiction of Defoe*, p. 25; Earle, *World of Defoe*, pp. 87-93, 138-39 et passim; and Geoffrey Sill's *Defoe and the Idea of Fiction*, pp. 29-53. These studies, however, are concerned almost exclusively with Defoe. So significant was the issue in contemporary eyes that men like Addison participated (see Addison's *The Trial and Conviction of Count Tariff*).

47. Defoe, *Considerations upon the Eighth and Ninth Articles of the Treaty of Commerce*, p. 35.

48. See Defoe, *Some Thoughts upon the Subject of Commerce with France*

and *A Letter from a Member of the House of Commons;* even *Considerations* does so when it concludes that the danger is in the way the articles might be interpreted in setting new tariffs rather than from the articles themselves (p. 37).

49. G.D.H. Cole, Introduction, *A Tour thro' the Whole Island of Great Britain,* p. x.

4. The Histories

1. James William Johnson, *The Formation of Neo-Classical Thought,* p. 43. See also, David Douglas, *English Scholars, 1660-1730,* esp. pp. 13-29; and James W. Thompson with B.J. Holm, *A History of Historical Writing,* 2: 3-61.

2. Thomas Hobbes, trans., *Eight Bookes of the Peloponnesian Warre Written by Thucydides,* p. 6.

3. This topic has been the subject of much recent research (see Geoffrey Holmes and W.A. Speck, eds., *The Divided Society,* and Henry Horwitz, "The Structure of Parliamentary Politics," in *Britain after the Glorious Revolution,* pp. 96-114). It was Henry St. John, Lord Bolingbroke, who acknowledged "that history has been purposely and systematically falsified in all ages" and yet "even those that are false serve to the discovery of the truth." His eloquent discussion of partisan history is in Letter IV of *On the Study and Use of History,* in *The Works of Lord Bolingbroke,* 2: 213-19. The impact of party on historiography came to be universally acknowledged and lauded; see, for example, [Peter Whalley], *An Essay on the Manner of Writing History* (pp. 12-15): "it is of great Moment to be assured from what Reigns we may date" the intermingling of party with our history (p. 13). James W. Thompson and B.J. Holm date the beginning of party historiography at 1625 (*History of Historical Writing,* 1: 628-29).

4. This manuscript is Moore no. 2 and is in the William Andrews Clark Library, UCLA. Daniel Defoe, *The Two Great Questions Further Considered,* p. 4.

5. The *History of the Union* was published in Edinburgh in 1709; a London edition with the names of the countries reversed followed soon after. Examination of dozens of first editions reveals differences almost great enough to warrant John R. Moore's comment: "No two copies seem to be exactly alike" (*A Checklist of the Writings of Daniel Defoe,* p. 66).

6. Defoe also had his "Proposals for Printing the History of the Union" printed separately (see J.H.P. Pafford, "Defoe's *Proposals* for Printing the *History of the Union*."

7. Defoe, *The History of the Union,* "A General History of Unions," p. 1.

8. John Chamberlayne, *Magnae Britanniae Notitia,* p. vi.

9. George MacKenzie, *The Lives and Characters of the most eminent Writers of the Scots Nation,* p. 1.

10. Chamberlayne, *Magnae Britanniae Notitia,* p. iii. Many people believed it their duty to assist historians. Andrew Colquhoun of Garscadden wrote James Robertoune after seeing an advertisement for information about the peerage of Scotland, "It is the duty of all good Scotts men to assist in this work if they are able. . . . And were I as I have been, I would have come in on it . . . [and encouraged its printing]. I shall wish the work may be well done, to the honour

of the nation" (Scottish Record Office [hereafter cited as S.R.O.], Ms. GD 124/15/1027, dated 19 February 1711).

11. I refer to the parts by means of section numbers for convenience; Defoe uses titles alone.

12. Defoe, *History of the Union,* "Of the Carrying on of the Treaty in Scotland," p. 45.

13. Defoe, *History of the Union,* "Of the Last Treaty," p. 71.

14. The passage reads: "Far be it from me to say, the Duke of *Hamilton* desired or encouraged this Tumultuary kind of Congratulations; That sort of Popularity must be too much below a Person of his Character; and his Grace knows the World too well, and is too Wise a Man, not to know, that such things always tend to Confusion, and to the Destruction of Civil Peace in the World" ("Of the Carrying on of the Treaty," p. 28; the account continues through p. 30).

15. Queensberry wrote: "So the greatest difficulty Treaty *[sic]* lies in the matter of Impositions on Salt and Malt," and "The opposers of the Union have so frightened the people about these Taxes, in representing them in Some cases three or four, and in others at least 5 or 6 times as heavy as they really are, or possibly can be, that there is hardly any persuading them to understand, or hear the truth, and had it not bin for the Committee of Parliament who have taken such hearty and unwearied pains to inform themselves and others, it had been Impossible to bring them to so good an issue as I still hope we shall" (S.R.O. Ms. GD 158/1153).

16. P.W.J. Riley, *The Union of England and Scotland,* p. 287.

17. No two sources agree on the exact vote, partly because Queensberry insisted upon being counted although he had no official vote (see William Ferguson, *Scotland,* p. 26; Riley, *Union of England and Scotland,* pp. 289, 328; James MacKinnon, *The Union of England and Scotland,* pp. 291-96; David Daiches, *Scotland and the Union,* pp. 146-51).

18. S.R.O. Ms. GD 90/2/172.

19. S.R.O. Ms. GD 124/14/449/44.

20. Mar to Nairn; 26 October 1706, S.R.O. Ms. GD 124/14/449/44 and 19 November 1706, S.R.O. Ms. GD 124/14/449/67 respectively.

21. Defoe, *History of the Union,* Part 4, p. 30, and George Lockhart, *Memoirs and Commentaries upon the Affairs of Scotland,* p. 164.

22. Defoe discusses the use of evidence in *A Reproof to Mr. Clark,* pp. 3-5, and *Advertisement From Daniel Defoe to Mr. Clark.*

23. Hugh Trevor-Roper, "The Historical Philosophy of the Enlightenment," pp. 1675-76.

24. Defoe's account compares favorably to those of T.C. Smout, "Union of Parliaments" in *The Scottish Nation,* pp. 149-58; Ferguson, *Scotland,* pp. 44-52; Maurice Lee, Jr., "The Anglo-Scottish Union of 1707: The Debate Re-opened"; T.C. Smout, *History of Scottish People,* pp. 216-23; James Rees Jones, *Country and Court: England 1658-1714,* pp. 329-33.

25. Maximillian E. Novak, "History, Ideology, and Method of Defoe's Historical Fiction" in *Studies in the Eighteenth Century,* 4: 105.

26. This is not to say that history and fiction writing can be distinguished absolutely. In fact, modern theorists continue to point out significant similarities. See, for example, Hayden White, *Metahistory,* esp. pp. 59-66, and his *Topics of Discourse: Essays in Cultural Criticism,* pp. 51, 91-115.

27. Ferguson says that "to his contemporaries Queensberry was simply a great

unprincipled operator on the make" (*Scotland*, p. 187; see also MacKinnon, *Union of England and Scotland*, pp. 47-50, 89-93, 284ff.).

28. This is the definition given by David Nichol Smith in *Characters from the Histories and Memoirs of the Seventeenth Century*, pp. x, li.

29. Gilbert Burnet, *History of My Own Time*, p. 5.

30. Lockhart, *Memoirs*, p. 5.

31. See, for example, Defoe, *A Short Narrative of the Life . . . of . . . Marlborough*, *The Memoirs of Major Ramkins*, and "Some Account of the Life of Sir Charles Sedley."

32. See the sections in *The Storm* on the Gisser's and Richards's houses, (pp. 237-38 and 246-48 respectively). Paul Alkon discusses *The Storm* in *Defoe and Fictional Time*, pp. 225-29.

33. In *Colonel Jack* the narrator argues that the reader shares the condition of the characters. In the first few pages, Jack reminds the reader that both greatness and misery develop slowly and that ambition occurs universally in men. The conclusion urges men to lead a reflective life in order to understand events and God's design for his creatures. Jack often points out that his story is an analogy and, therefore, separate from the reader but applicable. Furthermore, Jack recognizes his own story in the story the plantation master tells and in the life of his tutor. David Blewett explicates a scene in *Roxana* in which Defoe collapses time in "*Roxana* and the Masquerades."

34. See *A Paper Concerning Daniel Defoe*, and *A Just Reprimand to Daniel de Foe*. Defoe did make changes in the section on Clarke, "Of the Carrying on of the Treaty," p. 60 (see Backscheider, "Cross-Purposes: Defoe's *History of the Union*," p. 185).

35. See Defoe, *An Historical Account of the Voyages and Adventures of Sir Walter Raleigh*, *A General History of Discoveries and Improvements*, *A Plan of the English Commerce*, and *Atlas Maritimus*.

36. See Ferguson, *Scotland*, pp. 182, 240-43, 258. Ferguson finds Defoe's knowledge of Scotland "limited" and complains that he did not see the crucial nature of passing Article 1 first, yet he calls the *History* "a classical account" (p. 307). Riley complains that the *History* "has probably misled as many readers as Bismark's *Reflections and Reminiscences*" (*Union of England and Scotland*, p. 245). But see MacKinnon, who says that Defoe was "an enthusiastic and well-informed controversialist on the side of incorporation, and a painfully laborious and iterative historian of the movement" (*Union of England and Scotland*, p. 240); Basil Hall calls the *History* "full and careful" (in "Daniel Defoe and Scotland," in *Reformation, Conformity and Dissent*, p. 235); and John Clerk, a contemporary of Defoe, calls it "very exact" and says, "There is not one fact in it which I can challenge" (John Gray, ed., *Memoirs of the Life of Sir John Clerk of Penicuik*, pp. 63-65).

37. Defoe labels *Colonel Jack* and *Roxana* "histories" in the titles and *Moll Flanders* so in the introduction. Fielding calls *Joseph Andrews* and *Tom Jones* "histories"; Richardson so labels *Clarissa* and *Grandison*.

38. Voltair (Françis Marie Arouet), *Lion of the North, Charles XII of Sweden*, p. 49.

39. Charles Whitworth, *An Account of Russia As it was in the Year 1710*, pp. xxii-xxiii. Voltaire calls Charles XII and Peter I "by common accord the most remarkable men to have appeared in over two thousand years" (*Lion of the North*, p. 19).

40. Francis Bacon, *The Advancement of Learning,* p. 68, 72-73.

41. Edmund Calamy, Preface, *Memoirs of the Life of . . . Increase Mathers.*

42. Defoe, *Review,* no. 35 for 4 July 1704; 2, p. 153; see also 1, pp. 4, 81; Defoe consistently described the *Review*'s accounts as "real History."

43. Defoe, *The History of the Wars, of His Present Majesty Charles XII,* p. 17. All references refer to this edition rather than to the augmented 1720 *The History of the Wars, of His Late Majesty Charles XII.* Collation of the editions shows the 1720 edition to be identical except for the title page, the changing of the spelling of a few names, and the addition of an appendix called *A Continuation of the History of the Reign, and of the Wars, of His Late Majesty Charles the XII.* The preface, left the same, even states nonsensically that "the Second Part of his History, may render him more Glorious than the First."

44. See Ronald Weber, *The Literature of Fact,* pp. 2, 27-32; Tom Wolfe, introduction to *The New Journalism,* esp. pp. 21-34; John Hellman, *Fables of Fact,* pp. 3-9, 127-29, et passim; and John Hollowell, *Fact and Fiction.*

45. Michael Blowen, "Not all of the stuff in that movie was right," p. 1D.

46. Peace between Sweden and Poland was not made until 1731.

47. Defoe, *The Letters of Daniel Defoe,* pp. 450-54.

48. The minutes of the Russia Company in Guildhall are a graphic record of the economic and political complexities at this time. A number of copies of letters and memorials ask for convoys for merchant ships and refer to "great Losses" sustained at the hands of Sweden (Ms. 11741; see also Maurice Bruce, "Jacobite Relations with Peter the Great"; A.G. Cross, "By the Banks of the Thames" in *Russians in Eighteenth-Century Britain,* pp. 7-10). A full-scale pamphlet war including memorials written by two Russian ambassadors to England details the major quarrels; representative are *The Northern Crisis* and *A Memorial Presented to the King of Great-Britain, by M. Wesselofski, the Czar's Resident at London;* a bound collection of the official memorials and replies is in the British Library (8093.bb.12). On press coverage see Jeremy Black's "Russia and the British Press in the Early Eighteenth Century." A detailed study is in James F. Chance, *George I and the Northern War,* pp. 209-93. I thank A.G. Cross and Brenda Meehau-Waters for information about Russian sources.

49. Modern books in this tradition continue to reproduce some periodical and official documents (see, for example, Norman Mailer's *Armies of the Night,* particularly the second part, "The Novel as History"). Of Defoe's period, J. Franklin Jameson wrote, "The presentation of texts and of historical documents in the completest abundance is more esteemed than the production of narrative histories, or brilliant discourses on antiquity" (quoted in Thompson and Holm, *History of Historical Writing,* 2:7, from the 1905 University of Chicago Phi Beta Kappa address).

50. See Defoe, *History of the Wars,* pp. 156, 157, 162; in *The Life of Peter,* Charles is characterized as a meddler (see 76-83, 183-84, 305-11).

51. Defoe, *The Life of Peter,* pp. 39-40 correspond to [Jodocus Crull], *The Present Condition of the Muscovite Empire, Till the Year 1699,* pp. 35-36; Defoe summarizes and then quotes Crull's pp. 37-39 in *The Life of Peter,* pp. 41-43.

52. Defoe, *The Life of Peter,* pp. 88-91, 87, 40-43 correspond respectively to Perry, *The State of Russia,* pp. 183-87, 182, 153-55. Other contemporary books such as [F. Weber], *The Present State of Russia;* [Crull], *The Antient and Present State of Muscovy;* and Johann-Georg Korb, *Diary of an Austrian Secretary of Legation at the Court of Czar Peter the Great* corroborate Defoe's accounts. On

the similarity of composition of *Memoirs of a Cavalier*, see A.W. Secord, *Robert Drury's Journal and Other Studies*, pp. 73-133.

53. Compare:

History of the Wars	to	The Life of Peter
p. 20	Pathul	pp. 92-93
134ff.	Warsaw	152ff.
91-92	Narva	101-2
145-51	ravaging Livonia	121-28
283-312	Sweden's invasion	195-227
312-15	Augustus's designs	232-34
350	Pomerania	336-47
367-71	Ribitz	363-67

54. Cyprian A.G. Bridge notes that English and Scottish names are repeatedly encountered in seventeenth- and eighteenth-century Swedish histories (*History of the Russian Fleet during the Reign of Peter*, p. 41).

55. Defoe, Preface, *History of the Wars*.

56. Defoe, *History of the Wars*, pp. 91-92; *The Life of Peter*, pp. 101-2.

57. Defoe's word for such prose, given in the preface to his *Memoirs of a Cavalier*.

58. Peter Earle locates Defoe among the defeated troops in *Monmouth's Rebels*, p. 180 (*Calendar of State Papers, Domestic*, for 31 May 1687).

59. See Jean Norton Cru, *War Books* (excerpts from *Du Témoignage*): "Since Vauban all the improvements made in the instruments of warfare have been to the advantage of the defensive. . . . "; "a man entrenched is worth six who are not" (p. 34); Defoe's *Memoirs of a Cavalier*, p. 168. Any number of military histories describe Vauban's influence: see André Corvisier, *Armies and Societies in Europe, 1494-1789*; Barnett Corelli, *Britain and Her Army, 1509-1970*; Henry Guerlac, "Vauban: The Impact of Science on War" in *Makers of Modern Strategy*, pp. 26-48.

60. J.S. Bromley, ed., *New Cambridge Modern History*, 6: 742.

61. Cru, *War Books*, pp. 21-22. Paul Fussell makes the same statement in *The Great War and Modern Memory*.

62. This fact is made most obvious when comparing works as different in intention as

History of the Wars	and	Short View of the Conduct of the King of Sweden
preface	on truth and romance	p. 6
pp. 83-92	first campaign	13-20
106-10	Poland	20-25
117, 130-39	deposing Augustus	27-28

See also Herbert G. Wright, "Defoe's Writings on Sweden," and John J.

Murray, "Defoe: News Commentator and Analyst of Northern European Affairs."

63. See Defoe's *Review,* II, pp. 194, 206-7, and his attack on the *Spectator* in 21: 618-19.

64. Guerlac describes eighteenth-century warfare as "a relatively humane and well-regulated enterprise. These rules were known to commanders and were quite generally followed." "The whole tendency was to protect private persons and private rights" ("Vauban," p. 33).

65. Perry, *The State of Russia,* p. 219.

66. Defoe, *History of the Wars,* p. 150; Bromley, *New Cambridge Modern History,* 6: 659; R.M. Hatton, *Charles XII of Sweden,* pp. 160-61.

67. 1720 edition of *History of the Wars,* p. 250.

68. Revenge was an accepted if not approved motive for war. Voltaire, too, assigns it to Charles (*Lion of the North,* pp. 248-49; see also Bernard Mandeville, *The Fable of the Bees,* 1:207-20).

69. Defoe, *The Life of Peter,* p. 195. Again Voltaire agrees; Charles is "a unique rather than a great man" to him. Voltaire develops a number of personality characteristics, such as a passion for glory, stubbornness, and a desire to be singular, more systematically than does Defoe. Many of the differences in lives can be explained by the English association of history and biography in contrast to the French affinity for memoirs.

70. See, for example, *The Life of Peter,* pp. 121-29.

71. Based upon quotations in his works and his library sale catalog, Defoe may have owned most of these books. More than a dozen universal histories are in the Farewell/Defoe catalogue. *A History of Discoveries* was first published in four parts, the first in October 1725 and the fourth in May 1726. In December 1726, the four numbers were published as a single book with a new conclusion. All references here are to the 1726 compilation.

72. Diodorus of Sicily, *Bibliotheca,* 1: 5, 7.

73. See Sir Francis Bacon, *The Advancement of Learning,* p. 68, and Anne Robert Jacques Turgot, "On Universal History," in *Turgot on Progress, Sociology and Economics,* pp. 63-64.

74. The new preference for beginning with the Flood probably reflects the influence of French historians such as Scaliger who emphasized precise dating of events. Fabyan, however, had given his reason for beginning with the Flood to be the fact that he could count the years more exactly in his 1516 book. Defoe says he began at that point because the world was a "universal blank" (*History of Discoveries,* p. 1).

75. Petavius, To the Reader, in *The History of the World: or, an Account of Time.*

76. Bonded warehouses held imports free from duty until the time they were exported or sold for use in England; only those goods that remained and were used in England were taxable.

77. The Ostend clause opened the trade of the Americas, Indies, China, and Africa to the Company of the Austrian Low Countries. England objected to the economic competition and the presence of the Empire's ships in the Flemish port (see Basil Williams, *The Whig Supremacy, 1714-1760,* pp. 195-202; on England's economic conditions, see Earle, *World of Defoe,* pp. 107-53).

78. Lewis Theobald, *Memoirs of Sir Walter Raleigh,* pp. 39 and 5 respectively. Defoe's publication was *An Historical Account of the Voyages and Adventures of*

Sir Walter Raleigh. The year 1719 was not the first time Raleigh had been used for similar propaganda purposes; a number of works in the 1580s and 1590s had been dedicated to Raleigh "to inspire and encourage" projects similar to his (see Eleanor Rosenberg, "Giacopo Castelvetro, Italian Publisher in Elizabethan London and His Patrons," pp. 126-32). Defoe's life was widely quoted; see William Oldys's edition of *The History of the World* in which he credits "Philip Ralegh" with authorship.

79. On Raleigh's circle, see Rosenberg, "Giacopo Castelvetro," pp. 127-28, and Christopher Hill, *Intellectual Origins of the English Revolution*, pp. 154-55.

80. Quoted in Hill, *Intellectual Origins*, p. 210.

81. Thomas Twyne, *A Shorte Discourse of All Earthquakes in General.*

82. Raleigh, "Observations concerning the Royal Navy and Sea-Service" in *Works*, 8:350. This essay may not be entirely by Raleigh. All references here to Raleigh's works are from this edition.

83. See, for example, Defoe, *A History of Discoveries*, pp. 1-2, 79.

84. Hanno was a fifth-century Carthaginian explorer who sailed to West Africa and established five cities.

85. Bacon, *Advancement of Learning*, pp. 40-42.

86. Defoe's copy of *The Advancement of Learning* in the Taylor collection at Princeton. Defoe calls the reworking of the story about Solomon a "play" that is "innocent" (sig. H3; see also, sigs. H-I).

87. "Comment on the Eighth Book" by George Sandys in *Ovid's Metamorphosis English'd, Mythologiz'd, and Represented in Figures*, p. 385. The same interpretation is in Raleigh's *History of the World*, book II (see *The Works of Sir Walter Raleigh*, 4: 405-6).

88. [Peter Whalley], *An Essay*, p. 12.

89. Defoe cites, among many others, a contemporary *History of Navigation and Commerce.*

90. Quoted in Thompson and Holm, *History of Historical Writing*, 1: 612-13.

91. *Apparitions* was reissued in 1728 as *The Secrets of the Invisible World Disclos'd: Or, an Universal History of Apparitions Sacred and Prophane.*

92. Compare *A History of Discoveries*, pp. 223-25 and 82-83 with *Essay upon Literature*, pp. 120ff. and 31-32, respectively.

93. James Sutherland, *Defoe: A Critical Study*, p. 231. Isaac Newton's writings on alchemy have received the same treatment. His most recent biographer mentions, "those . . . who wish to pretend that Newton did not leave behind a vast collection of alchemical manuscripts" (Richard S. Westfall, *Never at Rest*, p. 284).

94. C.A. Patrides, *The Phoenix and the Ladder*, pp. 35, 43.

95. The leading character in Bunyan's psychomachia is "Mansoul." See Defoe, *Political History of the Devil*, p. 216.

96. Sir Walter Scott, "Daniel DeFoe" in *The Lives of the Novelists*, p. 370; the first part of this life is by John Ballantyne. The most complete study is still Rodney Baine, *Defoe and the Supernatural.*

97. Compare *Political History of the Devil*, pp. 361-62, and *History of Apparitions*, pp. 206-9, with *Moll Flanders*, 2: 7-8.

98. Sir Walter Scott, in *Essays on Chivalry, Romance, and The Drama*, p. 431.

99. Defoe, *History of Apparitions*, p. 494.

100. Keith Thomas, in *Religion and the Decline of Magic*, explains that "the disposition to see prodigies, omens and portents, sprang from a coherent view of the world as a moral order reflecting God's purposes" and that the "search for

correlations between disparate events is a valid form of inquiry" (p. 91). Aniela Jaffé, in *Apparitions and Precognition,* notes that "In most cases occult experiences are valued not only because they hint at a meaningful pattern in life, but because they make the writer feel there has been an intervention of fate . . ." (p. 35).

5. The Historical Novels

1. Although I obviously do not agree entirely with any of these theorists, my discussion of the historical novel has been deeply influenced by Herbert Butterfield, *The Historical Novel,* Georg Lukács, *The Historical Novel,* and Avrom Fleishman, *The English Historical Novel.* For other definitions and discussions of the historical novel, see also Alfred Sheppard, *The Art and Practice of Historical Fiction,* pp. 12-17; and Brander Matthews, *The Historical Novel and Other Essays,* pp. 18-21. John J. Burke, Jr., has also noted that some of Defoe's novels are historical (see his "Observing the Observer in the Historical Fictions by Defoe").

2. Sir Walter Scott, "Samuel Richardson" and "Daniel Defoe" in *Sir Walter Scott on Novelists and Fiction,* pp. 42-43, 167ff.

3. Lukács, *The Historical Novel,* p. 31.

4. See chapter one of Lukács, *The Historical Novel,* esp. pp. 33-34, 36, 42, 45, 47.

5. Lukács, *The Historical Novel,* p. 44.

6. Butterfield, *The Historical Novel,* p. 87.

7. Lukács, *The Historical Novel,* pp. 19-21.

8. Maximillian E. Novak offers a different political impulse (see his *Realism, Myth, and History in Defoe's Fiction,* pp. 56-60). The accuracy of Defoe's account of the Great Rebellion may be tested against Correlli Barnett, *Britain and Her Army 1509-1970,* pp. 79-99. Alfred Sheppard calls *Memoirs of a Cavalier* the "most striking example" of the historical novel in Defoe's century, in *The Art and Practice of Historical Fiction,* pp. 37, 181.

9. [John Dalrymple], *Memoirs of the Life, Family, and Character of John late Earl of Stair,* p. 29.

10. Bernard Mandeville, *Free Thoughts on Religion, the Church, and National Happiness,* pp. 352-54.

11. [J. Olivier], *Memoirs of the Life and Adventures of Signor Rozelli, Done in English, from the Second Edition of the French; and adorn'd with several curious Copper-Cuts;* [Courtilz de Sandras], *Memoirs of the Count de Rochefort, Made English from the French;* [Courtilz de Sandras], *The French Spy: or, the Memoirs of John Baptist De La Fontaine, Translated from the French Original,* p. 2; and [Anthony Hamilton], *Memoirs of the Life of Count de Grammont, Translated from the French By Mr. Boyer,* p. 282, respectively.

12. Typical amorous adventures may be found in *Memoirs . . . of de Grammont,* whose author writes, "Tis *Love* must compleat . . . Character" (pp. 31-32); see also [Eliza Haywood], *Memoirs of the Baron de Brosse,* pp. 1-3.

13. *The English Expositor Improv'd* (1719); Nathan Bailey's *An Universal Etymological English Dictionary* (1721); Benjamin Norton Defoe, *A New English Dictionary* (1735), s.v. "Memoirs."

14. [Olivier], *Memoirs of Signor Rozelli;* [Eliza Haywood], *Memoirs of the Baron de Brosse.*

15. *Memoirs of * * *. Commonly known by the Name of George Psalmanazar,* p. 11.

16. Adrian Drift, compiler, *The History of His Own Time. Compiled from the Original Mss Of his late Excellency Matthew Prior, Esq.,* p. 11.

17. Cuirassiers were cavalry soldiers wearing armored vests; in this case, they wore black ones.

18. See also Defoe, *Memoirs of a Cavalier,* pp. 16-17.

19. See especially *Mercurius Politicus,* Jan., p. 10; March, pp. 127-49; April, pp. 220-27, and May, pp. 265-74, for 1719. Significantly Defoe opens the March entry with "The Month begins with The Alarms of Civil War" (p. 127).

20. It is clear from Defoe's nonfiction that he knew these books well. The Defoe/Farewell catalogue suggests that he may have owned Castiglione's *Il libro del cortegiano [sic]* as well as the English edition, *The Courtyer,* and J. Bulteel's *The Apopthegms of the Ancients,* among others.

21. Thomas Elyot, *The Book Named the Governor* (1531); epistle dedicatory to Henry VIII. The statement is ubiquitous; Machiavelli says that he offers Lorenzo de Medici what he finds most precious: "that knowledge of the deeds of great men," which will allow him "to understand in a very short time all those things which I have learnt at the cost of privation and danger in the course of many years."

22. See Elyot, *The Book Named the Governor,* Book III, fol. 243ff.

23. The sources from which Defoe draws anecdotes suggest wide reading in such diverse works as Bede and Ælianus's *Register of Hystories.*

24. Elyot, *The Book Named the Governor,* Book II, fol. 145.

25. Goldsmith's edition, published in seven volumes between May and November 1762, emphasizes the usefulness of biography. The preface may be found in *The Collected Works of Oliver Goldsmith,* 5: 226-27.

26. Elyot, *The Book Named the Governor,* Book III, fol. 246-47.

27. *The Works of John Dryden,* 17: 271, 273-75. All quotations from Plutarch's *Lives* come from the edition called Dryden's as "corrected" by Arthur Hugh Clough.

28. See Plutarch, *Life of Pericles,* 1: 318-19. Representative references to Plutarch may be found in [Hamilton], *Memoirs . . . of de Grammont* ("the *Historian* to whom, of *all the Ancients,* we are most obliged," p. 3) and *Some Memoirs of The Life of Robert Feilding.*

29. Plutarch, *Life of Alexander,* 4: 159.

30. The title is *The Mirrour for Magistrates, wherein may bee seene, by examples passed in this Realme, with how greeuous plagues vices are punished in great Princes and Magistrates, and how fraile and unstable worldly prosperity is found, where Fortune seemeth most highly to fauour. . . .*

31. Compare Plutarch, *Alexander,* 4: 215, with Defoe, *Historical Collections,* p. 81, and Plutarch, *Marius,* 3: 85, with Defoe, *Historical Collections,* p. 64, and *Memoirs of a Cavalier,* p. 85. Novak identified another anecdote in *Memoirs of a Cavalier* from *Historical Collections* (this one not from Plutarch), *Realism,* p. 20.

32. *Les Essais de Montaigne,* 2: 92.

33. Abel Boyer, *Memoirs of the Life and Negotiations of Sir W. Temple,* p. iv. This book cites Plutarch as a model and was popular enough to warrant a second edition in 1715.

34. Courtilz de Sandras, for example, explicitly says that he trusts readers

more than the "experts." In the preface to *The French Spy,* he tells the reader
that he must examine the book to settle the dispute "amongst those who pretend
to be the most competent Judges of a matter of this nature, whether the Author's
intention had been to give us a true History, or a piece participating both of the
nature of a Novel and a History." Eliza Haywood admitted that her translation
of *Mary Stuart, Queen of Scots* (London, 1725) would be taken for fiction
because of the extraordinary events recorded but asserted that it was "not a
Romance, but a *True History*" (see pp. 1, 111); her biographer Whicher accepts
it as a compilation of information from fifteen or sixteen "known Authors,"
some of which she translated. In fact, the title pages, prefaces, and dedicatory
epistles habitually note the mixing of genres and give fairly reliable guides to the
amount of historical fact included. Even Charles Burman's *Memoirs of the Life
of that Learned Antiquary, Elias Ashmore, Esq; Drawn up himself by way of
Diary,* promises to give us a "secret History" (p. viii).

35. Prior was at work on *The History of His Own Time* (posthumously
published by A. Drift in London in 1740) at the time of his death. A number of
excerpts from state documents appear in the book as well as a "journal" Prior
wrote after Shrewsbury's departure from Paris in 1713, when the poet served as
the de facto ambassador to the court of Louis XIV. I am grateful to Linda
Merians of Bucknell for this footnote.

36. John Richetti, *Defoe's Narratives: Situations and Structures,* p. 234.

37. Quoted in John Hollowell, *Fact and Fiction,* p. 14.

38. G.A. Starr, "Defoe's Prose Style: 1. The Language of Interpretation."
Some fine discussions of the artistic strengths of the novels are Novak, *Realism,*
and Everett Zimmerman, *Defoe and the Novel.*

39. Louis A. Landa, Introduction to *A Journal of the Plague Year,* p. xxxiii.

40. Michael McKeon discusses contemporary criticism of professional men,
especially Anglican clergymen, who fled the plague in *Politics and Poetry in
Restoration England,* p. 95; see also *The Autobiography of Richard Baxter,* 3:
196-97; Landa, "Introduction," pp. xxix-xxxii; and Watson Nicholson, *The
Historical Sources of Defoe's Journal of the Plague Year,* p. 77.

41. Defoe himself does so in *Due Preparations for the Plague* (see pp. 148-49);
see also [Seth Ward, Bishop of Exeter], *A Sermon Preached before the Peers, in
the Abby-Church at Westminster: October 10th M.D.C. LXVI;* John Dryden,
Annus Mirabilis, "To the Metropolis," esp. stanzas 291 and 292. Zimmerman
treats both as typology (*Defoe and the Novel,* pp. 119-20).

42. Nicholson, *Historical Sources,* pp. 49, 70ff. and the bibliography at the
end. The most important sources include J. Roberts, bookseller, *A Collection of
Very Valuable and Scarce Pieces relating to the last Plague in the Year 1665*
(1721) which included the Lord Mayor's *Orders;* the pioneer statistician John
Graunt's *Reflections on the Weekly Bills* (1720), and Nathaniel Hodges's
Loimologia (1672; trans. 1720). Nicholson says that more than two score books
on the plague were published in 1722 alone.

43. *The Memoirs of the Honorable Sir John Reresby,* pp. 6-7; Defoe sets the
number at 97,306 in *Due Preparations* (p. 108).

44. Paul Fussell describes the devastating effect on morale the sense of
endlessness had on French soldiers in World War I (*The Great War and Modern
Memory,* pp. 9-10). See Paul Alkon on duration and tempo (*Defoe and Fictional
Time,* pp. 221-31).

45. Novak, "Defoe and the Disordered City," p. 243. Lukács says that the

proper hero of a historical novel is life itself, *The Historical Novel*, p. 156. The conception of a city functioning as a heroic character was not original with Defoe; see, for example, John Dryden's *Annus Mirabilis* and Sandra Clark's description of Renaissance plague pamphlets, *Elizabethan Pamphleteers*, p. 118.

46. J.G.A. Pocock, *The Machiavellian Moment*, pp. 462-64.

47. Alkon, *Defoe and Fictional Time*, pp. 38-39.

48. Defoe's introduction to *Due Preparations*, pp. x-xi; Abel Boyer, *Memoirs of the Life and Negotiations of Sir W. Temple*, p. viii.

49. Baxter, *Autobiography*, 3:195.

50. Landa, "Introduction," pp. xxiv-xxviii.

51. All lives record history, not all novels show the impact of events.

52. See Paula R. Backscheider, *A Being More Intense*, pp. 48-53, 77-82, for an elaboration of this point.

53. Basil Williams, *The Whig Supremacy, 1714-1760*, p. 208.

54. This is, of course, an illusion. The criminal justice system was notorious for its vagaries (see Backscheider, *A Being More Intense*, pp. 54-60).

55. *The History of the Life of Thomas Ellwood, Written by his own hand*, pp. 141-42, 155.

56. Pocock demonstrates that "commerce was an aggressive action" at that time (*Machiavellian Moment*, pp. 424-25, 458); E. Bloom and L. Bloom, *Joseph Addison's Sociable Animal*, pp. 67-83; Peter Earle writes, "Never can there have been so many ships at sea whose sole function was to seize or destroy other ships" (*The World of Defoe*, p. 59).

57. Frederick Monteser, *The Picaresque Element in Western Literature*, p. 16.

58. On the characteristics of the pre-eighteenth century Spanish picaresque, see Monteser, *Picaresque Element*, pp. 1-4, 5-19; Robert Alter, *Rogue's Progress*, pp. 8-10 et passim; and Richard Bjornson, *The Picaresque Hero in European Fiction, pp. 6-8*.

59. Bjornson, *Picaresque Hero*, pp. 213-27.

60. Jean Sgard, *Prévost, Romancier*, pp. 72-73.

61. Preface to the [Oliver] *Memoirs of Signor Rozelli*.

62. *Memoirs of ****, p. 11; [Marie Aulnoy], *Memoirs of the Countess of Dunois*, title page, p. 2, et passim.

63. [Courtilz de Sandras] *Memoirs of de Rochefort*, p. 7; see also Monteser, *Picaresque Element*, pp. 25-27.

64. The English translation was published in 1696, and there was a fourth edition by 1707.

65. Sgard calls the form "apocryphe et vaguement satirique"; Monteser, *Picaresque Element*, p. 28; Alter finds the combination a cause of ambiguity (*Rogue's Progress*, pp. 4-8).

66. Samuel Holt Monk, Introduction to *Colonel Jack*, p. xxii.

67. Pocock associates credit with "passion" with good reason (*Machiavellian Moment*, pp. 451-53, 459-500).

68. For a single example, see Earle, *The World of Defoe*, pp. 59-61, 101-2, for changed attitude toward privateering.

6. Crime and Adventure

1. By the 1720s many of these travelers were hard-working, honest mer-

chants. They were, however, often like the men described by Robinson Crusoe's father—the ambitious or the poor. Younger brothers often went to sea.

2. See Peter Linebaugh, "The Ordinary of Newgate and His *Account*," in *Crime in England 1550-1800,* p. 298, and Michael Harris, "Trials and Criminal Biographies: A Case Study in Distribution," in *Sale and Distribution of Books,* pp. 17, 20.

3. John Richetti, *Popular Fiction before Richardson,* p. 29; and Frank W. Chandler, *The Literature of Roguery,* pp. 139-40.

4. Andrew Knapp and William Baldwin, *The Newgate Calendar,*1:1.

5. Scott, *Essays on Chivalry,* p. 462. Edward Heawood's *A History of Geographical Discovery in the Seventeenth and Eighteenth Centuries* is still the best guide to contemporary geographical knowledge.

6. I do not intend to deny interest in the interior life of characters as treated by such critics as Blewett, Novak, and Zimmerman, but the focus of this chapter is upon action; in chapter 8, I return to the adventure novel and an analysis of character.

7. Some scholars have said that Defoe makes idleness a sin and, therefore, gives this theme a predominantly moral significance (see Ian Watt, *The Rise of the Novel,* pp. 73-74, and Timothy J. Reiss, *The Discourse of Modernism,* pp. 297-327).

8. Quoted in Harris, "Trials and Criminal Biographies," p. 15.

9. Pielmeier's play is loosely based on a murder that took place in Rochester, New York, in April 1975 and came to trial in March 1977. The play was performed in eight cities, including Rochester, before it opened on Broadway in 1982 (see "Newborn a Horricide: Found in Convent," *Rochester Democrat and Chronicle,* 29 April 1975, p. 6B; "Brighton Nun Charged in Death of Infant," *Rochester Democrat and Chronicle,* 30 April 1975, p. 1A; "Lee Remick in Drama," *New York Times,* 12 January 1982, p. C13.

10. J. Paul Hunter discusses the tradition of journalistic treatment of the "unusual, surprising, and wonderful" and its influence on the novel in a study in progress, tentatively titled "The Contexts of the Early English Novel."

11. [Eliza Haywood], *Tea Table,* no. 22 (4 May 1724).

12. Frantz Funck-Brentano, *Les Nouvellistes,* pp. 23-72.

13. Clara Reeve, *The Progress of Romance,* pp. 110-11; see also Pinkus, *Grub Street Stripped Bare,* pp. 15-17; Davis, *Factual Fictions,* pp. 45-51.

14. On newsbooks, see Davis, *Factual Fictions,* p. 72; G.A. Cranfield, *The Press and Society,* pp. 6, 13, 17; Herd, *The March of Journalism,* p. 13; Sandra Clark, *Elizabethan Pamphleteers,* pp. 23ff.

15. Knapp and Baldwin, *Newgate Calendar,* 1:18.

16. Richard Altick, *Lives and Letters,* p. 32.

17. Low is the subject of one of Defoe's lives in *The General History of the . . . Pyrates.* A cruel bully in this collection, Low is eventually marooned by his men and hanged. For a discussion of Defoe's "facts," see Manuel Schonhorn, *"Defoe's Four Years Voyages of Captain Roberts and Ashton's Memorial."*

18. Sarah Fielding, Introduction to *The Lives of Cleopatra and Octavia,* p. xlii.

19. Robert Knox, *An Historical Relation of Ceylon,* p. 18, and *The Life and Adventures of Captain John Avery,* p. 9. This life is one that Defoe "answers" in his *King of Pirates* (1719), respectively.

20. William Chetwood, *The Voyages, Dangerous Adventures and imminent*

Escapes of Captain Richard Falconer; see, for example, 1: 64-65 and 2: 97-103. Chetwood refers to Royal Society descriptions, 3:86.

21. A number of scholars have documented this practice. See, for example, A.W. Secord, *Studies in the Narrative Method of Defoe,* Percy Adams, *Travelers and Travel Liars,* esp. pp. 142-61, and idem, *Travel Literature and the Evolution of the Novel,* pp. 73, 163-64, 178. *Captain Singleton,* for example, simply copies pp. 188-271 of Knox's *Ceylon.* Boies Penrose dates the practice from Claudius Ptolemaeus's *Geography* (c. 150 A.D.) in *Travel and Discovery in the Renaissance,* p. 5.

22. The practice became standard. See, for example, Arthur Young's *Travels in France,* James Boswell's *Accounts of Corsica,* and Hester Thrale Piozzi's *Observations and Reflections Made in the Course of a Journey through France, Italy, and Germany.* An early example was John Lawson's *New Voyage to Carolina* (1709); even Dionisius Petavius's *The History of the World* is divided into a universal history and "A Geographical Description of the World."

23. John G. Cawelti, *Adventure, Mystery, and Romance,* chapter 1. John Richetti finds similar strains in travel and crime narratives, in chapter 3 of *Popular Fiction;* and see Frederick R. Karl, *The Adversary Literature,* pp. 52-54.

24. Watt, of course, says that *Moll Flanders* lacks such a moral framework (*The Rise of the Novel,* pp. 117ff). Others have found the structure of the spiritual autobiography in the novel; for the fullest argument, see G.A. Starr, *Defoe and Spiritual Autobiography,* chapter 4.

25. Richard Gilman, *The Confusion of Realms,* p. 121. See also Wayne Shumaker, *Literature and the Irrational:* "Aesthetic creativity . . . often breaks through the limits of the rationally comprehensible" (p. 147).

26. See the lives of Rackam and White in Defoe, *The General History of the . . . Pyrates.*

27. Compare this to Richard Baxter on how despair comes from the idea that "the Day of Grace is past" and leads to suicidal thoughts in *The Certainty of the Worlds of Spirits.* In one anecdote, a man hears a voice saying "Now cut thy Throat. . . . Do it, do it" (pp. 171-72).

28. *The English Rogue* by Richard Head was published in 1665; Francis Kirkman added a second part in 1668, and Head and Kirkman collaborated on the final two parts, which were published in 1671. The book enjoyed great popularity and saw many editions (see Chandler, *Literature of Roguery,* pp. 211-21). The quotation from *The English Rogue* is from the 1928 edition, pp. 67-68.

29. See Defoe's *System of Magick,* p. 326; Richard Baxter's *Saint's Everlasting Rest* in *The Practical Works of the Rev. Richard Baxter,* 22: 319, and *The Reasons of the Christian Religion,* 21: 87 and 90; Raleigh's *History of the World,* 2:399; and John Aubrey, *Miscellanies* in *Three Prose Works,* pp. 65-66. Aubrey's *Miscellanies* was in a new edition in 1721 and is listed with the books in the Defoe/Farewell library.

30. Baxter, "Witness to the Truth of Christianity," in *The Practical Works,* 2: 339-40; Baxter explains that the devil's "baits" are suited to the age, station, and situation of his victim. Compare this to Defoe, *The Political History of the Devil,* pp. 384-85.

31. The belief in the Devil's promptings was widespread and listed repetitiously in collections of spirit manifestations throughout the period (see, for example, Sir Thomas Browne, *Pseudodoxia Epidemica,* 1: 58). Charles Morton,

Defoe's schoolmaster, quoted Browne in his *Compendium Physicae*. Particularly brutal crimes were often ascribed to the devil's inspiration or labeled "devilish ideas" as too wicked for man to have conceived without help.

32. The debate over Moll's sincerity is long-standing. For a recent discussion concluding that Moll is a penitent see Novak, *Realism*, pp. 75-98. Arnold Weinstein finds "Moll's fundamental doubleness" the source of the power of her characterization (*Fictions of the Self, 1550-1800*, pp. 94-95).

33. Compare *Robinson Crusoe*, 1: 3-4 and 2: 111-16.

34. Defoe, *Political History of the Devil*, pp. 241, 423-25.

35. In *The History of Apparitions* Defoe discusses good spirits (see pp. 186, 190, 199). On theologians' unwillingness to deny the reality of spirits and the "threat" of atheism, see Keith Thomas, *Religion and the Decline of Magic*, pp. 591-93. Many pamphlets insisted that disbelief in spirits was a sign of atheism (see, for example, *Satan's Invisible World Discover'd*, p. xviii).

36. On premonitions, see Defoe, *History of Apparitions*, pp. 214-18, 223.

37. Quoted in Aubrey, *Miscellanies*, p. 69; Thomas Vaughan, *Magia Adamica*, p. 132; see also Morton, *Compendium Physicae*, p. 195.

38. Defoe, *History of Apparitions*, p. 192. Among others, Defoe cites Clarendon, Lucian, Tournefort, and Jeremy Taylor as sources. The universal nature of similar reports is always offered as evidence for spirit existence. See, for instance, John Dee, *A True and Faithful Relation*, in which Meric Casaubon argues that he published Dee's account to "promote Religion" and draws examples from Aristotle, Cicero, Remigius, and Bodin. For a modern account, see Aniela Jaffé, *Apparitions and Precognition*, pp. 1, 7-8, 183.

39. Compare, *Farther Adventures*, 3: 62-63: "we do not expect Returns from Heaven, in a miraculous and particular Manner." For a discussion of this central theme in *Robinson Crusoe*, see Backscheider, *A Being More Intense*, pp. 142-44, 168-69.

40. In fact, *Captain Roberts* throws additional doubt on the extent to which Defoe accepted the argument from necessity; in this book only the evil use it, and Roberts rejects it out of hand (see p. 56).

41. On page 84, Roberts remembers, "I humbly besought [God] . . . that in all Things I might through the Guidance of the holy Spirit, be directed so as to submit myself entirely to his Will." Roberts's efforts to survive, however, are the subject of his story.

7. Roxana

1. Charles C. Mish classifies 40 percent of the prose fiction published between 1700 and 1740 as "romances/love stories" in "Early Eighteenth-Century Best Sellers in English Prose Fiction," 414-15, 417; see also William McBurney, *A Check List of English Prose Fiction 1700-1739*, and "Mrs. Penelope Aubin and the Early Eighteenth-Century Novel."

2. This is now a familiar argument. See, for example, Katharine M. Rogers, *Feminism in Eighteenth-Century England*, pp. 22, 46-47; Elaine Showalter, *A Literature of Their Own*, pp. 4-12, 90-94; and Ellen Moers, *Literary Women*. The existence of satires such as [Charles Johnson], *The History of . . . Elizabeth Mann* argues the early recognition of the form.

3. Watt, *The Rise of the Novel*, p. 299.

4. Margaret Doody's article, "George Eliot and the Eighteenth-Century Novel," reinforces my point.

5. Barker, "To the Reader," in *A Patch-Work Screen for the Ladies,* p. iv.

6. Tom Brown, Preface, *Lindamira.* See also the preface to *The Jamaica Lady* by W.P., in *Four Before Richardson,* on a new sort of novel (p. 87).

7. Doody finds some of these characteristics in her "ur-model" of the new kind of novel developed by women in the late eighteenth century ("George Eliot," pp. 268-72).

8. Quoted in Judith Kegan Gardiner's "On Female Identity and Writing by Women" in *Writing and Sexual Difference,* ed. Elizabeth Abel, p. 185; see also pp. 186-87, and Annette Kolodny, "Turning the Lens on 'The Panther Captivity': A Feminist Exercise in Practical Criticism," in *Writing and Sexual Difference,* p. 169; Patricia Meyer Spacks, *The Female Imagination,* pp. 2-6, 412 et passim; Rachel M. Brownstein, *Becoming a Heroine,* pp. xvii, 24 et passim.

9. Fanny Burney, *The Wanderer; or Female Difficulties,* 1: xvi.

10. Defoe, *Roxana,* pp. 148-49; see also 150-58, and, with Sir Robert Clayton, pp. 167, 170-71.

11. Delariviére Manley, "The Physician's Stratagem," in *The Power of Love,* pp. 144-54; Barker, *A Patch-Work Screen,* p. 99.

12. Mary Davys, *The Reform'd Coquet,* p. 95.

13. Defoe, *Roxana,* p. 62; see also pp. 287-91, when Roxana encourages Susan to describe her beauty in great detail.

14. See Davys, *Reform'd Coquet,* pp. 94-96, and Eliza Haywood, *Idalia.* Roger Thompson notes that "the 'Misses' of the courtiers often lodged near Whitehall in Pall Mall" (*Unfit for Modest Ears,* p. 62).

15. "Interesting" has always been a mixed compliment when applied to women (see Tania Modleski, *Loving with a Vengeance,* pp. 52, 95; Annis Pratt, *Archetypal Patterns in Women's Fiction,* pp. 122-23; and Mary Anne Schofield, *Quiet Rebellion, pp. 49-50).*

16. Eliza Haywood, *Fantomina;* the women characters in the anonymous *Love upon Tick* object to the men's attention to frivolous girls (p. 5).

17. Haywood, *Fantomina,* p. 265.

18. Pratt, *Archetypical Patterns,* pp. 111-14; see my forthcoming essay, "Esteem in the Novels by Women," in *Fetter'd or Free.*

19. Schofield discusses such characters in the novels by Haywood, *Quiet Rebellion,* p. 60.

20. Eliza Haywood, *The British Recluse,* in her *Secret Histories, Novels, and Poems,* p. 114.

21. Barker, *A Patch-Work Screen,* pp. 80 and 79 respectively.

22. Manley's *The Happy Fugitives,* in *The Power of Love,* is adapted from Bandello's novella in William Painter's *The Palace of Pleasure.* These novellas were reworked by a number of writers; compare, for example, Manley's *The Wife's Resentment* to *The Cruel Revenge* in *Lovers Tales.*

23. The evidence from the book trade contradicts limitations on women's reading to some extent. Such books as Richard Steele's *The Ladies Library, The Ladies Dictionary* (1694), *The Ladies Diary* (1707), *The Ladies Tutor* (1720), and numerous periodicals and sections of periodicals designed for women argue some social encouragement of women's reading. The first numbers of *The Mirrour* (1719) were directed at women; *The Wanderer* (1717) included a

question/answer section from women; *The Visiter* stated, "The Ladies I design as my most peculiar Care" (18 June 1723).

24. See, for example, G.S. Rousseau's "Nymphomania, Bienville, and the Rise of Erotic Sensibility," in *Sexuality in Eighteenth-Century Britain*, pp. 126-27; he tells of the death sentence imposed and then revoked upon a nobleman who raped his servant woman.

25. John V. Price discusses the use of sexual signals in novels in "Patterns of Sexual Behaviour in Some Eighteenth-Century Novels," *Sexuality*, pp. 170-73.

26. Susan Staves has demonstrated that women were not, in fact, invariably "ruined" (see "British Seduced Maidens").

27. John Milton, *Paradise Lost*, book 4, l.75.

28. John Richetti, "The Family, Sex, and Marriage in Defoe's *Moll Flanders* and *Roxana*," pp. 34-35.

29. Ernest Bernbaum, *The Mary Carleton Narratives, 1663-1673*, pp. 11, 66-69, 74-75. Bernbaum points out the movement in the Carleton narratives to more description, elaboration of motive, character development, and moral commentary—all directions the developing novel took.

30. Swearing indicated great moral depravity to the Dissenters. Defoe condemns such language repeatedly in his conduct books and uses it to label characters "evil" in his tracts (see, for example, *A Letter to Andrew Snape*, *Review* 19, 14 August 1711, pp. 246-47; and *Colonel Jack*, p. 68).

31. Quoted in Modleski, *Loving with a Vengeance*, p. 37; see also p. 53; Gardiner, "On Female Identity," pp. 188-90; Sandra Lee Bartky, "On Psychological Oppression," in *Philosophy and Women*, p. 38; Erik Erikson, "Inner and Outer Space: Reflections on Womanhood"; Eva Figes, *Sex and Subterfuge: Women Novelists to 1850*, pp. 20-22.

32. Attempts to identify a specific model for Defoe's *Roxana* have failed (see, for example, David Blewett, *Defoe's Art of Fiction*, p. 123). Novak discusses some contemporary associations raised by her name in *Realism*, pp. 113-16, 165n.50.

33. *Memoirs of . . . Count de Grammont*, p. 124.

34. Montesquieu, C.L. de Secondat, *Lettres Persanes*, letters 26 and 151, 7: 72-77, 421. Frederick M. Keener points out the importance of the *Lettres Persanes* to the history of fiction in *The Chain of Becoming*, pp. 128, 131, 135-40 et passim.

35. Montesquieu, *Lettres Persanes*, letter 161, pp. 433-34. In Letter 76, Usbek does not condemn suicide when it ends "sorrow, misery, and contempt" (pp. 209-11).

36. On Roxana's representative nature, see Blewett, *Defoe's Art of Fiction*, pp. 121-27, and Novak, *Realism*, pp. 117-18. On Roxane's see Pocock, *Machiavellian Moment*, pp. 468, 476-77.

37. Evidence from psychological studies to some extent bears out women's superior ability to "read" other people; see, for example, Carol Tavis and Carole Offir, *The Longest War*, pp. 47-48; Modleski, *Loving with a Vengeance*, pp. 34-39.

38. Mary Jacobus, "The Question of Language," in *Writing and Sexual Difference*, p. 43; Doody, "George Eliot," pp. 280-91; Tavis and Offir, *Longest War*, p. 184; Spacks, *Female Imagination*, pp. 7-40; Figes, *Sex and Subterfuge*, pp. 17, 39, 64-65, 151; Mary Ann Caws, "Wariness and Women's Language," in *Gender and Literary Voice*, pp. 26-36; Brownstein, *Becoming a Heroine*, pp.

24, 26. The feature most often pointed out by contemporary feminist critics is the ironic tone found in so many novels by women.

39. Woolf called it "chattering and garrulous," in "Women and Fiction," in *Granite and Rainbow*, p. 84; Matthew Arnold, "Eugénie de Guérin," in *The Complete Prose Works of Matthew Arnold*, 3: 87; I would like to thank David Riede of Ohio State University for this reference.

40. Defoe makes a telling observation about the Huguenots in *A True-Born Englishman*: "H' invites the banish'd Protestants of *France*: / Hither for God's sake and their own they fled, / Some for Religion came, and some for Bread . . ." (Ellis, *Poems on Affairs of State*, 6: 175). The Huguenots began to arrive a few years before the revocation of the Edict of Nantes in October 1685.

41. William Congreve, Preface, *Incognita*, n.p.

42. Congreve, *Incognita*, p. 12; see also Henry Fielding, *Tom Jones*, book 2, chapter 1.

43. Several of Defoe's contemporaries wrote plays, but those who combined careers as novelists and journalists seem to have been more successful; for example, Eliza Haywood and Delariviére Manley. Most novelists also translated novellas and romances from the continent.

44. Pratt, *Archetypical Patterns*, p. 75; Rogers, *Feminism*, p. 23; and Spacks, *Female Imagination*, pp. 200-201, and "Reflecting Women," p. 32.

45. Aphra Behn, *The Dumb Virgin*, in *The Works*, vol. 5.

46. Delariviére Manley, *The Perjur'd Beauty*, in *The Power of Love*. The fascination with the incest theme lasted throughout the age; even accidental incest such as Rossano's with Victoria was not forgiven.

47. Tavis and Offir, *Longest War*, pp. 66-69.

48. Ibid., pp. 68-70, 172-76.

49. Spacks, *Female Imagination*, pp. 11-34, 80-84 et passim; Modleski, *Loving with a Vengeance*, p. 45; Paula R. Backscheider, "Woman's Influence"; Helen Hazen, *Endless Rapture: Rape, Romance, and the Female Imagination*, pp. 24-28, 90.

50. Compare this to fiction by men, such as *The Double Captive* (1718), in which the man suffers but the woman is entirely guiltless; in fact, she is unaware that he is fantasizing about her. *The Double Captive* is in Natascha Wurzback, *The Novel in Letters*, pp. 91-102.

51. See Backscheider, "Esteem," forthcoming.

52. Helen Hazen's *Endless Rapture* is a sustained study of rape in fiction and demonstrates the considerable differences in attitudes toward rape between male and female writers (see esp. pp. 79-84). Examples of male characters raping the women who have rejected them are fairly common in early fiction; see Manley's *Fair Hypocrite* in *The Power of Love* and Haywood's *Mercenary Lover*.

53. Brownstein, *Becoming a Heroine*, pp. 39-40; Gardiner, "On Female Identity," p. 190; Bartky, "On Psychological Oppression," pp. 34-38.

54. John Richetti argues that fiction before 1740 shows attitudes toward experience, the secular and religious, in conflict and sees *Robinson Crusoe* as an attack upon the secularism that denies providential control of creation (*Popular Fiction before Richardson*, pp. 11-17).

55. Penelope Aubin, *The Noble Slaves*, p. xii.

56. Richetti, *Popular Fiction before Richardson*, p. 17.

57. Starr, *Defoe and Spiritual Autobiography*, pp. 163-83. Compare the technique and structure of the form as discussed in Starr, *Defoe and Spiritual*

Autobiography, pp. 165-67, and J. Paul Hunter, *The Reluctant Pilgrim,* pp. 84-85, 90.

58. No Aubin heroine even flirts with Job's doubts. On the religious aspects of her novels, see McBurney, "Mrs. Aubin," pp. 259-61, and Richetti, *Popular Fiction before Richardson,* pp. 210, 215-18, 226-27.

59. Michael Foucault has said that the most significant act in the eighteenth century was interpretation. For a discussion of interpretation in *Robinson Crusoe,* see Backscheider, *A Being More Intense,* pp. 119, 161-75.

60. Richetti, "The Family, Sex, and Marriage," p. 34.

61. Every great religion and most regional philosophies warn men of this danger (see Tavis and Offir, *Longest War,* pp. 5, 22; Wolfgang Lederer, *The Fear of Women,* pp. 53-55, 73-74 et passim; and Robert Scholes, *Semiotics and Interpretation,* pp. 131-32).

62. Henry Kramer, *Malleus Maleficarum,* l.6.

63. Lederer, *Fear of Women,* pp. 194, 233; Tavis and Offir, *Longest War,* pp. 5-23, 144, 148-50.

64. Lederer, *Fear of Women,* pp. 99-102 (and see his illustrations of primitive art); Tavis and Offir, *Longest War,* pp. 144; Scholes discussed Lawrence on pp. 139-40 of *Semiotics and Interpretation.*

65. "Estate" here means position in the world or rank and carries the implication that people with "estate" govern and have assets such as property and capital (*OED*).

66. Ron Howell, "What Men Fear about Women," p. 72.

67. Lederer, *Fear of Women,* pp. 161, 194.

68. One of man's greatest fears about woman is her alleged ability to change shapes (see Lederer, *Fear of Women,* p. 194; Pratt, *Archetypical Patterns,* pp. 122-23).

69. Lederer, *Fear of Women,* p. 228.

70. Richetti, *Popular Fiction before Richardson,* pp. 21, 187.

71. Many prefaces to novels compared prose fiction to drama and included discussions of the value of poetic justice. See, for example, Congreve's preface to *Incognita,* Eliza Haywood's to her 1725 *Works,* and Mary Davys's to her *Works* (1725), in which she says she follows "the great rule prescribed by the criticks, not only in tragedy and other heroic poems but in comedy too." Defoe himself compares his technique to that of the drama in his preface to *Moll Flanders* and argues, "The Advocates for the Stage, have in all Ages made this the great Argument to perswade People that their Plays are useful" (1: ix).

8. Melted Down, Filled with Wonders

John Dunton said, "the best of the English histories were melted down, filled with wonders, rarities, and curiosities." Quoted in "Robinson Crusoe at Yale," *Yale University Library Gazette* 2 (1936-37): 23.

1. Defoe, *A New Family Instructor,* pp. 52-53.

2. William Lee, *Daniel Defoe: His Life and Recently Discovered Writings,* 3: 466-69; see also, Defoe, *Review,* 1: 79.

3. Defoe, *Review,* 7:25 for 11 April 1710.

4. Charles Morton, "Of Ethicks and Its End," p. 32. I am grateful to the Houghton Library, Harvard University, for permission to quote.

5. The discussion of fiction as "lie" was extended and heated, and much has been written on the subject by modern scholars. My intention is to discuss Defoe's use of story rather than to rehearse or enter into the debate. In addition to Defoe's discussion in *A New Family Instructor*, see his remarks on the uses of parable and allegory in "Of the Immorality of Conversation, and the Vulgar Errors of Behavior" in *Serious Reflections of Robinson Crusoe*, pp. 107-9. In this essay Defoe refers specifically to John Bunyan's *Pilgrim's Progress*, which includes a similar defense of fictions in the poetic introductions to both parts of *Pilgrim's Progress*. See also [Samuel Croxall], Preface to *A Select Collection of Novels*, pp. v, xlii, and li, for a typical defense of fiction; Croxall said, for example, that "St. Austin" explained "those Falsities, which are significative, and contain in them a hidden Sense, are not properly Lies, but figurative Truths . . ." and have always been used by wise, pious men including Christ (p. xlix). Novak has consistently pointed out the crucial importance of Defoe's fiction making (see, for example, his most recent book, *Realism, Myth and History in Defoe's Fiction*).

6. Novak has written extensively on the genesis of *Robinson Crusoe* (see, for example, "Imaginary Islands and Real Beasts: The Imaginative Genesis of *Robinson Crusoe*" and his forthcoming "Sincerity, Delusion, and Character").

7. On Curll's biographies, see Donald A. Stauffer, *The Art of Biography in Eighteenth-Century England*, p. 234.

8. Knox, *Historical Relation of Ceylon*, p. xxix, of "Autobiography." Percy Adams makes some references to the commonplace religious element in *Travel Literature and the Evolution of the Novel*, pp. 39, 59, 60, 113, 123, 126, 182.

9. Alan D. McKillop notes Defoe's tendency "to derive both setting and incident largely from his sources" in *The Early Masters of English Fiction*, p. 9. The authoritative study is still A.W. Secord, *Studies in the Narrative Method of Defoe*. Boies Penrose (*Travel and Discovery in the Renaissance*, p. 5) discusses the common practice of borrowing. Penrose points out that England excelled in collections of voyages, and her travel literature "alone aimed explicitly at stimulating expansion" (pp. 312-20).

10. My fullest discussions of *Robinson Crusoe* are in *A Being More Intense*, "Defoe's Prodigal Sons," and "Defoe and the Geography of the Mind," in *The First English Novelists*.

11. The term is Mas'ud Zavarzadeh's from *The Mythopoeic Reality*.

12. The preface to Part II of *The English Rogue* is nearly identical (see p. 269).

13. Charles Gildon, *The Life and Strange Surprizing Adventures of Mr. D . . . De F. . ., Of London, Hosier.*

14. [Anonymous], *The Highland Rogue*, p. iii.

15. William McBurney notes Defoe's influence on Aubin, in "Mrs. Penelope," pp. 245-67; Aubin, *Count de Vinevil*, pp. 6.

16. Aubin, *Count de Vinevil*, pp. 5-6.

17. Jerry C. Beasley tells us that Aubin's success was more enduring than Eliza Haywood's and suggests that Aubin deliberately combined the appeals of Defoe's and Haywood's work (*Novels of the 1740's*, pp. 164-65).

18. For a discussion of Crusoe's reproduction of England, see Backscheider, *A Being More Intense*, pp. 170-72.

19. Aubin, *The Life of Madame de Beaumont*, p. 143.

20. Barker, *A Patch-Work Screen*, p. iv.

21. Patricia Meyer Spacks, "Ev'ry Woman is at Heart a Rake," pp. 32-33.

22. Richetti contrasts Aubin's and Haywood's techniques in *Popular Fiction before Richardson*, pp. 219, 223-25, 227-28.

23. Watt, *Rise of the Novel*, p. 66.

24. This chapter and my first have been influenced by Colie's *Resources of Kind*, esp. pp. viii, 3, 30, 79-80, 117-28.

25. A few examples are Novak, *Realism, Myth, and History;* Everett Zimmerman, *Defoe and the Novel;* and Samuel L. Macey, *Money and the Novel.*

26. Watt, *Rise of the Novel*, pp. 30-34, 104. Robert Adolph finds the style of *Robinson Crusoe* to be the "logical culmination of everything we have been saying about the rise of a style for modern fiction" (*The Rise of Modern Prose Style*, pp. 278-83 and 302-3).

27. Burgess, "Modern Novels: The 99 Best," *New York Times Book Review* (5 Feb. 1984): 1.

28. Henry James, "Preface," *Roderick Hudson*, pp. vi-vii. I would like to thank Professor Sharon Cameron for bringing this edition to my attention.

29. Henry James, uses the term in "The Art of Fiction," in *The Portable Henry James*, p. 403.

30. Timothy J. Reiss, *The Discourse of Modernism*, pp. 294-327.

31. Burgess, "Modern Novels," pp. 36-37.

32. Fanny Burney, *The Wanderer*, 5: 394-95.

33. Joseph Conrad, "Preface," *The Nigger of the "Narcissus,"* p. x.

34. Josiah Woodward, *The Duty of Compassion to the Souls of Others*, pp. viii-x.

35. James, "Art of Fiction," p. 413.

36. William Faulkner, "To the Book Editor of the *Chicago Tribune*," in *Essays, Speeches, and Public Letters by William Faulkner*, p. 198.

BIBLIOGRAPHY

Works by Defoe

Note: With a few exceptions, I use only those works in the Defoe canon which I believe certain to be by Defoe. The exceptions have explanatory notes. Dates are those printed on Defoe's works and cited in CBEL; for example, "1700 (for 1701)" is cited as "1700."

An Account of the Proceedings against the Rebels. 1716.

The Address to the Pillory. London, [1704].

Advertisement from Daniel De Foe, to Mr. Clark. [Edinburgh, 1710].

And What if the Pretender Should Come? London, 1713.

The Annals of King George, Year the Second. London, 1717.

The Annals of King George, Year the Third. London, 1718.

An Answer to a Question that No Body thinks of, viz. But What if the Queen should die? London, 1713.

An Appeal to Honour and Justice. (1715). In *The Shortest Way with Dissenters and Other Pamphlets*. Shakespeare Head edition. Oxford: Blackwell, 1974.

An Argument Proving that the Design of Employing and Enobling Foreigners is a Treasonous Conspiracy. London, 1717.

Armageddon: Or, The Necessity of Carrying on the War. London, [1711].

Atlas Maritimus. London, 1728.

The Ballance of Europe. London, 1711.

A Brief Explanation of a Late Pamphlet entitled The Shortest Way with the Dissenters. London, 1703.

A Brief State of the Inland or Home Trade of England. London, 1730.

A Brief State of the Question, Between the Printed and Painted Calicoes and the Woollen and Silk Manufacture. London, 1719.

A Brief Survey of the Legal Liberties of the Dissenters. London, 1714.

The British Visions. London, 1711.

Caledonia. Edinburgh, 1706.

A Challenge of Peace. London, 1703.

The Character of the Late Dr. Samuel Annesley. London, 1697.

Colonel Jack. Introduction by Samuel Holt Monk. London: Oxford University Press, 1965.

The Complete English Tradesman. London, 1726.

A Conference with a Jacobite. London, 1716.

Considerations on the Present State of Affairs in Great Britain. London, 1718.

Considerations upon the Eighth and Ninth Articles of the Treaty of Commerce and Navigation. London, 1713.

The Consolidator. London, 1705.

The Dissenters Answer to the High-Church Challenge. London, 1704.

The Double Welcome. London, 1705.

Due Preparations for the Plague. London, 1722.

An Elegy on the Author of the True-Born English-man. London, 1704.

An Encomium upon Parliament. London, [1699].

The Englishman's Choice, and True Interest: In a Vigorous Prosecution of the War against France. London, 1694.

An Enquiry into Occasional Conformity. London, 1702.

An Essay at Removing National Prejudices against a Union with Scotland. Part I. London, 1706.

An Essay on the History and Reality of Apparitions. London, 1727.

An Essay on the Treaty of Commerce with France. London, 1713.

An Essay upon Literature. London, 1726.

An Essay upon Publick Credit. London, 1710.

Every-body's Business is No-body's Business. London, 1725.

Faction in Power. London, 1717.

The Family Instructor. Newcastle, 1715; London, 1715.

The Four Years Voyages of Captain George Roberts. London, 1726.

The Free-Holders Plea against Stock-Jobbing Elections. London, 1701.

A General History of Discoveries and Improvements. Bound together as *The History of the Principal Discoveries and Improvements.* London, 1727.

The General History of the . . . Pyrates. London, 1724.

Giving Alms No Charity. London, 1704.

Good Advice to the Ladies. 1702.

An Historical Account of the Voyages and Adventures of Sir Walter Raleigh. London, 1719.

Historical Collections. Los Angeles: UCLA, Clark Library Ms., 1682.

History of Apparitions. Oxford: Talboys, 1840.

A History of the Clemency of Our English Monarchs. London, 1717.

The History of the Kentish Petition. 1701. In *The Shortest Way with the Dissenters and Other Pamphlets.* Shakespeare Head edition. Oxford: Blackwell, 1974.

The History of the Reign of King George. London, 1719.

The History of the Union of Great Britain. Edinburgh, 1709.

The History of the Wars, of His Late Majesty Charles XII, King of Sweden. London, 1720.

The History of the Wars, of His Present Majesty Charles XII, King of Sweden. London, 1715.

A Hymn to the Pillory. London, 1703.

A Hymn to Victory. London, 1704.

Instructions from Rome. London, [1710].

An Impartial History of the Life and Actions of Peter Alexowitz, The Present Czar of Muscovy. London, 1723.

Introduction to *A Journal of the Earl of Marr's Proceedings*. London, [1716].

A Journal of the Plague Year. Introduction by Louis A. Landa. London: Oxford Univ. Press, 1969.

Jure Divino. London, 1706.

The King of Pirates. London, 1720.

Legion's Memorial. London, 1701. In *The Shortest Way with the Dissenters and Other Pamphlets*. Shakespeare Head edition.

A Letter Concerning Trade. [Edinburgh, 1706.]

A Letter from a Member of the House of Commons, . . . Relating to the Bill of Commerce. London, 1713.

A Letter from some Protestant Dissenting Laymen. London, 1718.

A Letter to a Dissenter from his friend at the Hague. London, [1688].

A Letter to Andrew Snape. London, 1717.

A Letter to Mr. Steele. London, 1714.

A Letter to the Dissenters. London, 1713.

The Letters of Daniel Defoe. Edited by George H. Healey. Oxford: Clarendon, 1969.

Meditations. Edited by G. H. Healey. Cummington, Mass.: Cummington Press, 1946.

(Mist's) *Weekly Journal*. London, 1716-1724.

Memoirs of Count Tariff. London, 1713.

Memoirs of the Church of Scotland. London, 1717.

The Memoirs of Major Alexander Ramkins. London, 1719.

Minutes of Mesnager. London, 1717.

The Mock Mourners. London, 1702.

More Reformation. London, 1703.

A New Discovery of an Old Intreague. London, 1691.

A New Family Instructor. London, 1727.

A New Test of the Church of England's Honesty. London, 1704.

Novels and Selected Writings. 2d ed. Shakespeare Head edition. Oxford: Blackwell, 1974.

Observations and Remarks upon the Declaration of War against Spain. London, 1719.

The Opinion of a Known Dissenter on the Bill for Preventing Occasional Conformity. London, 1703.

The Pacificator. London, 1700.

Peace without Union. London, 1703.

Persecution Anatomiz'd. London, 1705.

A Plan of the English Commerce. London, 1728, 1730.

The Political History of the Devil. Exeter: Davies and Eldridge, 1814.

The Political History of the Devil. London, 1726.

The Political State of Great Britain. London, Dec. 1729-Oct. 1730.

"Proposals for Printing by Subscription A compleat History Of The Union." [London, 1707].

The Question Fairly Stated. London, 1717.

Reasons against the Succession of the House of Hanover. London, 1713.

Reasons for a Royal Visitation. London, 1717.

Reasons Why This Nation Ought to Put a Speedy End to this Expensive War. London, 1711.

Reflections on the Prohibition Act. London, 1708.

Reformation of Manners. London, 1702.

A Reproof to Mr. Clark. Edinburgh, [1710].

Review. Facsimile edition. Edited by A.W. Secord. New York: Columbia Univ. Press, 1938.

Roxana. Edited by Jane Jack. London: Oxford University Press, 1964.

The Secret History of the Secret History of the White Staff. London, 1715.

A Serious Inquiry into This Grand Question. London, 1704.

Serious Reflections of Robinson Crusoe. Edited by G.H. Maynadier. New York: Crowell, 1903.

A Short Narrative of the Life . . . of . . . Marlborough. London, 1711.

A Short View of the Conduct of the King of Sweden. London, [1717].

The Shortest Way to Peace and Union. London, 1703.

The Shortest Way with the Dissenters. London, 1702.

The Six Distinguishing Characters of a Parliament-Man. London, 1700.

Some Account of the Life . . . of the Baron de Goertz. London, 1719.

"Some Account of the Life of Sir Charles Sedley." Prefixed to *The Works of Sedley.* London, 1722.

Some National Grievances. London, 1717.

Some Thoughts upon the Subject of Commerce with France. London, 1713.

The Spanish Descent. London, 1702.

[*A Speech of a Stone Chimney-Piece.*] London, [1711].

A Speech without Doors. London, 1710.

The Storm. London, 1704.

The Storm, An Essay. London, 1704.

A System of Magick. London, 1726.

"To the Athenian Society." In *The History of the Athenian Society,* by Charles Gildon. 1692.

A Tour Thro' the Whole Island of Great Britain. Edited by G.D.H. Cole. 1962. Reprint. London: Dent, 1974.

A True Account of the Proceedings at Perth. London, 1716.

A True, Authentick, and Impartial History of the Life and Glorious Actions of the Czar of Muscovy. London, 1725.

A True Collection of the Writings of the Author of the True-Born Englishman. London, 1703.

The True-Born Englishman. London, 1700.

Two Great Questions Considered . . . Being a Sixth Essay at Removing National Prejudices against the Union. [Edinburgh], 1707.

The Two Great Questions Further Considered. London, 1700.

A View of the Real Dangers of the Succession, from the Peace with France. London, 1713.

A View of the Scots Rebellion. London, 1715.

A Vindication of the Press. London, 1718.

Wise as Serpents. London, 1712.

Primary and Secondary Sources

Abel, Elizabeth, ed. *Writing and Sexual Difference.* Chicago: Univ. of Chicago Press, 1982.

Adams, Percy. *Travelers and Travel Liars.* Berkeley: Univ. of California Press, 1962.

_____. *Travel Literature and the Evolution of the Novel.* Lexington: Univ. Press of Kentucky, 1983.

Addison, Joseph. *The Campaign.* London, 1704.

_____. *The Late Tryal and Conviction of Count Tariff.* London, 1713.

_____. *Remarks on Several Parts of Italy.* London, 1705.

Adolph, Robert. *The Rise of Modern Prose Style.* Cambridge: MIT Press, 1968.

Alkon, Paul K. *Defoe and Fictional Time.* Athens: Univ. of Georgia Press, 1979.

_____. "Defoe's Argument in *The Shortest Way with the Dissenters.*" *Journal of Modern Philology* 73 (1976): 12-22.

Alter, Robert. *Rogue's Progress.* Cambridge: Harvard Univ. Press, 1965.

Altick, Richard. *Lives and Letters.* New York: Knopf, 1965.

Anderson, Robert, ed. *A Complete Edition of the Poets of Great Britain.* Vol. 8. London: Arch, 1795.

Arnold, Matthew. *The Complete Prose Works of Matthew Arnold.* Edited by R.H. Super. Vol. 3. Ann Arbor: University of Michigan Press, 1962.

Aubin, Penelope. *The Life of Madame de Beaumont.* London, 1721.

――――. *The Noble Slaves.* London, 1722.

――――. *The Strange Adventures of Count de Vinevil.* London, 1722.

Aubin, Robert A. *Topographical Poetry in XVIII-Century England.* New York: MLA, 1936.

Aubrey, John. *Miscellanies: Three Prose Works.* Edited by John Buchanan-Brown. Carbondale: Southern Illinois Univ. Press, 1972.

[Aulnoy, Marie.] *Memoirs of the Countess of Dunois.* London, 1699.

Backscheider, Paula R. *A Being More Intense: The Prose Works of Bunyan, Swift, and Defoe.* New York: AMS Press, 1984.

――――. "Cross-Purposes: Defoe's *History of the Union*." *CLIO*, 11 (1982): 165-86.

――――. "Defoe and the Geography of the Mind." In *The First English Novelists*, edited by J.M. Armistead, 41-65. Knoxville: Univ. of Tennessee Press, 1985.

――――. "Defoe as Solitary Reader." *Princeton Library Chronicle* 46 (1985): 178-91.

――――. "Defoe's Lady Credit." *Huntington Library Quarterly* 44 (1981): 89-100.

――――. "Defoe's Prodigal Sons." *Studies in the Literary Imagination* 15 (1982): 3-18.

――――. "Esteem in the Novels by Women." In *Fetter'd or Free*, edited by Mary Anne Schofield and Cecilia Macheski, 152-68. Athens: Ohio Univ. Press, 1986.

――――. "Personality and Biblical Allusion in Defoe's Letters." *South Atlantic Review* 47 (1982): 1-20.

――――. "Woman's Influence." *Studies in the Novel. North Texas State* 11 (1979): 3-22.

Bacon, Francis. *The Advancement of Learning.* London, 1605. Oxford: Clarendon, 1974. [Princeton University's Taylor Collection has Defoe's annotated copy.]

Bailey, Nathan. *An Universal Etymological English Dictionary.* London, 1721.

Baine, Rodney. *Defoe and the Supernatural.* Athens: Univ. of Georgia Press, 1968.

Barker, Jane. *A Patch-Work Screen for the Ladies.* London, 1723.

Bartky, Sandra Lee. "On Psychological Oppression." In *Philosophy and*

Women, edited by Sharon Bishop and Marjorie Weinzweig. Belmont, Calif.: Wadsworth, 1979.

Bastian, Frank. *Defoe's Early Life*. Totowa, N.J.: Barnes and Noble, 1981.

_____. "Defoe's Journal of the Plague Year Reconsidered." *Review of English Studies*, ser. 2, 16 (1965): 151-73.

Baxter, Richard. *The Autobiography of Richard Baxter*. Abridged by J.M. Lloyd Thomas. London: Dent, 1974.

_____. *The Certainty of the World of Spirits*. London, 1691.

_____. *The Practical Works of the Rev. Richard Baxter*. Vols. 2, 21 and 22. London: Duncan, 1830.

Beasley, Jerry C. *Novels in the 1740's*. Athens: Univ. of Georgia Press, 1982.

Beeckman, Daniel. *Voyage to and from the Island of Borneo*. London, 1718.

Behn, Aphra. *The Works*. Edited by Montague Summers. London: Heineman, 1915.

Bernbaum, Ernest. *The Mary Carleton Narratives, 1663-1673*. Cambridge: Harvard Univ. Press, 1914.

Bjornson, Richard. *The Picaresque Hero in European Fiction*. Madison: Univ. of Wisconsin Press, 1977.

Black, Jeremy. "Russia and the British Press in the Early Eighteenth Century." *Study Group on Eighteenth-Century Russia Newsletter* 11 (1983): 16-31.

Blewett, David. *Defoe's Art of Fiction*. Toronto: Univ. of Toronto Press, 1979.

_____. "Roxana and the Masquerades." *Modern Language Review* 65 (1970): 499-502.

Bloom, Edward, and L. Bloom. *Joseph Addison's Sociable Animal*. Providence: Brown Univ. Press, 1971.

Blowen, Michael. "Not all of the stuff in that movie was right." Reprinted from *The Boston Globe* in *The Democrat and Chronicle* (30 October 1983), p. 1D.

Bolingbroke, Henry St. John, Lord. "On the Study and Use of History." In *The Works of Lord Bolingbroke*, vol. 2. Philadelphia: Carey and Hart, 1841.

Bonnet, Henri. "Dichotomy of Artistic Genres." In *Theories of Literary Genre*, edited by Joseph P. Strelka. University Park: Pennsylvania State Univ. Press, 1978.

Boswell, James. *An Account of Corsica, the Journal of a Tour to that Island*. London, 1768.

_____. *Memoirs of Pascal Paoli*. Edinburgh, 1768.

Boyer, Abel. *Memoirs of the Life and Negotiations of Sir W. Temple.* London, 1714.

Bridge, Cyprian A.G., ed. *History of the Russian Fleet during the Reign of Peter.* Publications of the Navy Records Society, No. 15 [1899].

Bromley, J.S., ed. *New Cambridge Modern History.* Vol. 6. Cambridge: Cambridge Univ. Press, 1970.

Bronson, Bertrand. *Facets of the Enlightenment.* Berkeley: Univ. of California Press, 1968.

Browne, Thomas. *Pseudodoxia Epidemica.* Edited by Robin Robbins. 1646. Oxford: Clarendon, 1981.

Brownstein, Rachel. *Becoming a Heroine.* New York: Viking, 1982.

Bruce, Maurice. "Jacobite Relations with Peter the Great." *The Slavonic and East European Review* 14 (1936): 343-62.

Bulteel, J. *The Apopthegms of the Ancients.* [London], 1683.

Bunyan, John. "Apology for his Book." In *Pilgrim's Progress.* Edited by Roger Sharrock. London: Oxford Univ. Press, 1966.

———. *The Holy War.* Edited by James F. Forrest. New York: New York Univ. Press, 1967.

Burgess, Anthony. "Modern Novels: The 99 Best." *New York Times Book Review* (5 Feb. 1984): 1, 36-37.

Burke, John J., Jr. "Observing the Observer in the Historical Fictions by Defoe." *Philological Quarterly* 61 (1982): 13-32.

Burman, Charles. *Memoirs of the Life of that Learned Antiquary, Elias Ashmore.* London, 1717.

Burnet, Gilbert. *History of His Own Time.* 6 vols. Oxford: Clarendon, 1823.

———. *History of the Reformation.* 3 vols. London, 1679, 1681, 1715.

Burney, Fanny. *The Wanderer; or Female Difficulties.* London: Longman, Hurst, Rees, Orme, and Brown, 1814.

Butterfield, Herbert. *The Historical Novel.* Cambridge: Cambridge Univ. Press, 1924.

Calamy, Edmund. *Memoirs of the Life of the late Reverend Increase Mather, D.D.* London, 1725.

Campbell, M.E. *Defoe's First Poem.* Bloomington: Principia Press, 1938.

Castiglione, B. *The Courtyer.* [London], 1603.

Cawelti, John G. *Adventure, Mystery, and Romance.* Chicago: Univ. of Chicago Press, 1976.

Chalmers, George. *The Life of Defoe.* London: Stockdale, 1790.

Chamberlayne, John. *Magnae Britanniae Notitia.* London, 1708.

Chance, James F. *George I and the Northern War.* London: Smith, Elder, 1909.

Chandler, Frank W. *The Literature of Roguery*. Boston: Houghton, Mifflin, 1907.

Cherniak, Warren L. "The Heroic Occasional Poem." *Modern Language Quarterly* 26 (1965): 523-35.

Chetwood, William. *The Voyages, Dangerous Adventures and Imminent Escapes of Captain Richard Falconer*. London, 1720.

Clarendon, Edward Hyde. *History of the Rebellion*. London, 1702-1704.

Clark, Sandra. *The Elizabethan Pamphleteers*. Rutherford: Fairleigh Dickinson Univ. Press, 1983.

Clarke, Adam. *Memoirs of the Wesley Family*. New York: Bangs and Mason, 1824.

Colie, Rosalie. *The Resources of Kind*. Berkeley: Univ. of California Press, 1973.

Congreve, William. *The Complete Works*. Edited by Montague Summers. Vol. 4. London: Nonesuch, 1923.

_____. *Incognita*. Menston, Yorkshire: Scholar Press, 1971.

Conrad, Joseph. *The Nigger of the "Narcissus."* Edinburgh: Grant, 1925.

Corelli, Barnett. *Britain and Her Army, 1509-1970*. New York: William Morrow, 1970.

Corvisier, André. *Armies and Societies in Europe, 1494-1789*. Translated by Abigail T. Siddall. Bloomington: Indiana Univ. Press, 1979.

Cotton, Charles. *Compleat Gamester*. London, 1674.

Courthope, W.J. *A History of English Poetry*. Vol. 5. London: Macmillan, 1925.

Cowley, Abraham. *Poems*. Edited by A.R. Waller. Cambridge: Cambridge Univ. Press, 1905.

Cranfield, G.A. *The Press and Society*. London: Longman, 1978.

Cross, A.G. "By the Banks of the Thames." In *Russians in Eighteenth-Century Britain*. Newtonville, Mass.: Oriental Research Partners, 1980.

[Croxall, Samuel.] *A Select Collection of Novels*. London, 1720.

Cru, Jean Norton. *War Books*. 1931. Reprint. San Diego: State Univ. Press, 1976.

[Crull, Jodocus.] *The Antient and Present State of Muscovy*. London, 1698.

_____. *The Present Condition of the Muscovite Empire, Till the Year 1699*. London, 1699.

Daiches, David. *Scotland and the Union*. London: Murray, 1977.

[Dalrymple, John.] *Memoirs of the Life, Family, and Character of John late Earl of Stair*. London, [1748].

Dampier, William. *A New Voyage round the World*. London, 1717.

Davis, Lennard J. *Factual Fictions*. New York: Columbia Univ. Press, 1983.

Davys, Mary. *The Reform'd Coquet*. London, 1724.

_____. *Works*. London, 1725.

Dee, John. *A True and Faithful Relation*. London, 1659.

de F. Lord, George, ed. *Poems of Affairs of State*. Vol. 1. New Haven: Yale Univ. Press, 1963.

Defoe, Benjamin Norton. *A New English Dictionary*. London, 1735.

[de Sandras, Courtilz.] *The French Spy*. London, 1700.

_____. *Memoirs of the Count de Rochefort*. London, 1707.

Diodorus of Sicily. *Bibliotheca*. London: Heinemann, 1933.

Dobrée, Bonamy. "Some Aspects of Defoe's Prose." In *Pope and his Contemporaries*, edited by James L. Clifford and Louis Landa. Oxford: Clarendon, 1949.

Doody, Margaret. "George Eliot and the Eighteenth-Century Novel." *Nineteenth-Century Fiction* 35 (1967): 260-91.

The Double Captive. London, 1718.

Douglas, David. *English Scholars 1660-1730*. 1939. Reprint. London: Eyre and Spottiswoode, 1951.

Drayton, Michael. *Poly-Olbion*. In *Works*, edited by J.W. Hebel. Oxford: Blackwell, 1933.

Drift, Adrian. *The History of His Own Time. Compiled from the Original Mss Of . . . Matthew Prior*. London, 1740.

Dryden, John. *Plutarch's Lives*. Edited by Arthur Hugh Clough. Boston: Little, Brown, 1891.

_____. *The Works of John Dryden*. Edited by Earl Miner. Vol. 3. Berkeley: Univ. of California Press, 1969.

_____. *The Works of John Dryden*. Edited by Samuel Holt Monk. Vol. 17. Berkeley: Univ. of California Press, 1971.

Earle, Peter. *Monmouth's Rebels*. London: Weidenfeld and Nicolson, 1977.

_____. *The World of Defoe*. New York: Atheneum, 1977.

Ehrenpreis, Irvin. *Swift: The Man, His Works, and the Age*. Vols. 2 and 3. Cambridge: Harvard Univ. Press, 1969, 1983.

Ellis, Frank, ed. *Poems on Affairs of State*. Vols. 6 and 7. New Haven: Yale Univ. Press, 1970.

Ellwood, Thomas. *The History of the Life of Thomas Ellwood*. London, 1714.

Elyot, Thomas. *The Book Named the Governor*. 1531. Menston, England: Scolar Press, 1970.

The English Expositor Improv'd. London, 1719.

Erikson, Erik. "Inner and Outer Space: Reflections on Womanhood." *Daedalus* 93 (1961): 582-606.

Ermarth, Elizabeth D. *Realism and Consensus in the English Novel.* Princeton: Princeton Univ. Press, 1983.

Erskine-Hill, Howard. *The Augustan Idea in English Literature.* London: Edward Arnold, 1983.

Eves, Charles K. *Matthew Prior, Poet and Diplomat.* New York: Columbia Univ. Press, 1939.

Faulkner, William. "To the Editor of the *Chicago Tribune.*" In *Essays, Speeches, and Public Letters by William Faulkner,* edited by James B. Meriwether. New York: Random House, 1965.

Ferguson, William. *Scotland. 1689 to the Present.* Edinburgh: Oliver and Boyd, 1968.

Fielding, Henry. *Tom Jones.* New York: Norton, 1973.

Fielding, Sarah. "Introduction to *The Lives of Cleopatra and Octavia,*" edited by R. Brimley Johnson. N.p.: Scholartis Press, 1928.

Figes, Eva. *Sex and Subterfuge: Women Novelists to 1850.* London: Macmillan, 1982.

Fleishman, Avrom. *The English Historical Novel.* Baltimore: Johns Hopkins Univ. Press, 1971.

_____. *Fiction and the Ways of Knowing.* Austin: Univ. of Texas, 1978.

Forster, E.M. "Pattern and Rhythm." In *Myth and Method,* edited by James E. Miller, Jr. Lincoln: Univ. of Nebraska Press, 1960.

Foster, James R. *History of the Pre-Romantic Novel in England.* New York: MLA, 1949.

Funck-Brentano, Frantz. *Les Nouvellistes.* Paris: Librairie Hachette, 1905.

Fussell, Paul. *The Great War and Modern Memory.* London: Oxford Univ. Press, 1975.

_____. *The Rhetorical World of Augustan Humanism.* 1965. Reprint. London: Oxford Univ. Press, 1969.

Gardiner, Judith Kegan. "On Female Identity and Writing by Women." In *Writing and Sexual Difference,* edited by Elizabeth Abel. Chicago: Univ. of Chicago Press, 1982.

Garrison, James D. *Dryden and the Tradition of Panegyric.* Berkeley: Univ. of California Press, 1975.

Gildon, Charles. *The Golden Spy.* London, 1709.

_____. *The Life and Strange Surprizing Adventures of Mr. D . . . De F . . . , Of London, Hosier.* London, 1719.

_____. *Miscellanea Aurea.* London, 1721.

_____. *The Post-boy Rob'd of his Mail.* London, 1692.

Gilman, Richard. *The Confusion of Realms*. 1963. Reprint. New York: Random House, 1969.

Goldsmith, Oliver. *The Collected Works*. Vol. 5. Edited by Arthur Friedman. Oxford: Clarendon, 1966.

Graunt, John. *Reflections on the Weekly Bills*. London, 1720.

Gray, John M., ed. *Memoirs of the Life of Sir John Clerk of Penicuik*. [Edinburgh: Constable, 1892.]

Grimblot, Paul, ed. *The Letters of William III and Louis XIV*. Vol. 2. London, 1848.

Guerlac, Henry. "Vauban: The Impact of Science on War." In *Makers of Modern Strategy*, edited by E.M. Earle. Princeton: Princeton Univ. Press, 1943.

Hagstrum, Jean. *The Sister Arts*. Chicago: Univ. of Chicago Press, 1958.

Hall, Basil. "Daniel Defoe and Scotland." In *Reformation, Conformity and Dissent*, edited by R. Buick Knox. London: Epworth, 1977.

[Hamilton, Anthony.] *Memoirs of the Life of Count de Grammont*. London, 1714.

Harris, Michael. "Trials and Criminal Biographies: A Case Study in Distribution." In *Sale and Distribution of Books*, edited by Robin Myers and Michael Harris. Oxford: Oxford Polytechnic Press, 1982.

Hatton, R.M. *Charles XII of Sweden*. New York: Weybright and Talley, 1968.

Haywood, Eliza. *Fantomina*. London, 1725.

_____. *Idalia*. London, 1723.

_____. *Love in Excess*. London, 1719.

_____. *Mary Stuart, Queen of Scots*. London, 1725.

[_____.] *Memoirs of the Baron de Brosse*. London, 1725.

_____. *Mercenary Lover*. London, 1726.

_____. *Tea Table*. London, 1724.

_____. *The British Recluse*. In *Secret Histories, Novels, and Poems*. 2d ed. London, 1725.

Hazen, Helen. *Endless Rapture: Rape, Romance, and the Female Imagination*. New York: Scribner's, 1983.

Head, Richard, and Francis Kirkman. *The English Rogue*. New York: Dodd, Mead, 1928.

Healey, George, ed. *The Letters of Daniel Defoe*. 1955. Reprint. Oxford: Clarendon, 1969.

Hearne, Mary. *The Female Deserters*. London, 1719.

Heawood, Edward. *A History of Geographical Discovery in the Seventeenth and Eighteenth Centuries*. Cambridge: Cambridge Univ. Press, 1912.

Hellman, John. *Fables of Fact*. Urbana: Univ. of Illinois Press, 1981.

Herd, Harold. *The March of Journalism*. London: Allen and Unwin, 1952.

Herr, Michael. *Dispatches*. New York: Knopf, 1977.

The Highland Rogue. 1723.

Hill, Christopher. *Intellectual Origins of the English Revolution*. Oxford: Clarendon, 1980.

Hobbes, Thomas, trans. *Eight Bookes of the Peloponnesian Warre Written by Thucydides*. Edited by Richard Schlatter. New Brunswick: Rutgers Univ. Press, 1975.

Hodges, Nathaniel. *Loimologia*. London, 1672.

Hollowell, John. *Fact and Fiction*. Chapel Hill: Univ. of North Carolina Press, 1977.

Holmes, Geoffrey. *The Trial of Doctor Sacheverell*. London: Methuen, 1973.

Holmes, Geoffrey and W.A. Speck, eds. *The Divided Society*. London: Arnold, 1967.

Hooker, Edward N. "The Purpose of Dryden's *Annus Mirabilis*." *Huntington Library Quarterly* 10 (1946): 49-67.

Horwitz, Henry. "The Structure of Parliamentary Politics." In *Britain after the Glorious Revolution*, edited by Geoffrey Holmes. London: Macmillan, 1969.

Howell, Ron. "What Men Fear about Women." *Ebony* 34 (Feb. 1979): 65-66, 68, 70, 72.

Hunter, J. Paul. *The Reluctant Pilgrim*. Baltimore: Johns Hopkins Univ. Press, 1966.

Jaffé, Aniela. *Apparitions and Precognition*. New Hyde Park, N.Y.: University Books, 1963.

James, Henry. "The Art of Fiction." In *The Portable Henry James*, edited by Morton D. Zabel. 1951. Reprint. New York: Viking, 1962.

James, Henry. *Roderick Hudson*. The New York Edition. New York: Scribner's, 1907.

[Johnson, Charles.] *The History of . . . Elizabeth Mann*. London, 1724.

Johnson, James William. *The Formation of Neo-Classical Thought*. Princeton: Princeton Univ. Press, 1967.

Johnson, Samuel. *The Idler and The Adventurer*. Vol. 2. Edited by Walter Jackson Bate, John M. Bullitt, and L.F. Powell. New Haven: Yale Univ. Press, 1963.

———. *Life of Savage*. London, 1767.

Jones, James Rees. *Country and Court: England 1658-1714*. Cambridge: Harvard Univ. Press, 1979.

Jones, S. Paul. *A List of French Prose Fiction from 1700-1750*. New York: Wilson, 1939.

Jonson, Ben. *Under-Woods*. London, 1640.

Joyce, James. "Daniel Defoe." *Buffalo Studies* 1 (1964): 3-27.

A Just Reprimand to Daniel de Foe. Edinburgh, 1710.

Karl, Frederick R. *The Adversary Literature*. New York: Farrar, Straus, and Giroux, 1974.

Keener, Frederick M. *The Chain of Becoming*. New York: Columbia Univ. Press, 1983.

Knapp, Andrew, and William Baldwin. *The Newgate Calendar*. Vol. 1. London: Robins, 1824.

Knox, Robert. *An Historical Relation of Ceylon*. Glasgow: James MacLehose and Sons, 1911.

Kolodny, Annette. "Turning the Lens on 'The Panther Captivity': A Feminist Exercise in Practical Criticism." In *Writing and Sexual Difference*, edited by Elizabeth Abel. Chicago: Univ. of Chicago Press, 1982.

Korb, Johann-Georg. *Diary of an Austrian Secretary of Legation at the Court of Czar Peter the Great*. New York: Da Capo, 1968.

Kramer, Henry. *Malleus Maleficarum*. 1486.

The Ladies Diary. London, 1707.

The Ladies Dictionary. London, 1694.

The Ladies Tutor. London, 1720.

Lawson, John. *New Voyage to Carolina*. London, 1709.

Lederer, Wolfgang. *The Fear of Women*. New York: Grune and Stratton, 1968.

Lee, Maurice, Jr. "The Anglo-Scottish Union of 1707: The Debate Re-opened." *British Studies Monitor* 9 (1979): 23-34.

Lee, William. *Daniel Defoe: His Life and Recently Discovered Writings*. 3 vols. London: Hotten, 1869.

Leranbaum, Miriam. "'An Irony Not Unusual': Defoe's *Shortest Way with the Dissenters*." *Huntington Library Quarterly* 37 (1974): 227-50.

The Life and Adventures of Captain John Avery. ARS, no. 203-204. Los Angeles: UCLA, Clark Library, 1980.

Lindamira. Edited by Benjamin Boyce. Minneapolis: Univ. of Minnesota Press, 1949.

Linebaugh, Peter. "The Ordinary of Newgate and His *Account*." In *Crime in England, 1550-1800*, edited by J.S. Cockburn. London: Methuen, 1977.

Lockhart, George. *Memoirs and Commentaries upon the Affairs of Scotland*. London, 1817.

Love upon Tick. London, 1724.

Lukács, Georg. *Der Historische Roman*. Berlin: Aufbau-Verlag, 1955.

———. *The Historical Novel.* Translated by Hannah and Stanley Mitchell. 1962. Reprint. London: Merlin, 1965.

Lyles, Albert M. *Methodism Mocked.* London: Epworth, 1960.

McBurney, William. *A Check List of English Prose Fiction, 1700-1739.* Cambridge: Harvard Univ. Press, 1960.

———. "Mrs. Penelope Aubin and the Early Eighteenth-Century Novel." *Huntington Library Quarterly* 20 (1957): 249-52.

Macey, Samuel L. *Money and the Novel: Mercenary Motivation in Defoe and His Immediate Successors.* Victoria, B.C.: Sono Nis Press, 1983.

MacKenzie, George. *The Lives and Characters of the most eminent Writers of the Scots Nation.* Edinburgh, 1708.

McKeon, Michael. *Politics and Poetry in Restoration England.* Cambridge: Harvard Univ. Press, 1975.

McKillop, Alan D. *The Early Masters of English Fiction.* Lawrence: Univ. of Kansas Press, 1956.

MacKinnon, James. *The Union of England and Scotland.* London: Longmans, Green, 1896.

Mailer, Norman. *The Armies of the Night.* New York: Signet, 1968.

———. *Existential Errands.* Boston: Little, Brown, 1972.

Mandeville, Bernard. *The Fable of the Bees.* Edited by F.B. Kaye. Oxford: Clarendon, 1924.

———. *Free Thoughts on Religion, the Church, and National Happiness.* London, 1720.

Manley, Delariviere. *Lovers Tales.* London, 1722.

———. *The Power of Love.* London, 1720.

Matthews, Brander. *The Historical Novel and Other Essays.* New York: Scribners, 1901.

May, Georges. *Le Dilemme du roman au XVIIIme siècle.* New Haven: Yale Univ. Press, 1963.

Memoirs of ***. Commonly known by the Name of George Psalmanazar. London, 1764.

The Memoirs of the Honorable Sir John Reresby. London, 1734.

A Memorial Presented to the King of Great-Britain, by M. Wesselofski. London, 1719.

Milton, John. *Paradise Lost.* London, 1667.

The Mirrour. London, 1719.

The Mirrour for Magistrates. London, 1587.

Mish, Charles C. "Early Eighteenth-Century Best Sellers in English Prose Fiction." *Publications of the Bibliographic Society of America* 75 (1981): 413-18.

———. *English Prose Fiction, 1600-1700: A Chronological Checklist.*

Charlottesville, Va.: Bibliographical Society of the Univ. of Virginia, 1952.

Modleski, Tania. *Loving with a Vengeance*. Hamden: Archon, 1982.

Moers, Ellen. *Literary Women*. Garden City, N.Y.: Doubleday, 1976.

Monteser, Frederick. *The Picaresque Element in Western Literature*. University: Univ. of Alabama Press, 1975.

Montesquieu, C.L. de Secondat. *Lettres Persanes*. Paris: Chez Dalibon, 1826.

Moore, C.A. "Whig Panegyric Verse, 1700-1760." *PMLA* 41 (1926): 362-401.

Moore, John R. *A Checklist of the Writings of Daniel Defoe*. 1960. Reprint. Hamden, Conn.: Archon, 1971.

Morton, Charles. *Compendium Physicae*. In *Publications of the Colonial Society of Massachusetts*. Vol. 33. Boston: Merrymount, 1940.

_____. "Of Ethicks and Its End." Harvard Ms. Am. 911. Harvard University, Cambridge, Mass.

_____. "Pneumaticks or the Doctrine of Spirits." Harvard Ms. Am. 911. Harvard University, Cambridge, Mass.

_____. *System of Logick*. Boston: Massachusetts Historical Society Collection, Ms. C.81.11. (19.4), 1692/3.

Motheau, H., and D. Jouaust. *Les Essais de Montaigne*. Vol. 2. Paris: Librarie des Bibliophiles, 1873.

Murray, John J. "Defoe: News Commentator and Analyst of Northern European Affairs." *Indiana Quarterly for Bookmen* 3 (1947): 39-50.

Nevo, Ruth. *The Dial of Virtue*. Princeton: Princeton Univ. Press, 1963.

Newdigate, Bernard H. *Michael Drayton and His Circle*. Oxford: Blackwell, 1941.

Nicholson, Watson. *The Historical Sources of Defoe's Journal of the Plague Year*. Boston: Stratford Co., 1919.

The Northern Crisis. London, 1716.

Novak, Maximillian E. "Defoe and the Disordered City." *PMLA* 92 (1977): 241-52.

_____. *Defoe and the Nature of Man*. London: Oxford Univ. Press, 1963.

_____. *Economics and the Fiction of Defoe*. Berkeley: Univ. of California Press, 1962.

_____. "History, Ideology, and Method of Defoe's Historical Fiction." In *Studies in the Eighteenth Century*, edited by R.F. Brissenden and J.C. Eade, vol. 4. Canberra: Australian National Univ. Press, 1979.

_____. "Imaginary Islands and Real Beasts: The Imaginative Genesis of *Robinson Crusoe*." *Tennessee Studies in Literature* 19 (1974): 57-58.

_____. *Realism, Myth, and History in Defoe's Fiction*. Lincoln: Univ. of Nebraska Press, 1983.

_____. "Sincerity, Delusion, and Character." Forthcoming.

Oldmixon, John. *Memoirs of the Press*. London, 1742.

Oldys, William. *The History of the World*. 11th ed. London, 1736.

[Olivier, J.]. *Memoirs of the Life and Adventures of Signor Rozelli*. London, 1709.

P., W. *The Jamaica Lady*. In *Four before Richardson*, edited by William McBurney. Lincoln: Univ. of Nebraska Press, 1963.

Pafford, J.H.P. "Defoe's *Proposals* for Printing the *History of the Union*." *Library*, 5th ser., 11 (1956): 202-6.

A Paper Concerning Daniel Defoe. Edinburgh, 1708.

Patrides, C.A. *The Phoenix and the Ladder*. Berkeley: Univ. of California Press, 1964.

Penrose, Boies. *Travel and Discovery in the Renaissance*. Cambridge: Harvard Univ. Press, 1952.

Perry, John. *The State of Russia Under the Present Czar*. London, 1716.

Petavius. "To the Reader." In *The History of the World: or, an Account of Time*. London, 1659.

Pinkus, Philip. *Grub Street Stripped Bare*. London: Constable, 1968.

Pinto, Vivian de S. "Rochester and Dryden." *Renaissance and Modern Studies* 5 (1961): 29-48.

Piozzi, Hester Thrale. *Observations and Reflections Made in the Course of a Journal through France, Italy, and Germany*. London, 1789.

Pocock, J.G.A. *The Machiavellian Moment*. Princeton: Princeton Univ. Press, 1975.

Pope, Alexander. *The Poems of Alexander Pope*. Edited by John Butt. New Haven: Yale Univ. Press, 1963.

Pratt, Annis. *Archetypal Patterns in Women's Fiction*. Bloomington: Indiana Univ. Press, 1981.

Price, John V. "Patterns of Sexual Behaviour in Some Eighteenth-Century Novels." In *Sexuality in Eighteenth-Century Britain*, edited by Paul-Gabriel Bouce. Totowa, N.J.: Barnes and Noble, 1982.

_____. "The Reading of Philosophical Literature." In *Books and Their Readers in Eighteenth-Century England*, edited by Isabel Rivers. New York: St. Martin's, 1982.

Prior, Matthew. *Satyr on the Poets*. London, 1687.

The Prude. By Ma[demoiselle] A. London, 1724.

Raleigh, Walter. *History of the World*. In *Works*, vol. 8. Oxford: Oxford Univ. Press, 1829.

_____. "Observations concerning the Royal Navy and Sea-Service." In *Works*, vol. 4. Oxford: Oxford Univ. Press, 1829.

Reeve, Clara. *The Progress of Romance*. 1785. New York: Garland, 1970.

Reiss, Timothy J. *The Discourse of Modernism*. Ithaca: Cornell Univ. Press, 1982.

Richetti, John. *Defoe's Narratives: Situations and Structures*. Oxford: Clarendon, 1975.

——. "The Family, Sex, and Marriage in Defoe's *Moll Flanders* and *Roxana*." *Studies in the Literary Imagination* 15 (1982): 19-35.

——. *Popular Fiction before Richardson*. London: Oxford Univ. Press, 1969.

——. "The Portrayal of Women in Restoration and Eighteenth-Century English Literature." In *What Manner of Woman*, edited by Marlene Springer. New York: New York Univ. Press, 1977.

Riley, P.W.J. *The Union of England and Scotland: A Study in Anglo-Scottish Politics of the Eighteenth Century*. Totowa, N.J.: Rowman and Littlefield, 1978.

Roberts, J. *A Collection of Very Valuable and Scarce Pieces relating to the last Plague in the Year 1665*. London, 1721.

Rogers, Katharine M. *Feminism in Eighteenth-Century England*. Urbana: Univ. of Illinois Press, 1982.

Rogers, Pat. *The Augustan Vision*. London: Weidenfeld and Nicolson, 1974.

Rosenberg, Albert. "Defoe's *Pacificator* Reconsidered," *Philological Quarterly* 37 (1958): 433-39.

Rosenberg, Eleanor. "Giacopo Castelvetro, Italian Publisher in Elizabethan London and His Patrons." *Huntington Library Quarterly* 6 (1943): 119-48.

Rousseau, G.S. "Nymphomania, Bienville, and the Rise of Erotic Sensibility." In *Sexuality in Eighteenth-Century Britain*, edited by Paul-Gabriel Boucé. Totowa, N.J.: Barnes and Noble, 1982.

Russia Company Minutes. Guildhall Ms. 11741.

Rynell, Alarik. "Defoe's *Journal of the Plague Year*, the Lord Mayor's *Orders*, and O.E.D." *English Studies* 50 (1969): 452-64.

St. John, Henry, Lord Bolingbroke. "On the Study and Use of History." In *The Works*, vol. 2. Philadelphia: Carey and Hart, 1841.

Saintsbury, George. *A History of English Prose Rhythm*. 1912. Reprint. Bloomington: Indiana Univ. Press, 1965.

Sandys, George. *Ovid's Metamorphosis English'd, Mythologiz'd, and Represented in Figures*. Edited by Karl Hulley and Stanley Vandersall. 1632. Lincoln: Univ. of Nebraska Press, 1970.

Satan's Invisible World Discover'd. Edinburgh, 1685.

Schofield, Mary Anne. *Quiet Rebellion*. Washington, D.C.: Univ. Press of America, 1982.

Scholes, Robert. *Semiotics and Interpretation*. New Haven: Yale Univ. Press, 1982.

Scholes, Robert, and Robert Kellogg. *The Nature of Narrative*. 1966. Reprint. London: Oxford Univ. Press, 1979.

Schonhorn, Manuel. "Defoe's *Four Years Voyages of Captain Roberts* and *Ashton's Memorial*." *Texas Studies in Literature and Language* 17 (1975): 93-102.

_____. "Defoe's *Journal of the Plague Year*: Topography and Intention." *Review of English Studies*, ser. 2, 19 (1968): 387-402.

Scott, Walter. *Essays on Chivalry, Romance, and The Drama*. London: Ware, n.d.

_____. *The Lives of the Novelists*. London: Dent, 1928.

_____. "Samuel Richardson" and "Daniel Defoe." In *Sir Walter Scott on Novelists and Fiction*, edited by Ioan Williams. New York: Barnes and Noble, 1968.

_____. *Waverley; or, 'Tis Sixty Years since*. Edinburgh, 1814.

Secord, A.W. *Robert Drury's Journal and Other Studies*. Urbana: Univ. of Illinois Press, 1961.

_____. *Studies in the Narrative Method of Defoe*. New York: Russell and Russell, 1963.

Sgard, Jean. *Prévost, Romancier*. Paris: Librarie Jose Corti, 1968.

Sheppard, Alfred. *The Art and Practice of Historical Fiction*. London: Toulmin, 1930.

Showalter, Elaine. *A Literature of Their Own*. Princeton: Princeton Univ. Press, 1977.

Shumaker, Wayne. *Literature and the Irrational*. Englewood Cliffs, N.J.: Prentice-Hall, 1960.

Sidney, Phillip. *The Defense of Poesy*. London, 1595.

Sill, Geoffrey. *Defoe and the Idea of Fiction*. Newark: Associated Univ. Presses, 1983.

Smith, Alexander. *The Secret Lives of the Most Celebrated Beauties. . . .* London, 1715.

Smith, David Nichol. *Characters from the Histories and Memoirs of the Seventeenth Century*. Oxford: Clarendon, 1918.

Smithers, Peter. *The Life of Joseph Addison*. 1954. Reprint. Oxford: Clarendon, 1968.

Smout, T.C. *History of Scottish People*. London: Collins, 1969.

_____. "Union of Parliaments." In *The Scottish Nation*, edited by Gordon Menzies. London: BBC, 1972.

Some Memoirs of the Life of Robert Feilding. London, 1715.

Spacks, Patricia Meyer. "Ev'ry Woman is at Heart a Rake." *Eighteenth-Century Studies* 8 (1974): 27-46.

———. *The Female Imagination*. New York: Avon, 1976.

———. "Reflecting Women." *Yale Review* 63 (1973): 26-42.

Speck, W.A. *Stability and Strife*. Cambridge: Harvard Univ. Press, 1979.

Starr, G.A. *Defoe and Casuistry*. Princeton: Princeton Univ. Press, 1971.

———. *Defoe and Spiritual Autobiography*. Princeton: Princeton Univ. Press, 1965.

———. "Defoe's Prose Style: 1. The Language of Interpretation." *Modern Philology* 71 (1974): 277-94.

Stauffer, Donald A. *The Art of Biography in Eighteenth-Century England*. Princeton: Princeton Univ. Press, 1941.

Staves, Susan. "British Seduced Maidens." *Eighteenth-Century Studies* 14 (1980): 109-34.

[Steele, Richard.] *The Ladies Library*. London, 1714.

Summers, Joseph. "Some Apocalyptic Strains in Marvell's Poetry." In *Tricentenary Essays in Honor of Marvell*, edited by Kenneth Friedenreich. Hamden: Archon, 1977.

Sutherland, James. *Daniel Defoe: A Critical Study*. Boston: Houghton Mifflin, 1971.

———. *Defoe*. Philadelphia: Lippincott, 1938.

Swift, Jonathan. *Conduct of the Allies*. London, 1712.

———. *The Prose Works*. Edited by Herbert Davis. 12 vols. Oxford: Blackwell, 1948.

Tavis, Carol, and Carole Offir. *The Longest War*. New York: Harcourt, Brace, Jovanovich, 1977.

Theobald, Lewis. *Memoirs of Sir Walter Raleigh*. London, 1719.

Thomas, Keith. *Religion and the Decline of Magic*. New York: Scribners, 1971.

Thompson, James W., and B.J. Holm. *A History of Historical Writing*. Gloucester, Mass.: Peter Smith, 1967.

Thompson, Roger. *Unfit for Modest Ears*. Totawa: Rowman and Littlefield, 1979.

Todd, Janet, ed. *Gender and Literary Voice*. New York: Holmes and Meier, 1980.

Todorov, Tzvetan. "The Notion of Literature." *New Literary History* 5 (1973): 5-16.

Trevor-Roper, Hugh. "The Historical Philosophy of the Enlightenment." *Studies in Voltaire and the Eighteenth Century* 27 (1963): 1667-87.

Trickett, Rachel. *The Honest Muse*. Oxford: Clarendon, 1967.

Trotter, David. *The Poetry of Abraham Cowley*. London: Macmillan, 1979.

Turgot, Anne Robert Jacques. "On Universal History." In *Turgot on Progress, Sociology, and Economics*, translated by R.L. Meek. Cambridge: Cambridge Univ. Press, 1973.

Twyne, Thomas. *A Shorte Discourse of All Earthquakes in General.* London, 1580.

Vaughan, Thomas. *Magia Adamica.* London: Theosophical Publishing House, 1919.

The Visiter. London, 1723.

Voltaire [François Marie Arouet]. *Lion of the North: Charles XII of Sweden.* Translated by M.F.O. Jenkins. London and Toronto: Associated Univ. Presses, 1981.

Wallerstein, Ruth. *Studies in Seventeenth-Century Poetic.* Madison: Univ. of Wisconsin Press, 1950.

The Wanderer. London, 1717.

[Ward, Seth.] *A Sermon Preached before the Peers, in the Abby-Church at Westminster.* London, 1666.

Watt, Ian. *The Rise of the Novel.* 1957. Reprint. Berkeley: Univ. of California Press, 1967.

Watts, Michael. *The Dissenters.* Oxford: Clarendon, 1978.

[Weber, F.] *The Present State of Russia.* London, 1723.

Weber, Ronald. *The Literature of Fact.* Athens: Ohio Univ. Press, 1980.

Weinstein, Arnold. *Fictions of the Self, 1550-1800.* Princeton: Princeton Univ. Press, 1981.

Wesley, Samuel. "An Epistle to a Friend concerning Poetry." London, 1700.

Westfall, Richard S. *Never at Rest.* Cambridge: Cambridge Univ. Press, 1980.

[Whalley, Peter.] *An Essay on the Manner of Writing History.* [1746.], Augustan Reprint Society, no. 80, Los Angeles: UCLA, Clark Library, 1960.

White, Hayden. *Metahistory.* Baltimore: Johns Hopkins Univ. Press, 1973.

———. *Topics of Discourse: Essays in Cultural Criticism.* Baltimore: Johns Hopkins Univ. Press, 1978.

Whitworth, Charles. *An Account of Russia As it was in the Year 1710.* Strawberry Hill, England, 1758.

Wilkinson, Andrew. "Defoe's 'New Discovery' and 'Pacificator.'" *Notes and Queries* 195 (1950): 496-98.

Williams, Arthur S. "Panegyric Decorum in the Reigns of William III and Anne." *Journal of British Studies* 21 (1981): 56-87.

Williams, Basil. *The Whig Supremacy, 1714-1760.* Oxford: Clarendon, 1962.

Williams, Ioan. *The Idea of the Novel in Europe, 1600-1800*. London: Macmillan, 1979.

Wolfe, Tom. *The New Journalism*. New York: Harper and Row, 1973.

Woodward, Josiah. *The Duty of Compassion to the Souls of Others*. London, 1698.

Woolf, Virginia. *Granite and Rainbow*. New York: Harcourt, Brace, 1958.

Wright, Herbert G. "Defoe's Writings on Sweden." *Review of English Studies* 16 (1940): 25-32.

Wurzback, Natascha. *The Novel in Letters*. Coral Gables, Fla.: Univ. of Miami Press, 1969.

Yorke, P., ed. *Miscellaneous State Papers from 1501 to 1726*. Vol. 2. London, 1778.

Young, Arthur. *Travels in France*. Bury St. Edmunds, England, 1792.

Zavarzadeh, Mas'ud. *The Mythopoeic Reality*. Urbana: Univ. of Illinois Press, 1976.

Zimmerman, Everett. *Defoe and the Novel*. Berkeley: Univ of California Press, 1975.

INDEX